STATISTICAL ANALYSIS
MICROSOFT® EXCEL 2010

Contents at a Glance

D0565039

Conrad Carlberg

800 East 96th Street,
Indianapolis, Indiana 46240 USA

Statistical Analysis: Microsoft® Excel 2010

Copyright © 2011 by Pearson Education, Inc.

Library of Congress Cataloging-in-Publication Data is on file.

ISBN-13: 978-0-7897-4720-4
ISBN-10: 0-7897-4720-0

Printed in the United States of America

Sixth Printing: March 2014

Trademarks

All terms mentioned in this book that are known to be trademarks or service marks have been appropriately capitalized. Que Publishing cannot attest to the accuracy of this information. Use of a term in this book should not be regarded as affecting the validity of any trademark or service mark.

Microsoft is a registered trademark of Microsoft Corporation.

Warning and Disclaimer

Every effort has been made to make this book as complete and as accurate as possible, but no warranty or fitness is implied. The information provided is on an "as is" basis. The author and the publisher shall have neither liability nor responsibility to any person or entity with respect to any loss or damages arising from the information contained in this book.

Bulk Sales

Que Publishing offers excellent discounts on this book when ordered in quantity for bulk purchases or special sales. For more information, please contact

U.S. Corporate and Government Sales
1-800-382-3419
corpsales@pearsontechgroup.com

For sales outside the United States, please contact

International Sales
international@pearson.com

Editor in Chief
Greg Wiegand

Acquisitions Editor
Loretta Yates

Development Editor
Abshier House

Managing Editor
Sandra Schroeder

Senior Project Editor
Tonya Simpson

Copy Editor
Bart Reed

Indexer
Tim Wright

Proofreader
Leslie Joseph

Technical Editor
Linda Sikorski

Publishing Coordinator
Cindy Teeters

Book Designer
Anne Jones

Compositor
Jake McFarland

Table of Contents

About the Author

Conrad Carlberg started writing about Excel, and its use in quantitative analysis, before workbooks had worksheets. As a graduate student he had the great good fortune to learn something about statistics from the wonderfully gifted Gene Glass. He remembers much of it and has learned more since—and has exchanged the discriminant function for logistic regression—but it still looks like a rodeo. This is a book he has been wanting to write for years, and he is grateful for the opportunity. He expects to refer to it often while running his statistical consulting business.

Dedication

For Toni, who has been putting up with this sort of thing for 15 years now, with all my love.

Acknowledgments

I'd like to thank Loretta Yates, who guided this book between the Scylla of my early dithering and the Charybdis of a skeptical editorial board, and who treats my self-imposed crises with an unexpected sort of pragmatic optimism. And Debbie Abshier, who managed some of my early efforts for Que before she started her own shop—I can't express how pleased I was to learn that Abshier House would be running the development show. And Joell Smith-Bornc, for her skillful solutions to the problems I created when I thought I was writing. Linda Sikorski's technical edit was just right, and what fun it was to debate with her once more about statistical inference.

We Want to Hear from You!

As the reader of this book, you are our most important critic and commentator. We value your opinion and want to know what we're doing right, what we could do better, what areas you'd like to see us publish in, and any other words of wisdom you're willing to pass our way.

As an editor-in-chief for Que Publishing, I welcome your comments. You can email or write me directly to let me know what you did or didn't like about this book—as well as what we can do to make our books better.

Please note that I cannot help you with technical problems related to the topic of this book. We do have a User Services group, however, where I will forward specific technical questions related to the book.

When you write, please be sure to include this book's title and author as well as your name, email address, and phone number. I will carefully review your comments and share them with the author and editors who worked on the book.

Email: feedback@quepublishing.com

Mail: Greg Wiegand
            Editor in Chief
            Que Publishing
            800 East 96th Street
            Indianapolis, IN 46240 USA

Reader Services

Visit our website and register this book at quepublishing.com/register for convenient access to any updates, downloads, or errata that might be available for this book.

Introduction

There was no reason I shouldn't have already written a book about statistical analysis using Excel. But I didn't, although I knew I wanted to. Finally, I talked Pearson into letting me write it for them.

Be careful what you ask for. It's been a struggle, but at last I've got it out of my system, and I want to start by talking here about the reasons for some of the choices I made in writing this book.

Using Excel for Statistical Analysis

The problem is that it's a huge amount of material to cover in a book that's supposed to be only 400 to 500 pages. The text used in the first statistics course I took was about 600 pages, and it was purely statistics, no Excel. In 2001, I co-authored a book about Excel (no statistics) that ran to 750 pages. To shoehorn statistics *and* Excel into 400 pages or so takes some picking and choosing.

Furthermore, I did not want this book to be an expanded Help document, like one or two others I've seen. Instead, I take an approach that seemed to work well in an earlier book of mine, *Business Analysis with Excel*. The idea in both that book and this one is to identify a topic in statistical (or business) analysis, discuss the topic's rationale, its procedures and associated issues, and only then get into how it's carried out in Excel.

You shouldn't expect to find discussions of, say, the Weibull function or the gamma distribution here. They have their uses, and Excel provides them as statistical functions, but my picking and choosing forced me to ignore them—at my peril, probably—and to use the space saved for material on more bread-and-butter topics such as statistical regression.

About You and About Excel

How much background in statistics do you need to get value from this book? My intention is that you need none. The book starts out with a discussion of different ways to measure things—by categories, such as models of cars, by ranks, such as first place through tenth, by numbers, such as degrees Fahrenheit—and how Excel handles those methods of measurement in its worksheets and its charts.

This book moves on to basic statistics, such as averages and ranges, and only then to intermediate statistical methods such as t-tests, multiple regression, and the analysis of covariance. The material assumes knowledge of nothing more complex than how to calculate an average. You do not need to have taken courses in statistics to use this book.

As to Excel itself, it matters little whether you're using Excel 97, Excel 2010, or any version in between. Very little statistical functionality changed between Excel 97 and Excel 2003. The few changes that did occur had to do primarily with how functions behaved when the user stress-tested them using extreme values or in very unlikely situations.

The Ribbon showed up in Excel 2007 and is still with us in Excel 2010. But nearly all statistical analysis in Excel takes place in worksheet functions—very little is menu driven—and there was virtually no change to the function list, function names, or their arguments between Excel 97 and Excel 2007. The Ribbon does introduce a few differences, such as how to get a trendline into a chart. This book discusses the differences in the steps you take using the traditional menu structure and the steps you take using the Ribbon.

In a very few cases, the Ribbon does not provide access to traditional menu commands such as the pivot table wizard. In those cases, this book describes how you can gain access to those commands even if you are using a version of Excel that features the Ribbon.

In Excel 2010, several apparently new statistical functions appear, but the differences are more apparent than real. For example, through Excel 2007, the two functions that calculate standard deviations are STDEV() and STDEVP(). If you are working with a sample of values you should use STDEV(), but if you happen to be working with a full population you should use STDEVP(). Of course, the "P" stands for *population*.

Both STDEV() and STDEVP() remain in Excel 2010, but they are termed *compatibility functions*. It appears that they may be phased out in some future release. Excel 2010 adds what it calls *consistency functions*, two of which are STDEV.S() and STDEV.P(). Note that a period has been added in each function's name. The period is followed by a letter that, for consistency, indicates whether the function should be used with a sample of values or a population of values.

Other consistency functions have been added to Excel 2010, and the functions they are intended to replace are still supported. There are a few substantive differences between the compatibility version and the consistency version of some functions, and this book discusses those differences and how best to use each version.

Clearing Up the Terms

Terminology poses another problem, both in Excel and in the field of statistics, and, it turns out, in the areas where the two overlap. For example, it's normal to use the word *alpha* in a statistical context to mean the probability that you will decide that there's a true difference between the means of two groups when there really isn't. But Excel extends *alpha* to usages that are related but much less standard, such as the probability of getting some number of heads from flipping a fair coin. It's not wrong to do so. It's just unusual, and therefore it's an unnecessary hurdle to understanding the concepts.

The vocabulary of statistics itself is full of names that mean very different things in slightly different contexts. The word *beta*, for example, can mean the probability of deciding that a true difference does *not* exist, when it does. It can also mean a coefficient in a regression equation (for which Excel's documentation unfortunately uses the letter *m*), and it's also the name of a distribution that is a close relative of the binomial distribution. None of that is due to Excel. It's due to having more concepts than there are letters in the Greek alphabet.

You can see the potential for confusion. It gets worse when you hook Excel's terminology up with that of statistics. For example, in Excel the word *cell* means a rectangle on a worksheet, the intersection of a row and a column. In statistics, particularly the analysis of variance, *cell* usually means a group in a factorial design: If an experiment tests the joint effects of sex and a new medication, one cell might consist of men who receive a placebo, and another might consist of women who receive the medication being assessed. Unfortunately, you can't depend on seeing "cell" where you might expect it: *within cell error* is called *residual* in the context of regression analysis.

So this book is going to present you with some terms you might otherwise find redundant: I'll use *design cell* for analysis contexts and *worksheet cell* when I'm referring to the software context where there's any possibility of confusion about which I mean.

On the other hand, for consistency, I try always to use *alpha* rather than *Type I error* or *statistical significance*. In general, I will use just one term for a given concept throughout. I intend to complain about it when the possibility of confusion exists: when *mean square* doesn't mean *mean square*, you ought to know about it.

Making Things Easier

If you're just starting to study statistical analysis, your timing's much better than mine was. You have avoided some of the obstacles to understanding statistics that once—as recently as the 1980s—stood in the way. I'll mention those obstacles once or twice more in this book, partly to vent my spleen but also to stress how much better Excel has made things.

Suppose that 25 years ago you were calculating something as basic as the standard deviation of twenty numbers. You had no access to a computer. Or, if there was one around, it was a mainframe or a mini and whoever owned it had more important uses for it than to support a Psychology 101 assignment.

So you trudged down to the Psych building's basement where there was a room filled with gray metal desks with adding machines on them. Some of the adding machines might even have been plugged into a source of electricity. You entered your twenty numbers very carefully because the adding machines did not come with Undo buttons or Ctrl+Z. The electricity-enabled machines were in demand because they had a memory function that allowed you to enter a number, square it, and add the result to what was already in the memory.

It could take half an hour to calculate the standard deviation of twenty numbers. It was all incredibly tedious and it distracted you from the main point, which was the concept of a standard deviation and the reason you wanted to quantify it.

Of course, 25 years ago our teachers were telling us how lucky we were to have adding machines instead of having to use paper, pencil, and a large supply of erasers.

Things are different in 2010, and truth be told, they have been changing since the mid 1980s when applications such as Lotus 1-2-3 and Microsoft Excel started to find their way onto personal computers' floppy disks. Now, all you have to do is enter the numbers into a worksheet—or maybe not even that, if you downloaded them from a server somewhere. Then, type **=STDEV.S(** and drag across the cells with the numbers before you press Enter. It takes half a minute at most, not half an hour at least.

Several statistics have relatively simple *definitional* formulas. The definitional formula tends to be straightforward and therefore gives you actual insight into what the statistic means. But those same definitional formulas often turn out to be difficult to manage in practice if you're using paper and pencil, or even an adding machine or hand calculator. Rounding errors occur and compound one another.

So statisticians developed *computational* formulas. These are mathematically equivalent to the definitional formulas, but are much better suited to manual calculations. Although it's nice to have computational formulas that ease the arithmetic, those formulas make you take your eye off the ball. You're so involved with accumulating the sum of the squared values that you forget that your purpose is to understand how values vary around their average.

That's one primary reason that an application such as Excel, or an application specifically and solely designed for statistical analysis, is so helpful. It takes the drudgery of the arithmetic off your hands and frees you to think about what the numbers actually mean.

Statistics is conceptual. It's not just arithmetic. And it shouldn't be taught as though it is.

The Wrong Box?

But should you even be using Excel to do statistical calculations? After all, people have been moaning about inadequacies in Excel's statistical functions for twenty years. The Excel forum on CompuServe had plenty of complaints about this issue, as did the Usenet newsgroups. As I write this introduction, I can switch from Word to Firefox and see that some people are still complaining on Wikipedia talk pages, and others contribute angry screeds to publications such as *Computational Statistics & Data Analysis*, which I believe are there as a reminder to us all of the importance of taking our prescription medication.

I have sometimes found myself as upset about problems with Excel's statistical functions as anyone. And it's true that Excel has had, and continues to have, problems with the algorithms it uses to manage certain functions such as the inverse of the F distribution.

But most of the complaints that are voiced fall into one of two categories: those that are based on misunderstandings about either Excel or statistical analysis, and those that are based on complaints that Excel isn't accurate enough.

If you read this book, you'll be able to avoid those kinds of misunderstandings. As to inaccuracies in Excel results, let's look a little more closely at that. The complaints are typically along these lines:

> I enter into an Excel worksheet two different formulas that should return the same result. Simple algebraic rearrangement of the equations proves that. But then I find that Excel calculates two different results.

Well, the results differ at the fifteenth decimal place, so Excel's results disagree with one another by approximately five in 111 trillion.

Or this:

> I tried to get the inverse of the F distribution using the formula **FINV(0.025,4198986,1025419)**, but I got an unexpected result. Is there a bug in FINV?

No. Once upon a time, FINV returned the #NUM! error value for those arguments, but no longer. However, that's not the point. With so many degrees of freedom, over four million and one million, respectively, the person who asked the question was effectively dealing with populations, not samples. To use that sort of inferential technique with so many degrees of freedom is a striking instance of "unclear on the concept."

Would it be better if Excel's math were more accurate—or at least more internally consistent? Sure. But even the finger-waggers admit that Excel's statistical functions are acceptable at least, as the following comment shows.

> They can rarely be relied on for more than four figures, and then only for $0.001 < p < 0.999$, plenty good for routine hypothesis testing.

Now look. Chapter 6, "Telling the Truth with Statistics," goes into this issue further, but the point deserves a better soapbox, closer to the start of the book. Regardless of the accuracy of a statement such as "They can rarely be relied on for more than four figures," it's pointless to make it. It's irrelevant whether a finding is "statistically significant" at the 0.001 level instead of the 0.005 level, and to worry about whether Excel can successfully distinguish between the two findings is to miss the context.

There are many possible explanations for a research outcome other than the one you're seeking: a real and replicable treatment effect. Random chance is only one of these. It's one that gets a lot of attention because we attach the word *significance* to our tests to rule out chance, but it's not more important than other possible explanations you should be concerned about when you design your study. It's the design of your study, and how well you implement it, that allows you to rule out alternative explanations such as selection bias and disproportionate dropout rates. Those explanations—bias and dropout rates—are just two examples of possible explanations for an apparent treatment effect: explanations that might make a treatment look like it had an effect when it actually didn't.

Even the strongest design doesn't enable you to rule out a chance outcome. But if the design of your study is sound, and you obtained what looks like a meaningful result, then you'll want to control chance's role as an alternative explanation of the result. So you certainly want to run your data through the appropriate statistical test, which *does* help you control the effect of chance.

If you get a result that doesn't clearly rule out chance—or rule it in—then you're much better off to run the experiment again than to take a position based on a borderline outcome. At the very least, it's a better use of your time and resources than to worry in print about whether Excel's F tests are accurate to the fifth decimal place.

Wagging the Dog

And ask yourself this: Once you reach the point of planning the statistical test, are you going to reject your findings if they might come about by chance five times in 1000? Is that too loose a criterion? What about just one time in 1000? How many angels are on that pinhead anyway?

If you're concerned that Excel won't return the correct distinction between one and five chances in 1000 that the result of your study is due to chance, then you allow what's really an irrelevancy to dictate how, and using what calibrations, you're going to conduct your statistical analysis. It's pointless to worry about whether a test is accurate to one point in a thousand or two in a thousand. Your decision rules for risking a chance finding should be based on more substantive grounds.

Chapter 9, "Testing Differences Between Means: Further Issues," goes into the matter in greater detail, but a quick summary of the issue is that you should let the risk of making the wrong decision be guided by the costs of a bad decision and the benefits of a good one—not by which criterion appears to be the more selective.

What's in This Book

You'll find that there are two broad types of statistics. I'm not talking about that scurrilous line about lies, damned lies and statistics—both its source and its applicability are disputed. I'm talking about *descriptive* statistics and *inferential* statistics.

No matter if you've never studied statistics before this, you're already familiar with concepts such as averages and ranges. These are descriptive statistics. They describe identified groups: The average age of the members is 42 years; the range of the weights is 105 pounds; the median price of the houses is $270,000. A variety of other sorts of descriptive statistics exists, such as standard deviations, correlations, and skewness. The first five chapters of this book take a fairly close look at descriptive statistics, and you might find that they have some aspects that you haven't considered before.

Descriptive statistics provides you with insight into the characteristics of a restricted set of beings or objects. They can be interesting and useful, and they have some properties that aren't at all well known. But you don't get a better understanding of the world from descriptive statistics. For that, it helps to have a handle on inferential statistics. That sort of analysis is based on descriptive statistics, but you are asking and perhaps answering broader questions. Questions such as this:

> The average systolic blood pressure in this group of patients is 135. How large a margin of error must I report so that if I took another 99 samples, 95 of the 100 would capture the true population mean within margins calculated similarly?

Inferential statistics enables you to make inferences about a population based on samples from that population. As such, inferential statistics broadens the horizons considerably.

But you have to take on some assumptions about your samples, and about the populations that your samples represent, in order to make that sort of generalization. From Chapter 6 through the end of this book you'll find discussions of the issues involved, along with examples of how those issues work out in practice. And, by the way, how you work them out using Microsoft Excel.

About Variables and Values

Variables and Values

It must seem odd to start a book about statistical analysis using Excel with a discussion of ordinary, everyday notions such as variables and values. But variables and values, along with scales of measurement (covered in the next section), are at the heart of how you represent data in Excel. And how you choose to represent data in Excel has implications for how you run the numbers.

With your data laid out properly, you can easily and efficiently combine records into groups, pull groups of records apart to examine them more closely, and create charts that give you insight into what the raw numbers are really doing. When you put the statistics into tables and charts, you begin to understand what the numbers have to say.

When you lay out your data without considering how you will use the data later, it becomes much more difficult to do any sort of analysis. Excel is generally very flexible about how and where you put the data you're interested in, but when it comes to preparing a formal analysis, you want to follow some guidelines. In fact, some of Excel's features don't work at all if your data doesn't conform to what Excel expects. To illustrate one useful arrangement, you won't go wrong if you put different variables in different columns and different records in different rows.

A *variable* is an attribute or property that describes a person or a thing. Age is a variable that describes you. It describes all humans, all living organisms, all objects—anything that exists for some period of time. Surname is a variable, and so are weight in pounds and brand of car. Database jargon often refers to variables as *fields*, and some Excel tools use that terminology, but in statistics you generally use the term *variable*.

Variables have *values*. The number "20" is a value of the variable "age," the name "Smith" is a value of the variable "surname," "130" is a value of the variable "weight in pounds," and "Ford" is a value of the variable "brand of car." Values vary from person to person and from object to object—hence the term *variable*.

Recording Data in Lists

When you run a statistical analysis, your purpose is generally to summarize a group of numeric values that belong to the same variable. For example, you might have obtained and recorded the weight in pounds for 20 people, as shown in Figure 1.1.

Figure 1.1
This layout is ideal for analyzing data in Excel.

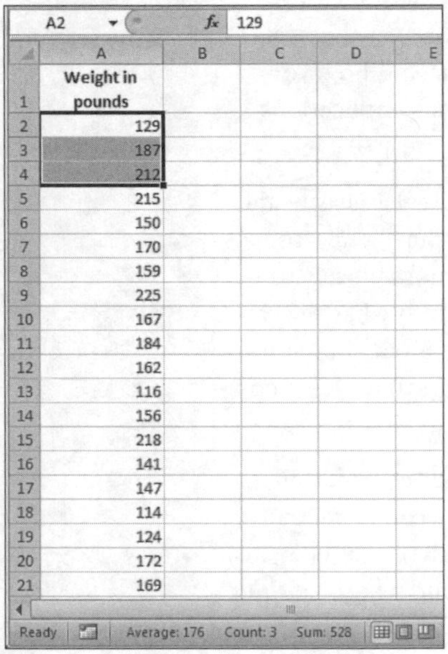

The way the data is arranged in Figure 1.1 is what Excel calls a *list*—a variable that occupies a column, records that each occupy a different row, and values in the cells where the records' rows intersect the variable's column. (The *record* is the individual being, object, location—whatever—that the list brings together with similar records. If the list in Figure 1.1 is made up of students in a classroom, each student constitutes a record.)

A list always has a *header*, usually the name of the variable, at the top of the column. In Figure 1.1, the header is the label "Weight in Pounds" in cell A1.

> **NOTE**
> A *list* is an informal arrangement of headers and values on a worksheet. It's not a formal structure that has a name and properties, such as a chart or a pivot table. Excel 2007 and 2010 offer a formal structure called a *table* that acts much like a list, but has some bells and whistles that a list doesn't have. This book will have more to say about tables in subsequent chapters.

There are some interesting questions that you can answer with a single-column list such as the one in Figure 1.1. You could select all the values and look at the status bar at the bottom of the Excel window to see summary information such as the average, the sum, and the count of the selected values. Those are just the quickest and simplest statistical analyses you might do with this basic single-column list.

> **TIP** You can turn the display of indicators such as simple statistics on and off. Right-click the status bar and select or deselect the items you want to see. However, you won't see a statistic unless the current selection contains at least two values. The status bar of Figure 1.1 shows the average, count, and sum of the selected values. (The worksheet tabs have been suppressed to unclutter the figure.)

Again, this book has much more to say about the richer analyses of a single variable that are available in Excel. But first, suppose that you add a second variable, "Sex," to the list in Figure 1.1.

You might get something like the two-column list in Figure 1.2. All the values for a particular record—here, a particular person—are found in the same row. So, in Figure 1.2, the person whose weight is 129 pounds is female (row 2), the person who weighs 187 pounds is male (row 3), and so on.

Figure 1.2
The list structure helps you keep related values together.

	A	B	C	D	E
	Weight in				
1	pounds	Sex			
2	129	Female			
3	187	Male			
4	212	Male			
5	215	Male			
6	150	Female			
7	170	Male			
8	159	Female			
9	225	Male			
10	167	Male			
11	184	Male			
12	162	Female			
13	116	Female			
14	156	Female			
15	218	Male			
16	141	Female			
17	147	Female			
18	114	Female			
19	124	Female			
20	172	Male			
21	169	Male			
22					

A1 f_x Weight in pounds

Using the list structure, you can easily do the simple analyses that appear in Figure 1.3, where you see a *pivot table* and a *pivot chart*. These are powerful tools and well suited to statistical analysis, but they're also very easy to use.

1

All that's needed for the pivot chart and pivot table in Figure 1.3 is the simple, informal, unglamorous list in Figure 1.2. But that list, and the fact that it keeps related values of weight and sex together in records, makes it possible to do the analyses shown in Figure 1.3. With the list in Figure 1.2, you're literally seven mouse clicks away from analyzing and charting weight by sex.

Figure 1.3
The pivot table and pivot chart summarize the individual records shown in Figure 1.2.

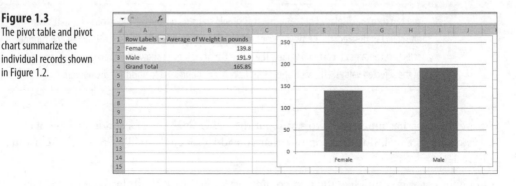

Note that you cannot create a column chart directly from the data as displayed in Figure 1.2. You first need to get the average weight of men and women, then associate those averages with the appropriate labels, and finally create the chart. A pivot chart is much quicker, more convenient, and more powerful.

Scales of Measurement

There's a difference in how weight and sex are measured and reported in Figure 1.2 that is fundamental to all statistical analysis—and to how you bring Excel's tools to bear on the numbers. The difference concerns scales of measurement.

Category Scales

In Figures 1.2 and 1.3, the variable Sex is measured using a *category* scale, sometimes called a *nominal* scale. Different values in a category variable merely represent different groups, and there's nothing intrinsic to the categories that does anything but identify them. If you throw out the psychological and cultural connotations that we pile onto labels, there's nothing about Male and Female that would lead you to put one on the left and the other on the right in Figure 1.3's pivot chart, the way you'd put June to the left of July.

Another example: Suppose that you wanted to chart the annual sales of Ford, General Motors, and Toyota cars. There is no order that's necessarily implied by the names themselves: They're just categories. This is reflected in the way that Excel might chart that data (see Figure 1.4).

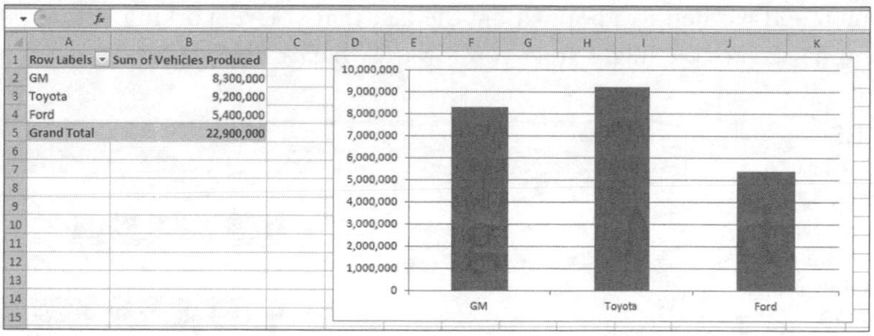

Figure 1.4

Excel's Column charts always show categories on the horizontal axis and numeric values on the vertical axis.

Notice these two aspects of the car manufacturer categories in Figure 1.4:

■ Adjacent categories are equidistant from one another. No additional information is supplied by the distance of GM from Toyota, or Toyota from Ford.

■ The chart conveys no information through the order in which the manufacturers appear on the horizontal axis. There's no implication that GM has less "car-ness" than Toyota, or Toyota less than Ford. You could arrange them in alphabetical order if you wanted, or in order of number of vehicles produced, but there's nothing intrinsic to the scale of manufacturers' names that suggests any rank order.

> **NOTE**   This is one of many quirks of terminology in Excel. The name "Ford" is of course a value, but Excel prefers to call it a category and to reserve the term *value* for numeric values only.

In contrast, the vertical axis in the chart shown in Figure 1.4 is what Excel terms a *value* axis. It represents numeric values.

Notice in Figure 1.4 that a position on the vertical, value axis conveys real quantitative information: the more vehicles produced, the taller the column. In general, Excel charts put the names of groups, categories, products, or any other designation, on a category axis and the numeric value of each category on the value axis. But the category axis isn't always the horizontal axis (see Figure 1.5).

The Bar chart provides precisely the same information as does the Column chart. It just rotates this information by 90 degrees, putting the categories on the vertical axis and the numeric values on the horizontal axis.

I'm not belaboring the issue of measurement scales just to make a point about Excel charts. When you do statistical analysis, you choose a technique based in large part on the sort of question you're asking. In turn, the way you ask your question depends in part on the scale of measurement you use for the variable you're interested in.

For example, if you're trying to investigate life expectancy in men and women, it's pretty basic to ask questions such as, "What is the average life span of males? of females?" You're examining two variables: sex and age. One of them is a category variable and the other is a numeric variable. (As you'll see in later chapters, if you are generalizing from a sample of men and women to a population, the fact that you're working with a category variable and a numeric variable might steer you toward what's called a *t-test*.)

Figure 1.5
In contrast to column charts, Excel's Bar charts always show categories on the vertical axis and numeric values on the horizontal axis.

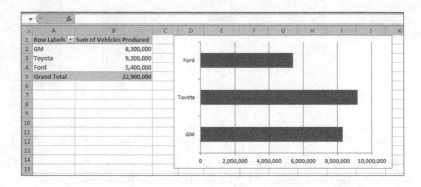

In Figures 1.3 through 1.5, you see that numeric summaries—average and sum—are compared across different groups. That sort of comparison forms one of the major types of statistical analysis. If you design your samples properly, you can then ask and answer questions such as these:

■ Are men and women paid differently for comparable work? Compare the average salaries of men and women who hold similar jobs.

■ Is a new medication more effective than a placebo at treating a particular disease? Compare, say, average blood pressure for those taking an alpha blocker with that of those taking a sugar pill.

■ Do Republicans and Democrats have different attitudes toward a given political issue? Ask a random sample of people their party affiliation, and then ask them to rate a given issue or candidate on a numeric scale.

Notice that each of these questions can be answered by comparing a *numeric* variable across different *categories* of interest.

Numeric Scales

Although there is only one type of category scale, there are three types of numeric scales: ordinal, interval, and ratio. You can use the value axis of any Excel chart to represent any type of numeric scale, and you often find yourself analyzing one numeric variable, regardless of type, in terms of another variable. Briefly, the numeric scale types are as follows:

■ Ordinal scales are often rankings. They tell you who finished first, second, third, and so on. These rankings tell you who came out ahead, but not how far ahead, and often you don't care about that. Suppose that in a qualifying race Jane ran 100 meters in 10.54 seconds, Mary in 10.83 seconds and Ellen in 10.84 seconds. Because it's a preliminary heat, you might care only about their order of finish, but not about how fast each woman ran. Therefore, you might well convert the time measurements to order of finish (1, 2 and 3), and then discard the timings themselves. Ordinal scales are sometimes used in a branch of statistics called *nonparametrics* but less so in the parametric analyses discussed in this book.

■ Interval scales indicate differences in measures such as temperature and elapsed time. If the high temperature Fahrenheit on July 1 is 100 degrees, 101 degrees on July 2, and 102 degrees on July 3, you know that each day is one degree hotter than the previous day. So an interval scale conveys more information than an ordinal scale. You know, from the order of finish on an ordinal scale, that in the qualifying race Jane ran faster than Mary and Mary ran faster than Ellen, but the rankings by themselves don't tell you how much faster. It takes elapsed time, an interval scale, to tell you that.

■ Ratio scales are similar to interval scales, but they have a true zero point, one at which there is a complete absence of some quantity. The Celsius temperature scale has a zero point, but it doesn't indicate that there is a complete absence of heat, just that water freezes there. Therefore, 10 degrees Celsius is not twice as warm as 5 degrees Celsius, so Celsius is not a ratio scale. Degrees kelvin does have a true zero point, one at which there is no molecular motion and therefore no heat. Kelvin is a ratio scale, and 100 degrees kelvin would be twice as warm as 50 degrees kelvin. Other familiar ratio scales are height and weight.

It's worth noting that converting between interval (or ratio) and ordinal measurement is a one-way process. If you know how many seconds it takes three people to run 100 meters, you have measures on a ratio scale that you can convert to an ordinal scale—gold, silver and bronze medals. You can't go the other way, though: If you know who won each medal, you're still in the dark as to whether the bronze medal was won with a time of 10 seconds or 10 minutes.

Telling an Interval Value from a Text Value

Excel has an astonishingly broad scope, and not only in statistical analysis. As much skill as has been built into it, though, it can't quite read your mind. It doesn't know, for example, whether the 1, 2, and 3 you just entered into a worksheet's cells represent the number of teaspoons of olive oil you use in three different recipes or 1st, 2nd, and 3rd place in a political primary. In the first case, you meant to indicate liquid measures on an interval scale. In the second case, you meant to enter the first three places in an ordinal scale. But they both look alike to Excel.

> **NOTE**
> This is a case in which you must rely on your own knowledge of numeric scales because Excel can't tell whether you intend a number as a value on an ordinal or an interval scale. Ordinal and interval scales have different characteristics—for one thing, ordinal scales do not follow a normal distribution, a "bell curve." Excel can't tell the difference, so you have to do so if you're to avoid using a statistical technique that's wrong for a given scale of measurement.

Text is a different matter. You might use the letters A, B, and C to name three different groups, and in that case you're using text values to represent a nominal, category scale. You can also use numbers: 1, 2, and 3 to represent the same groups. But if you use a number as a nominal value, it's a good idea to store it in the worksheet as a text value. For example, one way to store the number 2 as a text value in a worksheet cell is to precede it with an apostrophe: **'2**. You'll see the apostrophe in the formula box but not in the cell.

On a chart, Excel has some complicated decision rules that it uses to determine whether a number is only a number. Some of those rules concern the type of chart you request. For example, if you request a Line chart, Excel treats numbers on the horizontal axis as though they were nominal, text values. But if instead you request an XY chart using the same data, Excel treats the numbers on the horizontal axis as values on an interval scale. You'll see more about this in the next section.

So, as disquieting as it may sound, a number in Excel may be treated as a number in one context and not in another. Excel's rules are pretty reasonable, though, and if you give them a little thought when you see their results, you'll find that they make good sense.

If Excel's rules don't do the job for you in a particular instance, you can provide an assist. Figure 1.6 shows an example.

Figure 1.6
You don't have data for all the months in the year.

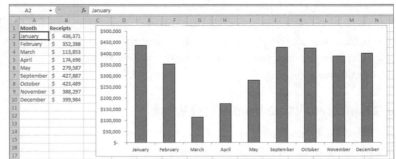

Suppose you run a business that operates only when public schools are in session, and you collect revenues during all months except June, July, and August. Figure 1.6 shows that Excel interprets dates as categories—but only if they are entered as text, as they are in the figure. Notice these two aspects of the chart in Figure 1.6:

■ The dates are entered in the worksheet cells A2:A10 as text values. One way to tell is to look in the formula box, just to the right of the f_x symbol, where you see the text value "January".

■ Because they are text values, Excel has no way of knowing that you mean them to represent dates, and so it treats them as simple categories—just like it does for GM, Ford, and Toyota. Excel charts the dates accordingly, with equal distances between them: May is as far from April as it is from September.

Compare Figure 1.6 with Figure 1.7, where the dates are real numeric values, not simply text:

■ You can see in the formula box that it's an actual date, not just the name of a month, in cell A2, and the same is true for the values in cells A3:A10.

■ The Excel chart automatically responds to the type of values you have supplied in the worksheet. The program recognizes that the numbers entered represent monthly intervals and, although there is no data for June through August, the chart leaves places for where the data would appear if it were available. Because the horizontal axis now represents a numeric scale, not simple categories, it faithfully reflects the fact that in the calendar, May is four times as far from September as it is from April.

Figure 1.7
The horizontal axis accounts for the missing months.

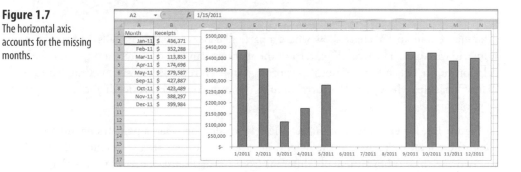

Charting Numeric Variables in Excel

Several chart types in Excel lend themselves beautifully to the visual representation of numeric variables. This book relies heavily on charts of that type because most people find statistical concepts that are difficult to grasp in the abstract are much clearer when they're illustrated in charts.

Charting Two Variables

Earlier this chapter briefly discussed two chart types that use a category variable on one axis and a numeric variable on the other: Column charts and Bar charts. There are other, similar types of charts, such as Line charts, that are useful for analyzing a numeric variable in terms of different categories—especially time categories such as months, quarters, and years. However, one particular type of Excel chart, called an *XY (Scatter)* chart, shows the relationship between two numeric variables. Figure 1.8 provides an example.

> **NOTE**
> Since the 1990s at least, Excel has called this sort of chart an *XY (Scatter) chart*. In its 2007 version, Excel started referring to it as an XY chart in some places, as a Scatter chart in others, and as an XY (Scatter) chart in still others. For the most part, this book opts for the brevity of *XY chart*, and when you see that term you can be confident it's the same as an XY (Scatter) chart.

Figure 1.8
In an XY (Scatter) chart, both the horizontal and vertical axes are value axes.

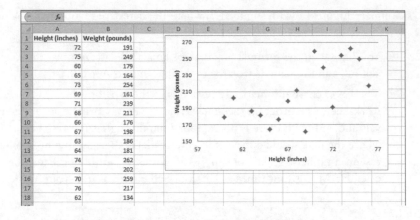

The markers in an XY chart show where a particular person or object falls on each of two numeric variables. The overall pattern of the markers can tell you quite a bit about the relationship between the variables, as expressed in each record's measurement. Chapter 4, "How Variables Move Jointly: Correlation," goes into considerable detail about this sort of relationship.

In Figure 1.8, for example, you can see the relationship between a person's height and weight: Generally, the greater the height, the greater the weight. The relationship between the two variables is fundamentally different from those discussed earlier in this chapter, where the emphasis is placed on the sum or average of a numeric variable, such as number of vehicles, according to the category of a nominal variable, such as make of car.

However, when you are interested in the way that two numeric variables are related, you are asking a different sort of question, and you use a different sort of statistical analysis. How are height and weight related, and how strong is the relationship? Does the amount of time spent on a cell phone correspond in some way to the likelihood of contracting cancer? Do people who spend more years in school eventually make more money? (And if so, does that relationship hold all the way from elementary school to post-graduate degrees?) This is another major class of empirical research and statistical analysis: the investigation of how different variables change together—or, in statistical lingo, how they *covary*.

Excel's XY charts can tell you a considerable amount about how two numeric variables are related. Figure 1.9 adds a trendline to the XY chart in Figure 1.8.

The diagonal line you see in Figure 1.9 is a *trendline*. It is an idealized representation of the relationship between men's height and weight, at least as determined from the sample of 17 men whose measures are charted in the figure. The trendline is based on this formula:

Weight = 5.2 * Height – 152

Excel calculates the formula based on what's called the *least squares* criterion. You'll see much more about this in Chapter 4.

Figure 1.9
A trendline graphs a numeric relationship, which is almost never an accurate way to depict reality.

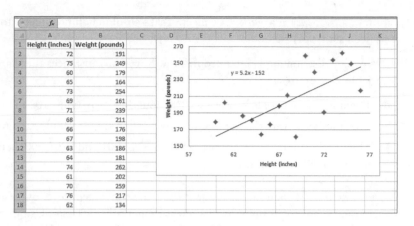

Suppose that you picked several—say, 20—different values for height in inches, plugged them into that formula, and then found the resulting weight. If you now created an Excel XY chart that shows those values of height and weight, you would get a chart that shows the straight trendline you see in Figure 1.9.

That's because arithmetic is nice and clean and doesn't involve errors. Reality, though, is seldom free from errors. Some people weigh more than a formula thinks they should, given their height. Other people weigh less. (Statistical analysis terms these discrepancies *errors*.) The result is that if you chart the measures you get from actual people instead of from a mechanical formula, you're going to get data that look like the scattered markers in Figures 1.8 and 1.9.

Reality is messy, and the statistician's approach to cleaning it up is to seek to identify regular patterns lurking behind the real-world measures. If those real-world measures don't precisely fit the pattern that has been identified, there are several explanations, including these (and they're not mutually exclusive):

- People and things just don't always conform to ideal mathematical patterns. Deal with it.

- There may be some problem with the way the measures were taken. Get better yardsticks.

- There may be some other, unexamined variable that causes the deviations from the underlying pattern. Come up with some more theory, and then carry out more research.

Understanding Frequency Distributions

In addition to charts that show two variables—such as numbers broken down by categories in a Column chart, or the relationship between two numeric variables in an XY chart—there is another sort of Excel chart that deals with one variable only. It's the visual representation of a *frequency distribution*, a concept that's absolutely fundamental to intermediate and advanced statistical methods.

A frequency distribution is intended to show how many instances there are of each value of a variable. For example:

- The number of people who weigh 100 pounds, 101 pounds, 102 pounds, and so on.
- The number of cars that get 18 miles per gallon (mpg), 19 mpg, 20 mpg, and so on.
- The number of houses that cost between $200,001 and $205,000, between $205,001 and $210,000, and so on.

Because we usually round measurements to some convenient level of precision, a frequency distribution tends to group individual measurements into classes. Using the examples just given, two people who weigh 100.2 and 100.4 pounds might each be classed as 100 pounds; two cars that get 18.8 and 19.2 mpg might be grouped together at 19 mpg; and any number of houses that cost between $220,001 and $225,000 would be treated as in the same price level.

As it's usually shown, the chart of a frequency distribution puts the variable's values on its horizontal axis and the count of instances on the vertical axis. Figure 1.10 shows a typical frequency distribution.

Figure 1.10
Typically, most records cluster toward the center of a frequency distribution.

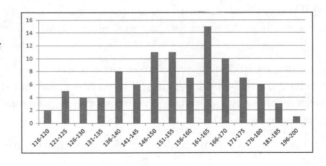

You can tell quite a bit about a variable by looking at a chart of its frequency distribution. For example, Figure 1.10 shows the weights of a sample of 100 people. Most of them are between 140 and 180 pounds. In this sample, there are about as many people who weigh a lot (say, over 175 pounds) as there are whose weight is relatively low (say, up to 130). The range of weights—that is, the difference between the lightest and the heaviest weights—is about 85 pounds, from 116 to 200.

There are lots of ways that a different sample of people might provide a different set of weights than those shown in Figure 1.10. For example, Figure 1.11 shows a sample of 100 vegans—notice that the distribution of their weights is shifted down the scale somewhat from the sample of the general population shown in Figure 1.10.

Figure 1.11
Compared to Figure 1.10, the location of the frequency distribution has shifted to the left.

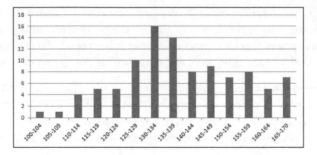

The frequency distributions in Figures 1.10 and 1.11 are relatively symmetric. Their general shapes are not far from the idealized normal "bell" curve, which depicts the distribution of many variables that describe living beings. This book has much more to say in future chapters about the normal curve, partly because it describes so many variables of interest, but also because Excel has so many ways of dealing with the normal curve.

Still, many variables follow a different sort of frequency distribution. Some are skewed right (see Figure 1.12) and others left (see Figure 1.13).

Figure 1.12
A frequency distribution that stretches out to the right is called positively skewed.

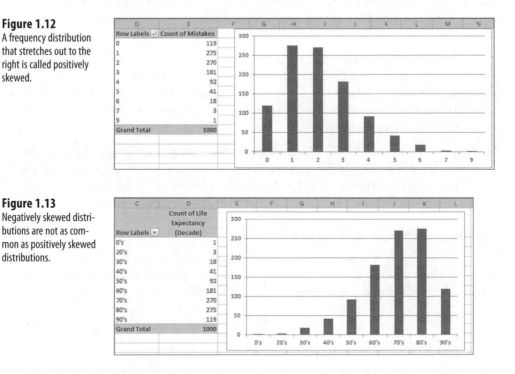

Figure 1.13
Negatively skewed distributions are not as common as positively skewed distributions.

Figure 1.12 shows counts of the number of mistakes on individual Federal tax forms. It's normal to make a few mistakes (say, one or two), and it's abnormal to make several (say, five or more). This distribution is positively skewed.

1

Another variable, home prices, tends to be positively skewed, because although there's a real lower limit (a house cannot cost less than $0) there is no theoretical upper limit to the price of a house. House prices therefore tend to bunch up between $100,000 and $200,000, with a few between $200,000 and $300,000, and fewer still as you go up the scale.

A quality control engineer might sample 100 ceramic tiles from a production run of 10,000 and count the number of defects on each tile. Most would have zero, one, or two defects, several would have three or four, and a very few would have five or six. This is another positively skewed distribution—quite a common situation in manufacturing process control.

Because true lower limits are more common than true upper limits, you tend to encounter more positively skewed frequency distributions than negatively skewed. But they certainly occur. Figure 1.13 might represent personal longevity: relatively few people die in their twenties, thirties, and forties, compared to the numbers who die in their fifties through their eighties.

Using Frequency Distributions

It's helpful to use frequency distributions in statistical analysis for two broad reasons. One concerns visualizing how a variable is distributed across people or objects. The other concerns how to make inferences about a population of people or objects on the basis of a sample.

Those two reasons help define the two general branches of statistics: *descriptive* statistics and *inferential* statistics. Along with descriptive statistics such as averages, ranges of values, and percentages or counts, the chart of a frequency distribution puts you in a stronger position to understand a set of people or things because it helps you visualize how a variable behaves across its range of possible values.

In the area of inferential statistics, frequency distributions based on samples help you determine the type of analysis you should use to make inferences about the population. As you'll see in later chapters, frequency distributions also help you visualize the results of certain choices that you must make, such as the probability of making the wrong inference.

Visualizing the Distribution: Descriptive Statistics

It's usually much easier to understand a variable—how it behaves in different groups, how it may change over time, and even just what it looks like—when you see it in a chart. For example, here's the formula that defines the normal distribution:

$$u = (1 / ((2\pi)^{.5}) \, \sigma) \, e \, \char94 \, (- (X - \mu)^2 / 2 \, \sigma^2)$$

And Figure 1.14 shows the normal distribution in chart form.

The formula itself is indispensable, but it doesn't convey understanding. In contrast, the chart informs you that the frequency distribution of the normal curve is symmetric and that most of the records cluster around the center of the horizontal axis.

Figure 1.14
The familiar normal curve is just a frequency distribution.

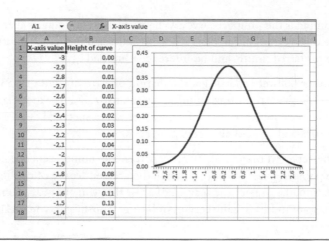

The formula was developed by a 17th century French mathematician named Abraham De Moivre. Excel simplifies it to this:

=NORMDIST(1,0,1,FALSE)

In Excel 2010, it's this:

=NORM.S.DIST(1,FALSE)

Those are *major* simplifications.

Again, personal longevity tends to bulge in the higher levels of its range (and therefore skews left as in Figure 1.13). Home prices tend to bulge in the lower levels of their range (and therefore skew right). The height of human beings creates a bulge in the center of the range, and is therefore symmetric and *not* skewed.

Some statistical analyses assume that the data comes from a normal distribution, and in some statistical analyses that assumption is an important one. This book does not explore the topic in detail because it comes up infrequently. Be aware, though, that if you want to analyze a skewed distribution there are ways to normalize it and therefore comply with the requirements of the analysis. In general, you can use Excel's SQRT() and LOG() functions to help normalize a negatively skewed distribution, and an exponentiation operator (for example, =A2^2 to square the value in A2) to help normalize a positively skewed distribution.

Visualizing the Population: Inferential Statistics

The other general rationale for examining frequency distributions has to do with making an inference about a population, using the information you get from a sample as a basis. This is the field of inferential statistics. In later chapters of this book you will see how to use Excel's tools—in particular, its functions and its charts—to infer a population's characteristics from a sample's frequency distribution.

A familiar example is the political survey. When a pollster announces that 53% of those who were asked preferred Smith, he is reporting a descriptive statistic. Fifty-three percent of the sample preferred Smith, and no inference is needed.

But when another pollster reports that the margin of error around that 53% statistic was plus or minus 3%, she is reporting an inferential statistic. She is extrapolating from the sample to the larger population and inferring, with some specified degree of confidence, that between 50% and 56% of all voters prefer Smith.

The size of the reported margin of error, six percentage points, depends in part on how confident the pollster wants to be. In general, the greater degree of confidence you want in your extrapolation, the greater the margin of error that you allow. If you're on an archery range and you want to be virtually certain of hitting your target, you make the target as large as necessary.

Similarly, if the pollster wants to be 99.9% confident of her projection into the population, the margin might be so great as to be useless—say, plus or minus 20%. And it's not headline material to report that somewhere between 33% and 73% of the voters prefer Smith.

But the size of the margin of error also depends on certain aspects of the frequency distribution in the sample of the variable. In this particular (and relatively straightforward) case, the accuracy of the projection from the sample to the population depends in part on the level of confidence desired (as just briefly discussed), in part on the size of the sample, and in part on the percent favoring Smith in the sample. The latter two issues, sample size and percent in favor, are both aspects of the frequency distribution you determine by examining the sample's responses.

Of course, it's not just political polling that depends on sample frequency distributions to make inferences about populations. Here are some other typical questions posed by empirical researchers:

- What percent of the nation's homes went into foreclosure last quarter?

- What is the incidence of cardiovascular disease today among persons who took the pain medication Vioxx prior to its removal from the marketplace in 2004? Is that incidence reliably different from the incidence of cardiovascular disease among those who did not take the medication?

- A sample of 100 cars from a particular manufacturer, made during 2010, had average highway gas mileage of 26.5 mpg. How likely is it that the average highway mpg, for all that manufacturer's cars made during that year, is greater than 26.0 mpg?

- Your company manufactures custom glassware and uses lasers to etch company logos onto wine bottles, tumblers, sales awards, and so on. Your contract with a customer calls for no more than 2% defective items in a production lot. You sample 100 units from your latest production run and find five that are defective. What is the likelihood that the entire production run of 1,000 units has a maximum of 20 that are defective?

In each of these four cases, the specific statistical procedures to use—and therefore the specific Excel tools—would be different. But the basic approach would be the same: Using the characteristics of a frequency distribution from a sample, compare the sample to a population whose frequency distribution is either known or founded in good theoretical work. Use the numeric functions in Excel to estimate how likely it is that your sample accurately represents the population you're interested in.

Building a Frequency Distribution from a Sample

Conceptually, it's easy to build a frequency distribution. Take a sample of people or things and measure each member of the sample on the variable that interests you. Your next step depends on how much sophistication you want to bring to the project.

Tallying a Sample

One straightforward approach continues by dividing the relevant range of the variable into manageable groups. For example, suppose you obtained the weight in pounds of each of 100 people. You might decide that it's reasonable and feasible to assign each person to a weight class that is ten pounds wide: 75 to 84, 85 to 94, 95 to 104, and so on. Then, on a sheet of graph paper, make a tally in the appropriate column for each person, as suggested in Figure 1.15.

Figure 1.15
This approach helps clarify the process, but there are quicker and easier ways.

	A	B	C	D	E	F	G
1							
2				✓			
3				✓			
4				✓			
5			✓	✓			
6			✓	✓	✓		
7			✓	✓	✓		
8			✓	✓	✓		
9			✓	✓	✓		
10			✓	✓	✓		
11			✓	✓	✓		
12			✓	✓	✓		
13			✓	✓	✓		
14			✓	✓	✓		
15			✓	✓	✓		
16		✓	✓	✓	✓		
17		✓	✓	✓	✓		
18		✓	✓	✓	✓		
19		✓	✓	✓	✓		
20		✓	✓	✓	✓	✓	
21		✓	✓	✓	✓	✓	
22		✓	✓	✓	✓	✓	
23	✓	✓	✓	✓	✓	✓	
24	✓	✓	✓	✓	✓	✓	✓
25	✓	✓	✓	✓	✓	✓	✓
26	✓	✓	✓	✓	✓	✓	✓
27	✓	✓	✓	✓	✓	✓	✓
28	75 to 84	85 to 94	95 to 104	105 to 114	115 to 124	125 to 134	135 to 144

The approach shown in Figure 1.15 uses a *grouped* frequency distribution, and tallying by hand into groups was the only practical option as recently as the 1980s, before personal computers came into truly widespread use. But using an Excel function named FREQUENCY(), you can get the benefits of grouping individual observations without the tedium of manually assigning individual records to groups.

Grouping with FREQUENCY()

If you assemble a frequency distribution as just described, you have to count up all the records that belong to each of the groups that you define. Excel has a function, FREQUENCY(), that will do the heavy lifting for you. All you have to do is decide on the boundaries for the groups and then point the FREQUENCY() function at those boundaries and at the raw data.

Figure 1.16 shows one way to lay out the data.

Figure 1.16
The groups are defined by the numbers in cells C2:C8.

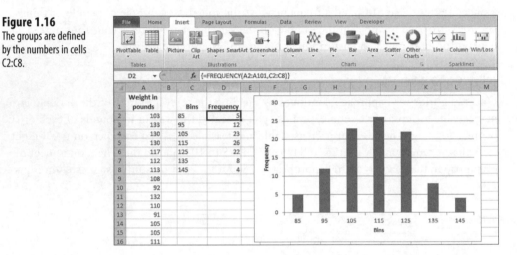

In Figure 1.16, the weight of each person in your sample is recorded in column A. The numbers in cells C2:C8 define the upper boundaries of what this section has called *groups*, and what Excel calls *bins*. Up to 85 pounds defines one bin; from 86 to 95 defines another; from 96 to 105 defines another, and so on.

> **NOTE**
> There's no special need to use the column headers shown in Figure 1.16, cells A1, C1, and D1. In fact, if you're creating a standard Excel chart as described here, there's no great need to supply column headers at all. If you don't include the headers, Excel names the data Series1 and Series2. If you use the pivot chart instead of a standard chart, though, you will need to supply a column header for the data shown in Column A in Figure 1.16.

The count of records within each bin appears in D2:D8. You don't count them yourself—you call on Excel to do that for you, and you do that by means of a special kind of Excel formula, called an *array formula*. You'll read more about array formulas in Chapter 2, "How Values Cluster Together," as well as in later chapters, but for now here are the steps needed to get the bin counts shown in Figure 1.16:

1. Select the range of cells that the results will occupy. In this case, that's the range of cells D2:D8.

2. Type, but don't yet enter, the formula

   =FREQUENCY(A2:A101,C2:C8)

   which tells Excel to count the number of records in A2:A101 that are in each bin defined by the numeric boundaries in C2:C8.

3. After you have typed the formula, hold down the Ctrl and Shift keys simultaneously and press Enter. Then release all three keys. This keyboard sequence notifies Excel that you want it to interpret the formula as an array formula.

>
>
> When Excel interprets a formula as an array formula, it places curly brackets around the formula in the formula box.

The results appear very much like those in cells D2:D8 of Figure 1.16, of course depending on the actual values in A2:A101 and the bins defined in C2:C8. You now have the frequency distribution but you still should create the chart. Here are the steps, assuming the data is located as in Figure 1.16:

1. Select the data you want to chart—that is, the range C1:D8.

2. Click the Insert tab, and then click the Column button in the Charts group.

3. Choose the Clustered Column chart type from the 2-D charts. A new chart appears, as shown in Figure 1.17. Because columns C and D on the worksheet both contain numeric values, Excel initially thinks that there are two data series to chart: one named Bins and one named Frequency.

Figure 1.17
Values from both columns are charted as data series at first because they're all numeric.

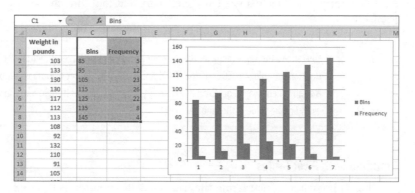

4. Fix the chart by clicking Select Data in the Design tab that appears when a chart is active. The dialog box shown in Figure 1.18 appears.

Figure 1.18
You can also use the
Select Data dialog box to
add another data series
to the chart.

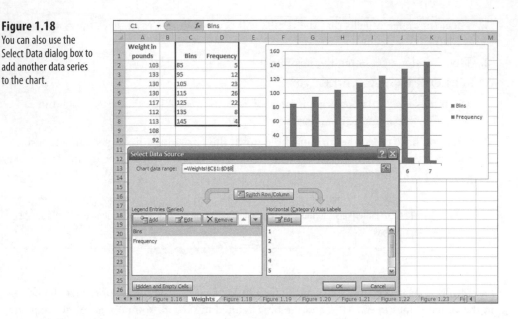

5. Click the Edit button under Horizontal (Category) Axis Labels. A new Axis Labels dialog box appears; drag through cells C2:C8 to establish that range as the basis for the horizontal axis. Click OK.

6. Click the Bins label in the left list box shown in Figure 1.18. Click the Remove button to delete it as a charted series. Click OK to return to the chart.

7. Remove the chart title and series legend, if you want, by clicking each and pressing Delete.

At this point you will have a normal Excel chart that looks much like the one shown in Figure 1.16.

> **TIP**
>
> You can use the same range for the Data argument and the Bins argument in the FREQUENCY() function: for example, =FREQUENCY(A1:A101,A1:A101). Don't forget to enter it as an array formula. This is a convenient way to get Excel to treat every recorded value as its own bin, and you get the count for every unique value in the range A1:A101.

Grouping with Pivot Tables

Another approach to constructing the frequency distribution is to use a pivot table. A related tool, the pivot chart, is based on the analysis that the pivot table does. I prefer this method to using an array formula that employs FREQUENCY() because once the initial groundwork is done, I can use the same pivot table to do analyses that go beyond the basic frequency distribution. But if all I want is a quick group count, FREQUENCY() is usually the faster way.

Again, there's more on pivot tables and pivot charts in Chapter 2 and later chapters, but this section shows you how to use them to establish the frequency distribution.

Building the pivot table (and the pivot chart) requires you to specify bins, just as the use of FREQUENCY() does, but that happens a little further on.

> **NOTE** A reminder: When you use the FREQUENCY() method described in the prior section, a header at the top of the column of raw data is helpful but not required. When you use the pivot table method, the header is required.

Begin with your sample data in A1:A101, just as before. Select any one of the cells in that range and then follow these steps:

1. Click the Insert tab. Click the PivotTable drop-down in the Tables group and choose PivotChart from the drop-down list. (When you choose a pivot chart, you automatically get a pivot table along with it.) The dialog box in Figure 1.19 appears.

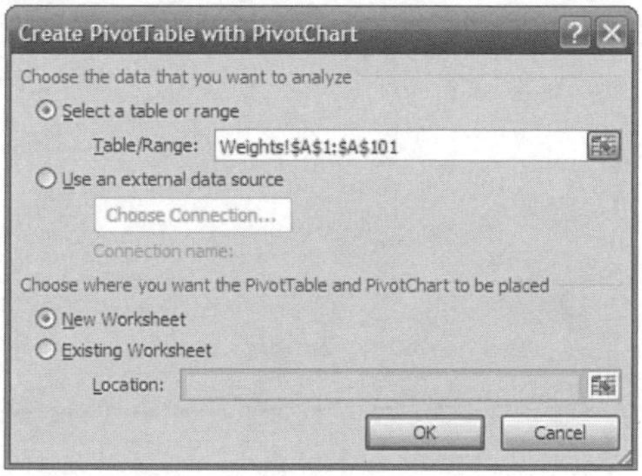

Figure 1.19
If you begin by selecting a single cell in the range containing your input data, Excel automatically proposes the range of adjacent cells that contain data.

2. Click the Existing Worksheet option button. Click in the Location range edit box and then click some blank cell in the worksheet that has other empty cells to its right and below it.

3. Click OK. The worksheet now appears as shown in Figure 1.20.

4. Click the Weight field in the PivotTable Field List and drag it into the Axis Fields (Categories) area.

5. Click the Weight field again and drag it into the **Σ Values** area. Despite the uppercase Greek sigma, which is a summation symbol, the **Σ Values** in a pivot table can show averages, counts, standard deviations, and a variety of statistics other than the sum. However, Sum is the default statistic for a numeric field.

6. The pivot table and pivot chart are both populated as shown in Figure 1.21. Right-click any cell that contains a row label, such as C2. Choose Group from the shortcut menu.

Figure 1.20
With one field only, you normally use it for both Axis Fields (Categories) and Summary Values.

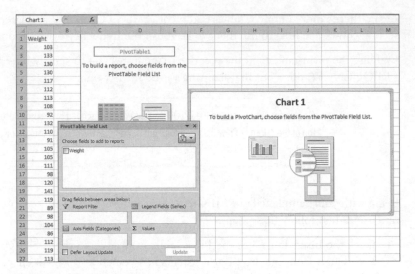

Figure 1.21
The Weight field contains numeric values only, so the pivot table defaults to Sum as the summary statistic.

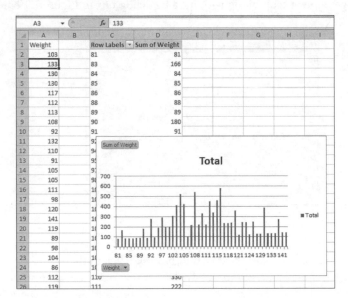

The Grouping dialog box shown in Figure 1.22 appears.

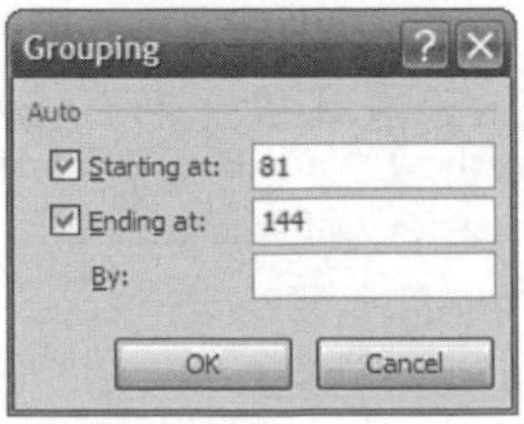

Figure 1.22
This step establishes the groups that the FREQUENCY() function refers to as *bins*.

7. In the Grouping dialog box, set the Starting At value to **81** and enter **10** in the By box. Click OK.

8. Right-click a cell in the pivot table under the header Sum of Weight. Choose Value Field Settings from the shortcut menu. Select Count in the Summarize Value Field By list box, and then click OK.

9. The pivot table and chart reconfigure themselves to appear as in Figure 1.23. To remove the field buttons in the upper- and lower-left corners of the pivot chart, select the chart, click the Analyze tab, click the Field Buttons button, and select Hide All.

Figure 1.23
This sample's frequency distribution has a slight right skew but is reasonably close to a normal curve.

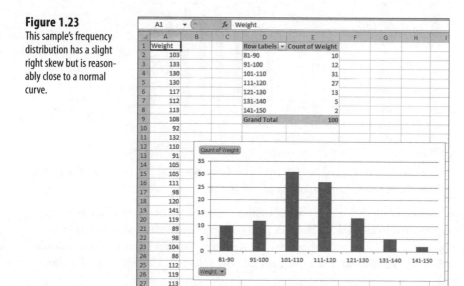

Building Simulated Frequency Distributions

It can be helpful to see how a frequency distribution assumes a particular shape as the number of underlying records increases. *Statistical Analysis: Excel 2010* has a variety of worksheets and workbooks for you to download from this book's website (www.informit.com/title/9780789747204). The workbook for Chapter 1 has a worksheet named Figure 1.24 that samples records at random from a population of values that follows a normal distribution. The following figure, as well as the worksheet on which it's based, shows how a frequency distribution comes closer and closer to the population distribution as the number of sampled records increases.

Begin by clicking the button labeled Clear Records in Column A. All the numbers will be deleted from column A, leaving only the header value in cell A1. (The pivot table and pivot chart will remain as they were: It's a characteristic of pivot tables and pivot charts that they do not respond immediately to changes in their underlying data sources.)

Decide how many records you'd like to add, and then enter that number in cell D1. You can always change it to another number.

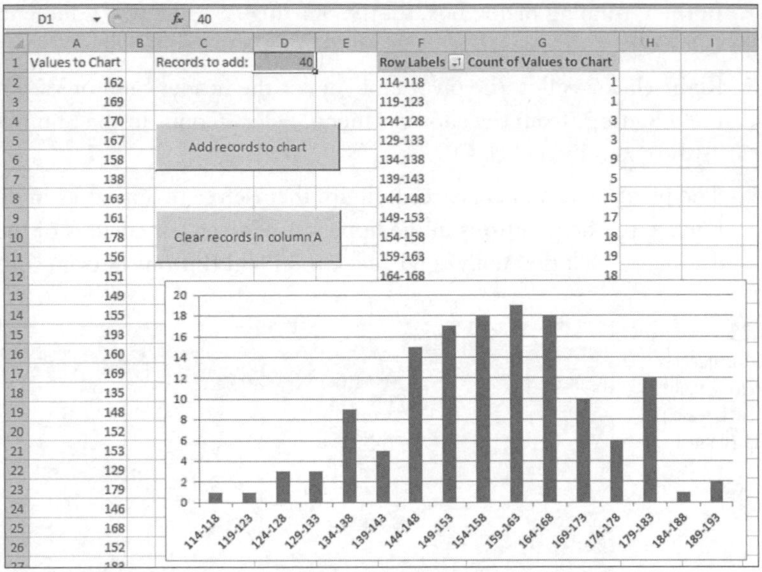

Figure 1.24
This frequency distribution is based on a population of records that follow a normal distribution.

D1		fx	40					
	A	B	C	D	E	F	G	H	I
1	Values to Chart		Records to add:	40		Row Labels	Count of Values to Chart		
2	162					114-118	1		
3	169					119-123	1		
4	170					124-128	3		
5	167		Add records to chart			129-133	3		
6	158					134-138	9		
7	138					139-143	5		
8	163					144-148	15		
9	161					149-153	17		
10	178		Clear records in column A			154-158	18		
11	156					159-163	19		
12	151					164-168	18		
13	149								
14	155								
15	193								
16	160								
17	169								
18	135								
19	148								
20	152								
21	153								
22	129								
23	179								
24	146								
25	168								
26	152								

Click the button labeled Add Records to Chart. When you do so, several events take place, all driven by Visual Basic procedures that are stored in the workbook:

- A sample is taken from the underlying normal distribution. The sample has as many records as specified in cell D1. (The underlying, normally distributed population is stored in a separate, hidden worksheet named Random Normal Values; you can display the worksheet by right-clicking a worksheet tab and selecting Unhide from the shortcut menu.)

- The sample of records is added to column A. If there were no records in column A, the new sample is written starting in cell A2. If there were already, say, 100 records in column A, the new sample would begin in cell A102.

- The pivot table and pivot chart are updated (or, in Excel terms, *refreshed*). As you click the Add Records to Chart button repeatedly, more and more records are used in the chart. The greater the number of records, the more nearly the chart comes to resemble the underlying normal distribution.

In effect, this is what happens in an experiment when you increase the sample size. Larger samples resemble more closely the population from which you draw them than do smaller samples. That greater resemblance isn't limited to the shape of the distribution: It includes the average value and measures of how the values vary around the average. Other things being equal, you would prefer a larger sample to a smaller one because it's likely to represent the population more closely.

But this effect creates a cost-benefit problem. It is usually the case that the larger the sample, the more accurate the experimental findings—and the more expensive the experiment. Many issues are involved here (and this book discusses them), but at some point the incremental accuracy of adding, say, ten more experimental subjects no longer justifies the incremental expense of adding them. One of the bits of advice that statistical analysis provides is to tell you when you're reaching the point when the returns begin to diminish.

With the material in this chapter—scales of measurement, the nature of axes on Excel charts, and frequency distributions—in hand, Chapter 2 moves on to the beginnings of practical statistical analysis, the measurement of central tendency.

1

How Values Cluster Together

When you think about a group that's measured on some numeric variable, you often start thinking about the group's average value. On a scale of 1 to 10, how well do registered Independents think the President is doing? What is the average market value of a house in Minneapolis? What's the most popular given name for boys born last year?

The answer to each of those questions, and questions like them, is usually expressed as an average, although the word *average* in everyday usage isn't well defined, and you would go about figuring each average differently. For example, to investigate Presidential approval, you might go to 100 Independent voters, ask them each for a rating from 1 to 10, add up all the ratings, and divide by 100. That's one kind of average, and it's more precisely termed the *mean*.

If you're after the average housing value in Minneapolis, you probably ask some group such as a board of realtors. They'll likely tell you what the *median* price is. The reason you're less likely to get the mean value is that in real estate sales, there are always a few houses that sell for really outrageous amounts of money. Those few houses pull the mean up so far that it isn't really representative of the price of a typical house in the region you're interested in.

The median, on the other hand, is right on the 50th percentile for house prices; half the houses sold for less than the median price and half sold for more (it's a little more complicated than this, and the complexities will be explained shortly). It isn't affected by how *far* some house values are from an average, just by how *many* are above an average. In that sort of situation, where the distribution of values isn't symmetric, the median often gives you a much better sense of the average, typical value than does the mean.

And if you're thinking of average as a measure of what's most popular, you're usually thinking in terms of a *mode*—the most frequently occurring value. For example, in 2009, Jacob was the modal boy's name among newborns.

Each of these measures—the mean, the median and the mode—is legitimately if imprecisely thought of as an average. More precisely, each of them is a measure of central tendency: that is, how a group of people or things tend to cluster in some way around a central value.

USING TWO SPECIAL EXCEL SKILLS

There are two particular skills in Excel that you will find indispensable for statistical analysis—and they're also handy for other sorts of work you do in Excel. One is the design and construction of pivot tables and pivot charts. The other is array-entering formulas.

This chapter spends more time than you might expect on the mechanics of creating a pivot chart that shows a frequency distribution—and therefore how to display the mode graphically. The material reviews and extends the information on pivot tables that is included in Chapter 1, "About Variables and Values."

You'll also find that this chapter details the rationale for array formulas and the techniques involved in designing them. There's a fair amount of information on how you can use Excel tools to peer inside these exotic formulas to see how they work. You saw some skimpy information about array formulas in Chapter 1.

You need to be familiar with pivot tables and charts, and with array formulas, if you are to use Excel for statistical analysis to any meaningful degree. This chapter, which concerns central tendency, discusses the techniques more than you might expect. But beginning to pick them up here will pay dividends later when you use them to run more sophisticated statistical analysis. They are easier to explore when you use them to calculate means and modes than when you use them to explore the effects of the Central Limit Theorem.

Calculating the Mean

When you're reading, talking, or thinking about statistics and the word *mean* comes up, it refers to the total divided by the count. The total of the heights of everyone in your family divided by the number of people in your family. The total price per gallon of gasoline at all the gas stations in your city, divided by the number of gas stations. The total number of a baseball player's hits divided by the number of at bats.

In the context of statistics, it's very convenient, and more precise, to use the word *mean* this way. It avoids the vagueness of the word *average*, which—as just discussed—can refer to the mean, to the median, or to the mode.

So it's sort of a shame that Excel uses the function name AVERAGE() instead of MEAN(). Nevertheless, Figure 2.1 gives an example of how you get a mean using Excel.

Figure 2.1
The AVERAGE() function calculates the mean of its arguments.

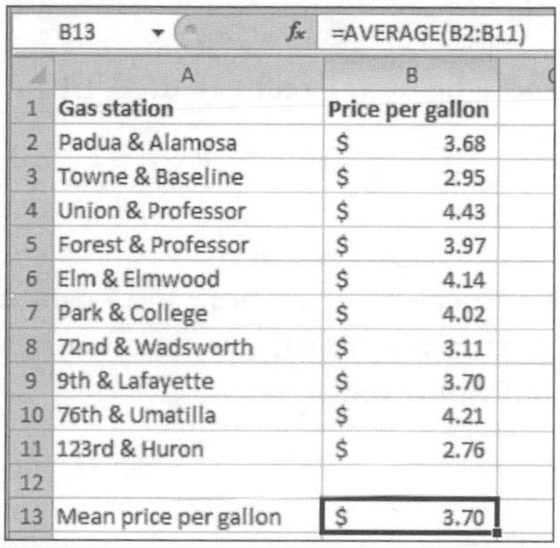

	A	B
1	Gas station	Price per gallon
2	Padua & Alamosa	$ 3.68
3	Towne & Baseline	$ 2.95
4	Union & Professor	$ 4.43
5	Forest & Professor	$ 3.97
6	Elm & Elmwood	$ 4.14
7	Park & College	$ 4.02
8	72nd & Wadsworth	$ 3.11
9	9th & Lafayette	$ 3.70
10	76th & Umatilla	$ 4.21
11	123rd & Huron	$ 2.76
12		
13	Mean price per gallon	$ 3.70

B13 =AVERAGE(B2:B11)

Understanding the elements that Excel's worksheet functions have in common with one another is important to using them properly, and of course you can't do good statistical analysis in Excel without using the statistical functions properly. There are more statistical worksheet functions in Excel, about one hundred, than any other function category. So I propose to spend some ink here on the elements of worksheet functions in general and statistical functions in particular. A good place to start is with the calculation of the mean, shown in Figure 2.1.

Understanding Functions, Arguments, and Results

The function that's depicted in Figure 2.1, AVERAGE(), is a typical example of statistical worksheet functions.

Defining a Worksheet Function

An Excel worksheet function—more briefly, a *function*—is just a formula that someone at Microsoft wrote to save you time, effort, and mistakes.

> **NOTE** Formally, a *formula* in Excel is an expression in a worksheet cell that begins with an equal sign (=); for example, =3+4 is a formula. Formulas often employ functions such as AVERAGE() and an example is =AVERAGE(A1:A20) + 5, where the AVERAGE() function has been used in the formula. Nevertheless, a worksheet function is itself a formula; you just use its name and arguments without having to deal with the way it goes about calculating its results.

Suppose that Excel had no AVERAGE() function. In that case, to get the result shown in cell B13 of Figure 2.1, you would have to enter something like this in B13:

=(B2+B3+B4+B5+B6+B7+B8+B9+B10+B11) / 10

Or, if Excel had a SUM() and a COUNT() function but no AVERAGE(), you could use this:

=SUM(B2:B11)/COUNT(B2:B11)

But you don't need to bother with those because Excel has an AVERAGE() function, and in this case you use it as follows:

=AVERAGE(B2:B11)

So—at least in the cases of Excel's statistical, mathematical, and financial functions—all the term *worksheet function* means is a prewritten formula. The function results in a summary value that's usually based on other, individual values.

Defining Arguments

More terminology: Those "other, individual values" are called *arguments*. That's a highfa-lutin name for the values that you hand off to the function—or, put another way, that you plug into the prewritten formula. In the instance of the function

=AVERAGE(B2:B11)

the range of cells represented by B2:B11 is the function's argument. The arguments *always* appear in parentheses following the function.

A single range of cells is regarded as one argument, even though the single range B2:B11 contains ten values. AVERAGE(B2:B11,C2:C11) contains two arguments: one range of ten values in column B and one range of ten values in column C. (Excel has a few functions, such as PI(), which take no arguments but you have to supply the parentheses anyway.)

> **NOTE**
> Excel 2010 enables you to specify as many as 255 arguments to a function. (Earlier versions, such as Excel 2003, allowed you to specify only 30 arguments.) But this doesn't mean that you can pass a maximum of 255 values to a function. Even AVERAGE(A1:A1048576), which calculates the mean of the values in over a million cells, has only one argument.

Many statistical and mathematical functions in Excel take the contents of worksheet cells as their arguments—for example, SUM(A2:A10). Some functions have additional arguments that you use to fine-tune the analysis. You'll see much more about these functions in later chapters, but a straightforward example involves the FREQUENCY() function, which was introduced in Chapter 1:

=FREQUENCY(B2:B11,E2:E6)

In this example, suppose that you wanted to categorize the price per gallon data in Figure 2.1 into five groups: less than $1, between $1 and $2, between $2 and $3 and so on. You could define the limits of those groups by entering the value at the upper limit of the range—that is, $1, $2, $3, $4, and so on—in cells E2:E6. The FREQUENCY() function expects that you will use its first argument to tell it where the individual observations are (here, they're in B2:B11, called the *data array* by Excel) and that you'll use its second argument to tell it where to find the boundaries of the groups (here, E2:E6, called the *bins array*).

So in the case of the FREQUENCY() function, the arguments have different purposes: The data array argument contains the range address of the values that you want to group, and the bins array argument contains the range address of the boundaries you want to use for the bins.

Contrast that with something such as =SUM(A1, A2, A3), where the SUM() function expects each of its arguments to contribute to the total. To use worksheet functions properly, you must be aware of the purpose of each one of a function's arguments.

Excel gives you an assist with that. When you start to enter a function into a cell in an Excel worksheet, Excel responds by prompting you for the remaining arguments. See Figure 2.2, where the user has just begun entering the FREQUENCY() function. Excel displays the names of the arguments in a small pop-up window.

Figure 2.2
The individual observations are found in the data_array and the bin boundaries are found in the bins_array.

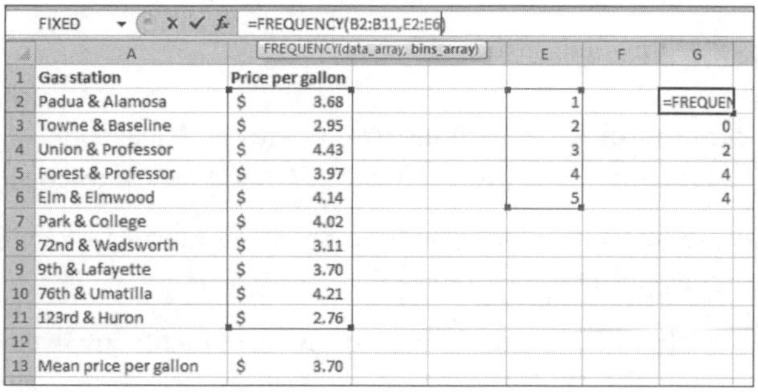

Excel is often finicky about the order in which you supply the arguments. In the prior example, for instance, you get a very different (and very wrong) result if you incorrectly give the bins array address first:

=FREQUENCY(E2:E6,B2:B11)

The order matters if the arguments serve different purposes, as they do in the FREQUENCY() function. If they all serve the same purpose, the order doesn't matter. For example, =SUM(A2:A10,B2:B10) is equivalent to =SUM(B2:B10,A2:A10) because the only arguments to the SUM() function are its addends.

Defining Return

One final bit of terminology used in functions: When a function calculates its result using the arguments you have supplied, it displays the result in the cell where you entered the function. This process is termed *returning* the result. For example, the AVERAGE() function *returns* the mean of the values you supply.

Understanding Formulas, Results, and Formats

It's important to be able to distinguish between a formula, the formula's results, and what the results look like in your worksheet. A friend of mine didn't bother to understand the distinctions and as a consequence he failed a very elementary computer literacy course.

My friend knew that among other learning objectives he was supposed to show how to use a formula to add together the numbers in two worksheet cells and show the result of the addition in a third cell. The numbers 11 and 14 were in A1 and A2, respectively. Because he didn't understand the difference between a formula and the result of a formula, he entered the actual sum, 25, in A3, instead of the formula =A1+A2. When he learned that he'd failed the test, he was surprised to find out that "There's some way they can tell that you didn't enter the formula."

What could I say? He was pre-law.

Earlier this chapter discussed the following example of the use of a simple statistical function:

=AVERAGE(B2:B11)

In fact, that's a formula. An Excel formula begins with an equal sign (=). This particular formula consists of a function name (here, AVERAGE) and its arguments (here, B2:B11).

In the normal course of events, after you have finished entering a formula into a worksheet cell, Excel responds as follows:

- The formula itself, including any function and arguments involved, appears in the Formula box.
- The result of the formula—in this case, what the function returns—appears in the cell where you entered the formula.
- The precise result of the formula might or might not appear in that cell, depending on the cell format that you have specified. For example, if you have limited how many decimal places show up in the cell, the result may appear less precise.

I used the phrase "normal course of events" just now because there are steps you sometimes take to override them (see Figure 2.3).

Notice these three aspects of the worksheet in Figure 2.3: The formula itself is visible, its result is visible, and its result can also be seen with a different appearance.

Visible Formulas

The formula itself appears in the Formula box. But if you wanted, you could set the protection for cell B13, or B15, to Hidden. Then, if you protect the worksheet, the formula would not appear in the Formula box. Usually, though, the formula box shows you the formula or the static value you've entered in the cell.

Figure 2.3
The Formula bar contains the Name box, on the left, and the Formula box, on the right.

MeanPrice	▾	f_x =AVERAGE(B2:B11)

	A	B	C
1	Gas station	Price per gallon	
2	Padua & Alamosa	$ 3.68	
3	Towne & Baseline	$ 2.95	
4	Union & Professor	$ 4.43	
5	Forest & Professor	$ 3.97	
6	Elm & Elmwood	$ 4.14	
7	Park & College	$ 4.02	
8	72nd & Wadsworth	$ 3.11	
9	9th & Lafayette	$ 3.70	
10	76th & Umatilla	$ 4.21	
11	123rd & Huron	$ 2.76	
12			
13	Mean price per gallon	$ 3.70	
14			
15		3.697	

Visible Results

The result of the formula appears in the cell where the formula is entered. In Figure 2.3, you see the average price per gallon for ten gas stations in cells B13 and B15. But you could instead see the formulas in the cells. There is a Show Formulas toggle button in the Formula Auditing section of the Ribbon's Formulas tab. Click it to change from values to formulas and back to values. If you don't find that button (perhaps someone has customized the Ribbon), click the File tab and choose Options from the navigation bar. Click Advanced in the Excel Options window and scroll down to the Display Options for This Worksheet area. Fill the check box labeled Show Formulas in Cells Instead of Their Calculated Results.

Same Result, Different Appearance

The same formula is in cell B15 as in cell B13, but the formula appears to return a different result. Actually, both cells contain 3.697. But cell B13 is formatted to show currency, and United States currency formats display two decimal values only, by convention. So, if you call for the currency format and your operating system is using U.S. currency conventions, the display is adjusted to show just two decimals. You can change the number of decimals displayed if you wish, by selecting the cell and then clicking either the Increase Decimal or the Decrease Decimal button in the Number group on the Home tab.

Minimizing the Spread

The mean has a special characteristic that makes it more useful for certain advanced statistical analyses than the median and the mode. That characteristic has to do with the distance of each individual observation from the mean of all observations included in calculating the mean.

Suppose you have a list of ten numbers—say, the ages of all your close relatives. Pluck another number out of the air. Subtract that number from each of the ten ages and square the result of each subtraction. Now, find the total of all ten squared differences.

If the number that you chose, the one that you subtracted from each of the ten ages, happens to be the mean of the ten ages, then the total of the squared differences is minimized, thus the term *least squares*. That total is smaller than it would be if you chose *any* number other than the mean. This outcome probably seems a strange thing to care about, but it turns out to be an important characteristic of many statistical analyses, as you'll see in later chapters of this book.

Here's a concrete example. Figure 2.4 shows the height of each of ten people in cells A2:A11.

Figure 2.4
Columns B, C and D are reserved for values that you supply.

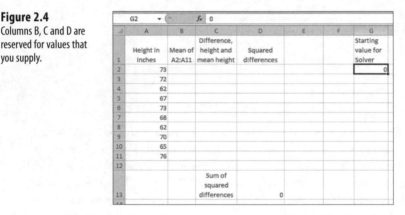

Using the workbook for Chapter 2 (see www.informit.com/title/9780789747204 for download information), you should fill in columns B, C, and D as described later in this section. The cells B2:B11 in Figure 2.4 will then contain a value—any numeric value—that's different from the actual mean of the ten observations in column A. You will see that if the mean is in column B, the sum of the squared differences in cell D13 is smaller than if any other number is in column B.

To see that, you will need to have made Solver available to Excel.

About Solver

Solver is an add-in that comes with Microsoft Excel. You can install it from the factory disc or from the software that you downloaded to put Excel on your computer. Solver helps you backtrack to underlying values when you want them to result in a particular outcome.

For example, suppose you have ten numbers on a worksheet, and their mean value is 25. You want to know what the tenth number must be in order for the mean to equal 30 instead of 25. Solver can do that for you. Normally, you know your inputs and you're seeking a result. When you know the result and want to find the necessary values of the inputs, Solver provides one way to do so.

The example in the prior paragraph is trivially simple, but it illustrates the main purpose of Solver: You specify the outcome and Solver determines the input values needed to reach the outcome.

You could use another Excel tool, Goal Seek, to solve the latter problem. But Solver offers you many more options than does Goal Seek. For example, using Solver, you can specify that you want an outcome maximized or minimized, instead of solving for a particular outcome. That's relevant here because we want to find a value that minimizes the sum of the squared differences.

Finding and Installing Solver

It's possible that Solver is already installed and available to Excel on your computer. To use Solver in Excel 2007 or 2010, click the Ribbon's Data tab and find the Analysis group. If you see Solver there you're all set. (In Excel 2003 or earlier, check for Solver in the Tools menu.)

If you don't find Solver on the Ribbon or the Tools menu, take these steps in Excel 2007 or 2010:

1. Click the Ribbon's File tab and choose Options.
2. Choose Add-Ins from the Options navigation bar.
3. At the bottom of the View and Manage Microsoft Office Add-Ins window, make sure that the Manage drop-down is set to Excel Add-Ins and then click Go.
4. The Add-Ins dialog box appears. If you see Solver Add-in listed, fill its check box and click OK.

You should now find Solver in the Analysis group on the Ribbon's Data tab.

If you're using Excel 2003 or earlier, start by choosing Add-Ins from the Tools menu. Then complete step 4 in the preceding list.

If you didn't find Solver in the Analysis group on the Data tab (or on the Tools menu in earlier Excel versions), and if you did not see it in the Add-Ins dialog box in step 4, then Solver was not installed with Excel. You will have to re-run the installation routine, and you can usually do so via the Programs item in the Windows Control Panel.

The sequence varies according to the operating system you're running, but you should choose to change features for Microsoft Office. Expand the Excel option by clicking the plus sign by its icon and then do the same for Add-ins. Click the drop-down by Solver and choose Run from My Computer. Complete the installation sequence. When it's through, you should be able to make the Solver add-in available to Excel using the sequence of four steps provided earlier in this section.

Setting Up the Worksheet for Solver

With the actual observations in A2:A11, as shown in Figure 2.4, continue by taking these steps:

1. Enter any number in cell G2. It is 0 in Figure 2.4, but you could use 10 or 1066 or 3.1416 if you prefer. When you're through with these steps, you'll find the mean of the values in A2:A11 has replaced the value you now begin with in cell G2.

2. In cell B2, enter this formula:

   =$G$2

3. Copy and paste the formula in B2 into B3:B11. Because the dollar signs in the cell address make it a fixed reference, you will find that each cell in B2:B11 contains the same formula. And because the formulas point to cell G2, whatever number is there also appears in B2:B11.

4. In cell C2, enter this formula:

   =A2 – B2

5. Copy and paste the formula in C2 into C3:C11. The range C2:C11 now contains the differences between each individual observation and whatever value you chose to put in cell G2.

6. In cell D2, enter the following formula, which uses the caret as an exponentiation operator to return the square of the value in cell C2:

   =C2^2

7. Copy and paste the formula in D2 into D3:D11. The range D2:D11 now contains the squared differences between each individual observation and whatever number you entered in cell G2.

8. To get the sum of the squared differences, enter this formula in cell D13:

   =SUM(D2:D11)

9. Now start Solver. With cell D13 selected, click the Data tab and locate the Analysis group. Click Solver to bring up the dialog box shown in Figure 2.5.

10. You want to minimize the sum of the squared differences, so choose the Min radio button.

11. Because D13 was the active cell when you started Solver, it is the address that appears in the Set Objective field. Click in the By Changing Variable Cells box and then click in cell G2. This establishes the cell whose value Solver will modify.

12. Click Solve.

Solver now iterates through a sequence of values for cell G2. It stops when its internal decision-making rules tell it that it has found a minimum value for cell D13 and that testing more values in cell G2 won't help.

Using the data given in Figure 2.4, Solver finishes with a value of 68.8 in cell G2 (see Figure 2.6). Because of the way that the worksheet was set up, that's the value that now appears in cells B2:B11, and it's the basis for the differences in C2:C11 and the squared differences in D2:D11. The sum of the squared differences in D13 is minimized, and the value in cell G2 that's responsible for the minimum sum of the squared differences—or, in more typical statistical jargon, *least squares*—is the mean of the values in A2:A11.

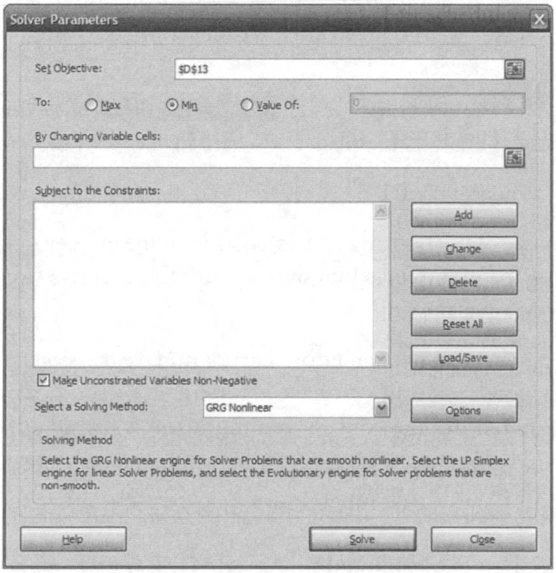

Figure 2.5
The Set Objective field should contain the cell you want Solver to maximize, minimize, or set to a specific value.

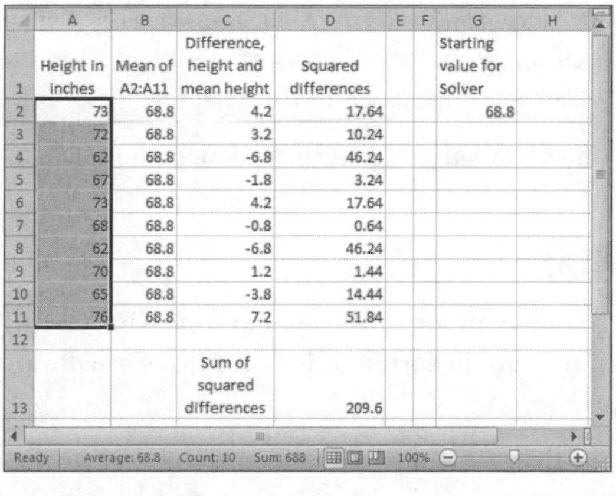

Figure 2.6
Compare cell G2 with the average of the values in A2:A11.

	A	B	C	D	E	F	G	H
1	Height in inches	Mean of A2:A11	Difference, height and mean height	Squared differences			Starting value for Solver	
2	73	68.8	4.2	17.64			68.8	
3	72	68.8	3.2	10.24				
4	62	68.8	-6.8	46.24				
5	67	68.8	-1.8	3.24				
6	73	68.8	4.2	17.64				
7	68	68.8	-0.8	0.64				
8	62	68.8	-6.8	46.24				
9	70	68.8	1.2	1.44				
10	65	68.8	-3.8	14.44				
11	76	68.8	7.2	51.84				
12								
13			Sum of squared differences	209.6				

Ready   Average: 68.8   Count: 10   Sum: 688   100%

TIP

If you take another look at Figure 2.6, you'll see a bar at the bottom of the Excel window with the word *Ready* at its left. This bar is called the *status bar*. You can arrange for it to display the mean of the values in selected cells. Right-click anywhere on the status bar to display a Customize Status Bar window. Select or deselect any of these to display or suppress them on the status bar: Average, Count, Numeric Count, Minimum, Maximum, and Sum. The Count statistic displays a count of all values in the selected range; the Numeric Count displays a count of only the numeric values in the range.

A few comments on this demonstration:

- It works with any set of real numbers, and any size set. Supply some numbers, total their squared differences from some other number, and then tell Solver to minimize that sum. The result will always be the mean of the original set.

- This is a demonstration, not a proof. The proof that the squared differences from the mean sums to a smaller total than from any other number is not complex and it can be found in a variety of sources.

- This discussion uses the terms *differences* and *squared differences*. You'll find that it's more common in statistical analysis to speak and write in terms of *deviations* and *squared deviations*.

This has to be the most roundabout way of calculating a mean ever devised. The AVERAGE() function, for example, is lots simpler. But the exercise using Solver in this section is important for two reasons:

- Understanding other concepts, including correlation, regression, and the general linear model, will come much easier if you have a good feel for the relationship between the mean of a set of scores and the concept of minimizing squared deviations.

- If you have not yet used Excel's Solver, you have now had a glimpse of it, although in the context of a problem solved much more quickly using other tools.

I have used a very simple statistical function, AVERAGE(), as a context to discuss some basics of functions and formulas in Excel. These basics apply to all Excel's mathematical and statistical functions, and to many functions in other categories as well. You'll need to know about some other aspects of functions, but I'll pick them up as we get to them: They're much more specific than the issues discussed in this chapter.

It's time to get on to the next measure of central tendency: the median.

Calculating the Median

The median of a group of observations is usually, and somewhat casually, thought of as the middle observation when they are in sorted order. And that's usually a good way to think of it, even if it's a little imprecise.

It's often said, for example, that half the observations lie below the median while half lie above it. The Excel documentation says so. So does my old college stats text. But no. Suppose that your observations consist of the numbers 1, 2, 3, 4, and 5. The middlemost number in that set is 3. But it is not true that half the numbers lie above it or below it. It *is* accurate to state that the same number of observations lie below the median as lie above it. In the prior example, two observations lie below 3 and two lie above 3.

If there is an even number of observations in the data set, then it's accurate to say that half lie below the median and half above it. But with an even number of observations there is no specific, middle record, and therefore there is no identifiable median record. Add one observation to the prior set, so that it consists of 1, 2, 3, 4, 5, and 6. There is no record in the middle of that set. Or make it 1, 2, 3, 3, 3, and 4. Although one of the 3's is the median, there is no specific, identifiable record in the middle of the set.

One way, used by Excel, to calculate the median with an even number of records is to take the mean of the two middle numbers. In this example, the mean of 3 and 4 is 3.5, which Excel calculates as the median of 1, 2, 3, 4, 5, and 6. And then, with an even number of observations, exactly half the observations lie below and half above the median.

> **NOTE** Other ways to calculate the median are available when there are tied values or an even number of values: One method is interpolation into a group of tied values. But the method used by Excel has the virtue of simplicity: It's easy to calculate, understand, and explain. And you won't go far wrong when Excel calculates a median value of 65.5 when interpolation would have given you 65.7.

The syntax for the MEDIAN() function echoes the syntax of the AVERAGE() function. For the data shown in Figure 2.7, you just enter **=MEDIAN(A2:A61)**.

Figure 2.7
The mean and the median are always different in asymmetric distributions.

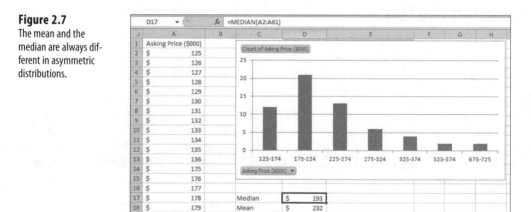

Choosing to Use the Median

The median is sometimes a more descriptive measure of central tendency than the mean. For example, Figure 2.7 shows what's called a *skewed* distribution—that is, the distribution isn't symmetric. Most of the values bunch up on the left side, and a few are located off to the right (of course, a distribution can skew either direction—this one happens to skew right). This sort of distribution is typical of home prices and it's the reason that the real-estate industry reports medians instead of means.

In Figure 2.7, notice that the median home price reported is $193,000 and the mean home price is $232,000. The median responds only to the number of ranked observations, but the mean also responds to the size of the observations' values.

Suppose that in the course of a week the price of the most expensive house increases by $100,000 and there are no other changes in housing prices. The median remains where it was, because it's still at the 50th percentile in the distribution of home prices. It's that 50% rank that matters, not the dollars associated with the most expensive house—or, for that matter, the cheapest.

In contrast, the mean would react if the most expensive house increased in price. In the situation shown in Figure 2.7, an increase of $120,000 in just one house's price would increase the mean by $2,000—but the median would remain where it is.

The median's relatively static quality is one reason that it's the preferred measure of central tendency for housing prices and similar data. Another reason is that when distributions are skewed, the median provides a better measure of how things tend centrally. Have another look at Figure 2.7. Which statistic seems to you to better represent the typical home price in that figure: the mean of $232,000 or the median of $193,000? It's a subjective judgment, of course, but many people would judge that $193,000 is a better summary of the prices of these houses than is $232,000.

Calculating the Mode

The mean gives you a measure of central tendency by taking all the actual values in a group into account. The median measures central tendency differently, by giving you the midpoint of a ranked group of values. The mode takes yet another tack: It tells you which one of several categories occurs most frequently.

You can get this information from the FREQUENCY() function, as discussed in Chapter 1. But the MODE() function returns the most frequently occurring observation only, and it's a little quicker to use. Furthermore, as you'll see in this section, a little work can get MODE() to work with data on a nominal scale—that's also possible with FREQUENCY() but it's a lot more work.

Suppose you have a set of numbers in a range of cells, as shown in Figure 2.8. The following formula returns the numeric value that occurs most frequently in that range (in Figure 2.8, the formula is entered in cell C1):

=MODE(A2:A21)

The pivot chart in Figure 2.8 provides the same information graphically. Notice that the mode returned by the function in cell C1 is the same value as the most frequently occurring value shown in the pivot chart.

The problem is that you don't usually *care* about the mode of numeric values. It's possible that you have at hand a list of the ages of the people who live on your block, or the weight of each player on your favorite football team, or the height of each student in your daughter's fourth grade class. It's even conceivable that you have a good reason to know the most frequently occurring age, weight, or height in a group of people. (In the area of inferential statistics, covered in the second half of this book, the mode of what's called a *reference distribution* is often of interest. At this point, though, we're dealing with more commonplace problems.) But you don't normally need the mode of people's ages, weights, or heights.

Figure 2.8
Excel's MODE() function works only with numeric values.

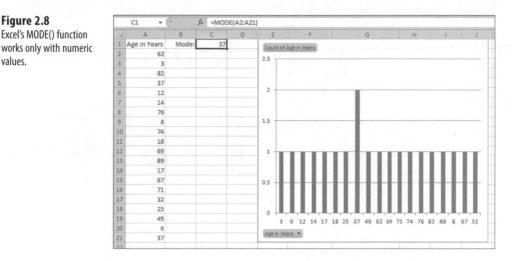

Among other purposes, numeric measures are good for recording small distinctions: Joe is 33 years old and Jane is 34; Dave weighs 230 pounds and Don weighs 232; Jake is 47 inches tall and Judy stands 48 inches. In a group of 18 or 20 people, it's quite possible that everyone is of a different age, or a different weight or a different height. The same is true of most objects and numeric measurements that you can think of.

In that case, it is not plausible that you would want to know the modal age, or weight, or height. The mean, yes, or the median, but why would you want to know that the most frequently occurring age is 47 years, when the next most frequently occurring age is 46 and the next is 48?

The mode is seldom a useful statistic when the variable being studied is numeric and ungrouped. It's when you are interested in nominal data—as discussed in Chapter 1, categories such as brands of cars or children's given names or political preferences—that the mode is of interest. It's worth noting that the mode is the only sensible measure of central tendency when you're dealing with nominal data. The modal boy's name for newborns in 2009 was Jacob; that statistic is interesting to some people in some way. But what's the mean of Jacob, Michael, and Ethan? The median of Emma, Isabella, and Emily? The mode is the only sensible measure of central tendency for nominal data.

But Excel's MODE() function doesn't work with nominal data. If you present to it, as its argument, a range that contains exclusively text data such as names, MODE() returns the #N/A error value. If one or more text values are included in a list of numeric values, MODE() simply ignores the text values.

I'll take this opportunity to complain that it doesn't make a lot of sense for Excel to provide analytic support for a situation that seldom occurs (for example, caring about the modal height of a group of fourth graders) while it fails to support situations that occur all the time ("Which model of car did we sell most of last week?").

Figure 2.9 shows a couple of solutions to the problem with MODE().

Figure 2.9
MODE() is much more useful with categories than with interval or ordinal scales of measurement.

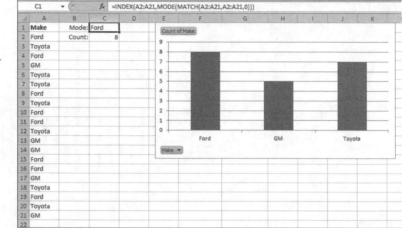

In contrast to the pivot chart shown in Figure 2.8, where just one value pokes up above the others because it occurs twice instead of once, the frequency distribution in Figure 2.9 is more informative. You can see that Ford, the modal value, leads Toyota by a slim margin and GM by somewhat more. (This report is genuine and was exported to Excel by a used car dealer from a popular small business accounting package.)

> **NOTE** Some of the steps that follow are similar, even identical, to the steps taken to create a pivot chart in Chapter 1. They are repeated here, partly for convenience and partly so that you can become accustomed to seeing how pivot tables and pivot charts are built. Perhaps more important, the values on the horizontal axis in the present example are measured on a nominal scale. Because you're simply looking for the mode, no ordering is implied, and the shape of the distribution is arbitrary. Contrast that with Figures 1.21 and 1.23, where the purpose is to determine whether the distribution is normal or skewed. There, you're after the shape of the distribution of an interval variable, so the left-to-right order on the horizontal axis is important.

To create a pivot chart that looks like the one in Figure 2.9, follow these steps:

1. Arrange your raw data in an Excel list format: the field name in the first column (such as A1) and the values in the cells below the field name (such as A2:A21).

2. Select a cell that has several empty columns to its right and several empty rows below it. This is to avoid overwriting any important data with the pivot table.

3. Click the Ribbon's Insert tab, and click the PivotTable drop-down in the Tables group. Choose PivotChart from the drop-down list. The dialog box shown in Figure 2.10 appears.

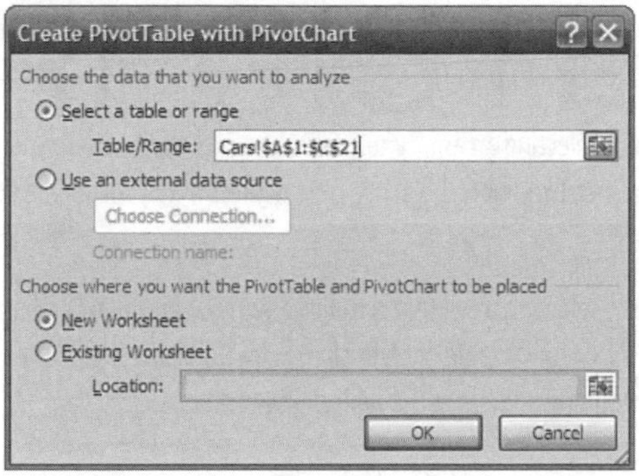

Figure 2.10
In this dialog box you indicate where Excel can find the underlying data set for the analysis, and where you want to pivot table to start.

4. Identify the range that contains your raw data (refer to step 1) by dragging through it with your mouse pointer, by typing its range address, or by typing its name if it's a named table or range. The location of the data should now appear in the Table/Range edit box. Click OK to get the layout shown in Figure 2.11.

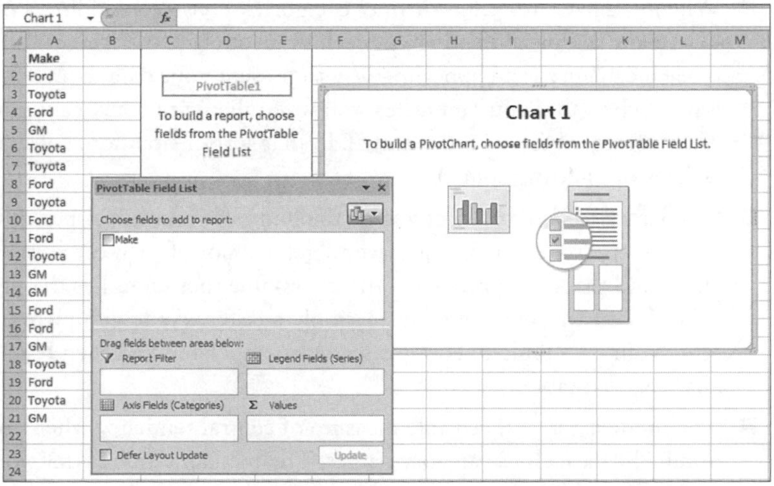

Figure 2.11
The PivotTable Field List pane appears automatically.

5. In the PivotTable Field List, drag the field or fields you're interested in down from the list and into the appropriate area at the bottom. In this example, you would drag Make down into the Axis Fields area and also drag it into the Values area.

The pivot chart and the pivot table that the pivot chart is based on both update as soon as you've dropped a field into an area. If you started with the data shown in Figure 2.9, you should get a pivot chart that's identical, or nearly so, to the pivot chart in that figure.

> **NOTE**
>
> Excel makes one of two assumptions, depending on whether the cell that's active when you begin to create the pivot table contains data.
>
> One, if you started by selecting an empty cell, Excel assumes that's where you want to put the pivot table's upper-left corner. Excel puts the active cell's address in the Location edit box, as shown in Figure 2.10.
>
> Two, if you started by selecting a cell that contains a value or formula, Excel assumes that cell is part of the source data for the pivot table or pivot chart. Excel finds the boundaries of the contiguous, filled cells and puts the resulting address in the Table/Range edit box.

A few comments on this analysis:

■ The mode is quite a useful statistic when it's applied to categories: political parties, consumer brands, days of the week, states in a region, and so on. Excel really should have a built-in worksheet function that returns the mode for text values. But it doesn't, and the next section shows you how to write your own worksheet formula for the mode, one that will work for both numeric and text values.

■ When you have just a few distinct categories, consider building a pivot chart to show how many instances there are of each. A pivot chart that shows the number of instances of each category is an appealing way to present your data to an audience. (There is no type of chart that communicates well when there are many categories to consider. The visual clutter obscures the message. In that sort of situation, consider combining categories or omitting some.)

■ Standard Excel charts do not show the number of instances per category without some preliminary work. You would have to get a count of each category before creating the chart, and that's the purpose of the pivot table that underlies the pivot chart. The pivot chart, based on the pivot table, is simply a faster way to complete the analysis than creating your own table to count category membership and then basing a standard Excel chart on that table.

■ The mode is the *only* sensible measure of central tendency when you're working with nominal data such as category names. The median requires that you rank order things in some way: shortest to tallest, least expensive to priciest, or slowest to fastest. In terms of the scale types introduced in Chapter 1, you need an ordinal scale to get a median, and many categories are nominal, not ordinal. What's the median value of Ford, GM, and Toyota? For that matter, what's their mean?

Getting the Mode of Categories with a Formula

I have pointed out that Excel's MODE() function does not work when you supply it with text values as its arguments. Here is a method for getting the mode using a worksheet formula. It tells you which text value occurs most often in your data set. You'll also see how to enter a formula that tells you how many instances of the mode exist in your data.

If you don't want to resort to a pivot chart to get the mode of a group of text values, you can get their mode with the formula

=INDEX(A2:A21,MODE(MATCH(A2:A21,A2:A21,0)))

assuming that the text values are in A2:A21. (The range could occupy a single column, as in A2:A21, or a single row, as in A2:Z2. It will not work properly with a multi-row, multi-column range such as A2:Z21.)

If you're somewhat new to Excel, that formula isn't going to make any sense to you at all. I structured it, I've been using Excel frequently since 1994, and I still have to stare at the formula and think it through before I see why it returns the mode. So if the formula seems baffling, don't worry about it. It will become clear in the fullness of time, and in the meantime you can use it to get the modal value for any set of text values in a worksheet. Simply replace the range address A2:A21 with the address of the range that contains your text values.

Briefly, the components of the formula work as follows:

- The MATCH() function returns the position in the array of values where each individual value first appears. The third argument to the MATCH() function, 0, tells Excel that in each case an exact match is required and the array is not necessarily sorted. So, for each instance of Ford in the array, MATCH() returns 1; for each instance of Toyota, it returns 2; for each instance of GM, it returns 4.
- The results of the MATCH() function are used as the argument to MODE(). In this example, there are twenty values for MODE() to evaluate: some equal 1, some equal 2 and some equal 4. MODE() returns the most frequently occurring of those numbers.
- The result of MODE() is used as the second argument to INDEX(). Its first argument is the array to examine. The second argument tells it how far into the array to look. Here, it looks at the first value in the array, which is Ford. If, say, GM had been the most frequently occurring text value, MODE() would have returned 4 and INDEX() would have used that value to find GM in the array.

Using an Array Formula to Count the Values

With the modal value (Ford, in this example) in hand, we still want to know how many instances there are of that mode. This section describes how to create the array formula that counts the instances.

Figure 2.9 also shows, in cell C2, the count of the number of records that belong to the modal value. This formula provides that count:

=SUM(IF(A2:A21=C1,1,0))

The formula is an array formula, and must be entered using the special keyboard sequence Ctrl+Shift+Enter. You can tell that a formula has been entered as an array formula if you see curly brackets around it in the formula box. If you array enter the prior formula, it will look like this in the formula box:

{=SUM(IF(A2:A21=C1,1,0))}

But don't supply the curly brackets yourself. If you do, Excel interprets this as text, not as a formula.

Here's how the formula works: As shown in Figure 2.9, cell C1 contains the value "Ford". So the following fragment of the array formula tests whether values in the range A2:A21 equal the value "Ford":

A2:A21=C1

Because there are 20 cells in the range A2:A21, the fragment returns an array of TRUE and FALSE values: TRUE when a cell contains "Ford" and FALSE otherwise. The array looks like this:

{TRUE;FALSE;TRUE;FALSE;FALSE;FALSE;TRUE;FALSE;TRUE;TRUE;

FALSE;FALSE;FALSE;TRUE;TRUE;FALSE;FALSE;TRUE;FALSE;FALSE}

Specifically, cell A2 contains "Ford" and so it passes the test: The first value in the array is therefore TRUE. Cell A3 does not contain "Ford" and so it fails the test: The second value in the array is therefore FALSE—and so on for all 20 cells.

> **NOTE**
> The array of TRUE and FALSE values is an intermediate result of this array formula (and of many others, of course). As such, it is not routinely visible to the user, who normally needs to see only the end result of the formula. If you want to see intermediate results such as this one, use the Formula Auditing tool. See "Looking Inside a Formula," later in this chapter, for more information.

Now step outside that fragment, which, as we've just seen, resolves to an array of TRUE and FALSE values. The array is used as the first argument to the IF() function. Excel's IF() function takes three arguments:

■ The first argument is a value that can be TRUE or FALSE. In this example, that's each value in the array just shown, returned by the fragment A2:A21=C1.

■ The second argument is the value that you want the IF() function to return when the first argument is TRUE. In the example, this is 1.

■ The third argument is the value that you want the IF() function to return when the first argument is FALSE. In the example, this is 0.

The IF() function examines each of the values in the array to see if it's a TRUE value or a FALSE value. When a value in the array is TRUE, the IF() function returns, in this example, a 1, and a 0 otherwise. Therefore, the fragment

IF(A2:A21=C1,1,0)

returns an array of 1's and 0's that corresponds to the first array of TRUE and FALSE values. That array looks like this:

{1;0;1;0;0;1;0;1;1;0;0;0;1;1;0;0;1;0;0}

A 1 corresponds to a cell in A2:A21 that contains the value "Ford" and a 0 corresponds to a cell in the same range that does not contain "Ford". Finally, the array of 1's and 0's is presented to the SUM() function, which totals the values in the array. Here, that total is 8.

Recapping the Array Formula

To review how the array formula counts the values for the modal category of Ford, consider the following:

- The formula's purpose is to count the number of instances of the modal category, Ford, whose name is in cell C1.
- The innermost fragment in the formula, A2:A21=C1, returns an array of 20 TRUE or FALSE values, depending on whether each of the 20 cells in A2:A21 contains the same value as is found in cell C1.
- The IF() function examines the TRUE/FALSE array and returns another array that contains 1's where the TRUE/FALSE array contains TRUE, and 0's where the TRUE/FALSE array contains FALSE.
- The SUM() function totals the values in the array of 1's and 0's. The result is the number of cells in A2:A21 that contain the value in cell C1, which is the modal value for A2:A21.

Using an Array Formula

Various reasons exist for using array formulas in Excel. Two of the most typical reasons are to support a function that requires it and to enable a function to work on more than just one value.

Accommodating a Function   One reason you might need to use an array formula is that you're employing a function that must be array-entered if it is to return results properly. For example, the FREQUENCY() function, which counts the number of values between a lower bound and an upper bound (see "Defining Arguments," earlier in this chapter) requires that you enter it in an array formula. Another function that requires array-entry is the LINEST() function, which will be discussed in great detail in several subsequent chapters.

Both FREQUENCY() and LINEST(), along with a number of other functions, return an array of values to the worksheet. You need to accommodate that array. To do so, begin by selecting a range of cells that has the number of rows and columns needed to show the function's results. (Knowing how many rows and columns to select depends on your knowledge of the function and your experience with it.) Then you enter the formula that calls the function by means of Ctrl+Shift+Enter instead of simply Enter; again, this sequence is called *array entering* the formula.

Accommodating a Function's Arguments   Sometimes you use an array formula because it employs a function that usually takes a single value as an argument, but you want to supply it with an array of values. The example in cell C2 of Figure 2.9 shows the IF() function, which usually expects a single condition as its first argument, accepting an array of TRUE and FALSE values as its first argument:

>   =SUM(IF(A2:A21=C1,1,0))

Typically, the IF() function deals with only one value as its first argument. For example, suppose you want cell C2 to show the value "Current" if cell A1 contains the value 2010; otherwise, B1 should show the value "Past". You could put this formula in B1, entered normally with the Enter key:

>   =IF(A1=2010,"Current","Past")

You can enter that formula normally, via the Enter key, because you're handing off just one value, 2010, to IF() as its first argument.

However, the example concerning the number of instances of the mode value is this:

>   =SUM(IF(A2:A21=C1,1,0))

The first argument to IF() in this case is an array of TRUE and FALSE values. To signal Excel that you are supplying an array rather than a single value as the first argument to IF(), you enter the formula using Ctrl+Shift+Enter, instead of the Enter key alone as you usually would for a normal Excel formula or value.

Looking Inside a Formula

Excel has a couple of tools that come in handy from time to time when a formula isn't working exactly as you expect—or when you're just interested in peeking inside to see what's going on. In each case you can pull out a fragment of a formula to see what it does, in isolation from the remainder of the formula.

Using Formula Evaluation   If you're using Excel 2002 or a more recent version, you have access to a formula evaluation tool. Begin by selecting a cell that contains a formula. Then start formula evaluation. In Excel 2007 and 2010, you'll find it on the Ribbon's Formulas tab, in the Formula Auditing group; in Excel 2002 and 2003, choose Tools, Formula Auditing, Evaluate Formula. If you were to begin by selecting a cell with the array formula that this section has discussed, you would see the window shown in Figure 2.12.

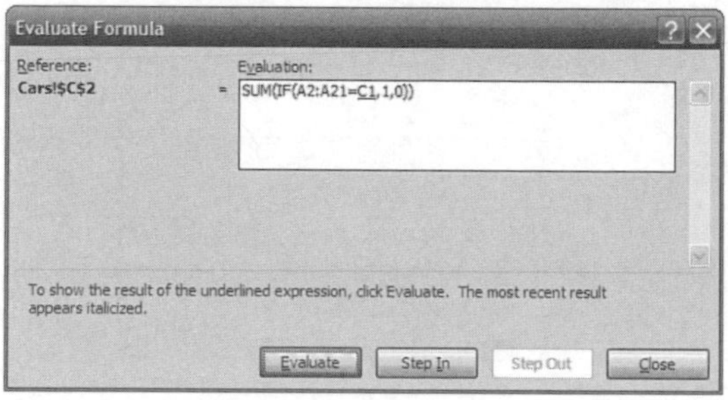

Figure 2.12
Formula evaluation starts with the formula as it's entered in the active cell.

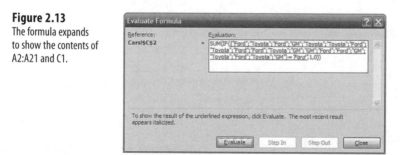

Now, if you click Evaluate, Excel begins evaluating the formula from the inside out and the display changes to what you see in Figure 2.13.

Figure 2.13
The formula expands to show the contents of A2:A21 and C1.

Click Evaluate again and you'll see the results of the test of A2:A21 with C1, as shown in Figure 2.14.

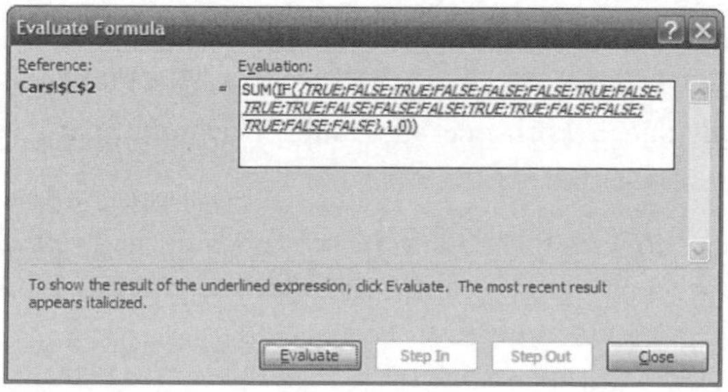

Figure 2.14
The array of cell contents becomes an array of TRUE and FALSE, depending on the contents of the cells.

Click Evaluate again and the window shows the results of the IF() function, which in this case replaces TRUE with 1 and FALSE with 0 (see Figure 2.15).

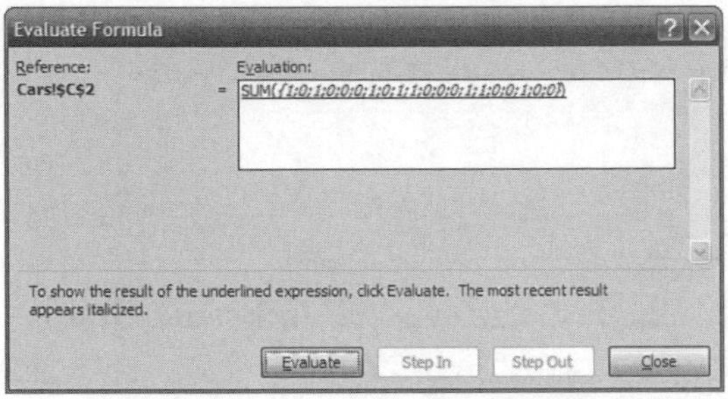

Figure 2.15
Each 1 represents a cell that equals the value in cell C1.

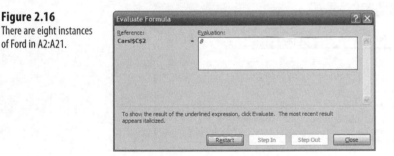

A final click of Evaluate shows you the final result, when the SUM() function totals the 1's and 0's to return a count of the number of instances of Ford in A2:A21, as shown in Figure 2.16.

Figure 2.16
There are eight instances of Ford in A2:A21.

You could use the SUMIF() or COUNTIF() function if you prefer. I like the SUM(IF()) structure because I find that it gives me more flexibility in complicated situations such as summing the results of multiplying two or more conditional arrays.

Using the Recalculate Key   Another method for looking inside a formula is available in all Windows versions of Excel, and makes use of the F9 key. The F9 key forces a calculation and can be used to recalculate a worksheet's formulas when automatic recalculation has been turned off.

If that were all you could do with the F9 key, its scope would be pretty limited. But you can also use it to calculate a portion of a formula. Suppose you have this array formula in a worksheet cell and its arguments as given in Figure 2.9:

```
=SUM(IF(A2:A21=C1,1,0))
```

If the cell that contains the formula is active, you'll see the formula in the Formula box. Drag across the A2:A21=C1 portion with your mouse pointer to highlight it. Then, while it's still highlighted, press F9 to get the result shown in Figure 2.17.

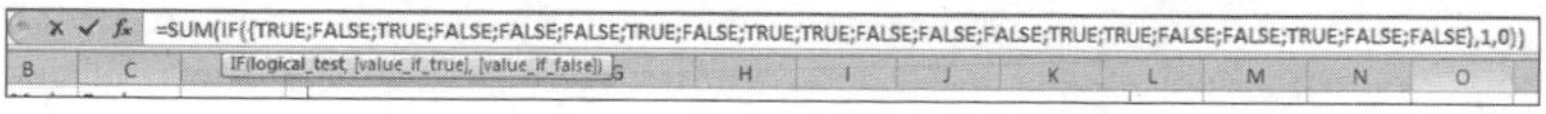

Figure 2.17
Notice that the array of TRUE and FALSE values is identical to the one shown in Figure 2.14.

> **NOTE**
> Excel formulas separate rows by semicolons and columns by commas. The array in Figure 2.17 is based on values that are found in different rows, so the TRUE and FALSE items are separated by semicolons. If the original values were in different columns, the TRUE and FALSE items would be separated by commas.

If you're using Excel 2002 or later, use formula evaluation to step through a formula from the inside out. Alternatively, using any Windows version, use the F9 key to get a quick look at how Excel evaluates a single fragment from the formula.

From Central Tendency to Variability

This chapter has examined the three principal measures of central tendency in a set of values. Central tendency is a critically important attribute in any sample or population, but so is variability. If the mean informs you where the values tend to cluster, the standard deviation and related statistics tell you how the values tend to disperse. You need to know both, and Chapter 3, "Variability: How Values Disperse," gets you started on variability.

Variability: How Values Disperse

Chapter 2, "How Values Cluster Together," went into some detail about measures of central tendency: the methods you can use to determine where on a scale of values you can find the value that's the most typical and representative of a group. Intuitively, an average value is often the most interesting statistic, certainly more interesting than a number that tells you how values *fail* to come together. But understanding their variation gives context to the central tendency of the values.

For example, people tend to be more interested in the median value of houses in a neighborhood than they are in the range of those values. However, a statistic such as the range, which is one way to measure variability, puts an average into context. Suppose you know that the median price of a house in a given neighborhood is $250,000. You also know that the range of home prices—the difference between the highest and the lowest prices—in the same neighborhood is $300,000. You don't know for sure, because you don't know how skewed the distribution is, but a reasonable guess is that the prices range from $100,000 to $400,000.

That's quite a spread in a single neighborhood. If you were told that the range of prices was $100,000, then the values might run from $200,000 to $300,000. In the former case, the neighborhood could include everything from little bungalows to McMansions. In the latter case, the houses are probably fairly similar in size and quality.

It's not enough to know an average value. To give that average a meaning—that is, a context—you also need to know how the various members of a sample differ from its average.

Measuring Variability with the Range

Just as there are three primary ways to measure the central tendency in a frequency distribution, there's more than one way to measure variability. Two of these methods, the standard deviation and the variance, are closely related and take up most of the discussion in this chapter.

A third way of measuring variability is the range: the maximum value in a set minus the minimum value. It's usually helpful to know the range of the values in a frequency distribution, if only to guard against errors in data entry. For example, suppose you have a list in an Excel worksheet that contains the body temperatures, measured in Fahrenheit, of 100 men. If the calculated range, the maximum temperature minus the minimum temperature, is 888 degrees, you know pretty quickly that someone dropped a decimal point somewhere. Perhaps you entered 986 instead of 98.6.

The range as a statistic has some attributes that make it unsuitable for use in much statistical analysis. Nevertheless, in part because it's much easier to calculate by hand than other measures of variability, the range can be useful.

> **NOTE**
>
> Historically, particularly in the area of statistical process control (a technique used in the management of quality in manufacturing), some well known practitioners have preferred the range as an estimate of variability. They claim, with some justification, that a statistic such as the standard deviation is influenced both by the underlying nature of a manufacturing system and by special events such as human errors that cause a system to go out of control.
>
> It's true that the standard deviation takes every value into account in calculating the overall variability in a set of numbers. It doesn't follow, though, that the range is sensitive only to the occasional problems that require detection and correction.

The use of the range as the sole measure of variability in a data set has some drawbacks, but it's a good idea to calculate it anyway to better understand the nature of your data. For example, Figure 3.1 shows a frequency distribution that can be sensibly described in part by using the range.

Because an appreciable number of the observations appear at each end of the distribution, it's useful to know that the range that the values occupy is 34. Figure 3.2 presents a different picture. It takes only one extreme value for the range to present a misleading picture of the degree of variability in a data set.

The size of the range is entirely dependent on the values of the largest and the smallest values. The range does not change until and unless there's a change in one or both of those values, the maximum and the minimum. All the other values in the frequency distribution could change and the range would remain the same. The other values could be distributed more homogeneously, or they could bunch up near one or two modes, and the range would still not change.

Figure 3.1

The distribution is approximately symmetric, and the range is a useful descriptor.

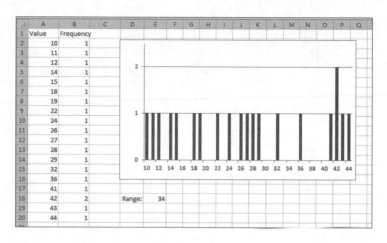

Figure 3.2

The solitary value at the top of the distribution creates a range estimate that misdescribes the distribution.

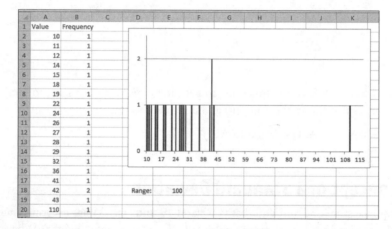

Furthermore, the size of the range depends heavily on the number of values in the frequency distribution. See Figure 3.3 for examples that compare the range with the standard deviation for samples of various sizes, drawn from a population where the standard deviation is 15.

Notice that the mean and the standard deviation are relatively stable across five sample sizes, but the range more than doubles from 27 to 58 as the sample size grows from 2 to 20. That's generally undesirable, particularly when you want to make inferences about a population on the basis of a sample. You would not want your estimate of the variability of values in a population to depend on the size of the sample that you take.

The effect that you see in Figure 3.3 is due to the fact that the likelihood of obtaining a relatively large or small value increases as the sample size increases. (This is true mainly of distributions such as the normal curve that contain many of their observations near the middle of the range.) Although the sample size has an effect on the calculated range, its effect on the standard deviation is much less pronounced because the standard deviation takes into account *all* the values in the sample, not just the extremes.

Figure 3.3
Samples of sizes from 2 to 20 are shown in columns B through F, and statistics appear in rows 22 through 24.

	A	B	C	D	E	F
1		110	71	84	99	72
2		83	85	67	70	128
3			94	89	89	97
4			116	79	104	104
5			98	108	100	102
6				109	124	118
7				85	75	88
8				81	75	130
9				112	102	105
10				119	109	122
11					88	110
12					111	80
13					82	96
14					114	109
15					112	98
16						87
17						118
18						99
19						99
20						84
21						
22	Mean	96.5	92.8	93.3	96.9	102.3
23	SD	19.1	16.6	17.3	16.3	15.8
24	Range	27	45	52	54	58

Excel has no RANGE() function. To get the range, you must use something such as the following, substituting the appropriate range address for the one shown:

=MAX(A2:A21) – MIN(A2:A21)

The Concept of a Standard Deviation

Suppose someone told you that you stand 19 units tall. What do you conclude from that information? Does that mean you're tall? short? of average height? What percent of the population is taller than you are?

You don't know, and you can't know, because you don't know how long a "unit" is. If a unit is four inches long, then you stand 76 inches, or 6'4" (rather tall). If a unit is three inches long, then you stand 57 inches, or 4'9" (rather short).

The problem is that there's nothing standard about the word *unit*. (In fact, that's one of the reasons it's such a useful word.) Now suppose further that the mean height of all humans is 20 units. If you're 19 units tall, you know that you're shorter than average.

But how much shorter is one unit shorter? If, say, 3% of the population stands between 19 and 20 units, then you're only a little shorter than average. Only 3% of the population stands between you and the average height.

If, instead, 34% of the population were between 19 and 20 units tall, then you'd be fairly short: Everyone who's taller than the mean of 20, plus another 34% between 19 and 20 units, would be taller than you.

Suppose now that you *know* the mean height in the population is 20 units, and that 3% of the population is between 19 and 20 units tall. With that knowledge, with the context provided by knowing the mean height and the variability of height, "unit" becomes a standard. Now when someone tells you that you're 19 units tall, you can apply your knowledge of the way that standard behaves, and immediately conclude that you're a skosh shorter than average.

Arranging for a Standard

A standard deviation acts much like the fictitious unit described in the prior section. In *any* frequency distribution that follows a normal curve, these statements are true:

■ You find about 34% of the records between the mean and one standard deviation from the mean.

■ You find about 14% of the records between one and two standard deviations from the mean.

■ You find about 2% of the records between two and three standard deviations from the mean.

These standards are displayed in Figure 3.4.

Figure 3.4
These proportions are found in all normal distributions.

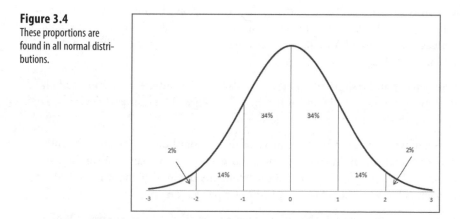

The numbers shown on the horizontal axis in Figure 3.4 are called *z-scores*. A z-score, or sometimes z-value, tells you how many standard deviations above or below the mean a record is. If someone tells you that your height in z-score units is +1.0, it's the same as saying that your height is one standard deviation above the mean height.

Similarly, if your weight in z-scores is –2.0, your weight is two standard deviations below the mean weight.

Because of the way that z-scores slice up the frequency distribution, you know that a z-score of +1.0 means that 84% of the records lie below it: Your height of 1.0 z means that you are as tall as or taller than 84% of the other observations. That 84% comprises the 50% below the mean, plus the 34% between the mean and one standard deviation above the mean. Your weight, –2.0 z, means that you outweigh only 2% of the other observations. Hence the term *standard deviation*. It's *standard* because it doesn't matter whether you're talking about height, weight, IQ, or the diameter of machined piston rings. If it's a variable that's normally distributed, then one standard deviation above the mean is equal to or greater than 84% of the other observations. Two standard deviations below the mean is equal to or less than 98% of the other observations.

It's a *deviation* because it expresses a distance from the mean: a departure from the mean value. And it's at this point in the discussion that we get back to the material in Chapter 2 regarding the mean, that it is the number that minimizes the sum of the squared deviations of the original values. More on that shortly, in "Dividing by N – 1," but first it's helpful to bring in a little more background.

Thinking in Terms of Standard Deviations

With some important exceptions, you are likely to find yourself thinking more about standard deviations than about other measures of variability. (Those exceptions begin to pile up when you start working with the analysis of variance and multiple regression, but those topics are a few chapters off.) The standard deviation is in the same unit of measurement as the variable you're interested in. If you're studying the distribution of miles per gallon of gasoline in a sample of cars, you might find that the standard deviation is four miles per gallon. The mean mileage of car brand A might be four mpg, or one standard deviation, greater than brand B's mean mileage.

That's very convenient and it's one reason that standard deviations are so useful. It's helpful to be able to think to yourself, "The mean height is 69 inches. The standard deviation is 3 inches." The two statistics are in the same metric.

The *variance* is a different matter. It's the square of the standard deviation, and it's fundamental to statistical analysis, and you'll see much more about the variance in this and subsequent chapters. But it doesn't lend itself well to statements in English about the variability of a measure such as blood serum cholesterol or miles per gallon.

For example, it's easy to get comfortable with statements such as "the mean was 20 miles per gallon and the standard deviation was 5 miles per gallon." It's a lot harder to feel comfortable with "the mean was 20 miles per gallon and the variance was 25 squared miles per gallon." What does a "squared mile per gallon" even mean?

Fortunately, standard deviations are more intuitively informative. Suppose you have the mpg of ten Toyota cars in B2:B11, and the mpg of ten GM cars in B12:B21. One way to express the difference between the two brands' mean gas mileage is this:

    =(AVERAGE(B2:B11) – AVERAGE(B12:B21)) / STDEV(B2:B21)

That Excel formula gets the difference in the mean values for the two brands, and divides by the standard deviation of the mpg for all 20 cars. It's shown in Figure 3.5.

Figure 3.5
The difference between two brands, expressed in standard deviation units.

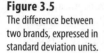

	A	B	C	D	E	F	G	H	I
	F20				f_x =(AVERAGE(B2:B11)-AVERAGE(B12:B21))/STDEV(B2:B21)				
1	Brand	MPG							
2	Toyota	27.94							
3	Toyota	27.51							
4	Toyota	22.22							
5	Toyota	20.55							
6	Toyota	23.13							
7	Toyota	28.79							
8	Toyota	27.36							
9	Toyota	24.96							
10	Toyota	28.95							
11	Toyota	29.23							
12	GM	17.34							
13	GM	24.55							
14	GM	22.46							
15	GM	22.41							
16	GM	24.11							
17	GM	24.22			Average, Toyota		26			
18	GM	25.10			Average, GM		23			
19	GM	21.06			Standard Deviation		3			
20	GM	24.75			Standardized Difference		1.0			
21	GM	22.98								

In Figure 3.5, the difference between the two brands in standard deviation units is 1.0. As you become more familiar and comfortable with standard deviations, you will find yourself automatically thinking things such as, "One standard deviation—that's quite a bit." Expressed in this way, you don't need to know whether 26 mpg vs. 23 mpg is a large difference or a small one. Nor do you need to know whether 5.6 mmol/L (millimoles per liter) of LDL cholesterol is high, low, or typical (see Figure 3.6). All you need to know is that 5.6 is more than one standard deviation above the mean of 4.8 to conclude that it indicates moderate risk of diseases associated with the thickening of arterial walls.

Figure 3.6
The difference between one observation and a sample mean, expressed in standard deviation units.

	A	B	C	D	E	F
	F6			f_x =(F5-F2)/F3		
1	LDL measure (mmol/L)					
2	5.3				Average LDL	4.8
3	4.3			Standard deviation of LDL		0.6
4	3.2					
5	5.7				My LDL	5.6
6	4.6			My LDL in standard deviations		1.41
7	3.2					
8	5.2					
9	5.0					
10	4.8					
11	4.9					
12	5.1					
13	4.9					
14	4.7					
15	4.6					
16	4.9					
17	4.9					
18	5.0					
19	4.9					
20	4.9					
21	5.0					

The point is that when you're thinking in terms of standard deviation units in an approximately normal distribution, you automatically know where a z-score is in the overall distribution. You know how far it is from another z-score. You know whether the difference between two means, expressed as z-scores, is large or small.

First, though, you have to calculate the standard deviation. Excel makes that very easy. There was a time when college students sat side by side at desks in laboratory basements, cranking out sums of squares on Burroughs adding machines with hand cranks. Now all that's needed is to enter something like =STDEV(A2:A21).

Calculating the Standard Deviation and Variance

Excel provides you with no fewer than six functions to calculate the standard deviation of a set of values, and it's pretty easy to get the standard deviation on a worksheet. If the values you're concerned with are in cells A2:A21, you might enter this formula to get the standard deviation:

=STDEV(A2:A21)

(Other versions of the function are discussed later in this chapter, in the section titled "Excel's Variability Functions.")

The *square* of a standard deviation is called the *variance*. It's another important measure of the variability in a set of values. Also, several functions in Excel return the variance of a set of values. One is VAR(). Again, other versions are discussed later in "Excel's Variability Functions." You enter a formula that uses the VAR() function just as you enter one that uses a standard deviation function:

=VAR(A2:A21)

That's so simple and easy, it might not seem sensible to take the wraps off a somewhat intimidating formula. But looking at how the statistic is defined often helps understanding.

So, although most of this chapter has to do with standard deviations, it's important to look more closely at the variance. Understanding one particular aspect of the variance makes it much easier to understand the standard deviation.

Here's what's often called the definitional formula of the variance:

$$s^2 = \sum_{i=1}^{N} \frac{(X_i - \overline{X})^2}{N}$$

Here's the definitional formula in words:

You have a sample of values, where the number of values is represented by N. The letter i is just an identifier that tells you which one of the N values you're using as you work your way through the sample. With those values in hand, Excel's standard deviation function takes the following steps. Refer to Figure 3.7 to see the steps as you might take them in a worksheet,

> **NOTE**
>
> Different formulas have different names, even when they are intended to calculate the same quantity. For many years, statisticians avoided using the definitional formula just shown because it led to clumsy computations, especially when the raw scores were not integers. Computational formulas were used instead, and although they tended to obscure the conceptual aspects of a formula, they made it much easier to do the actual calculations. Now that we use computers to do the calculations, yet a different set of algorithms is used. Those algorithms are intended to improve the accuracy of the calculations far into the tails of the distributions, where the numbers get so small that traditional calculation methods yield more approximation than exactitude.

if you wanted to treat Excel as the twenty-first-century equivalent of a Burroughs adding machine.

1. Calculate the mean of the N values ($\overline{X}$). In Figure 3.7, the mean is shown in cell C2.

2. Subtract the mean from each of the N values ($X_i - \overline{X}$). These differences (or *deviations*) appear in cells E2:E21 in Figure 3.7.

3. Square each deviation. See cells G2:G21.

4. Find the total (Σ) of the squared deviations, shown in cell I2.

5. Divide by N to find the mean squared deviation. See cell K2.

Figure 3.7
The long way around to the variance and the standard deviation.

	A	B	C	D	E	F	G	H	I	J	K	L	M	N
N5					=STDEVP(A2:A21)									
1	Values		Step 1, Mean		Step 2, Deviations		Step 3, Squared Deviations		Step 4, Sum of Squared Deviations		Step 5, Mean Squared Deviation or Variance		Step 6, Square Root of Variance to get the Standard Deviation	
2	9		56.55		-47.55		2261.0025		9596.95		479.85		21.91	
3	26				-30.55		933.3025							
4	28				-28.55		815.1025						Check:	
5	39				-17.55		308.0025						=STDEVP(A2:A21)	21.91
6	42				-14.55		211.7025							
7	42				-14.55		211.7025							
8	43				-13.55		183.6025							
9	51				-5.55		30.8025							
10	56				-0.55		0.3025							
11	57				0.45		0.2025							
12	58				1.45		2.1025							
13	59				2.45		6.0025							
14	62				5.45		29.7025							
15	68				11.45		131.1025							
16	68				11.45		131.1025							
17	75				18.45		340.4025							
18	76				19.45		378.3025							
19	82				25.45		647.7025							
20	92				35.45		1256.7025							
21	98				41.45		1718.1025							
22														

Step 5 results in the variance. If you think your way through those steps, you'll see that the variance is the average squared deviation from the mean. As we've already seen, this quantity is not intuitively meaningful. You don't say, for example, that John's LDL measure is one variance higher than the mean. But the variance is an important and powerful statistic, and you'll find that you grow more comfortable thinking about it as you work your way through subsequent chapters in this book.

If you wanted to take a sixth step in addition to the five listed above, you could take the square root of the variance. Step 6 results in the standard deviation, shown as 21.91 in cell M2 of Figure 3.7. The Excel formula is =SQRT(K2).

As a check, you find the same value of 21.91 in cell N5 of Figure 3.7. It's much easier to enter the formula **=STDEVP (A2:A21)** than to go through all the manipulations in the six steps just given. Nevertheless, it's a useful exercise to grind it out on the worksheet even just once, to help you learn and retain the concepts of squaring, summing, and averaging the deviations from the mean.

Figure 3.8 shows the frequency distribution from Figure 3.7 graphically.

Figure 3.8
The frequency distribution approximates but doesn't duplicate a normal distribution.

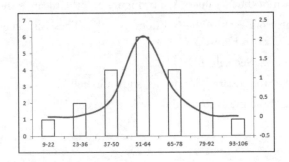

Notice in Figure 3.8 that the columns represent the count of records in different sets of values. A normal distribution is shown as a curve in the figure. The counts make it clear that this frequency distribution is close to a normal distribution; however, largely because the number of observations is so small, the frequencies depart somewhat from the frequencies that the normal distribution would cause you to expect.

Nevertheless, the standard deviation in this frequency distribution captures the values in categories that are roughly equivalent to the normal distribution.

For example, the mean of the distribution is 56.55 and the standard deviation is 21.91. Therefore, a z-score of −1.0 (that is, one standard deviation below the mean) represents a raw score of 34.64. Figure 3.4 says to expect that 34% of the observations will come between the mean and one standard deviation on each side of the mean.

If you examine the raw scores in cells A2:A21 in Figure 3.7, you'll see that six of them fall between 34.64 and 56.65. Six is 30% of the 20 observations, and is a good approximation of the expected 34%.

Squaring the Deviations

Why square each deviation and then take the square root of their total? One primary reason is that if you simply take the average deviation, the result is always zero. Suppose you have three values: 8, 5, and 2. Their average value is 5. The deviations are 3, 0, and –3. The deviations total to zero, and therefore the mean of the deviations must equal zero. The same is true of any set of real numbers you might choose.

Because the total deviation is always zero, regardless of the values involved, it's useless as an indicator of the amount of variability in a set of values. Therefore, each deviation is squared before totaling them. Because the square of any number is positive, you avoid the problem of always getting zero for the total of the deviations.

It is possible, of course, to use the absolute value of the deviations: that is, treat each deviation as a positive number. Then the sum of the deviations must be a positive number, just as is the sum of the squared deviations. And in fact there are some who argue that this figure, called the *mean deviation*, is a better way to calculate the variability in a set of values than the standard deviation.

But that argument, such as it is, goes well beyond the scope of this book. The standard deviation has long been the preferred method of measuring the amount of variability in a set of values.

Population Parameters and Sample Statistics

You normally use the word *parameter* for a number that describes a population and *statistic* for a number that describes a sample. So the mean of a population is a parameter, and the mean of a sample is a statistic.

This book tries to avoid using symbols where possible, but you're going to come across them sooner or later—one of the places you'll find them is in Excel's documentation. It's traditional to use Greek letters for parameters that describe a population and to use Roman letters for statistics that describe a sample. So, you use the letter *s* to refer to the standard deviation of a sample and σ to refer to the standard deviation of a population.

With those conventions in mind—that is, Greek letters to represent population parameters and Roman letters to represent sample statistics—the equation that defines the variance for a sample that was given above should read differently for the variance of a population. The variance as a parameter is defined in this way:

$$\sigma^2 = \sum_{i=1}^{N} \frac{(X_i - \mu)^2}{N}$$

The equation shown here is functionally identical to the equation for the sample variance given earlier. This equation uses the Greek σ, pronounced *sigma*. The lowercase σ is the symbol used in statistics to represent the standard deviation of a population, and σ^2 to represent the population variance.

The equation also uses the symbol μ. The Greek letter, pronounced *mew*, represents the population mean, whereas the symbol $\overline{X}$, pronounced *X bar*, represents the sample mean. (It's usually, but not always, related Greek and Roman letters that represent the population parameter and the associated sample statistic.)

The symbol for the number of values, N, is not replaced. It is considered neither a statistic nor a parameter.

Dividing by N − 1

Another issue is involved with the formula that calculates the variance (and therefore the standard deviation). It stays involved when you want to estimate the variance of a population by means of the variance of a sample from that population. If you wondered why Chapter 2 went to such lengths to discuss the mean in terms of minimizing the sum of squared deviations, you'll find the reason in this section.

Recall from Chapter 2 this property of the mean: if you calculate the deviation of each value in a sample from the mean of the sample, square the deviations and total them, then the result is smaller than it is if you use any number other than the mean. You can find this concept discussed at length in the section of Chapter 2 titled "Minimizing the Spread."

Suppose now that you have a sample of 100 piston rings taken from a population of, say, 10,000 rings that your company has manufactured. You have a measure of the diameter of each ring in your sample, and you calculate the variance of the rings using the definitional formula:

$$s^2 = \sum_{i=1}^{N} \frac{(X_i - \overline{X})^2}{N}$$

You'll get an accurate value for the variance in the sample, but that value is likely to *underestimate* the variance in the population of 10,000 rings. In turn, if you take the square root of the variance to obtain the standard deviation as an estimate of the population's standard deviation, the underestimate comes along for the ride.

Samples involve error: in practice, their statistics are virtually never precisely equal to the parameters they're meant to estimate. If you calculate the mean age of ten people in a statistics class that has 30 students, it is almost certain that the mean age of the ten student sample will be different from the mean age of the 30 student class.

Similarly, it is very likely that the mean piston ring diameter in your sample is different, even if only slightly, from the mean diameter of your population of 10,000 piston rings. Your sample mean is calculated on the basis of the 100 rings in your sample. Therefore, the result of the calculation

$$\sum_{i=1}^{N} \frac{(X_i - \overline{X})^2}{N}$$

which uses the sample mean $\overline{X}$, is different from, *and smaller than*, the result of this calculation:

$$\sum_{i=1}^{N} \frac{(X_i - \mu)^2}{N}$$

which uses the population mean μ.

The outcome is as demonstrated in Chapter 2.

Bear in mind that when you calculate deviations using the mean of the *sample's* observations, you minimize the sum of the squared deviations from the sample mean. If you use any other number, such as the population mean, the result will be different from, and larger than, when you use the sample mean.

Therefore, any time you estimate the variance (or the standard deviation) of a population using the variance (or standard deviation) of a sample, your statistic is virtually certain to underestimate the size of the population parameter.

There would be no problem if your sample mean happened to be the same as the population mean, but in any meaningful situation that's wildly unlikely to happen.

Is there some correction factor that can be used to compensate for the underestimate? Yes, there is. You would use this formula to accurately calculate the variance in a sample:

$$\sum_{i=1}^{N} \frac{(X_i - \overline{X})^2}{N}$$

But if you want to estimate the value of the variance of the population from which you took your sample, you divide by N – 1:

$$\sum_{i=1}^{N} \frac{(X_i - \overline{X})^2}{(N - 1)}$$

The quantity (N – 1) in this formula is called the *degrees of freedom*.

Similarly, this formula is the definitional formula to estimate a population's standard deviation on the basis of the observations in a sample (it's just the square root of the sample estimate of the population variance):

$$\sqrt{\sum_{i=1}^{N} \frac{(X_i - \overline{X})^2}{N - 1}}$$

If you look into the documentation for Excel's variance functions, you'll see that VAR() or, in Excel 2010, VAR.S() is recommended if you want to estimate a population variance from a sample. Those functions use the degrees of freedom in their denominators.

The functions VARP() and, in Excel 2010, VAR.P() are recommended if you are calculating the variance of a population by supplying the entire population's values as the argument to the function. Equivalently, if you do have a sample from a population but do not intend to infer the population variance—that is, you just want to know the sample's variance—you would use VARP() or VAR.P(). These functions use N, not the N – 1 degrees of freedom, in their denominators.

The same is true of STDEVP() and STDEV.P(). Use them to get the standard deviation of a population or of a sample when you don't intend to infer the population's standard deviation. Use STDEV() or STDEV.S() to infer a population standard deviation.

3

Bias in the Estimate

The main purpose of inferential statistics, the topic that's discussed in the second half of this book, is to infer population parameters such as μ and σ from sample statistics such as $\overline{X}$ and s. You will sometimes see $\overline{X}$ and s and other statistics referred to as *estimators*, particularly in the context of inferring population values.

Estimators have several desirable characteristics, and one of them is *unbiasedness*. The absence of bias in a statistic that's being used as an estimator is desirable. The mean is an unbiased estimator. No special adjustment is needed for $\overline{X}$ to estimate μ accurately.

But when you use N, instead of the N – 1 degrees of freedom, in the calculation of the variance, you are biasing the statistic as an estimator. It is then biased negatively: it's an underestimate of the variance in the population.

As discussed in the prior section, that's the reason to use the degrees of freedom instead of the actual sample size when you infer the population variance from the sample variance. So doing removes the bias from the estimator.

It's easy to conclude, then, that using N – 1 in the denominator of the standard deviation also removes its bias as an estimator of the population standard deviation. But it doesn't. The square root of an unbiased estimator is not itself necessarily unbiased.

Much of the bias in the standard deviation is in fact removed by the use of the degrees of freedom instead of N in the denominator. But a little is left, and it's usually regarded as negligible.

The larger the sample size, of course, the smaller the correction involved in using the degrees of freedom. With a sample of 100 values, the difference between dividing by 100 and dividing by 99 is quite small. With a sample of ten values, the difference between dividing by 10 and dividing by 9 can be meaningful.

Similarly, the degree of bias that remains in the standard deviation is very small when the degrees of freedom instead of the sample size is used in the denominator. The standard deviation remains a biased estimator, but the bias is only about 1% when the sample size is as small as 20, and the remaining bias becomes smaller yet as the sample size increases.

> **NOTE**
> You can estimate the bias in the standard deviation as an estimator of the population standard deviation that remains after the degrees of freedom has replaced the sample size in the denominator. In a normal distribution, this expression is an unbiased estimator of the population standard deviation:
>
> (1 + 1 / [4 * {n - 1}]) * s

Degrees of Freedom

The concept of degrees of freedom is important to calculating variances and standard deviations. But as you move from descriptive statistics to inferential statistics, you encounter the concept more and more often. Any inferential analysis, from a simple t-test to a complicated multivariate linear regression, uses degrees of freedom (df) as part of the math and to help evaluate how reliable a result might be. The concept of degrees of freedom is also important for understanding standard deviations, as the prior section discussed.

Unfortunately, degrees of freedom is not a straightforward concept. It's usual for people to take longer than they expect to become comfortable with it.

Fundamentally, degrees of freedom refers to the number of values that are free to vary. It is often true that one or more values in a set are constrained. The remaining values—the number of values in that set that are unconstrained—constitute the degrees of freedom.

Consider the mean of three values. Once you have calculated the mean and stick to it, it acts as a *constraint*. You can then set two of the three values to any two numbers you want, but the third value is constrained by the calculated mean.

Take 6, 8, and 10. Their mean is 8. Two of them are free to vary, and you could change 6 to 2 and 8 to 24. But because the mean acts as a constraint, the original 10 is constrained to become –2 if the mean of 8 is to be maintained.

When you calculate the deviation of each observation from the mean, you are imposing a constraint—the calculated mean—on the values in the sample. All of the observations but one (that is, N – 1 of the values) are free to vary, and with them the sum of the squared deviations. One of the observations is forced to take on a particular value, in order to retain the value of the mean.

In later chapters, particularly concerning the analysis of variance and linear regression, you will see that there are situations in which more constraints on a set of data exist, and therefore the number of degrees of freedom is fewer than the N – 1 value for the variances and standard deviations this chapter discusses.

Excel's Variability Functions

The 2010 version of Excel reorganizes and renames several statistical functions. The aim is to name the functions according to a more consistent pattern, and to make a function's purpose more apparent from its name.

Standard Deviation Functions

For example, Excel has since 1995 offered two functions that return the standard deviation:

- **STDEV()**—This function assumes that its argument list is a sample from a population, and therefore uses N – 1 in the denominator.
- **STDEVP()**—This function assumes that its argument list is the population, and therefore uses N in the denominator.

In its 2003 version, Excel added two more functions that return the standard deviation:

- **STDEVA()**—This function works like STDEV() except that it accepts alphabetic, text values in its argument list and also Boolean (TRUE or FALSE) values. Text values and FALSE values are treated as zeroes, and TRUE values are treated as ones.

- **STDEVPA()**—This function accepts text and Boolean values, just as does STDEVA(), but again it assumes that the argument list constitutes a population.

Microsoft decided that using P, for population, at the end of the function name STDEVP() was inconsistent because there was no STDEVS(). That would never do, and to remedy the situation, Excel 2010 includes two new standard deviation functions that append a letter to the function name in order to tell you whether it's intended for use with a sample or on a population:

- **STDEV.S()**—This function works just like STDEV—it ignores Boolean values and text.

- **STDEV.P()**—This function works just like STDEVP—it also ignores Boolean values and text.

STDEV.S() and STDEV.P() are termed *consistency* functions because they introduce a new, more consistent naming convention than the earlier versions. Microsoft also states that their computation algorithms bring about more accurate results than is the case with STDEV() and STDEVP().

Excel 2010 continues to support the old STDEV() and STDEVP() functions, although it is not at present clear how long they will continue to be supported. In recognition of their deprecated status, STDEV() and STDEVP() occupy the bottom of the list of functions that appears in a pop-up window when you begin to type **=STD** in a worksheet cell. Excel 2010 refers to them as *compatibility functions*.

Variance Functions

Similar considerations apply to the worksheet functions that return the variance. The function's name is used to indicate whether it is intended for a population or to infer a population value from a sample, and whether it can deal with nonnumeric values in its arguments.

- VAR() has been available in Excel since its earliest versions. It returns an unbiased estimate of a population variance based on values from a sample and uses degrees of freedom in the denominator. It is the square of STDEV().

- VARP() has been available in Excel for as long as VAR(). It returns the variance of a population and uses the number of records, not the degrees of freedom, in the denominator. It is the square of STDEVP().

- VARA() made its first appearance in Excel 2003. See the discussion of STDEVA(), earlier in this chapter, for the difference between VAR() and VARA().

FUNCTIONAL CONSISTENCY

The documentation for Excel 2010 stresses the notion of consistency in the naming of functions: If a function shows that it's intended for use with a population by means of an appended letter *P*, then the name of a function intended for use with a sample should behave the same way. It should have the letter *S* appended to it.

That's fair enough, so Excel 2010 offers its users STDEV.P for use with a population and STDEV.S for use with a sample. However, what if we want to include text and/or Boolean values in the argument to the function? In that case, we must resort to the 2003 functions STDEVA() and STDEVPA(). Notice, though, these points:

One, there is no STDEVSA(), as consistency with STDEVPA() would imply.

Two, there is no period separating STDEV from the rest of the function name in STDEVPA(), as there is with STDEV.P and STDEV.S.

Three, neither STDEVA() nor STDEVPA() is flagged as deprecated in the function pop-up window, so there is apparently no intent to supplant them with something such as STDEV.S.A() or STDEV.P.A().

As to the enhancement of STDEV() with STDEVA(), and STDEVP() with STDEVPA(), Microsoft documentation suggests that they were supplied for consistency with 2003's VARA() and COUNTA(), which also allow for text and Boolean values. If so, it is what Emerson referred to as "a foolish consistency." When a user finds that he or she needs to calculate the standard deviation of a set of values that might include the word *weasel* or the logical value FALSE, then that user has done a poor job of planning either the layout of the worksheet or the course of the analysis.

I do not put these complaints here in order to assert my right to rant. I put them here so that, if they have also occurred to you, you'll know that you're not alone in your thoughts.

3

- VARPA() also first appeared in Excel 2003 and takes the same approach to its nonnumeric arguments as does STDEVPA().

- VAR.S() is new in Excel 2010. Microsoft states that its computations are more accurate than are those used by VAR(). Its use and intent is the same as VAR().

- VAR.P() is new in Excel 2010. Its similarities to VARP() are analogous to those between VAR() and VAR.S().

How Variables Move Jointly: Correlation

4

Chapter 2, "How Values Cluster Together," discussed how the values on one variable can tend to cluster together at an average of some sort—a mean, a median, or a mode. Chapter 3, "Variability: How Values Disperse," discussed how the values of one variable fail to cluster together: how they disperse around a mean, as measured by the standard deviation and its close relative, the variance.

This chapter begins a look at how two or more variables *covary*: that is, how higher values on one variable are associated with higher values on another, and how lower values on the two variables are also associated. The reverse situation also occurs frequently, when higher values on one variable are associated with lower values on another variable.

Understanding Correlation

The degree to which two variables behave in this way—that is, the way they covary—is called *correlation*. A familiar example is height and weight They have what's called a *positive* correlation: High values on one variable are associated with high values on the other variable (see Figure 4.1).

The chart in Figure 4.1 has a marker for each of the 12 people whose height and weight appear in cells A2:B13. Generally, the lower the person's height (according to the horizontal axis), the lower the person's weight (according to the vertical axis), and the greater the weight, the greater the height.

The reverse situation appears in Figure 4.2, which charts the number of points scored in a game against the order of each player's finish. The higher the number of points, the lower (that is, the better) the finish. That's an example of a *negative* correlation: Higher values on one variable are associated with lower values on the other variable.

Figure 4.1
A positive correlation appears in a chart as a general lower-left to upper-right trend.

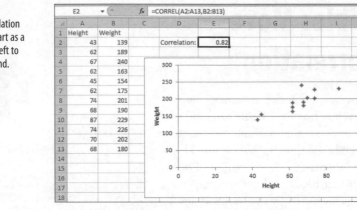

Figure 4.2
A negative correlation appears as a general upper-left to lower-right trend.

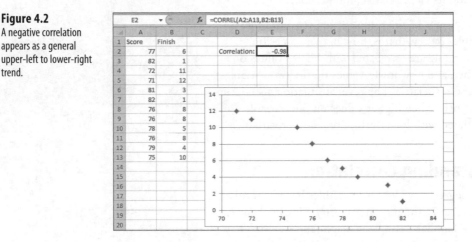

Notice the figure in cell E2 of both Figure 4.1 and 4.2. It is the *correlation coefficient*. It expresses the strength and direction of the relationship between the two variables. In Figure 4.1, the correlation coefficient is .82, a positive number. Therefore, the two variables vary in the same direction: Higher values on one variable are associated with higher values on the other variable.

In Figure 4.2, the correlation coefficient is –.98, a negative number. Therefore, the relationship between the two variables is a negative one, indicated by the direction of the trend in Figure 4.2's chart.

The correlation coefficient, or *r*, can take on values that range from –1.0 to +1.0. The closer that r is to plus or minus 1.0, the stronger the relationship. When two variables are unrelated, the correlation that you might calculate between the two of them should be close to 0.0. For example, Figure 4.3 shows the relationship between the number of letters in a person's last name and the number of gallons of water that person's household uses in a month.

Figure 4.3
Two uncorrelated variables tend to display a relationship such as this one: a random spray of markers on the chart.

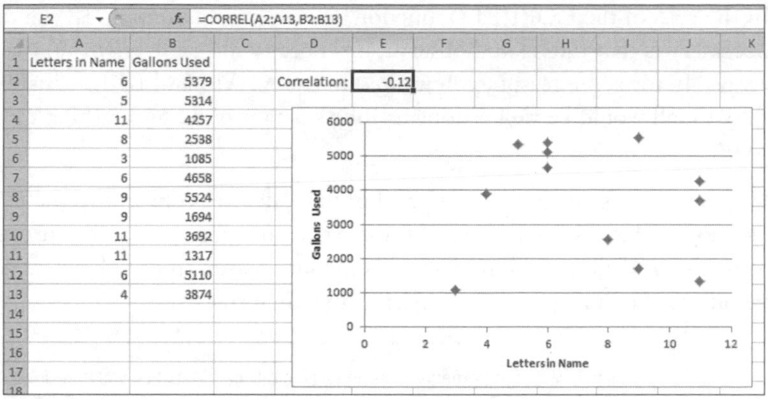

The Correlation, Calculated

Notice the formula in the formula bar shown in Figure 4.3:

=CORREL(A2:A13,B2:B13)

The fact that you're calculating a correlation coefficient at all implies that there are two or more variables to deal with—remember that the correlation coefficient r expresses the strength of a relationship between two variables. In Figures 4.1 through 4.3, two variables are found: one in column A, one in column B.

The arguments to the CORREL() function indicate where the values of those two variables are to be found in the worksheet. One variable, one set of values, is in the first range (here, A2:A13), and the other variable and its values is in the second range (here, B2:B13).

In the arguments to the CORREL() function it makes no difference which variable you identify first. The formula that calculates the correlation in Figure 4.3 could just as well have been this:

=CORREL(B2:B13,A2:A13)

In each row of the ranges that you hand off to CORREL() there should be two values associated with the same person or object. In Figure 4.1, which demonstrates the correlation between height and weight, row 2 could have John's height in column A and his weight in column B; it could have Pat's height in column A and weight in column B, and so on.

The important point to recognize is that r expresses the strength of a relationship between two variables. The only way to measure that relationship is to take the values of the variables on a set of people or things and then maintain the pairing for the statistical analysis. In Excel, you do that by putting the two measures in the same row. You could calculate a value for r if, for example, John's height were in A2 and his weight in B4—that is, the values could be scattered randomly through the rows—but the result of your calculation would be incorrect. Excel assumes that two values in the same row of a list go together and that they constitute a pair.

In the case of the CORREL() function, from a purely mechanical standpoint all that's really necessary is that the related observations occupy the same *relative* positions in the two arrays. If, for some reason, you wanted to use A2:A13 and B3:B14 instead of A2:A13 and B2:B13, all would be well as long as John's data is in A2 and B3, Pat's in A3 and B4, and so on.

However, that structure, A2:A13 and B3:B14, doesn't conform to the rules governing Excel's lists and tables. As I've described it that structure would work, but it could easily come back to bite you. Unless you have some compelling reason to do otherwise, keep measures that belong to the same person or object in the same row.

> **NOTE**
> If you have some experience using Excel to calculate statistics, you may be wondering when this chapter is going to get around to the PEARSON() function. The answer is that it won't. Excel has two worksheet functions that calculate r: CORREL() and PEARSON(). They take the same arguments and return precisely the same results. There is no good reason for this duplicated functionality: When I informed a product manager at Microsoft about it in 1995, he responded, "Huh."
>
> Karl Pearson developed the correlation coefficient that is returned by the Excel functions CORREL() and PEARSON() in the late nineteenth century. The abbreviations r (for the statistic) and ρ (rho, the Greek *r*, for the parameter) stand for *regression*, a measure that's closely related to correlation, and about which this book will have much more to say in this and subsequent chapters.
>
> Anything that this book has to say about CORREL() applies to PEARSON(). I prefer CORREL() simply because it has fewer letters to type.

So, as is the case with the standard deviation and the variance, Excel has a function that calculates the correlation on your behalf, and you need not do all the adding and subtracting, multiplying and dividing yourself. Still, a look at one of the calculation formulas for r can help provide some insight into what it's about. The correlation is based on the covariance, which is symbolized as s_{xy}:

$$s_{xy} = \sum_{i=1}^{N} \frac{\left(X_i - \overline{X}\right)\left(Y_i - \overline{Y}\right)}{(N-1)}$$

That formula may look familiar if you've read Chapter 3. There, you saw that the variance is calculated by subtracting the mean from each value and squaring the deviation—that is, multiplying the deviation by itself: $(X_i - \overline{X})^2$ or $(X_i - \overline{X})(X_i - \overline{X})$.

In the case of the *co*variance, you take a deviation score from one variable and multiply it by the deviation score from the other variable: $(X_i - \overline{X})(Y_i - \overline{Y})$.

To see the effect of calculating the covariance in this way, suppose that you have two variables, height and weight, and a pair of measurements of those variables for each of two men (see Figure 4.4).

Notice that the denominator in the formula for the covariance is N − 1. The reason is the same as it is with the variance, discussed in Chapter 3: In a sample, from which you want to make inferences about a population, degrees of freedom instead of N is used to make the estimate independent of sample size.

Along the same lines, notice from its formula that the covariance of a variable with itself is simply the variable's variance.

Figure 4.4
Large deviations on one variable paired with large deviations on the other result in a larger covariance.

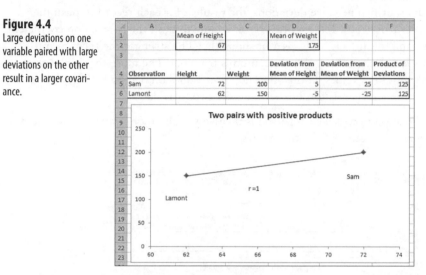

In Figure 4.4, one person (Sam) weighs more than the mean weight of 175, and he also is taller than the mean height of 67 inches. Therefore, both of Sam's deviation scores, his measure minus the mean of that measure, will be positive (see cells D5 and E5 of Figure 4.4). And therefore the product of his deviation scores must also be positive (see cell F5).

In contrast, Lamont weighs less than the mean weight and is shorter than the mean height. Therefore, both his deviation scores will be negative (cells D6 and E6). However, the rule for multiplying two negative numbers comes into play, and Lamont winds up with a positive product for the deviation scores in cell F6.

These two deviation products, which are both 125, are totaled in this fragment from the equation for the covariance (the full equation is given earlier in this section):

$$\sum_{i=1}^{N}(X_i - \overline{X})(Y_i - \overline{Y})$$

Their combined effect of summing the two deviation products is to move the covariance away from a value of zero: Sam's product of 125 moves it from zero, and Lamont's product, also 125, moves it even further from zero.

Notice the diagonal line in the chart in Figure 4.4. That's called a regression line (or, in Excel terms, a *trendline*). In this case (as is true of any case that has just two records), both markers on the chart fall directly on the regression line. When that happens, the correlation is perfect: either +1.0 or –1.0. Perfect correlations are the result of either the analysis of trivial outcomes (for example, the correlation between degrees Fahrenheit and degrees Celsius) or examples in statistics textbooks. The real world of experimental measurements is much more messy.

We can derive a general rule from this example: When each pair of values consists of two positive deviations, or two negative deviations, the result is for each record to push the covariance further from zero. The eventual result will be to push the correlation coefficient away from zero and toward +1.0. This is as it should be: The stronger the relationship between two variables, the further the correlation is from 0.0. The more that high values on one variable go with high values on the other (and low values on one go with low values on the other), the stronger the relationship between the two variables.

What about a situation in which each person is relatively high on one variable and relatively low on the other? See Figure 4.5 for that analysis.

Figure 4.5
The covariance is as strong as in Figure 4.4, but it's negative.

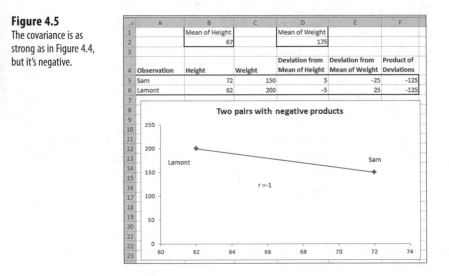

In Figure 4.5, the relationship between the two variables has been reversed. Now, Sam is still taller than the mean height (positive deviation in D5) but weighs less than the mean weight (negative deviation in E5). Lamont is shorter than the mean height (negative deviation in D6) but weighs more than the mean weight (positive deviation in E6).

The result is that both Sam and Lamont have negative deviation products in F5 and F6. When they are totaled, their combined effect is to push the covariance away from zero. The relationship is as strong as it is in Figure 4.4, but its direction is different.

The strength of the relationship between variables is measured by the size of the correlation and has nothing to do with whether the correlation is positive or negative. For example, the correlation between body weight and hours per week spent jogging might be a strong one. But it would likely be negative, perhaps –0.6, because you would expect that the more time spent jogging the lower the body weight.

Weakening the Relationship

Lastly, Figure 4.6 shows what happens when you mix positive with negative deviation products.

Figure 4.6
Peter's deviation product is negative, whereas Sam's and Lamont's are still positive.

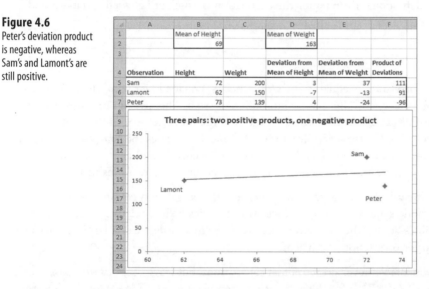

Figure 4.6 shows that Sam and Lamont's deviation products are still positive (cells F5 and F6). However, adding Peter to the mix weakens the observed relationship between height and weight. Peter's height is *above* the mean of height, but his weight is *below* the mean of weight. The result is that his height deviation is positive, his weight deviation is negative, and the product of the two is therefore negative.

This has the effect of pulling the covariance back toward zero, given that both Sam and Lamont have positive deviation products. It is evidence of a weaker relationship between height and weight: Peter's measurements tell us that we can't depend on tall height pairing with heavy weight and short height pairing with low weight, as is the case with Sam and Lamont.

When the observed relationship weakens, so does the covariance (it's closer to zero in Figure 4.6 than in Figures 4.4 and 4.5). Inevitably, the correlation coefficient gets closer to zero: It's shown as r in the charts in Figures 4.4 and 4.5, where it's a perfect 1.0 and –1.0.

In Figure 4.6, r is much weaker: .27 is a weak correlation for continuous variables such as height and weight.

Notice in Figure 4.6 that Sam and Peter's data markers do not touch the regression line. That's another aspect of an imperfect correlation: The plotted data points deviate from the regression line. Imperfect correlations are expected with real-world data, and deviations from the regression line are the rule, not the exception.

Moving from the Covariance to the Correlation

Even without Excel's CORREL() function, it's easy to get from the covariance to the correlation. The definitional formula for the correlation coefficient between variable x and variable y is as follows:

$$r = \frac{s_{xy}}{s_x s_y}$$

In words, the correlation is equal to the covariance (s_{xy}) divided by the product of the standard deviation of x (s_x) and the standard deviation of y (s_y). The division removes the effect of the standard deviations of the two variables from the measurement of their relationship. Taking the spread of the two variables out of the correlation fixes the limits of the correlation coefficient to a minimum of –1.0 (perfect negative correlation) and a maximum of +1.0 (perfect positive correlation) and a midpoint of 0.0 (no observed relationship).

I'm stressing the calculations of the covariance and the correlation coefficient because they can help you understand the nature of these two statistics. When relatively large values on both variables go together, the covariance is larger than otherwise. A larger covariance results in a larger correlation coefficient.

In practice, you almost never do the actual calculations, but leave them to the Excel worksheet functions CORREL() for the correlation coefficient and COVAR() for the covariance.

Using the CORREL() Function

Figure 4.7 shows how you might use the CORREL() function to look into the relationship between two variables that interest you. Suppose that you're a loan officer at a company that provides home loans and you want to examine the relationship between purchase prices and buyers' annual income for loans that your office has made during the past month.

You gather the necessary data and enter it into an Excel worksheet as shown in columns A through C of Figure 4.7.

Notice in Figure 4.7 that there's a value—here, the buyer's name in column A—that uniquely identifies each pair of values. Although an identifier like that isn't at all necessary for calculating a correlation coefficient, it can be a big help in verifying that a particular record's values on the two variables actually belong together. For example, without the buyer's name in column A, it would be more difficult to check that the Neil's house cost $195,000 and their annual income is $110,877. If you don't have the values on one variable paired with the proper values on the other variable, the correlation coefficient will be calculated correctly only by accident. Therefore, it's good to have a way of making sure that, for example, the Neil's income of $110,877 matches up with the cost of $195,000.

Figure 4.7
It's always a good idea to validate the correlation with a chart.

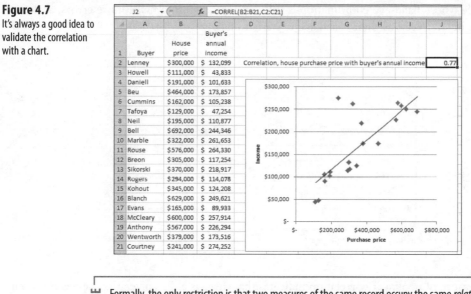

	A	B	C	D	E	F	G	H	I	J
			Buyer's							
		House	annual							
1	Buyer	price	income							
2	Lenney	$300,000	$ 132,099	Correlation, house purchase price with buyer's annual income						0.77
3	Howell	$111,000	$ 43,833							
4	Daniell	$191,000	$ 101,633							
5	Beu	$464,000	$ 173,857							
6	Cummins	$162,000	$ 105,238							
7	Tafoya	$129,000	$ 47,254							
8	Neil	$195,000	$ 110,877							
9	Bell	$692,000	$ 244,346							
10	Marble	$322,000	$ 261,653							
11	Rouse	$576,000	$ 264,330							
12	Breon	$305,000	$ 117,254							
13	Sikorski	$370,000	$ 218,917							
14	Rogers	$294,000	$ 114,078							
15	Kohout	$345,000	$ 124,208							
16	Blanch	$629,000	$ 249,621							
17	Evans	$165,000	$ 89,933							
18	McCleary	$600,000	$ 257,914							
19	Anthony	$567,000	$ 226,294							
20	Wentworth	$379,000	$ 173,516							
21	Courtney	$241,000	$ 274,252							

> **NOTE** Formally, the only restriction is that two measures of the same record occupy the same *relative position* in the two arrays, as noted earlier in "The Correlation, Calculated." I recommend that each value for a given record occupy the same row because that makes the data easier to validate, and because you frequently want to use CORREL() with columns in a list or table as its arguments. Lists and tables operate correctly only if each value for a given record is on the same row.

You would get the correlation between housing price and income in the present sample easily enough. Just enter the following formula in some worksheet cell, as shown in cell J2 in Figure 4.7:

=CORREL(B2:B21,C2:C21)

Simply getting the correlation isn't the end of the job, though. Correlation coefficients can be tricky. Here are two ways they can steer you wrong:

■ There's a strong relationship between the two variables, but the normal correlation coefficient, r, obscures that relationship.

■ There's no strong relationship between the two variables, but one or two highly unusual observations make it seem as though there is one.

Figure 4.8 shows an example of a strong relationship that r doesn't tell you about.

If you were to simply calculate the standard Pearson correlation coefficient by means of CORREL() on the data used for Figure 4.8, you'd miss what's going on. The Pearson r assumes that the relationship between the two variables is linear—that is, it calculates a regression line that's straight, as it is in Figure 4.7. Figure 4.8 shows the results you might get if you charted age against number of typographical errors per 1,000 words. Very young people whose hand-eye coordination is still developing tend to make more errors, as do those in later years as their visual acuity starts to fade.

Figure 4.8
The relationship is not linear, and r assumes linear relationships.

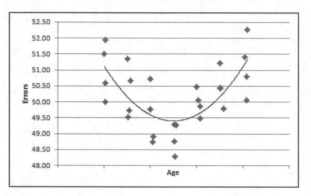

A measure of nonlinear correlation indicates that there is a .75 correlation between the variables. But the Pearson r is calculated by CORREL() at 0.08 because it's not designed to pick up on a nonlinear relationship. You might well miss an important result if you didn't chart the data.

Figure 4.9
Just one outlier can overstate the relationship between the variables.

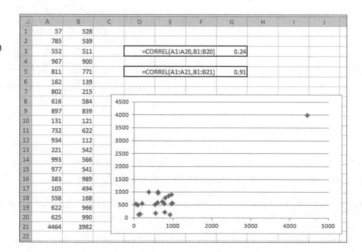

A different problem appears in Figure 4.9.

In Figure 4.9, two variables that are only weakly related are shown in cells A1:B20 (yes, B20, not B21). The correlation between them is shown in cell G3: It is only .24.

Somehow, because of a typo or incorrect readings on meters or a database query that was structured ineptly, two additional values appear in cells A21:B21. When those two values are included in the arguments to the CORREL() function, the correlation changes from a weak 0.24 to quite a strong 0.91.

This happens because of the way the covariance, and therefore the correlation, is defined. Let's review a covariance formula given earlier:

$$s_{xy} = \sum_{i=1}^{N} \frac{\left(X_i - \overline{X}\right)\left(Y_i - \overline{Y}\right)}{(N - 1)}$$

The expression in the numerator multiplies an observation's deviation from the mean of X times the observation's deviation from the mean of Y. The addition of that one record, where both the X and the Y values deviate by thousands of units from the means of the two variables, inflates the covariance and the correlation far above their values based on the first 20 records.

You might not have realized what was going on without the accompanying XY chart. There you can see the one observation that turns what is basically no relationship into a strong one. Of course, it's possible that the one outlier is entirely legitimate. But in that case, it might be that the standard correlation coefficient is not an appropriate expression of the relationship between the two variables (any more than the mean is an appropriate expression of central tendency in a distribution that's highly skewed).

Make it a habit to create XY charts of variables that you investigate via correlation analysis. The standard r, the Pearson correlation coefficient, is the basis for many sophisticated statistical analyses, but it was not designed to assess the strength of relationships that are either nonlinear or contain extreme outliers.

Fortunately, Excel makes it very easy to create the charts. For example, to create the XY chart shown in Figure 4.9, take these steps:

1. With raw data as shown in cells A1:B21, select any cell in that range.
2. Click the Insert tab.
3. Click the Scatter button in the Charts group.
4. Click the Scatter with Only Markers type in the drop-down.

Using the Analysis Tools

Since the 1990s, Excel has included an add-in that provides a variety of tools that perform statistical analysis. In several Excel versions, Microsoft's documentation has referred to it as the Analysis ToolPak. This book terms it the Data Analysis add-in, because that's the label you see in the Ribbon once the add-in has been installed.

Many of the tools in the Data Analysis add-in are quite useful. One of them is the Correlation tool. There isn't actually a lot of sense in deploying it if you have only two or three variables to analyze. Then, it's faster to enter the formula with the CORREL() function on the worksheet yourself than it is to jump through the few hoops that Data Analysis puts in the way. With more than two or three variables, consider using the Correlation tool.

You can use this formula to quickly calculate the number of unique correlation coefficients in a set of k variables:

$$k * (k - 1) / 2$$

If you have three variables, then, you would have to calculate three correlations (3 * 2 / 2). That's easy enough, but with four variables there are six possible correlations (4 * 3 / 2), and with five variables there are ten (5 * 4 / 2). Then, using the CORREL() function for each correlation gets to be time consuming and error prone, and that's where the Data Analysis add-in's Correlation tool becomes more valuable.

You get at the Data Analysis add-in much as you get at Solver; see Chapter 2 for an introduction to accessing and using the Solver add-in. With Excel 2007 or 2010, click the Ribbon's Data tab and look for Data Analysis in the Analysis group. (In Excel 2003 or earlier, look for Data Analysis in the Tools menu.) If you find Data Analysis you're ready to go, and you can skip forward to the next section, "Using the Correlation Tool."

If you don't see Data Analysis, you'll need to make it available to Excel, and you might even have to install it from the installation disc or the downloaded installation utility.

> **NOTE** The Data Analysis add-in has much more than just a Correlation tool. It includes a tool that returns descriptive statistics for a single variable, tools for several inferential tests that are discussed in detail in this book, moving averages, and several other tools. If you intend to use Excel to carry out beginning-to-intermediate statistical analysis, I urge you to install and become familiar with the Data Analysis add-in.

The Data Analysis add-in might have been installed on your working disk but not yet made available to Excel. If you don't see Data Analysis in the Analysis group of the Data tab, take these steps:

1. In Office 2010, click the File tab and click Options in its navigation bar. In Office 2007, click the Office button and click the Excel Options button at the bottom of the menu.
2. The Excel Options window opens. Click Add-Ins in its navigation bar.
3. If necessary, select Excel Add-Ins in the Manage drop-down, and then click Go.
4. The Add-Ins dialog box appears. If you see Analysis ToolPak listed, be sure its check box is filled. (*Analysis ToolPak* is an old term for this add-in.) Click OK.

You should now find Data Analysis in the Analysis group on the Data tab. Skip ahead to the section titled "Using the Correlation Tool."

Things are a little quicker in versions of Excel prior to 2007. Choose Add-Ins from the Tools menu. Look for Analysis ToolPak in the Add-Ins dialog box, and fill its check box if you see it. Click OK. You should now find Data Analysis in the Tools menu.

If you do not find Analysis ToolPak in the Add-Ins dialog box, regardless of the version of Excel you're using, you'll need to modify the installation. You can do this if you have access to the installation disc or downloaded installation file. It's usually best to start from the Control Panel. Choose Add or Remove Software, or Programs and Features, depending on the version of Windows that you're running. Choose to change the installation of Office.

When you get to the Excel portion of the installation, click Excel's expand box (the one with a plus sign inside a box). You'll see another expand box beside Add-Ins. Click it to display Analysis ToolPak. Use its drop-down to select Run From My Computer, and then Continue and OK your way back to Excel.

Now continue with step 1 in the preceding list.

Using the Correlation Tool

To use the Correlation tool in Data Analysis, begin with data laid out as shown in Figure 4.10.

Figure 4.10
The Correlation tool can deal with labels, so be sure to use them in the first row of your list.

▲	A	B	C	D
1	Age	Weight in pounds	Height in inches	Cholesterol
2	2	28	32	161
3	4	26	40	142
4	4	42	38	181
5	10	72	51	138
6	4	61	37	175
7	2	41	33	162
8	5	50	43	129
9	7	31	44	143
10	3	28	33	150
11	5	51	40	128
12	4	39	40	138
13	6	61	44	126
14	4	29	37	133

4

Then click Data Analysis in the Data tab's Analysis group, and choose Correlation from the Data Analysis list box. Click OK to get the Correlation dialog box shown in Figure 4.11, and then follow these steps:

1. Make sure that the Input Range box is active—if it is, you'll see a flashing cursor in it. Use your mouse pointer to drag through the entire range where your data is located.

> **TIP**
> For me, the fastest way to select the data range is to start with the range's upper-left corner. I hold down Ctrl+Shift and press the right arrow to select the entire first row. Then, without releasing Ctrl+Shift, I press the down arrow to select all the rows.

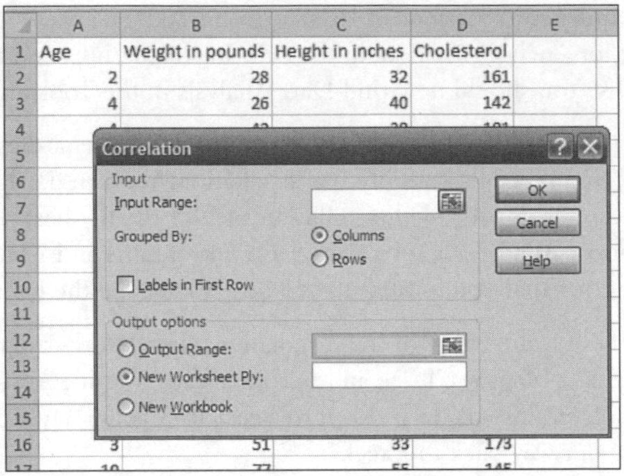

Figure 4.11
If you have labels at the top of your list, include them in the Input Range box.

2. If your data is laid out as a list, with different variables occupying different columns, make sure that the Columns option button is selected.

3. If you used and selected the column headers supplied in Figure 4.11, make sure the Labels in First Row check box is filled.

4. Click the Output Range option button if you want the correlation coefficients to appear on the same worksheet as the input data. (This is normally my choice.) Click in the Output Range edit box, and then click the worksheet cell where you want the output to begin. *See the Caution that follows this list.*

5. Click OK to begin the analysis.

> **CAUTION**
>
> The Correlation dialog box has a trap built into it, one that it shares with several other Data Analysis dialog boxes. When you click the Output Range option button, the Input Range edit box becomes active. If you don't happen to notice that, you can think that you have specified a cell where you want the output to start, but in fact you've told Excel that's where the input range is located.
>
> After clicking the Output Range option button, reactivate its associated range edit box by clicking in it.

Almost immediately after you click OK, you'll see the Correlation tool's output, as shown in Figure 4.12.

You need to keep some matters in mind regarding the Correlation tool. To begin, it gives you a square range of cells with its results (F1:J5 in Figure 4.12). Each row in the range, as well as each column, represents a different variable from your input data. The layout is an efficient way to show the matrix of correlation coefficients.

In Figure 4.12, the cells G2, H3, I4, and J5 each contain the value 1.0. Each of those four specific cells shows the correlation of one of the input variables with itself. That correlation is always 1.0. Those cells in Figure 4.12, and the analogous cells in other correlation matrixes, are collectively referred to as the *main diagonal.*

Figure 4.12
The numbers shown in cells G2:J5 are sometimes collectively called a *correlation matrix.*

	A	B	C	D	E	F	G	H	I	J
1	Age	Weight in pounds	Height in inches	Cholesterol			Age	Weight in pounds	Height in inches	Cholesterol
2	2	28	32	161		Age	1.00			
3	4	26	40	142		Weight in pounds	0.74	1.00		
4	4	42	38	181		Height in inches	0.97	0.72	1.00	
5	10	72	51	138		Cholesterol	-0.11	0.34	-0.19	1.00
6	4	61	37	175						
7	2	41	33	162						
8	5	50	43	129						
9	7	31	44	143						
10	3	28	33	150						
11	5	51	40	128						
12	4	39	40	138						

You don't see correlation coefficients above the main diagonal because they would be redundant with those below it. You can see in cell H4 that for this sample, the correlation between height and weight is 0.72. Excel could show the same correlation in cell I3, but doing so wouldn't add any new information: The correlation between height and weight is the same as the correlation between weight and height.

The suppression of the correlation coefficients above the main diagonal is principally to avoid visual clutter. More advanced statistical analyses such as factor analysis often require the fully populated square matrix.

The Correlation tool, like some other Data Analysis tools, reports static values. For example, in Figure 4.12, the numbers in the correlation matrix are not formulas such as

=CORREL(A2:A31,B2:B31)

but rather the results of the formulas. In consequence, if even one number in the input range changes, or if you add or remove even one record from the input range, the correlation matrix does not automatically update to reflect the change. You must run the Correlation tool again if you want a change in the input data to result in a change in the output.

The Data Analysis add-in has problems—problems that date all the way back to its introduction in Excel 95. One, the Output Range issue, is described in a Caution earlier in this section. Another, concerning the tool named F-Test: Two Sample for Variances is discussed in some detail in Chapter 6, "Telling the Truth with Statistics." The tool named ANOVA: Two Factor without Replication employs an old fashioned approach to repeated measures that involves some very restrictive assumptions. But the Data Analysis add-in is nevertheless a useful adjunct and I encourage you to install it and use it as needed.

Correlation Isn't Causation

It can be surprisingly easy to see that changes in one variable are associated with changes in another variable, and conclude that one variable's behavior causes changes in the other's. For example, it might very well be true that the regularity with which children eat breakfast has a direct effect on their performance in school. Certainly, TV commercials assert that eating breakfast cereals enhances concentration.

But there's an important difference between believing that one variable is related to another and believing that changes to one variable *cause* changes to another. Some observational research, relying on correlations between nutrition and achievement, concludes that eating breakfast regularly improves academic achievement. Other, more careful studies show that the question is more complicated: that variables such as absenteeism come into play, and that coaxing information out of a mass of correlation coefficients isn't as informative or credible as a manufacturer of sugar-coated cereal flakes might wish.

Besides the issue of the complexity of the relationships, there are two general reasons, discussed next, that you should be very careful of assuming that a correlational relationship is also causal.

A Third Variable

It sometimes happens that you find a strong correlation between two variables that suggests a causal relationship. The classic example is the number of books in school district libraries and scores on the standardized SAT exams. Suppose you found a strong correlation—say, 0.7—between the number of books per student in districts' libraries and the average performance by those districts' students on the SATs. A first-glance interpretation might be that the availability of a larger number of books results in more knowledge, thus better outcomes on standardized tests.

A more careful examination might reveal that communities where the annual household income is higher have more in the way of property taxes to spend on schools and their libraries. Such communities also tend to spend more on other important aspects of children's development, such as nutrition and stable home environments. In other words, children raised in wealthier districts are more likely to score well on standardized tests. In contrast, it is difficult to argue that simply adding more books to a school library will result in higher SAT scores. The third variable here, in addition to number of library books and SAT scores, is the wealth of the community.

Another example concerns the apparent relationship between childhood vaccinations and the incidence of autism. It has been argued that over the past several decades, vaccination has become more and more prevalent, as has autism. Some have concluded that childhood vaccines, or the preservatives used in their manufacture, cause autism. But close examination of studies that apparently supported that contention disclosed problems with the studies' methods, in particular the methods used to establish an increased prevalence of autism. Further study has suggested that a third variable, more frequent and sophisticated tests for autism, has been at work, bringing about an increase in the diagnoses of autism rather than an increase in the prevalence of the condition itself.

Untangling correlation and causation is a problem. In the 1950s and 1960s, the link between cigarette smoking and lung cancer was debated on the front pages of newspapers. Some said that the link was merely correlation, and not causation. The only way to convincingly demonstrate causation would be by means of a true experiment: Randomly assign people to smoking and nonsmoking groups and force those in the former group to smoke cigarettes. Then, after years of enforced smoking or abstinence, compare the incidence of lung cancer in the two groups.

That solution is obviously both a practical and ethical impossibility. But it is generally conceded today that smoking cigarettes causes lung cancer, even in the absence of a true experiment. Correlation does not by itself mean causation, but when it's buttressed by the findings of repeated observational studies, and when the effect of a third variable can be ruled out (both liquor and sleep loss were posited and then discarded as possible third variables causing lung cancer among smokers), it's reasonable to conclude that causation is present.

The Direction of the Effect

Another possibility to keep in mind when you consider whether a correlation represents causation is that you might be looking at the wrong variable as the cause. If you find that the incidence of gun ownership correlates strongly with the incidence of violent crime, you might come to the conclusion that there's a causal relationship. And there might be cause involved. However, without more rigorous experimentation, whether you conclude that "More guns result in more violent crime" or "People respond to more violent crime by buying more guns" is likely to depend more on your own political and cultural sensibilities than on empirical evidence.

Using Correlation

To this point, we have talked mostly about the concept of a correlation coefficient—how it is defined and how it can illuminate the nature of the relationship between two variables. That's useful information by itself, but things go much further than that. For example, it's probably occurred to you that if you know the value of one variable, you can predict the value of another variable that's correlated with the first.

That sort of prediction is the focus of the remainder of this chapter. The basics discussed here turn out to be the foundation of several analyses discussed in later chapters. Used in this way, the technique goes by the name *regression*, which is the basis for the designation of the correlation coefficient, r.

> **NOTE**
>
> Why the word *regression*? In the nineteenth century, a scientist and mathematician named Francis Galton studied heredity and noticed that numeric relationships exist between parents and children as measured by certain standard variables. For example, Galton compared the heights of fathers to the heights of their sons, and he came to an interesting finding: Sons' heights tended to be closer to their own mean than did the heights of their fathers.
>
> Put another way, fathers who stood, say, two standard deviations above the mean height of their generation tended to have sons whose mean height was just one standard deviation above their own

generation's mean height. Similarly, fathers who were shorter than average tended to have sons who were also shorter than average, but who were closer to the average than their fathers were. The sons' height *regressed* toward the mean.

Subsequent work by Karl Pearson, mentioned earlier in this chapter, built on Galton's work and developed the concepts and methods associated with the correlation coefficient. Figure 4.13 shows some heights, in inches, of fathers and sons, and an XY chart showing visually how the two variables are associated.

Figure 4.13
The regression line shows where the data points would fall if the correlation were a perfect 1.0.

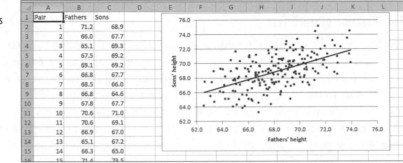

Given that two variables—here, fathers' height and sons' height—are correlated, it should be possible to predict a value on one variable from a value on the other variable. And it is possible, but the hitch is that the prediction will be perfectly accurate only when the relationship is of very limited interest, such as the relationship between weight in ounces and weight in grams. The prediction can be perfect only when the correlation is perfect, and that happens only in highly artificial or trivial situations.

The next section discusses how to make that sort of prediction without relying on Excel. Then I'll show how Excel does it quickly and easily.

Removing the Effects of the Scale

Chapter 3 discussed the standard deviation and z-scores, and showed how you can express a value in terms of standard deviation units. For example, if you have a sample of ten people whose mean height is 68 inches with a standard deviation of four inches, then you can express a height of 72 inches as one standard deviation above the mean—or, equivalently, as a z-score of +1.0. So doing removes the attributes of the original scale of measurement and makes comparisons between different variables much clearer.

The z-score is calculated, and thus standardized, by subtracting the mean from a given value and dividing the result by the standard deviation. The correlation coefficient uses an analogous calculation. To review, the definitional formula of the correlation coefficient is

$$r = \frac{s_{xy}}{s_x s_y}$$

or, in words, the correlation is the covariance divided by the product of the standard deviations of the two variables. It is therefore standardized to range from 0 to plus or minus 1.0, uninfluenced by the unit of measure used in the underlying variables.

The covariance, like the variance, can be difficult to visualize. Suppose you have the weights in pounds of the same ten people, along with their heights. You might calculate the mean of their weights at 150 pounds and the standard deviation of their weights at 25 pounds. It's easy to see a distance of 25 pounds on the horizontal axis of a chart. It's more difficult to visualize the variance of your sample, which is 625 squared pounds—or even to comprehend its meaning.

Similarly, it can be difficult to comprehend the meaning of the covariance (unless you're used to working with the measures involved, which is often the case for physicists and engineers—they're usually familiar with the covariance of measures they work with, and sometimes term the correlation coefficient the *dimensionless covariance*).

In your sample of ten people, for example, you might have height measures as well as weight measures. If you calculate the covariance of height and weight in your sample, you might wind up with some value such as 58.5 foot-pounds. But this is not one of the classical meanings of "foot-pound," a measure of force or energy. It is a measure of how pounds and feet combine in your sample. And it's not always clear how you visualize or otherwise interpret that measurement.

The correlation coefficient resolves that difficulty in a way that's similar to the z-score. You divide the covariance by the standard deviation of each variable, thus removing the effect of the two scales—here, height and weight—and you're left with an expression of the strength of the relationship that isn't affected by your choice of measure, whether feet or inches or centimeters, or pounds or ounces or kilograms. A perfect, one-to-one relationship is plus or minus 1.0. The absence of a relationship is 0.0. The correlations of most variables fall somewhere between the extremes.

In the z-score you have a way to measure how far from the mean a person or object is found, without reference to the unit of measurement. Perhaps John's height is 70.8 inches, or a z-score on height of 0.70. Perhaps the correlation between height and weight in your sample—again, uncontaminated by the scales of measurement—is 0.65. You can now predict John's weight with this equation:

$$Z_{Weight} = r Z_{Height}$$

Put into words, John's distance from the mean on weight is the product of the correlation coefficient and his distance from the mean on height. John's z-score on weight equals the correlation r times his z-score on height, or .65 * .70, or .455. See Figure 4.14 for the specifics.

Figure 4.14
The regression line shows where the data points would fall if the correlation were a perfect 1.0.

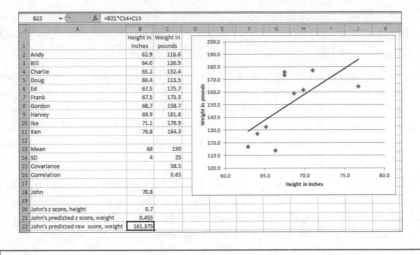

> **NOTE**
> John's z-score on weight (.455) is smaller than his z-score on height (.70). He has *regressed* toward the mean on weight, just as a son's predicted height is closer to the mean than his father's height. This regression *always* takes place when the correlation is not perfect: that is, when it is less than ±1.0. That's inherent in the equation given above for weight and height, repeated here in a more general form: $z_y = r_{xy} z_x$. Consider that equation and keep in mind that r is always between −1.0 and +1.0.

The mean weight in your sample is 150 pounds, and the standard deviation is 25. You have John's predicted z-score for weight, 0.455, from the prior formula. You can change that into pounds by rearranging the formula for a z-score:

$$z = \frac{X - \overline{X}}{s}$$
$$X = sz + \overline{X}$$

In John's case, you have the following:

$$161.375 = 25 * 0.455 + 150$$

To verify this result, see cell B22 in Figure 4.14.

So, the correlation of .65 leads you to predict that John's weighs 161.375 pounds. But then John tells you that he actually weighs 155 pounds. When you use a reasonably strong correlation to make predictions, you don't expect your predictions to be exactly correct with any real frequency, any more than you expect the prediction for a tenth of an inch of rain tomorrow to be exactly correct. In both situations, though, you expect the prediction to be reasonably close most of the time.

Using the Excel Function

The prior section described how to use a correlation between two variables, plus a z-score on each variable, to predict a person's weight in pounds from his height in inches. This involved multiplying one z-score by a correlation to get another z-score, and then converting the latter z-score to a weight in pounds by rearranging the formula for a z-score. Behind the scenes, it was also necessary to calculate the mean and standard deviation of both variables as well as the correlation between the two.

I inflicted all this on you because it helps illuminate the relationship between raw scores and covariances, between z-scores and correlations. As you would expect, Excel relieves you of the tedium of doing all that formulaic hand-waving.

Figure 4.15 shows the raw data and some preliminary calculations that the preceding discussion was based on.

Figure 4.15
The TREND() function takes care of all the calculations for you.

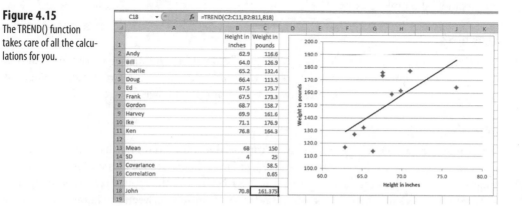

To predict John's weight using the data as shown in Figures 4.14 and 4.15, enter this formula in some empty cell (it's C18 in Figure 4.15):

=TREND(C2:C11,B2:B11,B18)

With this data set, the formula returns the value 161.375. To get the same value using the scenic route used in Figure 4.14, you could also enter the formula

=((B18-B13)/B14)*C16*C14+C13

which carries out the math that was sketched in the prior section: Calculate John's z-score for height, multiply it by the correlation, multiply that by the standard deviation for weight, and add the mean weight. Fortunately, the TREND() function relieves you of all those opportunities to make a mistake.

The TREND() function's syntax is as follows:

=TREND(known_y's, known _x's, new_x's, const)

The first three arguments to TREND() are discussed next.

> **NOTE** The fourth argument, const, is optional. A section in Chapter 13, "Dealing with the Intercept," discusses the reason you should omit the const argument, which is the same as setting it to FALSE. It's best to delay that discussion until more groundwork has been laid.

known_y's

These are values that you already have in hand for the variable you want to predict. In the example from the prior section, that variable is weight: the idea was to predict John's weight on the basis of the correlation between height and weight, combined with knowledge of John's height. It's conventional in statistical writing to designate the predicted variable as Y, and its individual values as y's.

known_x's

These are values of the variable you want to predict from. Each must be paired up with one of the known_y's. You'll find that the easiest way to do this is to align two adjacent ranges as in Figure 4.15, where the known_x's are in B2:B11 and the known_y's are in C2:C11.

new_x's

This value (or values) belongs to the predictor variable, but you do not have, or are not supplying, associated values for the predicted variable. There are various reasons that you might have new_x's to use as an argument to TREND(), but the typical reason is that you want to predict y's for the new_x's, based on the relationship between the known_y's and the known_x's. For example, the known_x's might be years: 1980, 1981, 1982, and so on. The known_y's might be company revenue for each of those years. And your new_x might be next year's number, such as 2012, for which you'd like to predict revenue.

Getting the Predicted Values

If you have only one new_x value to predict from, you can enter the formula with the TREND() function normally, just by typing it and pressing Enter. This is the situation in Figure 4.15, where you would enter =TREND(C2:C11,B2:B11,B18) in a blank cell such as C18 to get the predicted weight given the height in B18.

But suppose you want to know what the predicted weight of *all* the subjects in your sample would be, given the correlation between the two variables. TREND() does this for you, too: You simply need to *array-enter* the formula.

You start by selecting a range of cells with the same dimensions as is occupied by your known_x's. In Figure 4.15, that's B2:B11, so you might select D2:D11. Then type the formula =TREND(C2:C11,B2:B11) and array-enter it with Ctrl+Shift+Enter instead of simply Enter.

> **NOTE** Array formulas are discussed in more detail in Chapter 2, in the section titled "Using an Array Formula to Count the Values."

The result appears in Figure 4.16.

Figure 4.16
The curly brackets around the formula in the formula box indicate that it's an array formula.

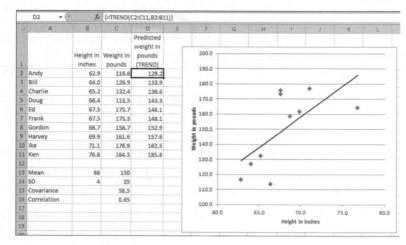

You can get some more insight into the meaning of the trendline in the chart if you use the predicted values in D2:D11 of Figure 4.16. If you create an XY chart using the values in B2:B11 and D2:D11, you'll find that you have a chart that duplicates the trendline in Figure 4.16's chart.

So a linear trendline in a chart represents the unrealistic situation in which all the observations obediently follow a formula that relates two variables. But Ed eats too much and Doug isn't eating enough. They, along with the rest of the subjects, stray to some degree from the perfect trendline.

If it's unrealistic, what's the point of including a trendline in a chart? It's largely a matter of helping you visualize how far individual observations fall from the mathematical formula. The larger the deviations, the lower the correlation. The more that the individual points hug the trendline, the greater the correlation. Yes, you can get that information from the magnitude of the result returned by CORREL(). But there's nothing like seeing it charted.

> **NOTE** Because so many options are available for chart trendlines, I have waited to even mention how you get one. For a trendline such as the one shown in Figures 4.14 through 4.16, click the chart to select it and then click the Layout tab in the Chart Tools section of the Ribbon. Click Trendline and then click Linear Trendline on the drop-down.

Getting the Regression Formula

An earlier section in this chapter, "Removing the Effects of the Scale," discussed how you can use z-scores, means and standard deviations, and the correlation coefficient to predict one variable from another. The subsequent section, "Using the Excel Function," described how to use the TREND() function to go directly from the observed values to the predicted values.

Neither discussion dealt with the formula that you can use on the raw data. In the examples that this chapter has used—predicting one variable on the basis of its relationship with another variable—it is possible to use two Excel functions, SLOPE() and INTERCEPT(), to generate the formula that returns the predicted values that you get with TREND().

There is a related function, LINEST(), that is more powerful than either SLOPE() or INTERCEPT(). It can handle many more variables and return much more information, and subsequent chapters of this book, particularly Chapter 12, regression analysis, and Chapter 13, on the analysis of covariance, discuss it in depth.

However, this chapter discusses SLOPE() and INTERCEPT() briefly, so that you'll know what their purpose is and because they serve as an introduction of sorts to LINEST().

A formula that best describes the relationship between two variables, such as height and weight in Figures 4.14 through 4.16, requires two numbers: a slope and an intercept. The slope refers to the regression line's steepness (or lack thereof). Back in geometry class your teacher might have referred to this as the "rise over the run." The slope indicates the number of units that the line moves up for every unit that the line moves right. The slope can be positive or negative: If it's positive, the regression line slopes from lower left to upper right, as in Figure 4.16; if it's negative, the slope is from upper left to lower right.

You calculate the value of the slope directly in Excel with the SLOPE() function. For example, using the data in Figures 4.14 through 4.16, the value returned by the formula

    =SLOPE(C2:C11,B2:B11)

is 4.06. That is, for every unit increase (each inch) in height in this sample, you expect slightly over four pounds increase in weight.

But the slope isn't all you need: You also need what's called the *intercept*. That's the value of the predicted variable—here, weight—at the point that the regression line crosses its axis. In Figure 4.17, the regression line has been extended to the left, to the zero point on the horizontal axis where it crosses the vertical axis. The point where the regression line crosses the vertical axis is the value of the intercept.

The values of the regression line's slope and intercept are shown in B18 and B19 of Figure 4.17. Notice that the intercept value shown in cell B19 matches the point in the chart where the regression line crosses the vertical axis.

The predicted values for weight are shown in cells D2:D11 of Figure 4.17. They are calculated using the values for the slope and intercept in B18 and B19, and are identical to the predicted values in Figure 4.16 that were calculated using TREND(). Notice these three points about the formula, shown in the formula box:

■ You multiply a known_x value by the value of the slope, and add the value of the intercept.

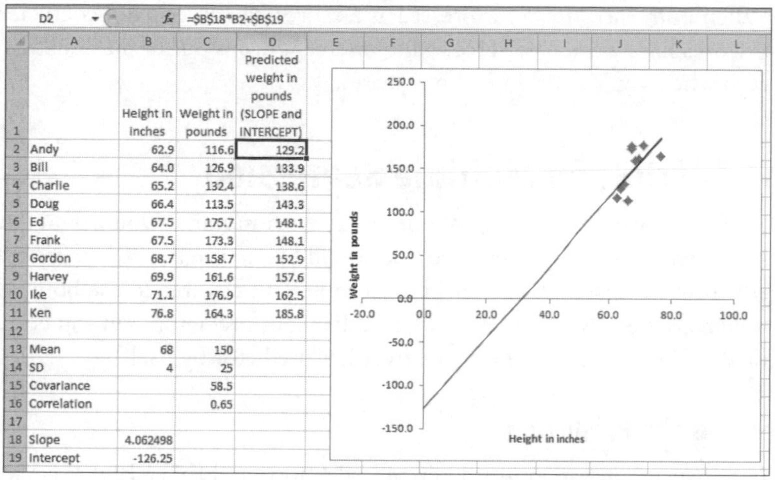

D2 =$B$18*B2+$B$19

	A	B	C	D
1		Height in inches	Weight in pounds	Predicted weight in pounds (SLOPE and INTERCEPT)
2	Andy	62.9	116.6	129.2
3	Bill	64.0	126.9	133.9
4	Charlie	65.2	132.4	138.6
5	Doug	66.4	113.5	143.3
6	Ed	67.5	175.7	148.1
7	Frank	67.5	173.3	148.1
8	Gordon	68.7	158.7	152.9
9	Harvey	69.9	161.6	157.6
10	Ike	71.1	176.9	162.5
11	Ken	76.8	164.3	185.8
12				
13	Mean	68	150	
14	SD	4	25	
15	Covariance		58.5	
16	Correlation		0.65	
17				
18	Slope	4.062498		
19	Intercept	-126.25		

Figure 4.17
The ranges of values on the axes have been increased so as to show the intercept.

- No curly brackets appear around the formula. Therefore, in contrast to the instance of the TREND() function in Figure 4.16, you can enter the formula normally.
- You enter the formula in one cell—in the figure, you might as well start in cell D2—and either copy and paste or drag and drop into the remaining cells in the range (here, that's D3:D11). So doing adjusts the reference to the known_x value. But because you don't want to adjust the references to the cell with the slope and the cell with the intercept, dollar signs are used to make those references absolute prior to the copy-and-paste operation.

> **NOTE** Yet another way is to begin by selecting the entire D2:D11 range, typing the formula (including the dollar signs that make two of the cell references absolute), and finishing with Ctrl+Enter. This sequence enters the formula in a range of selected cells, with the references adjusting accordingly. It is *not* an array formula: you have not finished with Ctrl+Shift+Enter.

It's also worth noting that an earlier section in this chapter, "Removing the Effects of the Scale," shows how to work with z-scores and the correlation coefficient to predict the z-score on one variable from the z-score on the other. In that context, both variables have been converted to z-scores and therefore have a standard deviation of 1.0 and a mean of 0.0. Therefore, the formula

Predicted value = Slope * Predictor value + Intercept

reduces to this formula:

Predicted z-score = Correlation Coefficient * Predictor z-score

When both variables are expressed as z-scores, the correlation coefficient *is* the slope. Also, z-scores have a mean of zero, so the intercept drops out of the equation: Its value is always zero when you're working with z-scores.

Using TREND() for Multiple Regression

It often happens that you have one variable whose values you would like to predict, and more than just one variable that you would like to use as predictors. Although it's not apparent from the discussion so far in this chapter, it's possible to use both variables as predictors *simultaneously*. Using two or more simultaneous predictors can sometimes improve the accuracy of the prediction, compared to either predictor by itself.

Combining the Predictors

In the sort of situation just described, SLOPE() and INTERCEPT() won't help you, because they weren't designed to handle multiple predictors. Excel instead provides you with the functions TREND() and LINEST(), which can handle both the single predictor and the multiple predictor situations. That's the reason you won't see SLOPE() and INTERCEPT() discussed further in this book. They serve as a useful introduction to the concepts involved in regression, but they are underpowered and their capabilities are available in TREND() and LINEST() when you have only one predictor variable.

> **NOTE**
>
> It's easy to conclude that TREND() and LINEST() are analogous to SLOPE() and INTERCEPT(), but they are not. The results of SLOPE() and INTERCEPT() combine to form an equation based on a single predictor. LINEST() by itself takes the place of SLOPE() and INTERCEPT() for both single and multiple predictors. TREND() returns only the results of applying the prediction equation. Just as in the case of the single predictor variable, you can use TREND() with more than one predictor variable to return the predictions directly to the worksheet.
>
> LINEST() does not return the predicted values directly, but it does provide you with the equation that TREND() uses to calculate the predicted values (and it also provides a variety of statistics that are discussed in Chapters 12 and 13). The function name LINEST is a contraction of *linear estimation*.

Figure 4.18 shows a multiple regression analysis along with two standard regression analyses.

Figure 4.18
The predicted values in columns E, F, and G are all based on TREND().

	J4			f_x	=CORREL(C2:C31,G2:G31)				
	A	B	C	D	E	F	G	H	I	J
1	Education	Age	Income ($000)		Income predicted by Education	Income predicted by Age	Income predicted by Education and Age		Correlations	Income
2	13	32	$ 28		$ 46.6	$ 27.1	$ 30.5		Income predicted by Education	0.63
3	14	40	$ 26		$ 52.3	$ 47.0	$ 49.0		Income predicted by Age	0.72
4	11	38	$ 42		$ 35.3	$ 42.1	$ 35.1		Income predicted by Education and Age	0.80
5	13	51	$ 72		$ 46.6	$ 74.5	$ 66.4			
6	9	37	$ 61		$ 23.9	$ 39.6	$ 26.4			

In Figure 4.18, columns E and F each contain values, predicted from a single variable, of the sort that this chapter has already discussed. Column E shows the results of regressing Income on Education, and Column F shows the results of regressing Income on Age.

One way of assessing the accuracy of predicted values is to calculate their correlation with the actual values, and you'll find those correlations in Figure 4.18, cells J2 and J3. In this sample, the correlation of Education with Income is .63 and Age with Income is .72. These are good, strong correlations and indicate that both Education and Age are useful predictors of Income, but it may be possible to do better yet.

In Figure 4.18, column G contains this array formula:

=TREND(C2:C31,A2:B31)

Notice the difference between that formula and, say, the one in Column E:

=TREND(C2:C31,A2:A31)

Both formulas use the Income values in C2:C31 as the known_y's. But the formula in Column E, which predicts Income from Education, uses only the Education values in Column A as the known_x's. The formula in Column G, which predicts Income from both Education and Age, uses the Education values in Column A *and* the Age values in Column B as the known_x's.

The correlation of the actual income values in Column C with those predicted by Education and Age in column G is shown in cell J4 of Figure 4.18. That correlation, .80, is a bit stronger than the correlation of either Income with Income predicted by Education (0.63), or of Income with Income predicted by Age (0.72). This means that—to the degree that this sample is representative of the population—you can do a more accurate job of predicting Income when you do so using both Education and Age than you can using either variable alone.

Understanding "Best Combination"

The prior section shows that you can use TREND() with two or more predictor variables to improve the accuracy of the predicted values. Understanding how that comes about involves two general topics: the mechanics of the process, and the concept of *shared variance*.

Creating a Linear Combination

You sometimes hear multiple regression discussed in terms of a "best combination" or "optimal combination" of variables. Multiple regression's principal task is to combine the predictor variables in such a way as to maximize the correlation of the combined variables with the predicted variable.

Consider the problem discussed in the prior section, in which education and age were used first separately, then jointly to predict income. In the joint analysis, you handed education and age to TREND() and asked for—and got—the best available predictions of income given those predictors in that sample.

In the course of completing that assignment, TREND() figured out the coefficient needed for education and the coefficient needed for age that would result in the most accurate predictions. More specifically, TREND() derived and used (but did not show you) this equation:

Predicted Income = 3.39 * Education + 1.89 * Age + (−73.99)

Figure 4.19
The predictions use the regression equation instead of TREND().

	J6		fx	=CORREL(C6:C35,H6:H35)						
	A	B	C	D	E	F	G	H	I	J	K
1	1.889928	3.388934	-73.9935		b₂	b₁	a				
2	0.45	1.173826	18.23959		1.89	3.39	-73.99				
3	0.6373	15.03106	#N/A							Correlation, Income	
4										with Predicted Income	
5	Education	Age	Income ($000)		b₁ X Education	b₂ X Age	a	Predicted Income		R	R²
6	13	32	$ 28		44.06	60.48	-73.99	$ 30.5		0.7983	0.6373
7	14	40	$ 26		47.45	75.60	-73.99	$ 49.0			
8	11	38	$ 42		37.28	71.82	-73.99	$ 35.1			
9	13	51	$ 72		44.06	96.39	-73.99	$ 66.4			

With the data as given in Figure 4.18 and 4.19, that equation (termed the *regression equation*) results in a set of predicted income values that correlate in this sample with the actual income values better than any other combination of education and age.

How do you get that equation, and why would you want to? One way to get the equation is to use the LINEST() function, shown next. As to why you would want to know the regression equation, a fuller answer to that has to wait until Chapter 12. For now, it's enough to know that you don't want to use a predictor variable that doesn't contribute much to the accuracy of the prediction. The regression equation, in combination with some associated statistics, enables you to decide which predictor variables to use and which to ignore.

Using LINEST() for the Regression Equation

Figure 4.19 contains quite a bit of information starting with cells A1:C3, which show most of the results of running LINEST() on the raw data in the range A6:C35.

> **NOTE**
> LINEST() can return two more rows, not shown here. They have been omitted because the meaning of their contents won't become clear until Chapter 12.

The first row of results returned by LINEST() includes the regression coefficients and the intercept. Compare the contents of A1:C1 in Figure 4.19 with the equation given toward the end of the prior section. The final column in the first row of the results always contains the intercept. Here, that's −73.99, found in cell C1.

Still in the first row of any result returned by LINEST(), the columns that precede the final one always contain the regression coefficients. These are the values that are multiplied by the predictor variables in the regression equation. In this example, there are only two predictor variables—education and age—so there are only two regression coefficients, found in cells A1 and B1.

Figure 4.19 uses the labels b_2, b_1 and a in cells E1, F1 and G1. The letters a and b are standard symbols used in much of the literature concerning regression analysis. I'm inflicting them on you only so that when you encounter them elsewhere you'll know what they refer to. ("Elsewhere" does not include Microsoft's Help documentation on LINEST(), which is highly idiosyncratic.) If this example used a third predictor variable, standard sources would refer to it as b_3. The intercept is normally referred to as a.

LINEST() RUNS BACKWARD

On the topic of idiosyncrasies, here's one that has been making me nuts since Excel 3. LINEST() returns the regression coefficients in the reverse of the order that they appear on the worksheet.

Figure 4.19 shows this pretty clearly. There, you find Education in the first column of the input data, and Age in the second column. But LINEST() returns the regression coefficient for Age first (cell A1) and then Education (cell A2). As just noted, LINEST() always returns the intercept last, in the final column, first row of its output.

This reversal can be hugely inconvenient. It's easy enough to handle when you have only a couple of predictor variables. However, when you have as many as five or six, making use of the equation on the worksheet becomes very tricky. Suppose your raw data for the predictor variables were in the range A6:E100, and you enter the LINEST() function in A1:F3. To get a predicted value for the first record, you'd need this:

=A1*E6 + B1*D6 + C1*C6 + D1*B6 + E1*A6 + F1

Notice how the order of the coefficients in row 1 runs one way and the order of the predictor variables runs in the opposite direction. If Microsoft had gotten it right in the 1990s, your equation could have been along these lines (which is much easier to compose and understand):

=A1*A6 + B1*B6 + C1*C6 + D1*D6 + E1*E6 + F1

There is absolutely no good reason, statistical or programmatic, for this situation. It is the sort of thing that happens from time to time when the programmers and the subject matter experts aren't talking the same language (assuming that they're talking at all).

If Microsoft had gotten it right to begin with, we wouldn't be saddled with this nonsense 20 years later. But once the function hit the marketplace, Microsoft couldn't take it back. By the time the next release appeared, there were too many workbooks out there that depended on finding LINEST's regression coefficients in a particular order.

TREND() gets it right and calculates the predicted values properly, but TREND() returns only the predicted values, not the regression coefficients. The Data Analysis add-in has a Regression tool that returns the regression equation with the coefficients in the proper order. But the Regression tool writes static values to the worksheet, so if your data change at all and you want to see the results, you have to run the Regression tool again.

4

The reversal of the order of the regression coefficients imposed by LINEST() is the reason you see b_2 as a label in cell E1 of Figure 4.19, and b_1 in cell F1. If you want to derive the predicted values yourself directly from the raw data and the regression coefficients—and there are times you want to do that rather than relying on TREND() to do it for you—you need to be sure you're multiplying the correct variable by the correct coefficient.

Figure 4.19 does this in columns E through G. It then adds the values in those columns to get the predicted income in column H. For example, the formula in cell E6 is

=A6*$F$2

In F6:

=B6*$E$2

And in G6, all you need is the intercept:

=$G$2

In H6, you can add them up to get the predicted income for the first record:

=E6+F6+G6

> **NOTE**
>
> I have used the coefficients in cells E2, F2, and G2 in these prediction equations, rather than the identical coefficients in A1, B1, and C1. The reason is that if you're using the workbook that you can download from this book's website (www.informit.com/title/9780789747204), I want you to be able to change the values of the coefficients used in the formulas. If you change any of the coefficients, you'll see that the correlation in cell J6 becomes smaller. That's the correlation between the actual and predicted income values, and is a measure of the accuracy of the prediction.
>
> Earlier, I said that multiple regression returns the best combination of the predictor variables, so if you change the value of any coefficient you will reduce the value of the correlation. You need to modify the values in E2, F2, and G2 if you want to try this experiment. But the coefficients in A1, B1, and C1 are what LINEST() returns and so you can't conveniently change them to see what happens in cell J6. (You cannot change individual values returned by an array formula.)

Understanding Shared Variance

Toward the beginning of this chapter there is a discussion of a statistic called the *covariance*. Recall that it is analogous to the variance of a single variable. That is, the variance is the average of the squared deviations of each value from the mean, whereas the covariance is the average of the cross products of the deviations of each of two variables from its mean:

$$s_{xy} = \sum_{i=1}^{N} \frac{\left(X_i - \overline{X}\right)\left(Y_i - \overline{Y}\right)}{(N - 1)}$$

If you divide the covariance by the product of the two standard deviations, you get the correlation coefficient:

$$r = \frac{s_{xy}}{s_x s_y}$$

Another way to conceptualize the covariance is in terms of set theory. Imagine that Income and Education each represent a set of values associated with the people in your sample. Those two sets *intersect*: that is, there is a tendency for income to increase as education increases. And the covariance is actually the variance of the intersection of, in this example, income and education.

Viewed in that light, it's both possible and useful to say that education shares some variance with income, that education and income have some amount of variance in common. But how much?

You can easily determine what proportion of variance is shared by the two variables by squaring the values in the prior formula:

$$r^2 = \frac{s_{xy}^2}{s_x^2 s_y^2}$$

Now we're standardizing the measure of the covariance by dividing its square by the two variances. The result is the proportion of one variable's variance that it has in common with the other variable. This is usually termed r^2 and, perhaps obviously, pronounced *r-squared*. It's usual to capitalize the r when there are multiple predictor variables: then you have a *multiple R^2*.

Figure 4.19 has the correlation between the actual income variable in column C and the predicted income variable in column H. That correlation is returned by =CORREL(C6:C35,H6:H35). Its value is .7983 and it appears in cell J6. It is the multiple R for this regression analysis.

The square of the multiple R, or the multiple R^2, is shown in cell K6. Its value is .6373. Let me emphasize that the multiple R^2, here .6373, is *the proportion of variance in the Income variable that is shared with the income as predicted by education and age*. It is a measure of the usefulness of the regression equation in predicting, in this case, income. Close to two-thirds of the variability in income, almost 64% of income's variance, can be predicted by (a) knowing a person's education and age, and (b) knowing how to combine those two variables optimally with the regression equation.

> **NOTE**
> The multiple R^2 is also returned by LINEST() in cell A3 of Figure 4.19.

You might see R^2 referred to as the *coefficient of determination*. That's not always a meaningful designation. It is often true that changes in one variable cause changes in another, and in that case it's appropriate to say that one variable's value determines another's. But when you're running a regression analysis outside the context of a true experimental design, you usually can't infer causation (see this chapter's earlier section on correlation and causation). In that very common situation, the term *coefficient of determination* probably isn't apt, and "R^2" does just fine.

Is there a difference between r^2 and R^2? Not much. The symbol r^2 is normally reserved for a situation where there's a single predictor variable, and R^2 for a multiple predictor situation. With a simple regression, you're calculating the correlation r between the single predictor and the known_y's; with multiple regression, you're calculating the multiple correlation R between the known_y's and a composite—the best combination of the individual predictors.

After that best combination has been created in multiple regression, the process of calculating the correlation and its square is the same whether the predictor is a single variable or a composite of more than one variable. So the use of R^2 instead of r^2 is simply a way to inform the reader that the analysis involved multiple regression instead of simple regression. (The Regression tool in the Data Analysis add-in does not distinguish and always uses R and R^2 in its labeling.)

Shared Variance Isn't Additive

It's easy to assume, intuitively, that you could simply take the r^2 between education and income, and the r^2 between age and income, and then total those two r^2 values to come up with the correct R^2 for the multiple regression. Unfortunately, it's not quite that simple.

In the example given in Figure 4.19, the simple correlation between education and income is .63; between age and income it's .72. The associated r^2 values are .40 and .53, which sum to .93. But the actual R^2 is .6373.

The problem is that the values used for age and education are themselves correlated—there is shared variance in the predictors. Therefore, to simply add their r^2 values with income is to add the same variance more than once. Only if the predictors are uncorrelated will their simple r^2 values with the predicted variable sum to the multiple R^2.

The process of arranging for predictor variables to be uncorrelated with one another is a major topic in Chapter 12. It is often required when you're designing a true experiment and when you have unequal group sizes.

A Technical Note: Matrix Algebra and Multiple Regression in Excel

The remaining material in this chapter is intended for readers who are well versed in statistics but may be somewhat new to Excel. If you're not familiar with matrix algebra and see no particular need to use it—which is the case for the overwhelming majority of those who do high-quality statistical analysis using Excel—then by all means head directly for Chapter 5, "How Variables Classify Jointly: Contingency Tables."

Figure 4.20 repeats the raw data shown in Figure 4.19 but uses matrix multiplication and matrix determinants to obtain the regression coefficients and the intercept. It has the advantage of returning the regression coefficients and the intercept in the proper order.

Begin by inserting a column of 1's immediately following the columns with the predictor variables. This is a computational device to make it easier to calculate the intercept. Figure 4.20 shows the vector of unities in column C.

Figure 4.20
Excel's matrix functions are used to create the regression coefficients.

	F10	▾		fx	{=TRANSPOSE(MMULT(F6:H8,J6:J8))}				
◢	A	B	C	D	E	F	G	H	I	J
1	Education	Age	Unities	Income ($000)						
2	13	32	1	$ 28		5785	17131	409		
3	14	40	1	$ 26		17131	52510	1238		
4	11	38	1	$ 42		409	1238	30		
5	13	51	1	$ 72						
6	9	37	1	$ 61		0.006099	-0.00108	-0.03837514		21718
7	15	33	1	$ 41		-0.00108	0.000896	-0.022196395		65692
8	14	43	1	$ 50		-0.03838	-0.0222	1.472485654		1506
9	8	44	1	$ 31						
10	12	33	1	$ 28		3.388934	1.889928	-73.99349453		
11	15	40	1	$ 51						

Cells F2:H4 in Figure 4.20 show the sum of squares and cross products (SSCP) for the predictor variables, perhaps more familiar in matrix notation as $\mathbf{X'X}$. Using Excel, you obtain that matrix by selecting a square range of cells with as many columns and rows as you have predictors, plus the intercept. Then array-enter this formula (modified, of course, according to where you have stored the raw data):

=MMULT(TRANSPOSE(A2:C31),A2:C31)

Excel's MMULT() function must be array-entered for it to return the results properly, and it always postmultiplies the first argument by the second.

To get the inverse of the SSCP matrix, use Excel's MINVERSE() function, also array-entered. Figure 4.20 shows the SSCP inverse in cells F6:H8, using the formula

=MINVERSE(F2:H4)

to return $(\mathbf{X'X})^{-1}$.

The vector that contains the summed cross products of the predictors and the predicted variable, $\mathbf{X'y}$, appears in Figure 4.20 in cells J6:J8 using this array formula:

=MMULT(TRANSPOSE(A2:C31),D2:D31)

Finally, the matrix multiplication that returns the regression coefficients and the intercept, *in the same order as they appear on the worksheet*, is array-entered in cells F10:H10:

=TRANSPOSE(MMULT(F6:H8,J6:J8))

Alternatively, the entire analysis could be managed in a range of one row and three columns with this array formula, which combines the intermediate arrays into a single expression:

4

=TRANSPOSE(MMULT(MINVERSE(MMULT(TRANSPOSE(A2:C31),
A2:C31)),MMULT(TRANSPOSE(A2:C31),D2:D31)))

This is merely a lengthy way in Excel to express $(\mathbf{X'X})^{-1} \mathbf{X'y}$.

Moving on to Statistical Inference

Chapter 5 takes a step back from the continuous variables that are emphasized in this chapter, to simpler, nominal variables with only a few possible values each. They are often best studied using two-way tables that contain simple counts in their cells.

However, when you start to make inferences about populations using contingency tables built on samples, you start getting into some very interesting areas. This is the beginning of statistical inference and it will lead very quickly to issues such as gender bias in university classes.

4

How Variables Classify Jointly: Contingency Tables

5

In Chapter 4, "How Variables Move Jointly: Correlation," you saw the ways in which two continuous variables can covary: together in a direct, positive correlation, and apart in an indirect, negative correlation—or not at all when no relationship between the two exists.

This chapter explores how two *nominal* variables can vary together, or fail to do so. Recall from Chapter 1, "About Variables and Values," that variables measured on a nominal scale have names (such as Ford or Toyota, Republican or Democrat, Smith or Jones) as their values. Variables measured on an ordinal, interval, or ratio scale have numbers as their values and their relationships can be measured by means of covariance and correlation. For nominal variables, we have to make do with tables.

Understanding One-Way Pivot Tables

As the quality control manager of a factory that produces sophisticated, cutting-edge cell phones, one of your responsibilities is to see to it that the phones leaving the factory conform to some standards for usability. One of those standards is the phone's ability to establish a connection with a cell tower when it is being held in a fashion that most users find natural and comfortable (rather than as your company's CEO tells them to hold it).

Your factory is producing the phones at a phenomenal rate and you just don't have the staff to check every phone. Therefore, you arrange to have a sample of 50 phones tested daily, checking for connection problems. You know that zero-defect manufacturing is both terribly expensive and a generally impossible goal: Your company will be satisfied if only 1% of its phones fail to establish a connection with a cell tower that's within reach.

Today your factory produced 1,000 phones. Did you meet your goal of at most ten defective units in 1,000?

You can't possibly answer that question yet. First, you need more information about the sample you had tested: In particular, how many failed the test? See Figure 5.1.

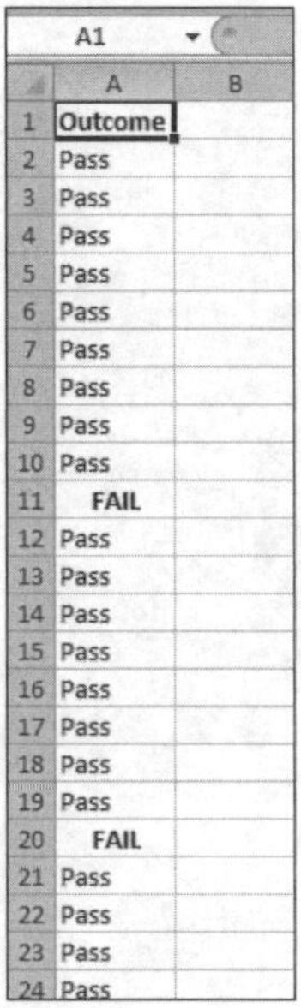

Figure 5.1
A standard Excel list, with a variable occupying column A, records occupying different rows, and a value in each cell of column A.

	A	B
1	Outcome	
2	Pass	
3	Pass	
4	Pass	
5	Pass	
6	Pass	
7	Pass	
8	Pass	
9	Pass	
10	Pass	
11	FAIL	
12	Pass	
13	Pass	
14	Pass	
15	Pass	
16	Pass	
17	Pass	
18	Pass	
19	Pass	
20	FAIL	
21	Pass	
22	Pass	
23	Pass	
24	Pass	

To create a pivot table with category counts, take these steps:

1. Select cell A1 to help Excel find your input data.

2. Click the Insert tab and choose PivotTable in the Tables group.

3. In the Create PivotTable dialog box, click the Existing Worksheet option button, click in the Location edit box, and then click in cell C1 on the worksheet. Click OK.

4. In the PivotTable Fields list, click Outcome and drag it into the Row Labels area.

5. Click Outcome again and drag it into the Summary Values area, designated in Excel 2010 by Σ **Values**. Because at least one value in the input range is text, the summary statistic is Count.

6. It's often useful to show the counts in the pivot table as percentages. If you're using Excel 2010, right-click any cell in the pivot table's Count column and choose Show Values As from the shortcut menu. See the following note if you're using an earlier version of Excel.

7. Click % of Column Total in the cascading menu.

You now have a statistical summary of the pass/fail status of the 50 phones in your sample, as shown in Figure 5.2.

NOTE Microsoft made significant changes to the user interface for pivot tables between Excel 2003 and 2007, and again between Excel 2007 and 2010. In this book I try to provide instructions that work regardless of the version you're using. That's not always feasible.

In this case, you could do the following in either Excel 2007 or 2010. Right-click one of the Count or Total cells in the pivot table, such as D2 or D3 in this example. Choose Value Field Settings from the shortcut menu and click the Show Values As tab. Click % of Column Total in the Show Values As drop-down. Then click OK. In Excel 2003 or earlier, right-click one of the pivot table's value cells and choose Field Settings from the shortcut menu. Use the drop-down labeled Show Data As in the Field Settings dialog box.

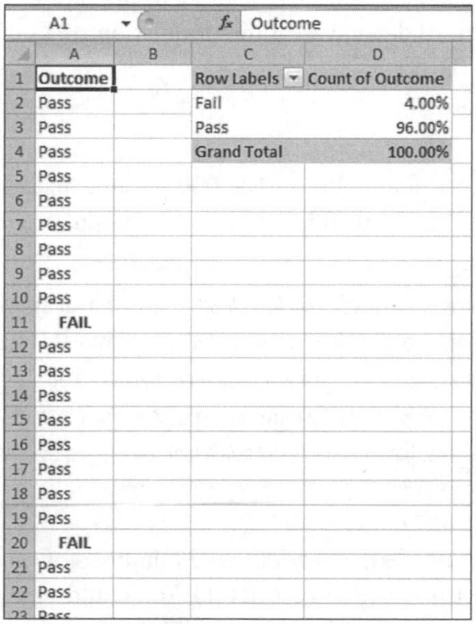

Figure 5.2
A quick-and-easy summary of your sample results.

The results shown in Figure 5.2 aren't great news. Your target is this: Out of the entire population of 1,000 phones that were made today, no more than 1% (10 total) should be defective if you're to meet your target. But in a sample of 50 phones you found 2 defectives. In other words, a 5% sample (50 of 1,000) got you 20% (2 of 10) of the way toward your self-imposed limit.

You could take another nineteen 50-unit samples from the population. At the rate of 2 defectives in 50 units, you'd wind up with 40 defectives overall, and that's four times the number you can tolerate from the full population.

On the other hand, it is a random sample. As such, there are limits to how representative the sample is of the population it comes from. It's possible that you just happened to get your hands on a sample of 50 phones that included 2 defective units when the full population has a smaller defective rate. How likely is that?

Here's how Excel can help you answer that question.

Running the Statistical Test

A large number of questions in the areas of business, manufacturing, medicine, social science, gambling, and so on are based on situations in which there are just two typical outcomes: succeeds/fails, breaks/doesn't break, cures/sickens, Republican/Democrat, wins/loses. In statistical analysis, these situations are termed *binomial*: "bi" referring to "two," and "nomial" referring to "names." Several hundred years ago, due largely to a keen interest in the outcomes of bets, mathematicians started looking closely at the nature of those outcomes. We now know a lot more than we once did about how the numbers behave in the long run.

And you can use that knowledge as a guide to an answer to the question posed earlier: How likely is it that there are at most 10 defectives in the population of 1,000 phones, when you found two in a sample of just 50?

Framing the Hypothesis

Start by supposing that you had a population of 100,000 phones that has 1,000 defectives—thus the same 1% defect rate as you hope for in your actual population of 1,000 phones.

> **NOTE** This sort of supposition is often called a *null hypothesis*. It assumes that there is no difference between two values, such as a value obtained from a sample and a value assumed for a population; another type of null hypothesis assumes that there is no difference between two population values. The assumption of no difference is behind the term *null* hypothesis. You often see that the researcher has framed another hypothesis that contradicts the null hypothesis, called the *alternative hypothesis*.

If you had all the resources you needed, you could take hundreds of samples, each sample consisting of 50 units, from that population of 100,000. You could examine each sample and determine how many defective units were in it. If you did that, you could create a special kind of frequency distribution, called a *sampling distribution*, based on the number of defectives in each sample.

Under your supposition of just 1% defective in the population, one of those hypothetical samples would have zero defects; another sample would have two (just like the one you took in reality); another sample would have one defect; and so on until you had exhausted all those resources in the process of taking hundreds of samples. You could chart the number of defects in each sample, creating a sampling distribution that shows the frequency of the number of defects in each sample.

Using the BINOM.DIST() Function

Because of all the research and theoretical work that was done by those mathematicians starting in the 1600s, you know what that frequency distribution looks like *without having to take all those samples*. You'll find it in Figure 5.3.

Figure 5.3
A sampling distribution of the number of defects in each of many, many samples would look like this.

E3 =BINOM.DIST(D3,$B$1,$B$2,FALSE)

	A	B	C	D	E	F
1	Sample size	50				
2	Target Percent Defective in Population	1%		Number of defectives	Percent of samples	Cumulative percent of samples
3				0	60.50%	60.50%
4				1	30.56%	91.06%
5				2	7.56%	98.62%
6				3	1.22%	99.84%
7				4	0.15%	99.99%
8				5	0.01%	100.00%
9				6	0.00%	100.00%
10				7	0.00%	100.00%
11				8	0.00%	100.00%
12				9	0.00%	100.00%
13				10	0.00%	100.00%

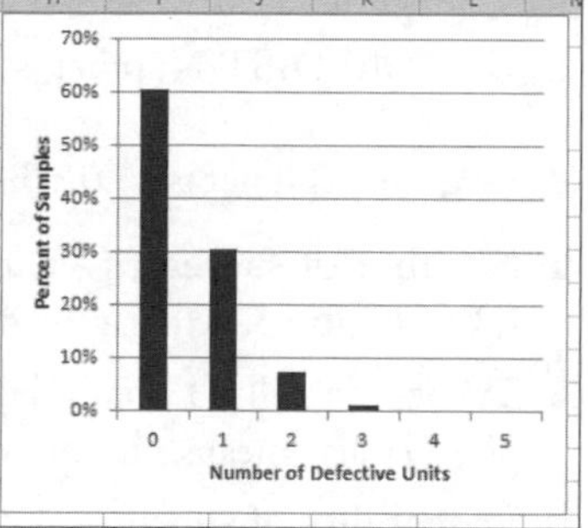

The distribution that you see charted in Figure 5.3 is one of many *binomial distributions*. The shape of each binomial distribution is different, depending on the size of the samples and the probability of each alternative in the population. The binomial distribution you see in Figure 5.3 is based on a sample size of 50 and a probability (in this example, of defective units) of 1%. For contrast, Figure 5.4 shows an example of the binomial distribution based on a sample size of 100 and a probability of 3%.

Figure 5.4
Compare with Figure 5.3: The distribution has shifted to the right.

E3 =BINOM.DIST(D3,$B$1,$B$2,FALSE)

	A	B	C	D	E	F
1	Sample size	100				
2	Target Percent Defective in Population	3%		Number of defectives	Percent of samples	Cumulative percent of samples
3				0	4.76%	4.76%
4				1	14.71%	19.46%
5				2	22.52%	41.98%
6				3	22.75%	64.72%
7				4	17.06%	81.79%
8				5	10.13%	91.92%
9				6	4.96%	96.88%
10				7	2.06%	98.94%
11				8	0.74%	99.68%
12				9	0.23%	99.91%
13				10	0.07%	99.98%

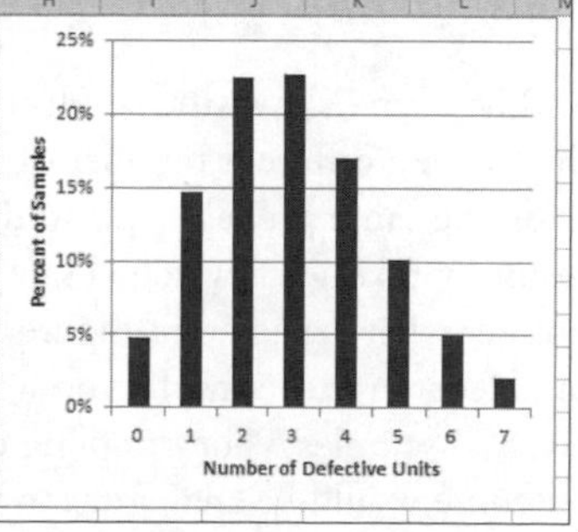

The distributions shown in Figures 5.3 and 5.4 are based on the theory of binomial distributions and are generated directly using Excel's BINOM.DIST()function.

For example, in Figure 5.4, the formula in cell E3 is as follows:

=BINOM.DIST(D3,$B$1,$B$2,FALSE)

> **NOTE**
> If you are using a version of Excel prior to 2010, you must use the compatibility function BINOMDIST().
> Notice that there is no period in the function name, as there is with the consistency function
> BINOM.DIST(). The arguments to the two functions are identical as to both argument name and
> argument meaning.

or, using argument names instead of cell addresses:

=BINOM.DIST(Number_s,Trials,Probability_s,Cumulative)

Here are the arguments to the BINOM.DIST() function:

- **Number of successes**—Excel calls this *Number_s*. In BINOM.DIST(), as found in cell E3 of Figure 5.4, that's the value found in cell D3: 0.

- **Trials**—In cell E3, that's the value found in cell $B$1: 100. In the context of this example, "Trials" means number of cell phones in a sample.

- **Probability of success**—Excel calls this *Probability_s*. This is the probability of a success—of finding a defective unit—in the population. In this example, we're assuming that the probability is 3%, which is the value found in cell $B$2.

- **Cumulative**—This argument takes either a TRUE or FALSE value. If you set it to TRUE, Excel returns the probability for this number of successes plus the probability of all smaller numbers of successes. That is, if the number of successes cited in this formula is 2, and if Cumulative is TRUE, then BINOM.DIST() returns the probability for 2 successes plus the probability of 1 success plus the probability of zero successes (in Figure 5.4, that is 41.98% in cell F5). When Cumulative is set to FALSE, Excel returns the probability of one particular number of successes. As used in cell E4, for example, that is the probability of the number of successes found in D4 (1 success in D4 leads to 14.71% of samples in cell E4).

So Figure 5.4 shows the results of entering the BINOM.DIST() function 11 times, each time with a different number of successes but the same number of trials (that is, sample size), the same probability, and the same cumulative option. If you tried to replicate this result by taking a few actual samples of size 50 with a success probability of 3%, you would not get what is shown in Figure 5.4. After taking 20 or 30 samples and charting the number of defects in each sample, you would begin to get a result that looks like Figure 5.4. After, say, 500 samples, your sampling distribution would look very much like Figure 5.4. (That outcome would be analogous to the demonstration for the normal distribution shown at the end of Chapter 1, in "Building Simulated Frequency Distributions.")

But because we know the characteristics of the binomial distribution, under different sample sizes and with different probabilities of success in the population, it isn't necessary to get a new distribution by repeated sampling each time we need one. (We know those characteristics by understanding the math involved, not from trial and error.) Just giving the required information to Excel is enough to generate the characteristics of the appropriate distribution.

So, in Figure 5.3, there is a binomial distribution that's appropriate for this question: Given a 50-unit sample in which we found two defective units, what's the probability that the sample came from a population in which just 1% of its units are defective?

Interpreting the Results of BINOM.DIST()

In Figure 5.3, you can see that you expect to find zero defective units in a sample of 50 in 60.50% of samples you might take. You expect to find one defective unit in a sample of 50 in another 30.56% of possible samples. That totals to 91.06% of 50-unit samples that you might take from this population of units. The remaining 8.94% of 50-unit samples would have two defective units, 4% of the sample, or more, when the population has only 1%.

What conclusion do you draw from this analysis? Is the one sample that you obtained part of the 8.94% of 50-unit samples that have two or more defectives when the population has only 1%? Or is your assumption that the population has just 1% defective a bad assumption?

If you decide that you have come up with an unusual sample—that yours is one of the 8.94% of samples that has 4% defectives when the population has only 1%—then you're laying odds of 10 to 1 on your decision-making ability. Most rational people, given exactly the information discussed in this section, would conclude that their initial assumption about the population was in error—that the population does not in fact have 1% defective units. Most rational people don't lay 10 to 1 on themselves without a pretty good reason, and this example has given you no reason at all to take the short end of that bet.

If you decide that your original assumption, that the population has only 1% defectives, was wrong—if you decide that the population has more than 1% defective units—that doesn't necessarily mean you have persuasive evidence that the percentage of defects in the population is 4%, as it is in your sample (although that's your best estimate right now). All your conclusion says is that you have decided that the population of 1,000 units you made today includes more than ten defective units.

Setting Your Decision Rules

Now, it can be a little disturbing to find that almost 9% (8.94%) of the samples of 50 phones from a 1% defective population would have at least 4% defective phones. It's disturbing because most people would not regard 9% of the samples as absolutely conclusive. They would normally decide that the population has more than a 1% defect rate, but there would be a nagging doubt. After all, we've seen that almost one sample in ten from a 1% defective population would have 4% defects or more, so it's surely not impossible to get a bad sample from a good population.

Let's eavesdrop: "I have 50 phones that I sampled at random from the 1,000 we made today—and we're hoping that there are no more than 10 defective units in that entire production run. Two of the sample, or 4%, are defective. Excel's BINOM.DIST() function, with those arguments, tells me that if I took 10 samples of 50 each, roughly one of them

(8.94% of the samples) would be likely to have two or even more defectives. Maybe that's the sample I have here. Maybe the full production run only has 1% defective."

Tempting, isn't it? This is why you should specify your decision rule *before* you've seen the data, and why you shouldn't fudge it after the data has come in. If you see the data and then decide what your criterion will be, you are allowing the data to influence your decision rule after the fact. That's called *capitalizing on chance.*

Traditional experimental methods advise you to specify the likelihood of making the wrong decision about the population before you see the data. The idea is that you should bring a cost-benefit approach to setting your criterion. Suppose that you sell your 1,000 phones to a wholesaler at a 5% markup. The terms of your contract with the wholesaler call for you to refund the price of an entire shipment if the wholesaler finds more than 1% defective units in the shipment. The cost of that refund has to be borne by the profits you've made.

So if you make a bad decision (that is, the population of items from which we drew our sample has 1% or fewer defective units, when in fact it has, say, 3%) the 21st sale could cost you all the profits you've made on the first 20 sales. Therefore, you want to make your criterion for deciding to a ship the 1,000-unit lot strong enough that at *most* one shipment in 20 will fail to meet the wholesaler's acceptance criterion.

> **NOTE**
> The approach discussed in this book can be thought of as a more traditional one, following the methods developed in the early part of the twentieth century by theoreticians such as R. A. Fisher. It is sometimes termed a *frequentist approach.* Other statistical theorists and practitioners follow a Bayesian model, under which the hypotheses themselves can be thought of as having probabilities. The matter is a subject of some controversy and is well beyond the scope of a book on Excel. Be aware, though, that where there is a choice that matters in the way functions are designed and the Data Analysis add-in works, Microsoft has taken a conservative stance and adopted the frequentist approach.

Making Assumptions

You must be sure to meet two basic assumptions if you want your analysis of the defective phone problem—and other, similar problems—to be valid. You'll find that all problems in statistical inference involve assumptions; sometimes there are more than just two, and sometimes it turns out that you can get away with violating the assumptions. In this case, there are just two, but you can't get away with any violations.

Random Selection

The analysis assumes that you take samples from your population at random. In the phone example, you can't look at the population of phones and pick the 50 that look least likely to be defective.

Well, more precisely, you *can* do that if you want to. But if you do, you are creating a sample that is systematically different from the population. You need a sample that you can use to make an inference about all the phones you made, and your judgment about which phones look best was not part of the manufacturing process. If you let your judgment interfere with random selection of phones for your sample, you'll wind up with a sample that isn't truly representative of the population.

And there aren't many things more useless than a nonrepresentative sample (just ask George Gallup about his prediction that Truman would lose to Dewey in 1948). If you don't pick a random sample of phones, you make a decision about the population of phones that you have manufactured on the basis of a nonrepresentative sample. If your sample has not a single defective phone, how confident can you be that the outcome is due to the quality of the population, and not the quality of your judgment in selecting the sample?

Using Excel to Help Sample Randomly

The question of using Excel to support a random selection comes up occasionally. Here's the approach that I use and prefer. Start with a worksheet list of values that uniquely identify members of a population. In the example this chapter has used, those values might be serial numbers.

If that list occupies, say, A1:A1001, you can continue by taking these steps:

1. In cell B1, enter a label such as **Random Number**.
2. Select the range B2:B1001.
3. Type the formula **=RAND()** and enter it into B2:B1001 using Ctrl+Enter. This generates a list of random values in random order. The values returned by RAND() are unrelated to the identifying serial numbers in column A. Leave the range B2:B1001 selected.
4. So that you can sort them, convert the formulas to values by clicking the Copy button on the Ribbon's Home tab, then clicking Paste, choosing Paste Special, selecting the Values option, and then clicking OK. You now have random numbers in B2:B1001.
5. Select any cell in the range A1:B1001. Click the Ribbon's Data tab and click the Sort button.
6. In the Sort By drop-down, choose Random Number. Accept the defaults for the Sort On and the Order drop-downs and click OK.

The result is to sort the unique identifiers into random order, as shown in Figure 5.5. You can now print off the first 50 (or the size of the sample you want) and select them from your population.

5

Figure 5.5
Instead of serial number, the unique identifier in column A could be name, social security number, phone number—whatever is most apt for your population of interest.

	A	B
1	**Serial Number**	**Random Number**
2	0755	0.001689476
3	0543	0.002009872
4	0036	0.003269631
5	0180	0.005764236
6	0592	0.006447337
7	0075	0.00688983
8	0738	0.008381166
9	0398	0.008724755
10	0333	0.010579213
11	0558	0.011353086
12	0370	0.011771092
13	0237	0.012935051
14	0230	0.016904888
15	0958	0.018583868

NOTE

Random numbers that you generate in this way are really pseudo-random numbers. Computers have a relatively limited instruction set, and execute their instructions repeatedly. This makes them very fast and very accurate but not very random. Nevertheless, the pseudo-random numbers produced by Excel's RAND() function pass some rigorous tests for nonrandomness and are well suited to any sort of random selection you're at all likely to need.

Independent Selections

It's important that the individual selections be independent of one another: that is, the fact that Phone 0001 is selected for the sample must not change the likelihood that another specific unit will be selected.

Suppose that the phones leave the factory floor packaged in 50-unit cartons. It would obviously be convenient to grab one of those cartons, even at random, and declare that it's to be your 50-unit sample. But if you did that, you could easily be introducing some sort of systematic dependency into the system.

For example, if the 50 phones in a given carton were manufactured sequentially—if they were, say, the 51st through 100th phones to be manufactured that day—then a subset of them might be subject to the same calibration error in a piece of equipment. In that case, the lack of independence in making the selections again introduces a nonrandom element into what is assumed to be a random process.

A corollary to the issue of independence is that the probability of being selected must remain the same through the process. In practice, it's difficult to adhere slavishly to this requirement, but the difference between 1/1,000 and 1/999, or between 1/999 and 1/998 is so small that they are generally taken to be equivalent probabilities.

The Binomial Distribution Formula

If these assumptions—random and independent selection with just two possible values—are met, then the formula for the binomial distribution is valid:

$$\text{Probability} = \binom{n}{r} p^r q^{n-r}$$

In this formula:

- **n** is the number of trials.
- **r** is the number of successes.
- $\binom{n}{r}$ is the number of combinations.
- **p** is the probability of a success in the population.
- **q** is (1 – p), or the probability of a failure in the population.

(The number of combinations is often called the "nCr" formula, or "n things taken r at a time.")

You'll find the formula worked out in Figure 5.6 for a specific number of trials, successes, and probability of success in the population. Compare Figure 5.6 with Figure 5.4. In both figures:

- The number of trials, or *n*, representing the sample size, is 100.
- The number of successes, or *r*, representing the number of defects in the sample, is 4 (cell D7 in Figure 5.4).
- The probability of a success in the population, or *p*, is .03.

Figure 5.6
Building the results of BINOM.DIST() from scratch.

	A	B	C	D	E
			fx	=C5*(C3^C2)*(C4^(C1-C2))	
1		Trials (n)	100		
2		Successes (r)	4		
3		Population Probability (p)	0.03		
4		1-Population Probability (q)	0.97		
5		n (trials) taken r (successes) at a time	3921225		=COMBIN(C1,C2)
6		Probability of 4 successes	17.06%		

In Figure 5.6:

- The value of q is calculated simply by subtracting p from 1 in cell C4.
- The value of $\binom{n}{r}$ is calculated in cell C5 with the formula =COMBIN(C1,C2).
- The formula for the binomial distribution is used in cell C6 to calculate the probability of four successes in a sample of 100, given a probability of success in the population of 3%.

Note that the probability calculated in cell C6 of Figure 5.6 is identical to the value returned by BINOM.DIST() in cell E7 of Figure 5.4.

Of course, it's not necessary to use the nCr formula to calculate the binomial probability; that's what BINOM.DIST() is for. Still, I like to calculate it from scratch from time to time as a check that I have used BINOM.DIST() and its arguments properly.

Using the BINOM.INV() Function

You have already seen Excel's BINOM.DIST() function, in Figures 5.3 and 5.4. There, the arguments used were as follows:

- **Number of successes**—More generally, that's the number of times something occurred—here, that's the number of instances that phones are defective. Excel terms this argument *successes* or *number_s*.
- **Number of trials**—The number of opportunities for *successes* to occur. In the current example, that's the sample size.
- **Probability of success**—The percent of times something occurs *in the population*. In practice, this is usually the probability that you are testing for by means of a sample: "How likely is it that the probability of success in the population is 1%, when the probability of success in my sample is 4%?"
- **Cumulative**—TRUE to return the probability associated with this number of successes, plus all smaller numbers down to and including zero. FALSE to return the probability associated with this number of successes only.

BINOM.DIST() returns the probability that a sample with the given number of defectives can be drawn from a population with the given probability of success. The older function BINOMDIST() takes the same arguments and returns the same results.

As you'll see in this and later chapters, a variety of Excel functions that return probabilities for different distributions have a form whose name ends with .DIST(). For example, NORM.DIST() returns the probability of observing a value in a normal distribution, given the distribution's mean and standard deviation, and the value itself.

Another form of these functions ends with .INV() instead of .DIST(). The INV stands for *inverse*. In the case of BINOM.INV(), the arguments are as follows:

- **Trials**—Just as in BINOM.DIST(), this is the number of opportunities for successes (here, the sample size).
- **Probability**—Just as in BINOM.DIST(), this is the probability of successes in the population.
- **Alpha**—This is the value that BINOM.DIST() returns: the cumulative probability of obtaining some number of successes in the sample, with the sample size and the population probability. (The term *alpha* for this value is nonstandard.)

Given these arguments, BINOM.INV() returns the number of successes (here, defective phones) associated with the alpha argument you supply. I know that's confusing, and this may help clear it up: Look back to Figure 5.4. Suppose you enter this formula on that worksheet:

=BINOM.INV(B1,B2,F9)

That would return the number 7. Here's what that means and what you can infer from it, given the setup in Figure 5.4:

> You've told me that you have a sample of 100 phones (cell B1). The sample comes from a population of phones where the probability of a phone being defective is 3% (cell B2). You want to hold on to a correct assumption that the sample came from that population 96.88% of the time (cell F9). Thus, you're willing to make a mistake, to reject your assumption when it's correct, 3.12% of the time: 3.12% of 100-unit samples from a population with 3% defective will have 7 or more defective units.

> Given all that, you should conclude that the sample did *not* come from a population with only 3% defective if you get 7 or more defective units in your sample—if you get that many, you're into the 3.12% of the samples that have 7 or more defectives. Although your sample could certainly be among the 3.12% of samples with 7 defectives from a 3% defective population, that's too unlikely a possibility to suit most people. Most people would decide instead that the population has more than 3% defectives.

So the .INV() form of the function turns the .DIST() form on its head. With BINOM.DIST(), you supply the number of successes and the function returns the probability of that many successes in the population you defined. With BINOM.INV(), you supply the largest percent of samples beyond which you would cease to believe the sample comes from a population that has a given defect rate. Then, BINOM.INV() returns the number of successes that would satisfy your criteria for sample size, for percent defective in the population, and for the percent of the area in the binomial distribution that you're interested in.

Therefore, you would supply the probability .99 if you decided that a sample with so many defects that it could come from a 3% defective population only 1% of the time, the sample must come from a population with a higher defect rate. Or you would supply the probability .90 if you decided that a sample with so many defects that it could come from a 3% defective population only 10% of the time, the sample must come from a population with a higher defect rate.

You'll see all this depicted in Figure 5.7, based on the data from Figure 5.4.

In Figure 5.7, as in Figure 5.4, a sample of 100 units (cell B1) is taken from a population that is assumed to have 3% defective units (cell B2). Cells G2:I13 replicate the analysis from Figure 5.4, using BINOM.DIST() to determine the percent (H2:H13) and cumulative percent (I2:I13) of samples that you would expect to have different numbers of defective units (cells G2:G13).

Columns D and E use BINOM.INV() to determine the number of defects (column D) you would expect in a given percent of samples. That is, in anywhere from 82% to 91% of samples from the population, you would expect to find as many as five defective units. This finding is consistent with the BINOM.DIST() analysis, which shows that a cumulative 91.92% of samples have as many as five defects.

Figure 5.7
Comparing BINOM.INV()
with BINOM.DIST().

	A	B	C	D	E	F	G	H	I
				D3		fx	=BINOM.INV($B$1,$B$2,E3)		
1	Sample size	100							
2	Target Percent Defective in Population	3%		Number of defectives	Percent of samples		Number of defectives	Percent of samples	Cumulative percent of samples
3				8	99%		0	4.76%	4.76%
4				7	98%		1	14.71%	19.46%
5				7	97%		2	22.52%	41.98%
6				6	96%		3	22.75%	64.72%
7				6	95%		4	17.06%	81.79%
8				6	94%		5	10.13%	91.92%
9				6	93%		6	4.96%	96.88%
10				6	92%		7	2.06%	98.94%
11				5	91%		8	0.74%	99.68%
12				5	90%		9	0.23%	99.91%
13				5	89%		10	0.07%	99.98%
14				5	88%				
15				5	87%				
16				5	86%				
17				5	85%				
18				5	84%				
19				5	83%				
20				5	82%				
21				4	81%				

The following sections offer a few comments on all this information.

Somewhat Complex Reasoning

Don't let the complexity throw you. It usually takes several trips through the reasoning before the logic of it begins to settle in. The general line of thought pursued here is somewhat more complicated than the reasoning you follow when you're doing other kinds of statistical analysis, such as whether two samples indicate that the means are likely to be different in their populations. The reasoning about mean differences tends to be less complicated than is the case with the binomial distribution.

Three issues complicate the logic of a binomial analysis. One is the cumulative nature of the outcome measure: the number of defective phones in the sample. To test whether the sample came from a population with an acceptable number of defectives, you need to account for zero defective units, one defective unit, two defective units, and so on.

Another complicating issue is that more percentages than usual are involved. In most other kinds of statistical analysis, the only percentage you're concerned with is the percent of the time that you would observe a sample like the one you obtained, given that the population is as you assume it to be. In the current discussion, for example, you consider the percent of the time you would get a sample of 100 with four defects, assuming the population has only 1% defective units.

It complicates the reasoning that you're working with percentages as the measures themselves. Putting things another way, you consider the percent of the time you would get 4% defects in a sample when the population has 1% defects. It's only when you're working with a nominal scale that you must work with outcome percentages: X% of patients survived one year; Y% of cars had brake failure; Z% of registered voters were Republicans.

The other complicating factor is that the outcome measure is an integer, and the associated probabilities jump, instead of increasing smoothly, as the number of successes increases. Refer back to Figure 5.4 and notice how the probabilities increase by dwindling amounts as the number of success increases.

The General Flow of Hypothesis Testing

Still, the basic reasoning followed here is analogous to the reasoning used in other situations. The normal process is as follows:

The Hypothesis   Set up an assumption (often called an *hypothesis*, sometimes a *null hypothesis*, to be contrasted with an *alternative hypothesis*). In the example discussed here, the null hypothesis is that the population from which the sample of phones came has a 1% defect rate; the term *null* suggests that nothing unusual is going on, that 1% is the normal expectation. The alternative hypothesis is that the population defect rate is higher than 1%.

The Sampling Distribution   Determine the characteristics of the sampling distribution that would result if the hypothesis were true. There are various types of distributions, and your choice is usually dictated by the question you're trying to answer and by the level of measurement available to you. Here, the level of measurement was not only nominal (acceptable vs. defective) but binomial (just two possible values). You use the functions in Excel that pertain to the binomial distribution to determine the probabilities associated with different numbers of defects in the sample.

The Error Rate   Decide how much risk of incorrectly rejecting the hypothesis is acceptable. This chapter has talked about that decision without actually making it in the phone quality example; it advises you to take into account issues such as the costs of making an incorrect decision versus the benefits of making a correct one. (This book discusses other related issues, such as statistical power.)

In many branches of statistical analysis, it is conventional to adopt levels such as .05 and .01 as error rates. Unfortunately, the choice of these levels is often dictated by tradition, not the logic and mathematics of the situation. But whatever the rationale for adopting a particular error rate, note that it's usual to make that decision prior to analyzing the data. You should decide on an error rate before you see any results; then you have more confidence in your sample results because you have specified beforehand what percent of the time (5%, 1%, or some other figure) your result will be in error.

Hypothesis Acceptance or Rejection   In this fourth phase of hypothesis testing, take the sample and calculate the pertinent statistic (here, number of defective phones). Compare the result with the same result in the sampling distribution that was derived in step 2. If your sample result appears in the sampling distribution less often than implied by the error rate you chose in step 3, reject the null hypothesis. For example, if the error rate you chose is .05 (5%) and you would get as many defective units as you did only .04 (4%) of the time when the null is true, reject the null; otherwise, retain the null hypothesis that your sample comes from a population of phones with 1% defectives.

Figure 5.3 represents the hypothesis that the population has 1% defective units. A sample of 50 with zero, one, or two defective units would occur in 98.62% of the possible samples. Therefore, if you adopted .05 as your error rate, two sample defects would cause you to reject the hypothesis of 1% defects in the population. The presence of two defective units in the 50-unit sample bypasses the .95 criterion, which is the complement of the .05 error rate.

This logic can get tortuous, so let's look at it again using different words. You have said that you're willing to make the wrong decision about your population of phones 5% of the time; that's the error rate you chose. You are willing to conclude 5% of the time that the population has more than 1% defective when it actually has 1% defective. That 5% error rate puts an upper limit on the number of defective phones you can find in your sample and still decide it came from a population with only 1% defectives.

Your sample of 50 comes in with two defective phones. You would get up to two defectives in 98.62% of samples from a population with 1% defective units. That's more than you can put up with when you want to limit your error rate to 5%. So you conclude that the population actually has more than 1% defective—you reject the null hypothesis.

Figure 5.4 shows the distribution of samples from a population with a 3% defect rate. In this case, two defects in a sample of 100 would not persuade you to reject the hypothesis of 3% defects in the population if you adopt a .05 error rate. Using that error rate, you would need to find six defective units in your sample to reject the hypothesis that the population has a 3% defect rate.

Choosing Between BINOM.DIST() and BINOM.INV()

The functions BINOM.DIST() and BINOM.INV() are two sides of the same coin. They deal with the same numbers. The difference is that you supply BINOM.DIST() with a number of successes and it tells you the probability, but you supply BINOM.INV() with a probability and it tells you the number of successes.

You can get the same set of results either way, but I prefer to create analyses such as Figures 5.3 and 5.4 using BINOM.DIST(). In Figure 5.4, you could supply the integers in D3:D13 and use BINOM.DIST() to obtain the probabilities in E3:E13. Or you could supply the cumulative probabilities in F3:F13 and use BINOM.INV() to obtain the number of successes in D3:D13.

But just in terms of worksheet mechanics, it's easier to present a series of integers to BINOM.DIST() than it is to present a series of probabilities to BINOM.INV().

Alpha: An Unfortunate Argument Name

Standard statistical usage reserves the name *alpha* for the probability of incorrectly rejecting a null hypothesis, of deciding that something unexpected is going on when it's really business as usual. But in the BINOM.INV() function, Excel uses the argument name *alpha* for the probability that your data will tell you that the null hypothesis is true, when it is in fact true, and in standard statistical usage, that is not alpha but 1 – alpha. If you're used to the standard usage, or even if you're not yet used to it, don't be misled by the idiosyncratic Excel terminology.

> **NOTE** In versions of Excel prior to 2010, BINOM.INV() was named CRITBINOM(). Like all the "compatibility functions," CRITBINOM() is still available in Excel 2010.

Understanding Two-Way Pivot Tables

Two-way pivot tables are, on the surface, a simple extension of the one-way pivot table discussed at the beginning of this chapter. There, you obtained data on some nominal measure—the example that was used was acceptable vs. defective—and put it into an Excel list. Then you used Excel's pivot table feature to count the number of instances of acceptable units and defective units. Only one field, acceptable vs. defective, was involved, and the pivot table had only row labels and a count, or a percent, for each label (refer back to Figure 5.2).

A two-way pivot table adds a second field, also normally measured on a nominal scale. Suppose that you have at hand data from a telephone survey of potential voters, many of whom were willing to disclose both their political affiliation and their attitude (approve or disapprove) of a proposition that will appear on the next statewide election ballot. Your data might appear as shown in Figure 5.8.

To create a two-way pivot table with the data shown in Figure 5.8, take these steps:

1. Select cell A1 to help Excel find your input data.
2. Click the Insert tab and choose PivotTable in the Tables group.
3. In the Create PivotTable dialog box, click the Existing Worksheet option button, click in the Location edit box, and then click in cell D1 on the worksheet. Click OK.
4. In the PivotTable Fields list, click Party and drag it into the Row Labels area.
5. Still in the PivotTable Fields list, click Proposition and drag it into the Column Labels area.
6. Click Proposition again and drag it into the Σ Values area in the PivotTable Fields list. Because at least one value in the input range is text, the summary statistic is Count. (You could equally well drag Party into the Σ Values area.)

The result is shown in Figure 5.9.

Figure 5.8
The relationship between
these two sets of data can
be quickly analyzed with
a pivot table.

	A	B
1	Party	Proposition
2	Republican	Oppose
3	Democrat	Oppose
4	Republican	Approve
5	Democrat	Oppose
6	Republican	Approve
7	Democrat	Oppose
8	Republican	Approve
9	Democrat	Approve
10	Democrat	Approve
11	Democrat	Oppose
12	Democrat	Oppose
13	Republican	Oppose
14	Republican	Approve
15	Democrat	Approve
16	Democrat	Oppose
17	Republican	Oppose
18	Democrat	Approve
19	Republican	Oppose
20	Republican	Oppose
21	Republican	Approve
22	Republican	Oppose
23	Republican	Approve

A1 — fx Party

Figure 5.9
By displaying the Party
and the Proposition fields
simultaneously, you can
tell whether there's a
joint effect.

	A	B	C	D	E	F	G	H
1	Party	Proposition			Count of Proposition	Proposition		
2	Republican	Oppose			Party	Approve	Oppose	Grand Total
3	Democrat	Oppose			Democrat	63	142	205
4	Republican	Approve			Republican	133	162	295
5	Democrat	Oppose			Grand Total	196	304	500
6	Republican	Approve						
7	Democrat	Oppose						
8	Republican	Approve						

There is another way to show two fields in a pivot table that some users prefer—and that some report formats make necessary. Instead of dragging Proposition into the Column Labels area in step 5, drag it into the Row Labels area along with Party (see Figure 5.10).

Figure 5.10
Reorienting the table in
this way is called "pivot-
ing the table."

Party	Proposition	Count of Proposition
⊟ Democrat	Approve	63
	Oppose	142
Democrat Total		205
⊟ Republican	Approve	133
	Oppose	162
Republican Total		295
Grand Total		500

The term *contingency table* is sometimes used for this sort of analysis because it can happen that the results for one variable are contingent on the influence of the other variable. For example, you would often find that attitudes toward a ballot proposition are contingent on the respondents' political affiliations. From the data shown in Figure 5.10, you can infer that more Republicans oppose the proposition than Democrats. How many more? More than can be attributed to the fact that there are simply more Republicans in this sample? One way to answer that is to change how the pivot table displays the data. Follow these steps, which are based on the layout in Figure 5.9:

1. Right-click one of the summary data cells. In Figure 5.9, that's anywhere in the range F3:H5.

2. In the shortcut menu, choose Show Values As.

3. In the cascading menu, choose % of Row Total.

The pivot table recalculates to show the percentages, as in cells E1:H5 in Figure 5.11, rather than the raw counts that appear in Figures 5.9 and 5.10, so that each row totals to 100%. Also in Figure 5.11, the pivot table in cells E8:H12 shows that you can also display the figures as percentages of the grand total for the table.

Figure 5.11
You can instead show the percent of each column in a cell.

	E	F	G	H
Count of Proposition	Proposition ▾			
Party ▾	Approve	Oppose	Grand Total	
Democrat		30.73%	69.27%	100.00%
Republican		45.08%	54.92%	100.00%
Grand Total		39.20%	60.80%	100.00%
Count of Proposition	Proposition ▾			
Party ▾	Approve	Oppose	Grand Total	
Democrat		12.60%	28.40%	41.00%
Republican		26.60%	32.40%	59.00%
Grand Total		39.20%	60.80%	100.00%

TIP If you don't like the two decimal places in the percentages any more than I do, right-click one of them, choose Number Format from the shortcut menu, and set the number of decimal places to zero.

Viewed as row percentages—so that the cells in each row total to 100%—it's easy to see that Republicans oppose this proposition by a solid but not overwhelming margin, whereas Democrats are more than two-to-one against it. The respondents' votes may be *contingent* on their party identification. Or there might be sampling error going on, which could mean that the sample you took does not reflect the party affiliations or attitudes of the overall electorate. Or Republicans might oppose the proposition, but in numbers less than you would expect given their simple numeric majority.

Put another way, the cell frequencies and percentages shown in Figures 5.9 through 5.11 aren't what you'd expect, given the overall Republican vs. Democratic ratio of 295 to 205. Nor do the observed cell frequencies follow the overall pattern of Approve versus Oppose, which at 304 oppose to 196 approve approximates the ratio of Republicans to Democrats. How can you tell what the frequencies in each cell would be if they followed the overall, "marginal" frequencies?

To get an answer to that question, we start with a brief tour of your local card room.

Probabilities and Independent Events

Suppose you draw a card at random from a standard deck of cards. Because there are 13 cards in each of the four suits, the probability that you draw a diamond is .25. You put the card back in the deck.

Now you draw another card, again at random. The probability that you draw a diamond is still .25.

As described, these are two independent events. The fact that you first drew a diamond has no effect at all on the denomination you draw next. Under that circumstance, the laws of probability state that the chance of drawing two consecutive diamonds is .0625, or .25 times .25. The probability that you draw two cards of any two named suits, under these circumstances, is also .0625, because all four suits have the same number of cards in the deck.

It's the same concept with a fair coin, one that has an equal chance of coming up heads or tails when it's tossed. Heads is a 50% shot, and so is tails. When you toss the coin once, it's .5 to come up heads. When you toss the coin again, it's still .5 to come up heads. Because the first toss has nothing to do with the second, the events are independent of one another and the chance of two heads (or a heads first and then a tail, or two tails) is .5 * .5, or .25.

> **NOTE**
> The *gambler's fallacy* is relevant here. Some people believe that if a coin, even a coin known to be fair, comes up heads five times in a row, the coin is "due" to come up tails. Given that it's a fair coin, the odds on heads is still 50% on the sixth toss. People who indulge in the gambler's fallacy ignore the fact that *the unusual event has already occurred*. That event, the streak of five heads, is in the past, and has no say about the next outcome.

This rule of probabilities—that the likelihood of occurrence of two independent events is the product of their respective probabilities—is in play when you evaluate contingency tables. Notice in Figure 5.11 that the probability in the sample of being a Democrat is 41% (cell H10) and a Republican is 59% (cell H11).

Similarly, irrespective of political affiliation, the probability that a respondent approves of the proposition is 39.2% (cell F12) and opposes it 60.8% (cell G12). *If approval is independent of party*, the rule of independent events states that the probability of, say, being a Republican and approving the proposition is .59 * .392, or .231. See cell E16 in Figure 5.12.

You can complete the remainder of the table, the other three cells F16, E17, and F17, as shown in Figure 5.12. Then, by multiplying the percentages by the total count, 500, you wind up with the number of respondents you would expect in each cell if party affiliation were independent of attitude toward the proposal. These expected counts are shown in cells E21:F22.

Figure 5.12
Moving from observed counts to expected counts.

	A	B	C	D	E	F	G
1		Observed counts		Count of Proposition	Proposition		
2				Party	Approve	Oppose	Grand Total
3				Democrat	63	142	205
4				Republican	133	162	295
5				Grand Total	196	304	500
6							
7		Observed Counts as		Percent of total	Proposition		
8		proportion of total		Party	Approve	Oppose	Grand Total
9				Democrat	12.6%	28.4%	41.0%
10				Republican	26.6%	32.4%	59.0%
11				Grand Total	39.2%	60.8%	100.0%
12							
13		Cells as product of		Product of marginals	Proposition		
14		marginal proportions		Party	Approve	Oppose	Grand Total
15		(expected proportions)		Democrat	16.1%	24.9%	41.0%
16				Republican	23.1%	35.9%	59.0%
17				Grand Total	39.2%	60.8%	100.0%
18							
19		Expected proportions		Expected Count of Proposition	Proposition		
20		as counts		Party	Approve	Oppose	Grand Total
21				Democrat	80.36	124.64	205
22				Republican	115.64	179.36	295
23				Grand Total	196	304	500

In Figure 5.12, you see these tables:

- **D1:G5**—These are the original counts as shown in the pivot table in Figure 5.9.

- **D7:G11**—These are the original counts displayed as percentages of the total count. For example, 41.0% in cell G9 is 205 divided by 500, and 12.6% in cell E9 is 63 divided by 500.

- **D13:G17**—These are the cell percentages as obtained from the marginal percentages. For example, 35.9% in cell F16 is the result of multiplying 60.8% in cell F17 (the column percentage) by 59.0% in cell G16 (the row percentage). To review, if party affiliation is independent of attitude toward the proposition, then their joint probability is the product of the two individual probabilities. The percentages shown in E15:F16 are the probabilities that are expected if party and attitude are independent of one another.

- **D19:G23**—The expected counts are in E21:F22. They are obtained by multiplying the expected percentages in E15:G16 by 500, the total number of respondents.

Now you are in a position to determine the likelihood that the observed counts would have been obtained under an assumption: that in the population, there is no relationship between party affiliation and attitude toward the proposition. The next section shows you how that's done.

Testing the Independence of Classifications

Prior sections of this chapter discussed how you use the binomial distribution to test how likely it is that an observed proportion comes from an assumed, hypothetical distribution. The theoretical binomial distribution is based on the use of one field that has only two possible values.

5

But when you're dealing with a contingency table, you're dealing with at least two fields (and each field can contain two or more categories). The example that's been discussed so far concerns two fields: party affiliation and attitude toward a proposition. As I'll explain shortly, the appropriate distribution that you refer to in this and similar cases is called the *chi-square* (pronounced *kai square*) distribution.

Using the CHISQ.TEST() function

Excel has a special chi-square test that is carried out by a function named CHISQ.TEST(). It is new in Excel 2010, but all that's new is the name. If you're using an earlier version of Excel, you can use CHITEST() instead. The two functions take the same arguments and return the same results. CHITEST() is retained as a so-called "compatibility function" in Excel 2010.

You use CHISQ.TEST() by passing the observed and the expected frequencies to it as arguments. With the data layout shown in Figure 5.12, you would use CHISQ.TEST() as follows:

    =CHISQ.TEST(E3:F4,E21:F22)

The observed frequencies are in cells E3:F4, and the expected frequencies, derived as discussed in the prior section, are in cells E21:F22. The result of the CHISQ.TEST() function is the probability that you would get observed frequencies that differ by as much as this from the expected frequencies, if political affiliation and attitude toward the proposition are independent of one another. In this case, CHISQ.TEST() returns 0.001. That is, assuming that the population's pattern of frequencies is as shown in cells E21:F22 in Figure 5.12, you would get the pattern in cells E3:F4 in only 1 of 1,000 samples obtained in a similar way.

What conclusion can you draw from that? The expected frequencies are based on the assumption that the frequencies in the individual cells (such as E3:F4) follow the marginal frequencies. If there are twice as many Republicans as Democrats, then you would expect twice as many Republicans in favor than Democrats in favor. Similarly, you would expect twice as many Republicans opposed as Democrats opposed.

In other words, your null hypothesis is that the expected frequencies are influenced by nothing other than the frequencies on the margins: that party affiliation is independent of attitude toward the proposal, and the differences between observed and expected frequencies is due solely to sampling error. If, however, something else is going on, that might push the observed frequencies away from what you'd expect if attitude is independent of party. The result of the CHISQ.TEST() function suggests that something else is going on.

It's important to recognize that the chi-square test itself does not pinpoint the observed frequencies whose departure from the expected causes this example to represent an improbable outcome. All that CHISQ.TEST() tells us is that the pattern of observed frequencies differs from what you would expect on the basis of the marginal frequencies for affiliation and attitude.

It's up to you to examine the frequencies and decide why the survey outcome indicates that there is an association between the two variables, that they are not in fact independent of one another.

For example, is there something about the proposition that makes it even more unattractive to Democrats than to Republicans? Certainly that's a reasonable conclusion to draw from these numbers. But you would surely want to look at the proposition and the nature of the publicity it has received before you placed any confidence in that conclusion.

This situation highlights one of the problems with nonexperimental research. Surveys entail self-selection. The researcher cannot randomly assign respondents to either the Republican or the Democratic party and then ask for their attitude toward a political proposition. If one variable were diet and the other variable were weight, it would be possible—in theory at least—to conduct a controlled experiment and draw a sound conclusion about whether differences in food intake cause differences in weight. But survey research is almost never so clear cut.

There's another difficulty that this chapter will deal with in the section titled "The Yule Simpson Effect."

Understanding the Chi-Square Distribution

Figures 5.3 and 5.4 show how the shape of the binomial distribution changes as the sample size changes and the number of successes (in the example, the number of defects) in the population changes. The distribution of the chi-square statistic also changes according to the number of observations involved (see Figure 5.13).

Figure 5.13

The differences in the shapes of the distributions are due solely to their degrees of freedom.

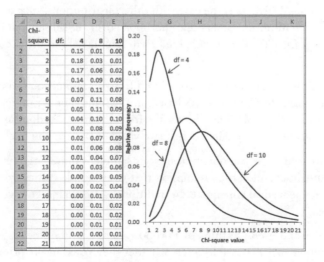

The three curves in Figure 5.13 show the distribution of chi-square with different numbers of degrees of freedom. Suppose that you sample a value at random from a normally distributed population of values with a known mean and standard deviation. You create a z-score, as described in Chapter 3, "Variability: How Values Disperse," subtracting the mean from the value you sampled, and dividing by the standard deviation. Here's the formula once more, for convenience:

$$z = \frac{X - \overline{X}}{s}$$

Now you square the z-score. When you do so, you have a value of chi-square. In this case, it has one degree of freedom. If you square two independent z-scores and sum the squares, the sum is a chi-square with two degrees of freedom. Generally, the sum of n squared independent z-scores is a chi-square with n degrees of freedom.

In Figure 5.13, the curve that's labeled df = 4 is the distribution of randomly sampled groups of four squared, summed z-scores. The curve that's labeled df = 8 is the distribution of randomly sampled groups of eight squared, summed z-scores, and similarly for the curve that's labeled df = 10. As Figure 5.13 suggests, the more the degrees of freedom in a set of chi-squares, the more closely the theoretical distribution resembles a normal curve.

Notice that when you square the z-score, the difference between the sampled value and the mean is squared and is therefore always positive:

$$z^2 = \left[\frac{X - \overline{X}}{s} \right]^2$$

So the farther away the sampled values are from the mean, the larger the calculated values of chi-square.

The mean of a chi-square distribution is n, its degrees of freedom. The standard deviation of the distribution is $\sqrt{2n}$. As is the case with other distributions, such as the normal curve, the binomial distribution, and others that this book covers in subsequent chapters, you can compare a chi-square value that is computed from sample data to the theoretical chi-square distribution.

If you know the chi-square value that you obtain from a sample, you can compare it to the theoretical chi-square distribution that's based on the same number of degrees of freedom. You can tell how many standard deviations it is from the mean, and in turn that tells you how likely it is that you will obtain a chi-square value as large as the one you have observed.

If the chi-square value that you obtain from your sample is quite large relative to theoretical mean, you might abandon the assumption that your sample comes from a population described by the theoretical chi-square. In traditional statistical jargon, you might reject the null hypothesis.

It is both possible and useful to think of a proportion as a kind of mean. Suppose that you have asked a sample of 100 possible voters whether they voted in the prior election. You find that 55 of them tell you that they did vote. If you assigned a value of 1 if a person voted and 0 if not, then the sum of the variable Voted would be 55, and its average would be 0.55.

Of course, you could also say that 55% of the sample voted last time out, and in that case the two ways of looking at it are equivalent. Therefore, you could restate the z-score formula in terms of proportions instead of means:

$$z = (p - \pi) / s_\pi$$

In this equation, the letter p (for proportion) replaces X and the letter π replaces $\overline{X}$. The standard deviation in the denominator, s_π, depends on the size of π. When your classification scheme is binomial (such as voted versus did not vote), the standard deviation of the proportion is:

$$\sqrt{\frac{\pi(1 - \pi)}{n}}$$

where n is the sample size.

So the z score based on proportions becomes:

$$z = \frac{(p - \pi)}{\sqrt{\dfrac{\pi(1 - \pi)}{n}}}$$

Here's the chi-square value that results:

$$\chi^2 = (p - \pi)^2 / (\pi * (1 - \pi) / n)$$

In many situations, the value of p is the proportion that you observe in your sample, whereas the value of π is a hypothetical value that you're investigating. The value of π can also be the value of a proportion that you would expect if two methods of classification, such as political party and attitude toward a ballot proposal, are independent of one another. That's the meaning of π discussed in this section.

The discussion in this section has been fairly abstract. The next section shows how to put the concepts into practice on a worksheet.

Using the CHISQ.DIST() and CHISQ.INV() Functions

The CHISQ.TEST() function returns a probability value only. That can be very handy if all you're after is the probability of observing the actual frequencies assuming there is no dependence between the two variables. But it's usually best to do the spadework and calculate the value of the chi-square statistic. If you do so, you'll get more information back and you can be clearer about what's going on. Furthermore, it's easier to pinpoint the location of any problems that might exist in your source data.

The process of using chi-square to test a null hypothesis is described very sparingly in the prior section. This section goes more fully into the matter.

Figure 5.14 repeats some of the information in Figure 5.12.

In this example, Excel tests the assumption that you would have observed the counts shown in cells E3:F4 of Figure 5.14 if political party and attitude toward the proposition were unrelated to one another. If they were, if the null hypothesis were true, then the counts you would expect to obtain are the ones shown in cells E9:F10.

Figure 5.14
The expected counts are based on the hypothesis that political party and attitude toward the proposition are independent of one another.

	E16	▼		f_x	=SUM(E13:F14)	
	A	B	C	D	E	F	G
1		Observed counts		Count of Proposition		Proposition	
2				Party	Approve	Oppose	Grand Total
3				Democrat	63	142	205
4				Republican	133	162	295
5				Grand Total	196	304	500
6							
7		Expected counts		Expected Count of Proposition		Proposition	
8				Party	Approve	Oppose	Grand Total
9				Democrat	80.36	124.64	205
10				Republican	115.64	179.36	295
11				Grand Total	196	304	500
12							
13					3.75	2.42	
14					2.61	1.68	
15							
16				Chi-square	10.45		
17				=CHISQ.DIST.RT(E16,1)	0.001		

There are several algebraically equivalent ways to go about calculating a chi-square statistic when you're working with a *contingency table* (a table such as the ones shown in Figure 5.14). Some methods work directly with cell frequencies, some work with proportions instead of frequencies, and one simplified formula is intended for use only with a 2-by-2 table. I chose to use the one used here because it emphasizes the comparison between the observed and the expected cell frequencies.

The form of the equation used in Figure 5.14 is

$$\sum_{k=1}^{K}[(f_{o,k} - f_{e,k})^2/f_{e,k}]$$

where

- k indexes each cell in the table.
- $f_{o,k}$ is the observed count, or the frequency, in each cell.
- $f_{e,k}$ is the expected frequency in each cell.

So, for each cell:

1. Subtract the expected frequency from the observed frequency.
2. Square the difference.
3. Divide the result by the cell's expected frequency.

Total the results to get the value of chi-square. This procedure is shown in Figure 5.14, where cells E13:F14 show the results of the three steps just given for each cell. Cell E16 contains the sum of E13:F14 and is the chi-square value itself.

> **TIP**
>
> You can combine the three steps just given for each cell, plus totaling the results, into one step by using an array formula. As the data is laid out in Figure 5.14, this array formula provides the chi-square value in one step:
>
> =SUM((E3:F4-E9:F10)^2/E9:F10)
>
> Recall that to array-enter a formula, you use Ctrl+Shift+Enter instead of simply Enter.

Cell E17 contains the CHISQ.DIST.RT() function, with the chi-square value in E16 as one argument and the degrees of freedom for chi-square, which is 1 in this case, as the second argument.

Chi-square, when used in this fashion, has degrees of freedom that is the product of the number of categories in one field, minus 1, and the number of categories in the other field, minus 1. In other words, suppose that there are J levels of political party and K levels of attitude toward the ballot proposition. Then this chi-square test has (J – 1) * (K – 1) degrees of freedom. Because each field has two categories, the test has (2 – 1) * (2 – 1) or 1 degree of freedom. The probability of observing these frequencies if the two categories are independent is about 1 in 1,000.

Note that the number of cases in the cells has no bearing on the degrees of freedom for this test. All that matters is the number of fields and the number of categories in each field.

The Yule Simpson Effect

In the early 1970s, a cause célèbre put a little-known statistical phenomenon on the front pages—at least on the front pages of the Berkeley student newspapers. A lawsuit was brought against the University of California, alleging that discrimination against women was occurring in the admissions process at the Berkeley campus. Figure 5.15 presents the damning evidence.

Figure 5.15
Men were admitted to graduate study at Berkeley with disproportionate frequency.

C8 fx {=SUM((B3:C4-H3:I4)^2/H3:I4)}

	A	B	C	D	E	F	G	H	I	J
1			Observed						Expected	
2		Admitted	Denied	Total	Percent admitted			Admitted	Denied	Total
3	Men	3738	4704	8442	44%		Men	3461	4981	8442
4	Women	1494	2827	4321	35%		Women	1771	2550	4321
5	Total	5232	7531	12763	41%		Total	5232	7531	12763
6										
7										
8		Chi-square	111.24971							
9		Probability	< .001							

Forty-four percent of men were admitted to graduate study at Berkeley in 1973, compared to only 35% of women. This is pretty clear prima facie evidence of sex discrimination. The expected frequencies are shown in cells H3:I4 and are tested against the observed frequencies, returning a chi-square of 111.24 in cell C8. The CHISQ.DIST.RT() function returns a probability of less than .001 for such a large chi-square with 1 degree of freedom. This makes it very unlikely that admission and sex were independent of one another. The OJ Simpson jury took longer than a Berkeley jury would have.

Some Berkeley faculty and staff (Bickel, Hammel, and O'Connell, 1975) got involved and, using work done by Karl Pearson (of the Pearson correlation coefficient) and a Scot named Udny Yule, dug more deeply into the numbers. They found that when information about admissions to specific departments was included, the apparent discrimination disappeared. Furthermore, more often than not women enjoyed higher admission rates than did men. Figure 5.16 shows some of that additional data.

Figure 5.16

Information about department admission rates shows that women applied more often where admission rates were lowest.

		Males			Females			Admission Rate			Application Rate		
	Department	Admitted	Denied		Admitted	Denied		Males	Females	Overall		Males	Females	Overall
	1	512	313		89	19		62%	82%	64%		18%	2%	21%
	2	353	207		17	8		63%	68%	63%		12%	1%	13%
	3	120	205		202	391		37%	34%	35%		7%	13%	20%
	4	138	279		131	244		33%	35%	34%		9%	8%	17%
	5	53	138		94	299		28%	24%	25%		4%	9%	13%
	6	22	351		24	317		6%	7%	6%		8%	8%	16%
	Total	45%	55%		30%	70%								

There were 101 graduate departments involved. The study's authors found that women were disproportionately more likely to apply to departments that were overall more difficult to gain admission to. This is illustrated in Figure 5.16, which provides the data for six of the largest departments. (The pattern was not substantially different across the remaining 95 departments.)

Notice cells C3:D8 and F3:G8, which show the raw numbers of male and female applicants as well as the outcomes of their applications. That data is summarized in row 9, where you can see that the aggregated outcome for these six departments echoes that shown in Figure 5.15 for all departments. About 45% of men and about 30% of women were admitted.

Compare that with the data in cells I3:J8 in Figure 5.16. There you can see that women's acceptance rates were higher than men's in Departments 1, 2, 4, and 6. Women's acceptance rates lagged men's by 3% in Department 3 and by 4% in Department 5.

This pattern reversal is so striking that some have termed it a "paradox," specifically *Simpson's paradox* after the statistician who wrote about it a half century after Yule and Pearson's original work. But it is not in fact a paradox. Compare the application rates with the admission rates in Figure 5.16.

> **NOTE** This effect is not limited to contingency tables. It affects the results of tests of two or more means, for example, and in that context is called the *Behrens-Fisher problem*. It is discussed in that guise in Chapter 9, "Testing Differences Between Means: Further Issues."

Departments 1 and 2 have very high admission rates compared with the other four departments. But it's the two departments with the highest admission rates that have the lowest application rates from females. About ten times as many males applied to those departments as females, and that's where the admission rates were highest.

Contrast that analysis with Departments 5 and 6, which had the two lowest admission rates. There, women were twice as likely as men to apply (Department 5) or just as likely to apply (Department 6).

So one way of looking at the data is suggested in Figure 5.15, which ignores departmental differences in admission rates: Women's applications are disproportionately rejected.

Another way of looking at the data is suggested in Figure 5.16: Some departments have relatively high admission rates, and a disproportionately large number of men apply to those departments. Other departments have relatively low admission rates, regardless of the applicant's sex, and a disproportionately large number of women apply to those departments.

Neither this analysis nor the original 1975 paper proves *why* admission rates differ, either in men's favor in the aggregate or in women's favor when department information is included. All they prove is that you have to be very careful about assuming that one variable causes another when you're working with survey data or with "grab samples"—that is, samples that are simply close at hand and therefore convenient. The Berkeley graduate admissions data is far from the only published example of the Yule Simpson effect. Studies in the areas of medicine, education, and sports have exhibited similar outcomes.

I don't mean to imply that the use of a true experimental design, with random selection and random assignment to groups, would have prevented the initial erroneous conclusion in the Berkeley case. An experimenter would have to direct students to apply to randomly selected departments, which is clearly impractical. (Alternatively, bogus applications would have to be made and evaluated, after which the experimenter would have difficulty finding another test bed for future research.) Although a true experimental design usually makes it possible to interpret results sensibly, it's not always feasible.

Summarizing the Chi-Square Functions

In versions of Excel prior to Excel 2010, just three functions are directly concerned with chi-square: CHIDIST(), CHIINV(), and CHITEST(). Their purposes, results, and arguments are completely replicated by functions introduced in Excel 2010. Those new functions are discussed next, and their relationships to the older, "compatibility" functions are also noted.

Using CHISQ.DIST()

The CHISQ.DIST() function returns information about the left side of the chi-square distribution. You can call for either the relative frequency of a chi-square value or the cumulative frequency—that is, the cumulative area or probability—at the chi-square value you supply.

> **NOTE** Excel functions return cumulative areas that are directly interpretable as the proportion of the total area under the curve. Therefore, they can be treated as cumulative probabilities, from the leftmost point on the curve's horizontal axis through the value that you have provided to the function, such as the chi-square value to CHISQ.DIST().

The syntax of the CHISQ.DIST() function is

=CHISQ.DIST(X, Df, Cumulative)

where:

- *X* is the chi-square value.
- *Df* is the degrees of freedom for chi-square.
- *Cumulative* indicates whether you want the cumulative area or the relative frequency.

If you set Cumulative to TRUE, the function returns the cumulative area to the left of the chi-square you supply, and is the probability that this chi-square or a smaller one will occur among the chi-square values with a given number of degrees of freedom.

Because of the way most hypotheses are framed, it's usual that you want to know the area—the probability—to the *right* of a given chi-square value. Therefore, you're more likely to want to use CHISQ.DIST.RT() than CHISQ.DIST()—see "Using CHISQ.DIST.RT() and CHIDIST()" for a discussion of CHISQ.DIST.RT().

If you set Cumulative to FALSE, the function returns the relative frequency of the specific chi-square value in the family of chi-squares with the degrees of freedom you specified. You seldom need this information for hypothesis testing, but it's very useful for charting chi-square, as shown in Figure 5.17.

> **NOTE** The only chi-square function with a Cumulative argument is CHISQ.DIST(). There is no Cumulative argument for CHISQ.INV() and CHISQ.INV.RT() because they return axis points, not values that represent either relative frequencies (the height of the curve) or probabilities (the area under the curve, which you call for by setting the Cumulative argument to TRUE). There is no Cumulative argument for CHISQ. DIST.RT because the cumulative area is the default result; you can get the curve height at a given chi-square value using CHISQ.DIST().

Using CHISQ.DIST.RT() and CHIDIST()

The Excel 2010 function CHISQ.DIST.RT() and the "compatibility" function CHIDIST() are equivalent as to arguments, usage, and results. The syntax is

=CHISQ.DIST.RT(X, Df)

Figure 5.17
CHISQ.DIST() returns the height of the curve when Cumulative is FALSE, and returns the area under the curve when Cumulative is TRUE.

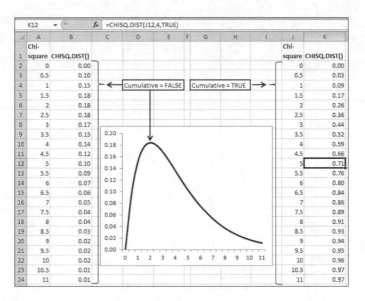

where:

■ *X* is the chi-square value.

■ *Df* is the degrees of freedom for chi-square.

There is no Cumulative argument. CHISQ.DIST.RT() and CHIDIST() both return cumulative areas only, and do not return relative frequencies. To get relative frequencies you would use CHISQ.DIST() and set Cumulative to FALSE.

When you want to test a null hypothesis using chi-square, as has been done earlier in this chapter, it's likely that you will want to use CHISQ.DIST.RT() or, equivalently, CHIDIST(). The larger the departure of a sample observation from a population parameter such as a proportion, the larger the associated value of chi-square. (Recall that to calculate chi-square, you square the difference between the sample observation and the parameter, thereby eliminating negative values.)

Therefore, under a null hypothesis such as that of the independence of two fields in a contingency table, you would want to know the likelihood of a relatively large observation. As you can see in Figure 5.18, a chi-square of 10 (cell A22) is found in the rightmost 4% (cell B22) of a chi-square distribution that has 4 degrees of freedom (cell E1).

That tells you that only 4% of samples from a population where two variables, of three levels each, are independent of one another would result in a chi-square value as large as 10. So it's 96% to 4%, or 24 to 1, against a chi-square of 10 under whatever null hypothesis you have adopted: for example, no association between classifications in a 3-by-3 contingency table.

5

Figure 5.18

The farther to the right you get in a chi-square distribution, the larger the value of chi-square and the less likely you are to observe that value purely by chance.

	A	B	C	D	E
	B22	▾	f_x	=CHISQ.DIST.RT(A22,$E$1)	
	Chi-			Degrees of	
1	square	CHISQ.DIST.RT()		Freedom:	4
2	0	1.00			
3	0.5	0.97			
4	1	0.91			
5	1.5	0.83			
6	2	0.74			
7	2.5	0.64			
8	3	0.56			
9	3.5	0.48			
10	4	0.41			
11	4.5	0.34			
12	5	0.29			
13	5.5	0.24			
14	6	0.20			
15	6.5	0.16			
16	7	0.14			
17	7.5	0.11			
18	8	0.09			
19	8.5	0.07			
20	9	0.06			
21	9.5	0.05			
22	10	0.04			
23	10.5	0.03			
24	11	0.03			

Using CHISQ.INV()

CHISQ.INV() returns the chi-square value that defines the right border of the area in the chi-square distribution that you specify, for the degrees of freedom that you specify. The syntax is

=CHISQ.INV(Probability, Df)

where:

■ *Probability* is the area in the chi-square distribution to the left of the chi-square value that the function returns.

■ *Df* is the number of degrees of freedom for the chi-square value.

So the expression CHISQ.INV(.3, 4) returns the chi-square value that divides the leftmost 30% of the area from the rightmost 70% of the area under the chi-square curve that has 4 degrees of freedom.

CHISQ.INV()_is closely related to CHISQ.INV.RT(), as you might expect. CHISQ.INV() equals 1 – CHISQ.INV.RT(), which is discussed next.

Recall that the chi-square distribution is built on squared z-scores, which themselves involve the difference between an observation and a mean value. Your interest in the probability of observing a given chi-square value, and your interest in that chi-square value itself, usually centers on areas that are in the right tail of the distribution. This is because the larger the difference between an observation and a mean value—whether that difference is positive or negative—the larger the value of chi-square, because the difference is squared.

Therefore, you normally ask, "What is the probability of obtaining a chi-square this large if my null hypothesis is true?" You do not tend to ask, "What is the probability of obtaining a chi-square value this *small* if my null hypothesis is true?"

In consequence, and as a practical matter, you will not have much need for the CHISQ.INV() function. It returns chi-square values that bound the left end of the distribution, but your interest is normally focused on the right end.

Using CHISQ.INV.RT() and CHIINV()

As is the case with BINOM.DIST(), CHISQ.DIST.RT() returns the probability; you supply the chi-square value and degrees of freedom. And as with BINOM.INV(), CHISQ.INV.RT() returns the chi-square value; you supply the probability and the degrees of freedom. (So does the CHIINV() compatibility function.)

This can be helpful when you know the probability that you will require to reject a null hypothesis, and simply want to know what value of chi-square is needed to do so, given the degrees of freedom.

These two procedures come to the same thing:

Determine a Critical Value for Chi-Square Before Analyzing the Experimental Data   Decide in advance on a probability level to reject a null hypothesis. Determine the degrees of freedom for your test based on the design of your experiment. Use CHISQ.INV.RT() to fix a critical value of chi-square in advance, given the probability level you require and the degrees of freedom implied by the design of your experiment. Compare the chi-square from your experimental data with the critical value of chi-square from CHISQ.INV.RT() and retain or reject the null hypothesis accordingly.

This is a formal, traditional approach, and enables you to state with a little more assurance that you settled on your decision rules before you saw the experimental outcome.

Decide Beforehand on the Probability Level Only   Select the probability level to reject a null hypothesis in advance. Calculate the chi-square from the experimental data and use CHISQ.DIST.RT() and the degrees of freedom to determine whether the chi-square value falls within the area in the chi-square distribution implied by the probability level you selected. Retain or reject the null hypothesis accordingly.

This approach isn't quite so formal, but it results in the same outcome as deciding beforehand on a critical chi-square value. Both approaches work, and it's more important that you see why they are equivalent than for you to decide which one you prefer.

Using CHISQ.TEST() and CHITEST()

The CHISQ.TEST() consistency function and the CHITEST() compatibility function both return the probability of observing a pattern of cell counts in a contingency table when the classification methods that define the table are independent of one another.

For example, in terms of the Berkeley study cited earlier in this chapter, those classifications are sex and admission status.

The syntax of CHISQ.TEST() is

=CHISQ.TEST(observed frequencies, expected frequencies)

where each argument is a worksheet range of values such that the ranges have the same dimensions. The arguments for CHITEST() are identical to those for CHISQ.TEST().

The expected frequencies are found by taking the product of the associated marginal values and dividing by the total frequency. Figure 5.19 shows one way that you can generate the expected frequencies.

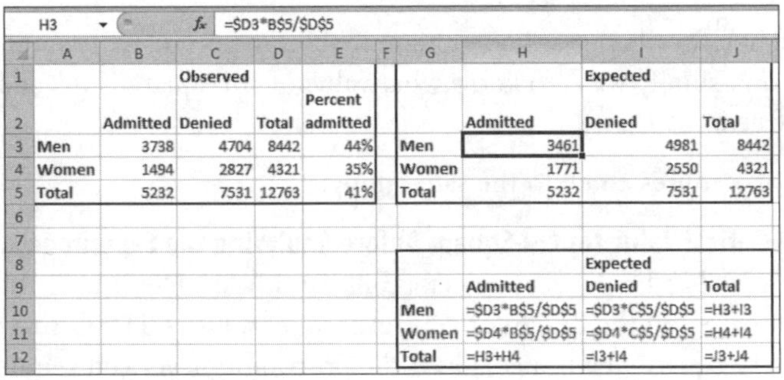

H3 =$D3*B$5/$D$5

	A	B	C	D	E	F	G	H	I	J
1			Observed						Expected	
2		Admitted	Denied	Total	Percent admitted			Admitted	Denied	Total
3	Men	3738	4704	8442	44%		Men	3461	4981	8442
4	Women	1494	2827	4321	35%		Women	1771	2550	4321
5	Total	5232	7531	12763	41%		Total	5232	7531	12763
6										
7										
8									Expected	
9								Admitted	Denied	Total
10							Men	=$D3*B$5/$D$5	=$D3*C$5/$D$5	=H3+I3
11							Women	=$D4*B$5/$D$5	=$D4*C$5/$D$5	=H4+I4
12							Total	=H3+H4	=I3+I4	=J3+J4

Figure 5.19
If you set up the initial formula properly with mixed and absolute references, you can easily copy and paste it to create the remaining formulas.

In Figure 5.19, cells H3:J5 display the results of formulas that make use of the observed frequencies in cells B3:E5. The formulas in H3:J5 are displayed in cells H10:J12.

5

The formula in cell H3 is =$D3*B$5/$D$5.

Ignore for a moment the dollar signs that result in mixed and absolute cell references. This formula instructs Excel to multiply the value in cell D3 (the total men) by the value in cell B5 (the total admitted) and divide by the value in cell D5 (the total of the cell frequencies). The result of the formula, 3461, is what you would estimate to be the number of male admissions if all you knew was the number of men, the number of admissions, the number applying, and that sex and admission status were independent of one another.

The other three estimated cells are filled in via the same approach: Multiply the marginal frequencies for each cell and divide by the total frequency.

Using Mixed and Absolute References to Calculate Expected Frequencies Now notice the mixed and absolute referencing in the prior formula for cell H3. The column marginal, cell D3, is made a mixed reference by anchoring its column only. Therefore, you can copy and paste, or drag and drop, the formula to the right without changing the reference to the males' column, column D.

Similarly, the row marginal, cell B5, is made a mixed reference by anchoring its row only. You can copy and paste it down without changing its row.

Lastly, the total frequencies cell, D5, is made absolute by anchoring both its row and column. You can copy the formula anywhere and the pasted formula will still divide by the value in D5.

Notice how easy this makes things. If you take the prior formula

    =$D3*B$5/$D$5

and drag it one column to the right, you get this formula:

    =$D3*C$5/$D$5

The result is to multiply by C5 instead of B5, by total denied instead of total admitted. You continue to use D3, total men. And the result is the estimate of the number of men denied admission.

And if you drag it one row down, you get this formula:

    =$D4*B$5/$D$5

Now you are using cell D4, total women instead of total men. You continue to use B5, total admitted. And the result is the estimate of the number of women admitted.

In short, if you set up your original formula properly with mixed and absolute references, it's the only one you need to write. Once you've done that, drag it right to fill in the remaining cells in its row. Then drag those cells down to fill in the remaining cells in their columns.

With the range that contains the observed frequencies and the range that contains the computed, expected frequencies, you can use CHISQ.TEST() to determine the probability of observing those frequencies given the expected frequencies, which assume no dependence between sex and admission status:

    =CHISQ.TEST(B3:C4,H3:I4)

As noted earlier in the chapter, you bypass the calculation of the chi-square value itself and get the probability directly in the cell where you enter the CHISQ.TEST() function. There's no need to supply the degrees of freedom because CHISQ.TEST() can calculate them itself, noting the number of rows and columns in either the observed or in the expected frequencies range.

Using the Pivot Table's Index Display

As easy as it is to generate the expected frequencies in a 2-by-2 contingency table, it can get complicated when you're dealing with more rows and columns, or with a different number of rows and columns, or with a third classification.

5

If your original data is in the form of a list that you've used to create a pivot table, you can display the counts as an Index. This simplifies the task of getting the expected frequencies. Figure 5.20 shows an example.

Figure 5.20
The Index display helps you move from observed to expected frequencies.

	F14	▼	fx	{=F3:G4/F10:G11}			
	A	B	C D	E	F	G	H
1	Party	Proposition		Count of Proposition	Proposition ▼		
2	Republican	Oppose		Party ▼	Approve	Oppose	Grand Total
3	Democrat	Oppose		Democrat	63	142	205
4	Republican	Approve		Republican	133	162	295
5	Democrat	Oppose		Grand Total	196	304	500
6	Republican	Approve					
7	Democrat	Oppose					
8	Republican	Approve		Count of Proposition	Proposition ▼		
9	Democrat	Approve		Party ▼	Approve	Oppose	Grand Total
10	Democrat	Approve		Democrat	0.78	1.14	1.00
11	Democrat	Oppose		Republican	1.15	0.90	1.00
12	Democrat	Oppose		Grand Total	1.00	1.00	1.00
13	Republican	Oppose					
14	Republican	Approve			80.36	124.64	205
15	Democrat	Approve			115.64	179.36	295
16	Democrat	Oppose			196	304	500

The first pivot table in Figure 5.20 shows the normal result of showing the count in cells defined by two nominal variables. It repeats the analysis shown in Figure 5.9.

The second pivot table, found in E8:H12, uses the same source data as the first pivot table and is structured identically. However, it shows what Excel terms the *Index*. To get that display, take these steps:

1. Replicate the first pivot table. You can either build a second pivot table from scratch or simply copy and paste the first pivot table.

2. Right-click in any one of the summary cells of the second pivot table. The shortcut menu contains a Show Values As item.

3. Move your mouse pointer over the Show Values As item to display a cascading menu that contains the Index item. Click Index.

> **NOTE** If you're using Excel 2007, follow the instructions in the note in this chapter's section, "Understanding One-Way Pivot Tables." Choose Index from the Show Values As drop-down.

The final task is to divide the observed frequencies by the index values. That is done in cells F14:G15 of Figure 5.20 by means of this array formula:

=F3:G4/F10:G11

The result is the expected cell frequencies, based on the marginal frequencies, assuming no dependency between sex and admission status. There is no need to structure an initial formula properly, either as to pointing it at the correct marginal frequencies or as to changing the correct cell references from relative to mixed.

Telling the Truth with Statistics

Several decades ago a man named Darrell Huff wrote a book titled *How to Lie with Statistics*. The book describes a variety of amusing ways that some people, often unintentionally, use statistics in ways that mislead other people.

I glanced through Huff's book again as I was preparing this book (although I wasn't yet in kindergarten when it was published) and it reminded me that many of the ways there are to go wrong with statistics have to do with context. I'm going to spend half this chapter talking about the context of statistical analysis: how you go about creating a situation in which statistics can have actual meaning. When numbers are gathered outside the context of a strong experimental design, their meaning is suspect. Worse, as Huff noted, they can easily mislead.

Problems with Excel's Documentation

Most of the other ways to go wrong with statistics have to do with misunderstanding the nuts and bolts of statistical analysis. It's unfortunate that Excel gives that sort of misunderstanding an assist here and there. But those assists are principally found in an add-in that has accompanied Excel since the mid-1990s. It used to be known as the Analysis ToolPak (sic), or ATP, and more recently as the Data Analysis add-in.

The add-in is a collection of statistical tools. Its intent is to provide the user with a way to create (mostly) inferential statistical analyses such as analysis of variance and regression analysis. These are analyses that you can do directly on a worksheet, using Excel's native worksheet functions. But the add-in's tools organize and lay out the analysis for you, using sensible formats and dialog box choices instead of somewhat clumsy function arguments. As such, the add-in's tools can make your life easier.

However, the tools can also mislead, or simply fail to inform you of the consequences of making certain decisions. Any statistical software can do that, of course, but the Data Analysis add-in is especially prone to that sort of problem because its documentation is terribly sparse.

A good example is the add-in's Exponential Smoothing tool. Exponential smoothing is a kind of moving average used to forecast the next value in a time series. It relies heavily on a numeric factor called the "smoothing constant," which helps the forecasts correct themselves by taking prior errors in the forecasts into account.

But selecting a smoothing constant can be a fairly complicated procedure, involving choices between fast tracking versus smoothing, and whether the time series has an up or down trend. Making things more difficult is that the standard approach is to supply the smoothing constant, but the Exponential Smoothing tool unaccountably asks the user to supply the damping factor instead. The term *smoothing constant* appears in perhaps ten times as many texts as the term *damping factor*, and there's no reason to expect the new user to know what a damping factor is. The damping factor is just 1 minus the smoothing constant, so it's a trivial problem, but it's also an unnecessary complication. Considerate, informed documentation would use the more common term (smoothing constant), or at least tell the user how to calculate the damping factor, but the add-in's documentation does neither—and never has.

The various tools in the Data Analysis add-in tend to exhibit this sort of hurdle, and making things more difficult yet is the fact that most of the tools provide results as values, not as formulas. This makes it more difficult to trace exactly what a given tool is trying to accomplish.

For example, suppose one of the Data Analysis add-in's tools tells you that the mean value of a particular variable is 4.5: the add-in puts the value 4.5 into the cell. If that value doesn't look right to you, you'll have to do some spadework to find the source of the discrepancy. But if the add-in showed you the *formula* behind the result of 4.5, you're on your way to solving the problem a lot quicker.

A couple of the tools are just fine: The Correlation and Covariance tools provide output that is otherwise tedious to generate using the built-in worksheet functions, they do not mislead or obfuscate, and their output is useful in a practical sense. They are the exception. (But they provide results as static values rather than as formulas, and that's inconvenient.) To give you an in-depth example of the sort of problem I'm describing, I take the second half of this chapter to discuss one of the tools, the F-Test Two-Sample for Variances, in some depth. I do so for two reasons:

- At one time, statisticians ran this analysis to avoid violating an assumption made in testing for differences between means. It has since been shown that violating the assumption has a negligible effect, at most, in many situations. There are still good reasons to use this tool, particularly in manufacturing applications that depend on statistical analysis. But there's almost no documentation on the technique, especially as it's managed in Excel's Data Analysis add-in.

■ Working through the problems with the add-in gives a good sense of the sort of thing you should look out for whenever you're starting to use unfamiliar statistical software—and that includes Excel. If something about it puzzles you, don't take it on faith. Question it.

Before discussing the sort of problem you can encounter with Excel's Data Analysis add-in and its documentation, it's helpful to review the context that makes statistical analysis meaningful. The way you design an experiment provides that context and usually determines whether the statistics have any meaning.

A Context for Inferential Statistics

Statistics provides a way to study how people and things respond to the world and, as such, it's a fascinating, annoying, and sometimes contrary field to work in. Descriptive statistics in particular seems to exercise a peculiar hold over some people. Some sports fans are able to rattle off the yearly batting averages, quarterback ratings, and/or assists per game achieved by their favorite players.

In the closely related area of inferential statistics, there are specialties such as test construction that depend heavily on the measurement of means, standard deviations, and correlations to create tests that not only measure what they are supposed to but do so with good accuracy.

But it's the area of hypothesis testing that most people reading this book think of when they encounter the term *statistics*. That's natural because they first encountered statistical inference when they read about experiments in their introductory psychology classes, and later on in psych labs where they conducted their own research, collected their own data, and used inferential statistics to summarize the numbers and generalize from them.

And that's a shame—but it's understandable because statistics is usually badly taught as an undergraduate course. Perhaps your experience was different—I hope so—but many people want never to take another course in statistics after completing their college or department's requirement. Certainly that was my own experience at a small, fairly well regarded liberal arts college quite a few years ago. It wasn't until I reached graduate school and started taking statistics from people who actually knew what they were talking about that I developed a real interest in the topic.

Still, statistics seems to exert a stranglehold on empirical research at colleges and universities, and that's a case of the tail wagging the dog. When it comes to actually doing research, it's arguable that statistics is the *least* important tool in your kit.

I feel entirely comfortable making that argument. I've spent years reading reports of research that expended large amounts of effort on statistical analysis. But the same research

6

spent very little effort building and carrying out an experimental design that would enable the statistics to actually mean something.

Almost 50 years ago, in the mid-1960s, Donald Campbell and Julian Stanley published a monograph titled "Experimental and Quasi-Experimental Designs for Research." Known more broadly by its authors' surnames, this paper explored and distinguished between two types of validity: generalizability or external validity, and internal validity.

Campbell and Stanley held that both types of validity are necessary for experimental research to be useful. It must be internally valid: that is, it must be designed so that we can have confidence in the comparisons the experiment makes.

At the same time the experiment must be externally valid or generalizable: The subjects must be chosen so that we can generalize the experimental results to the populations we're interested in. A pharmaceutical manufacturer might conduct an experiment that shows with impeccable internal validity that its new drug has no significant side effects. But if its experimental subjects were fire ants, then I'm not going to take the drug.

Understanding Internal Validity

A valid experiment, the so-called "gold standard" of experimental design, begins with the random selection of subjects from the population that you want to generalize to. (Therefore, they ought not all be college students if you're testing a drug for the general population.) Then you adopt an alpha or error rate: the risk you're willing to run of deciding, mistakenly, that your treatment has an effect.

> **NOTE** Several excellent references on building good sampling plans exist; they include William Cochran's *Sampling Techniques* (1977) and Leslie Kish's *Survey Sampling* (1995).

Establishing Internal Validity

Your next step is to randomly assign your subjects to one of two or more groups. In the simplest designs, there is one treatment group and one "control" or "comparison" group. You carry out your treatment on the treatment group and administer some other treatment to the comparison group—or just leave it alone. Finally, you make some sort of measure related to the treatment: If you administered a statin, you might measure the subjects' cholesterol levels. If you showed one group an inflammatory political blog, you might ask them about their attitude toward a politician. If you applied different kinds of fertilizer to different sets of planted citrus trees, you might wait and see how their fruits differed a month later.

Finally, you would run your outcome measures through one statistical routine or another to see whether the data contradicts an hypothesis of no treatment effect, at the error rate (the *alpha*) you adopted at the outset.

The whole point of all this rigmarole is to wind up with two groups that are equivalent in all respects but one: the effect of the treatment that one of them received and that the other didn't. The random assignment to groups at the outset helps to prevent any systematic difference between the groups. Then treating both groups the same with the exception of the treatment itself helps ensure that you can isolate the treatment as the only source of a difference between the groups. It is that difference that your outcome measure is intended to quantify.

If the way you have managed the groups makes it plausible that the only meaningful difference between them is due to the treatment, your experiment is said to have internal validity. The internal comparison between the groups is a valid one.

If your subjects were representative of the population you want to generalize to, your experiment is said to have external validity. It's then valid to generalize your findings from your sample to the population.

Threats to Internal Validity

Campbell and Stanley identified and wrote about seven threats, in addition to sampling error, to the internal validity of an experiment. The establishment via random selection (and the management via experimental design) of equivalent treatment and control groups is meant to eliminate most of these threats.

Selection   The way that subjects are selected for the treatment and comparison groups can threaten the internal validity of the experiment—particularly if they select themselves. Suppose that a researcher wanted to compare the success rates of two medical procedures, each of which is conducted at a different hospital in a major city.

If the results of the two procedures are compared, it's impossible to determine whether any difference in, say, survival rates is due to the procedure or to differences in the populations from which the hospitals draw their patients. It may not be feasible to do so, but the usual recommendation is to assign participants randomly to treatment groups, which in this case would be expected to equalize the effect of belonging to one population or the other. A large-scale study might control selection bias by pooling the results obtained from many hospitals, randomly assigning each institution to one treatment or another. (This approach can raise other problems.)

History   An event of major proportions may take place and have an effect on how subjects respond to a treatment. Perhaps you are field-testing the effect of a political campaign on the attitudes of the electorate toward an incumbent. At the same time, a financial disaster occurs that harms everyone's income prospects, regardless of political leanings. It now becomes very difficult to tease the effects of the campaign out from the effects of the disaster. However, under the assumption that the disaster exerts a roughly equivalent impact on both the group that sees the campaign and the group that does not, you hope to be able to attribute any difference to the effect of the campaign. Without equivalent treatment and comparison groups, the researcher has no hope of quantifying the campaign's effects, as distinct from the effects of the event.

If the people who interact with the subjects are aware of who is in which group, it's possible that their awareness can contaminate the effects of the treatment if they (usually unintentionally) behave in ways that signal their expectations to subjects or subtly direct the subjects' behavior to desired outcomes. To prevent that—to keep an awareness of who is being treated from becoming part of a differential history for the groups—you often see double-blind procedures, which prevent both the person administering the treatment and the subject receiving it from knowing which treatment, including a placebo, is being given to a particular subject.

Instrumentation As used here, the term *instrumentation* goes beyond measuring instruments such as calipers and includes any sort of device that can return quantitative information, including a simple questionnaire. A change in the way that an outcome is measured can make interpretation very difficult. For instance, quite apart from the question of treatment versus control group comparisons, many of those who have researched the prevalence of autism believe the apparent increase in autism rates over the past several decades is due primarily to changes in how it is diagnosed, which have led to higher per-capita estimates of its incidence.

Testing Repeatedly submitting the subjects in the groups to testing can cause changes in the way they respond, and it's not just human or other living subjects who are susceptible to this effect. Metals that are subject to repeated stress-testing can end up with different physical characteristics than they otherwise would have. And yet some testing at least is an inevitable part of any quantitative research.

Maturation Maturation rates differ across different age spans, and this can make some comparisons suspect. Even when a treatment and a comparison group have been equated on age by means of random assignment and covariance (see Chapter 14, "Analysis of Covariance: The Basics," and 15, "Analysis of Covariance: Further Issues"), it's possible that the maturation that occurs during the course of the treatment makes it difficult to be sure how much difference is due to treatment and how much to maturation.

Regression Regression toward the mean (see Chapter 4, "How Variables Move Jointly: Correlation") can have a pronounced effect on experimental results, particularly when the subjects are chosen *because* of their extreme scores on some measure related to the outcome. They will drift toward the mean regardless of any treatment effect. The use of matched pairs, with one member of each pair assigned to a different group, is intended to do a more efficient job than randomization in equating two groups prior to a treatment. However, it often happens that the regression effect undoes this good intent, due to the imperfect correlation on outcome measures across pairs.

Mortality   Experimental mortality comes about when subjects in either a treatment or a comparison group fail to complete their participation in the experiment. (In this context, mortality does not necessarily mean the loss of participants due to death; instead, it refers to any effect or effects that cause subjects to stop participating.) Although random assignment at the outset helps to equate groups as to the likelihood of losing subjects in this fashion, it can be very difficult to distinguish dropping out due to the treatment from dropping out for any other reason. The problem is particularly acute in medical research, where many experiments take as subjects people whose life expectancy is relatively short.

Chance   Toward the end of the experiment, when the protocols have all been met, treatments applied, and measurements taken, statistical analysis enters the picture. You usually employ a statistical analysis to test how likely it is that you obtained the results you did in your samples just by chance, when the results for the full populations would be different if you had access to them.

If you have employed the so-called gold standard of random selection and assignment, you have done as much as you can to constitute equivalent groups—groups that have these properties:

- They are not the results of self-selection, or of any sort of systematic assignment that would introduce a preexisting bias.
- They are subject to the same historical occurrences that come to pass during the course of the experiment, from political unrest to the accidental introduction of dust into a delicate manufacturing environment.
- They are measured by the same set of instruments through the course of the experiment.
- They are not differentially sensitized by the administration of tests.
- They mature at equivalent rates during the course of the experiment.
- They have not been differentially assigned to groups on the basis of extreme scores.
- They do not drop out of the experiment at differential rates.

Random selection and assignment are, together, the best ways to ensure that your experimental groups have these properties. But these techniques are imperfect. It can be entirely plausible that some outside occurrence has a greater impact on one group than on another, or that randomization did not eliminate the effect of a preexisting bias, or that more than chance is involved in differential dropout rates…and so on.

So those threats to the internal validity of your experiment exist, and you do your best to mitigate them by means of randomization, but they can never be completely ruled out as competing explanations for the results you observe.

6

And to the degree that these threats are present, statistical analysis loses much of its point. As traditionally used in the testing of hypotheses, statistical analysis serves to quantify the role of chance in the outcome of the experiment. But the accurate assessment of the degree to which chance plays a part depends on the presence of two or more groups that are equivalent except for the presence or absence of an experimental treatment.

Consider this situation: For one month you have administered a new drug to a treatment group and withheld it, instead using a placebo, from another group. The drug is intended to reduce the level of low density lipoproteins (LDL) in the blood. At the end of the month, blood samples are taken and you conduct a statistical analysis of the results. Your analysis shows that the likelihood is about 1 chance in 1,000 that the mean LDL of the treatment group and that of the control group came from the same population.

If you conclude that the group means had come from the same population, then the administration of the treatment did not bring about populations whose mean LDL levels parted ways as a result of taking the drug. However, your statistical analysis strongly indicates that the groups are now representative of two different populations. This seems like great news…*unless* you have not carefully equated the two groups at the outset, and maintained that degree of equivalence. In that case you cannot state that the difference was due to your drug. It could have come about because the members of the control group became friendly and went out for cheeseburgers every day after taking their placebos.

There are reasons to carry out statistical analyses that don't involve true or even quasi-experimentation. For example, the development and analysis of psychological tests and political surveys involve extensions to regression analysis (which is the basis for most of the analyses described in the second half of this book). Those tests are by no means restricted to tests of cognitive abilities or political attitudes, but can involve other areas—from medical and drug testing to quality control in manufacturing environments. Their development and interpretation depends in large measure on the kinds of statistical analysis that this book discusses, using Excel as the platform. But these analyses involve no hypotheses.

Nevertheless, the use of statistical analysis to rule out chance as an explanation of an experimental outcome is normal, typical, and standard. When we hear about the results of an experiment regarding a condition, situation, or even a disease that we're interested in, we want to know something about the nature of the statistical analysis that was used. And in experimentation, a statistical analysis is *pointless* if it is not done in the context of a solid experimental design, one that is carefully managed.

The F-Test Two-Sample for Variances

Now that I've spent several pages discussing why understanding statistics is unimportant—at least as compared to experimental design—I want to turn the telescope around and look at why understanding statistics is important: If you don't understand the concepts, you can't possibly interpret the analyses. And, given that the data was obtained sensibly, the analysis of the numbers *is* important.

But sometimes the software available does a good job of running the numbers but a bad job of explaining what it has done. We expect the software's documentation to provide clarification, but we're often disappointed. One of the tools in the Data Analysis add-in, F-Test Two-Sample for Variances, provides a great example of why it's a bad idea to simply take documentation at its word. Here is the meat of its documentation, from the Excel 2010 Help documents:

> The tool calculates the value f of an F-statistic (or F-ratio). A value of f close to 1 provides evidence that the underlying population variances are equal. In the output table, if f < 1 "P(F <= f) one-tail" gives the probability of observing a value of the F-statistic less than f when population variances are equal, and "F Critical one-tail" gives the critical value less than 1 for the chosen significance level, Alpha. If f > 1, "P(F <= f) one-tail" gives the probability of observing a value of the F-statistic greater than f when population variances are equal, and "F Critical one-tail" gives the critical value greater than 1 for Alpha.

Got that? Neither did I.

Among other uses, the F test—the statistical concept, not the Excel tool—helps determine whether the variances of two different samples are equal in the populations from which they were taken. The F-Test tool attempts to perform this test for you. However, as you'll see, it takes more background than that to get the tool to yield useful information.

Why Run the Test?

As you'll see in Chapter 9, "Testing Differences Between Means: Further Issues," and Chapter 10, "Testing Differences Between Means: The Analysis of Variance," one of the basic assumptions made by some statistical tests is that different groups have the same variance—or, equivalently, the same standard deviation—on the outcome measure. In the first half of the last century, textbooks advised you to run an F test for equal variances before testing whether different groups had different means. If the F test indicated that the groups had different variances, the advice was that you should not move ahead to test the difference between means, because you would be violating a basic assumption of that test.

Then along came the "robustness studies" of the 1950s and 1960s. That work tested the effects of violating the basic assumptions that underlie many statistical tests. The statisticians who studied those issues were interested in determining whether the assumptions that were used to develop the theoretical models were important when it came time to actually apply the models.

Some of the assumptions, as you'd expect, are important. For example, it's usually important that observations be independent of one another: that John's score on a test have no bearing on Jane's score, as they might if John and Jane were siblings and the measure was some biochemical trait.

6

But the assumption of equal variances is frequently unimportant. When all groups have the same number of observations, their variances can differ widely without harming the validity of the statistical test. But the combination of different group sizes with different group variances can cause problems. Suppose that one group has 20 observations and a variance of 5; another group has 10 observations and a variance of 2.5. So one group is twice as large as the other *and* its variance is twice as large as the other's. In that situation, statistical tables and functions might tell you that the probability of an incorrect decision is 5%, when it's actually 3%. That's quite a small impact for sample sizes and variances that are so discrepant. Therefore, statisticians usually regard these tests as *robust* with respect to the violation of the assumption of equal variances.

This doesn't mean that you shouldn't use an F test to help decide whether two sample *variances* are equal in the population. But if your purpose is to test differences in group *means*, then you wouldn't usually bother to do so if your group sizes were roughly equal. Or, if both the group sizes and the variances are very discrepant, your time is usually better spent determining why random selection and random assignment resulted in those discrepancies. It's always more important to make sure you have designed valid comparisons than it is to cross the last statistical *t*.

In the absence of that rationale—as a preliminary to a test of group means—the rationale for running an F test when its end purpose is to compare variances is fairly restricted. Certainly some disciplines, such as operations research and process control, test the variability of quality measures frequently. But other areas such as medicine, business, and behavioral sciences focus much more often on differences in means than on differences in variability.

> **NOTE**
>
> It's easy to confuse the F test discussed here with the F test used in the analysis of variance and covariance, discussed in Chapters 10 through 15. An F test is *always* based on the ratio of two variances. As used here, the focus is on the question of whether two sampled groups have different variances in the populations. As used in the analysis of variance and covariance, the focus is on the variability of group means divided by the variability of values within groups. In both cases, the inferential statistic is F, a ratio of variances. In both cases, you compare that F ratio to a curve that's almost as well known as the normal curve. Only the purpose of the test differs: testing differences in variances as an end in itself, versus testing differences in variances in order to make inferences about differences in means.

I suspect that unless you're in a manufacturing environment, you'll have only occasional use for the F-Test Two-Sample for Variances tool. If you do, you'll want to know how to protect yourself in the situations where it can mislead you. If you don't, you may want to understand a little more about how Excel's own documentation can steer you wrong.

Using the Tool: A Numeric Example

Figure 6.1 shows an example of how you might use the F-Test tool.

Figure 6.1
Your choice of the set of observations to designate as Variable 1 makes a difference in the results.

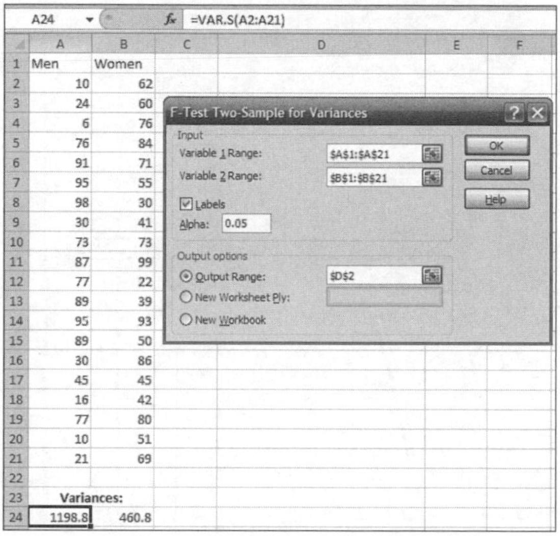

Suppose that you specify the range A1:A21 (Men) for Variable 1 in the dialog box, and B1:B21 (Women) as Variable 2. You fill the Labels check box, accept the default .05 value for alpha, and select cell D2 as the location to start the output.

> **NOTE**
>
> Notice in Figure 6.1 that you can accept the default value of .05 for alpha, or change it to some other value. Excel's documentation, including the Data Analysis documentation, uses the term *alpha* inconsistently in different contexts. In Excel's documentation for the F-Test tool, the term *alpha* is used correctly.
>
> As used by the F-Test Two-Sample for Variances tool, the concept of *alpha* is as discussed in Chapter 5, "How Variables Classify Jointly: Contingency Tables," and as I will pick it up again in Chapter 8, "Testing Differences Between Means: The Basics." It is the likelihood that you will conclude a difference exists when in fact there is no difference. In the present context, it is the likelihood that your sample data will convince you that the populations from which you drew the two samples have different variances, when in fact they have the same variance. That usage agrees with the normal statistical interpretation of the term.
>
> It's also worth noting that two assumptions that underlie the F test, the assumptions that the samples come from normally distributed populations and that they are independent of one another, are critically important. If either assumption is violated, there's good reason to suspect that the F test is not valid.

After you click OK, the F-Test tool runs and displays the results shown in D2:F11 of Figure 6.2.

Figure 6.2

Notice that the variance of Men is greater than the variance of Women in the samples, and that the F ratio is larger than 1.0.

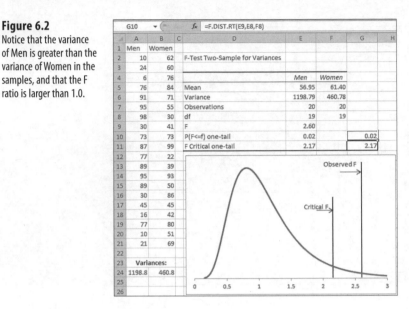

No one tells you—not the documentation, not the dialog box, not other books that deal with the Data Analysis add-in—that the data you designate as Variable 1 in the F-Test tool's dialog box is always treated as the numerator in the F ratio.

The F-Test Tool Always Divides Variable 1 by Variable 2   Why is it important to know that? Suppose that your research hypothesis was that men have greater variability than women on whatever it is that you've measured in Figures 6.1 and 6.2. If you arranged things as shown in Figure 6.2, with the men's measures in the numerator of the F ratio, then all is well. Your research hypothesis is that men have greater variability on this measure and the way you set up the F test conforms to that hypothesis. The test as you have set it up asks whether men's variability is so *much* greater than women's that you can rule out chance—that is, sampling error—as an explanation for the difference in their variances.

But now suppose that you didn't know that the F-Test tool always places Variable 1 in the numerator and Variable 2 in the denominator. In that case, you might in all innocence instruct the F-Test tool to treat the women's measures as Variable 1 and the men's as Variable 2. With the data in Figures 6.1 and 6.2 you would get an F ratio of less than 1. You would be hypothesizing that men exhibit greater variability on the measure, and then proceeding to test the opposite.

As long as you knew what was going on, no great harm would come from that. It's easy enough to interpret the results properly. But it could be confusing, particularly if you tried to interpret the meaning of the critical value reported by the F-Test tool. More on that in the following section.

The F-Test Tool Changes the Decision Rule   The F-Test tool changes the way the F ratio is calculated, depending on which data set is identified as Variable 1 and which as Variable 2. The tool also changes the way that it calculates the inferential statistics, according to whether the calculated F statistic is greater or less than 1.0. Notice the chart in Figure 6.2. The chart is not part of the output produced by the F-Test tool. I have created it using Excel's F.DIST() worksheet function.

> **TIP**   If you download the Excel workbooks for this book from the publisher's website (www.informit.com/title/9780789747204), you can see exactly how the chart was created by opening the workbook for Chapter 6 and activating the worksheet for Figure 6.2.

The curve in the chart represents all the possible F ratios you could calculate using samples of 20 observations each, assuming that both samples come from populations that have the same variance. (The shape of an F distribution depends on the number of observations in each sample).

At some point, the ratio of the sample variances gets so large that it becomes irrational to believe that the underlying populations have the same variance. If those populations have the same variance, you would have to believe that sampling error is responsible when you get an F ratio that doesn't equal 1. It doesn't take much sampling error to get an F ratio of, say, 1.05 or 1.10. But when you get a sample whose variance is twice that of the other sample—well, either an improbably large degree of sampling error is at work or the underlying populations have different variances.

"Improbably large" is a subjective notion. What is wildly unlikely to me might be somewhat out of the ordinary to you. So each researcher decides what constitutes the dividing line between the improbable and the unbelievable (often guided by the cost of making an incorrect decision). It's conventional to express that dividing line in terms of probability. In the F-Test dialog box shown in Figure 6.1, if you accept the default value of .05 for Alpha, you are saying that you will regard it as unbelievable if something could occur only 5% of the time. In the case of the F-Test, you would be saying that you regard it as unbelievable to get a ratio so large that it could occur only 5% of the time when both populations have the same variance.

That's what the vertical line labeled "Critical F" in Figure 6.2 is about. It shows where the largest 5% of the F ratios would begin. Any F ratio you obtained that was larger than the critical F value would belong to that 5% and, therefore, because you selected .05 as your Alpha criterion, would serve as evidence that the underlying populations had different variances.

6

The other vertical line, labeled "Observed F," is the value of the actual F ratio calculated from the data in A2:B21. It's the ratio of the variances, which are shown as the result of the VAR.S() function in A24:B24 and as returned by the F-Test tool as static, calculated values in E6:F6. The F-Test tool also returns the F ratio in E9, and it's that value that appears in the chart as the vertical line labeled "Observed F."

The observed F ratio of 2.60 in Figure 6.2 is even farther from a ratio of 1.0 than is the critical value of 2.17. So if you had used an alpha of .05, your decision rule would lead you to reject the hypothesis that the two populations that underlie the samples have equal variances.

But what happens if the investigator, not knowing what Excel will do about forming the F ratio, happens to identify the measures of women as Variable 1? Then the F-Test tool puts the variance for women, 460.8, in the numerator and the variance for men, 1198.8, in the denominator. The F ratio is now less than 1.0 and you get the output shown in Figure 6.3.

Figure 6.3
With the smaller variance now in the numerator of the F ratio, the results are still "significant" but reversed.

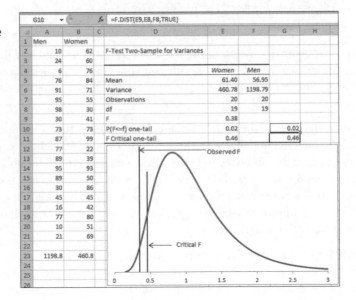

If you know what's going on—and you do now—it's not too hard to conclude that the observed F ratio of 0.38 is just as unlikely as 2.60. If the population variances are equal, the most likely results of dividing one sample variance by the other are close to 1.0. Looking at the two critical values in Figures 6.2 and 6.3, 2.17 at the high end and 0.46 at the low end cut off 5% of the area under the curve: 5% at each end. Whether you put the larger variance in the numerator by designating it as Variable 1, or in the denominator by designating it Variable 2, the ratio is unlikely to occur when the populations have equal variances, so if you accept 5% as a rational criterion you reject that hypothesis.

Understanding the F Distribution Functions   The cells G10:G11 in both Figures 6.2 and 6.3 contain worksheet functions that pertain to the F distribution. The F-Test tool does not supply them—I have done so—but notice that the values shown in G10:G11 are identical to those in E10:E11, which the F-Test tool does supply. However, the F-Test tool does not supply the formulas or functions it uses to calculate results: It supplies only the static results. Therefore, to more fully understand what's being done by a tool such as the F-Test in the Data Analysis add-in, you need to know and understand the worksheet functions the tool uses.

Cell G10 in Figure 6.2 uses this formula:

=F.DIST.RT(E9,E8,F8)

The F.DIST.RT function returns a probability, which you can interpret as an area under the curve. The RT suffix on the function informs Excel that an area in the right tail of the curve is needed; if you use F.DIST() instead, Excel returns an area in the left tail of the curve.

The function's first argument, which here is E9, is an F value. Used as an argument to the F.DIST.RT() function, the value in cell E9 calls for the area under the curve that lies to the right of that value. In Figure 6.2, the value in E9 is 2.60, so Excel returns 0.02: 2% of the area under this curve lies to the right of an F value of 2.60.

As noted in the prior section, the shape of an F distribution depends on the number of observations that form the variance in the numerator and in the denominator of the F ratio. More formally, you use the degrees of freedom instead of the actual number of observations: The degrees of freedom is the number of observations, minus 1. The second and third arguments to the F.DIST.RT() function are the degrees of freedom for the numerator and for the denominator, respectively.

You can conclude from the result returned by this function that, assuming men and women have the same variance in the populations, you would see an F ratio at least as large as 2.60 in only 2% of the samples you might take from the populations. You might regard it as more rational to conclude that the assumption of equal population variances is incorrect than to conclude that you obtained a fairly unlikely F ratio.

The formula in cell G11 of Figure 6.2 is as follows:

=F.INV(0.95,E8,F8)

Instead of returning an area under the curve, as F.DIST() and F.DIST().RT do, the F.INV() function accepts an area as an argument and returns an F value. Here, the second and third arguments in E8 and F8 are the same as in the F.DIST.RT() function: the degrees of freedom for the numerator and the denominator. The 0.95 argument tells Excel that the F value that corresponds to 95% of the area under the curve is needed. The function returns 2.17 in cell G11, so 95% of the curve lies to the left of the value 2.17 in an F distribution with 19 and 19 degrees of freedom. The F-Test tool returns the same value, as a value, in cell E11.

6

(The function's INV suffix is short for *inverse*. The value of the statistic is conventionally regarded as the inverse of the area.)

Compare the functions in Figure 6.2 that were just discussed with the versions in Figure 6.3. There, this formula is in cell G10:

=F.DIST(E9,E8,F8,TRUE)

This time, the F.DIST() function is used instead of the F.DIST.RT() function. The F.DIST() function returns the area to the *left* of the F value that you supply (here, that value is 0.38, which is the value in cell E9, the ratio of the women's variance to the men's variance).

> **NOTE** The F.DIST() function takes a fourth argument that the F.DIST.RT() function does not take. In F.DIST() you can supply the value TRUE, as before, to request the area to the left of the F value. If you instead supply FALSE, Excel returns the height of the curve at the point of the F value. Among other uses, this height value is indispensable for charting an F distribution. Similar considerations apply to the charting of normal distributions, t-distributions, chi-square distributions, and so on.

You can see by comparing the charts in Figures 6.2 and 6.3 that it's as unlikely to get a ratio of 0.38 (women's to men's variance) as it is to get a ratio of 2.60 (men's to women's variance). But it can confuse the issue that the critical value is different in the two sets of output. It is 2.17 in Figure 6.2 because the F-Test tool is working with an F ratio that's larger than 1.0, so the question is how much larger than 1.0 must the observed F ratio be in order to cut off the upper 5% of the distribution (or whatever alpha you choose instead of 0.05).

The critical value is 0.46 in Figure 6.3 because the F-Test tool is working with an F ratio that's smaller than 1.0, so the question is how much smaller than 1.0 must the observed F ratio be in order that you consider it improbably small—smaller than the smallest 5% of the ratios you observe if the populations have the same variance?

That critical value of 0.46 in cell G11 of Figure 6.3 is returned by this formula:

=F.INV(0.05,E8,F8)

Whereas, as noted earlier, the formula in cell G11 of Figure 6.2 is this:

=F.INV(0.95,E8,F8)

In the latter version the function returns the F value that cuts off the lower 95% of the area under the curve: Thus, larger values have a 5% or smaller chance of occurring.

In the former version, the function returns the F value that cuts off the lower 5% of the area under the curve. This is the critical value you want if you've set up the observed F ratio so that the smaller variance is in the numerator.

There is an F.INV.RT() function that you might use instead of =F.INV(0.95,E8,F8). It's simply a matter of personal preference. The F.INV.RT() function returns the F value that cuts off the right tail, not the left tail as the F.INV() function does. Therefore, these two functions are equivalent:

=F.INV(0.95,E8,F8)

and

=F.INV.RT(0.05,E8,F8)

> **NOTE** Again, the F-Test tool does *not* supply a chart. It's a good idea to view the test results in a chart so that you're more sure about what's going on, but you have to construct that yourself. Download the workbook from the publisher's website to see how to define the chart.

Making a Nondirectional Hypothesis

So far we've been interpreting the F-Test tool's results in terms of two mutually exclusive hypotheses:

- There is no difference between the two populations, as measured by their variances.
- The population of men has a larger variance than does the population of women.

The second hypothesis is called a *directional* hypothesis, because it specifies which of the two variances you expect to be the larger. (This is also called, somewhat carelessly, a *one-tailed* hypothesis, because you pay attention to only one tail of the distribution. It's a slightly careless usage because, as you'll see in later chapters, many nondirectional hypotheses make reference to one tail only in the F distribution.)

What if you didn't want to take a position about which variance is greater? Then your two, mutually exclusive hypotheses might be the following:

- There *is no* difference between the two populations, as measured by their variances.
- There *is a* difference between the two populations, as measured by their variances.

Notice that the second hypothesis doesn't specify which population variance is greater—simply that the two population variances are not equal. It's a *nondirectional* hypothesis. That has major implications for the way you go about structuring and interpreting your F test (and your t-tests, as you'll see in Chapter 9).

Looking at It Graphically   Figure 6.4 shows how the nondirectional situation differs from the directional situation shown in Figures 6.2 and 6.3.

Figure 6.4
In a nondirectional situation, the alpha area is split between the two tails.

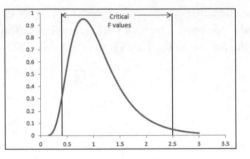

In a case like the one shown in Figure 6.4, you do not take a position regarding which population has the larger variance, just that one of them does. So, if you decide that you're willing to regard an outcome with a 5% likelihood as improbable enough to reject the null hypothesis, then that 5% probability must be shared by both tails of the distribution. The lower tail gets 2.5% and the upper tail gets 2.5%. (Of course, you could decide that 1%, not 5%, is necessary to reject an hypothesis, or any other value that your personal and professional judgment regards as "improbable." The important point to note is that in a nondirectional situation, you divide that improbable alpha percentage between the two tails of the distribution.)

One of the consequences of adopting a nondirectional alternative hypothesis is that the critical values move farther into the tails. In Figure 6.4, the nondirectional hypothesis moves the upper critical value to about 2.5, whereas in Figure 6.2 the directional hypothesis placed the critical value at 2.17. (It is solely coincidence that the upper critical value is about 2.5 and cuts off 2.5% of the area.)

The reason the critical value moves is that in Figure 6.4, the critical values cut off the lower and upper 2.5% of the distributions, rather than the lower 5% or the upper 5%, as in Figures 6.2 and 6.3. Therefore, the critical values are farther from the center of the distribution in Figure 6.4.

Running the F-Test Tool for a Nondirectional Hypothesis   If you want to use a nondirectional hypothesis, halve the alpha level accordingly. Adjust the alpha level in the F-Test tool's dialog box. If you want the overall alpha level to be 5%, enter **0.025** when you run the tool.

Specifying an alpha level affects *only* the critical F value returned by the F-Test tool. You can always look at the p-value for the observed F value returned by the tool (for example, cell E10 in Figure 6.3); then, decide whether the p-value is small enough to regard as improbable the hypothesis that the result is due to sampling error. In practice, it's a matter of whether you want to think in terms of the probabilities (pay attention to alpha and the p-value) or in terms of the F values (think in terms of the observed and critical F ratios).

A Trap to Avoid   One thing you must *not* do if you have made a *nondirectional hypothesis* is to look at the data before deciding which group's data to put in the F ratio's numerator, by using that group as Variable 1 in the F-Test tool's dialog box.

It's legitimate to decide before seeing the data that you will treat whichever group has the larger variance as Variable 1. Not this: "I see that men have the greater variance, so I'll treat their data as Variable 1." But instead this: "I will put whichever group has the greater variance in the numerator of the F ratio by designating that group as Variable 1."

It's also legitimate to assign one of the two sets of data to Variable 1 with a coin flip or some other random event.

If you decide that you will always put the larger variance in the F ratio's numerator, you will never get an F ratio that's less than 1.0. You're asking the upper tail of the distribution to stand in for the lower tail too. Therefore, if the test is nondirectional, you must be sure to put half the alpha that you really want in the dialog box. Notice that this is consistent with the advice I gave you in the prior section, to specify half the alpha you really want when you're dealing with the F-Test tool's dialog box, and you're making a nondirectional alternative hypothesis.

The Available Choices

In summary, the way you set things up in the Data Analysis add-in's F-Test tool depends on whether you make a directional or nondirectional hypothesis. The next two sections briefly discuss each alternative given that you set alpha, the probability that your observed result is due to chance, to 0.05.

Directional Hypotheses   Make the directional hypothesis that your theory leads you to support. If theory tells you that men should have a larger variance on some measure than women, let your alternative hypothesis be a directional one: that men have the larger variance. Use the F-Test tool's dialog box to put the men's variance in the numerator of the F ratio (set the men's data as Variable 1) and set alpha to 0.05. Conclude that your alternative hypothesis is correct only if the observed F ratio exceeds the critical F ratio.

Do not reject the null hypothesis of no difference even if the men's sample variance is significantly smaller than the women's. Once you've made a directional hypothesis that points in a particular direction, you must live with it. It's capitalizing on chance to make a directional hypothesis after you've seen what the outcome is.

Nondirectional Hypotheses   Make a nondirectional hypothesis that the sampled populations have different variances, but don't specify which is greater. For convenience, treat the group with the larger variance as Variable 1, cut the alpha in half when you complete the dialog box entries, and run the F-Test tool once. If the reported p-value is less than half the nominal alpha, adopt your alternative hypothesis that the populations have different variances.

6

A Final Point

Ignore the F-Test's output label "P(F<=f) one-tail." The label itself is misleading, the symbols are undefined, and it remains the same whether the obtained F ratio is larger or smaller than the critical value. Furthermore, the probability that one value is less than or equal to another is either 1.0 or 0.0: Either it is or it isn't. The values "F" and "f" are two specific numbers, and a statement such as "The probability that 2.60 is greater than 2.17 is .02" has no meaning.

To the contrary: in the F-Test tool's output, the quantity labeled "P(F<=f) one-tail" is the probability of obtaining the observed F ratio under the assumption that the populations from which the samples were taken have the same variance.

Using Excel with the Normal Distribution

7

About the Normal Distribution

You cannot go through life without encountering the normal distribution, or "bell curve," on an almost daily basis. It's the foundation for grading "on the curve" when you were in elementary and high school. The height and weight of people in your family, in your neighborhood, in your country each follow a normal curve. The number of times a fair coin comes up heads in ten flips follows a normal curve. The title of a contentious and controversial book published in the 1990s. Even that ridiculously abbreviated list is remarkable for a phenomenon that was only starting to be perceived 300 years ago.

The normal distribution occupies a special niche in the theory of statistics and probability, and that's a principal reason Excel offers more worksheet functions that pertain to the normal distribution than to any other, such as the t, the binomial, the Poisson, and so on. Another reason Excel pays so much attention to the normal distribution is that so many variables that interest researchers—in addition to the few just mentioned—follow a normal distribution.

Characteristics of the Normal Distribution

There isn't just one normal distribution, but an infinite number. Despite the fact that there are so many of them, you never encounter one in nature.

Those are not contradictory statements. There is a normal curve—or, if you prefer, normal distribution or bell curve or Gaussian curve—for every number, because the normal curve can have any mean and any standard deviation. A normal curve can have a mean of 100 and a standard deviation of 16, or a mean of 54.3 and a standard deviation of 10. It all depends on the variable you're measuring.

The reason you never see a normal distribution in nature is that nature is messy. You see a huge number of variables whose distributions follow a normal distribution very closely. But the normal distribution is the result of an equation, and can therefore be drawn precisely. If you attempt to emulate a normal curve by charting the number of people whose height is 56", all those whose height is 57", and so on, you will start seeing a distribution that resembles a normal curve when you get to somewhere around 30 people.

As your sample gets into the hundreds, you'll find that the frequency distribution looks pretty normal—not quite, but nearly. As you get into the thousands you'll find your frequency distribution is not visually distinguishable from a normal curve. But if you apply the functions for skewness and kurtosis discussed in this chapter, you'll find that your curve just misses being perfectly normal. You have tiny amounts of sampling error to contend with, for one; for another, your measures won't be perfectly accurate.

Skewness

A normal distribution is not skewed to the left or the right but is symmetric. A skewed distribution has values whose frequencies bunch up in one tail and stretch out in the other tail.

Skewness and Standard Deviations   The asymmetry in a skewed distribution causes the meaning of a standard deviation to differ from its meaning in a symmetric distribution, such as the normal curve or the t-distribution (see Chapters 8 and 9, for information on the t-distribution). In a symmetric distribution such as the normal, close to 34% of the area under the curve falls between the mean and one standard deviation below the mean. Because the distribution is symmetric, an additional 34% of the area also falls between the mean and one standard deviation above the mean.

But the asymmetry in a skewed distribution causes the equal percentages in a symmetric distribution to become unequal. For example, in a distribution that skews right you might find 45% of the area under the curve between the mean and one standard deviation below the mean; another 25% might be between the mean and one standard deviation above it.

In that case, you still have about 68% of the area under the curve between one standard deviation below and one standard deviation above the mean. But that 68% is split so that its bulk is primarily below the mean.

Visualizing Skewed Distributions   Figure 7.1 shows several distributions with different degrees of skewness.

The normal curve shown in Figure 7.1 (based on a random sample of 5,000 numbers, generated by Excel's Data Analysis add-in) is not the idealized normal curve but a close approximation. Its skewness, calculated by Excel's SKEW() function, is –0.02. That's very close to zero; a purely normal curve has a skewness of exactly 0.

Figure 7.1
A curve is said to be skewed in the direction that it tails off: The log X curve is "skewed left" or "skewed negative."

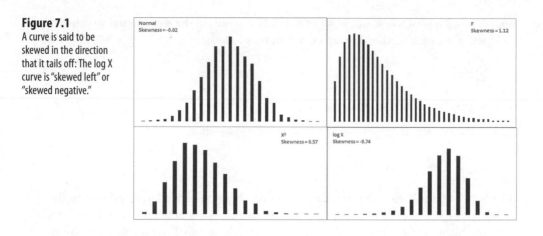

The X^2 and log X curves in Figure 7.1 are based on the same X values as form the figure's normal distribution. The X^2 curve tails to the right and skews positively at 0.57. The log X curve tails to the left and skews negatively at –0.74. It's generally true that a negative skewness measure indicates a distribution that tails off left, and a positive skewness measure tails off right.

The F curve in Figure 7.1 is based on a true F-distribution with 4 and 100 degrees of freedom. (This book has much more to say about F-distributions beginning in Chapter 10, "Testing Differences Between Means: The Analysis of Variance." An F-distribution is based on the ratio of two variances, each of which has a particular number of degrees of freedom.) F-distributions always skew right. It is included here so that you can compare it with another important distribution, t, which appears in the next section on a curve's kurtosis.

Quantifying Skewness   Several methods are used to calculate the skewness of a set of numbers. Although the values they return are close to one another, no two methods yield exactly the same result. Unfortunately, no real consensus has formed on one method. I mention most of them here so that you'll be aware of the lack of consensus. More researchers report some measure of skewness than was once the case, to help the consumers of that research better understand the nature of the data under study. It's much more effective to report a measure of skewness than to print a chart in a journal and expect the reader to decide how far the distribution departs from the normal. That departure can affect everything from the meaning of correlation coefficients to whether inferential tests have any meaning with the data in question.

For example, one measure of skewness proposed by Karl Pearson (of the Pearson correlation coefficient) is shown here:

Skewness = (Mean – Mode) / Standard Deviation

7

But it's more typical to use the sum of the cubed z-scores in the distribution to calculate its skewness. One such method calculates skewness as follows:

$$\sum_{i=1}^{N} z^3/N$$

This is simply the average cubed z-score.

Excel uses a variation of that formula in its SKEW() function:

$$N\sum_{i=1}^{N} z^3/((N-1)(N-2))$$

A little thought will show that the Excel function always returns a larger value than the simple average of the cubed z-scores. If the number of values in the distribution is large, the two approaches are nearly equivalent. But for a sample of only five values, Excel's SKEW() function can easily return a value half again as large as the average cubed z-score. See Figure 7.2, where the original values in Column A are simply replicated (twice) in Column E. Notice that the value returned by SKEW() depends on the number of values it evaluates.

Figure 7.2
The mean cubed z-score is not affected by the number of values in the distribution.

	A	B	C	D	E	F	G
	Original values	z scores	Cubed z scores		Original values	z scores	Cubed z scores
1							
2	2	-0.682288239	-0.31762		2	-0.682288239	-0.31762
3	2	-0.682288239	-0.31762		2	-0.682288239	-0.31762
4	3	-0.303239217	-0.02788		3	-0.303239217	-0.02788
5	3	-0.303239217	-0.02788		3	-0.303239217	-0.02788
6	9	1.971054913	7.657662		9	1.971054913	7.657662
7					2	-0.682288239	-0.31762
8		Mean cubed z score:	1.393332		2	-0.682288239	-0.31762
9		=SKEW(A2:A6)	2.077057		3	-0.303239217	-0.02788
10					3	-0.303239217	-0.02788
11					9	1.971054913	7.657662
12					2	-0.682288239	-0.31762
13					2	-0.682288239	-0.31762
14					3	-0.303239217	-0.02788
15					3	-0.303239217	-0.02788
16					9	1.971054913	7.657662
17							
18						Mean cubed z score:	1.393332
19						=SKEW(E2:E16)	1.553177

Kurtosis

A distribution might be symmetric but still depart from the normal pattern by being taller or flatter than the true normal curve. This quality is called a curve's *kurtosis*.

Types of Kurtosis   Several adjectives that further describe the nature of a curve's kurtosis appear almost exclusively in statistics textbooks:

- A *platykurtic* curve is flatter and broader than a normal curve. (A platypus is so named because of its broad foot.)

- ■ A *mesokurtic* curve occupies a middle ground as to its kurtosis. A normal curve is mesokurtic.

- ■ A *leptokurtic* curve is more peaked than a normal curve: Its central area is more slender. This forces more of the curve's area into the tails. Or you can think of it as thicker tails pulling more of the curve's area out of the middle.

The t-distribution (see Chapter 8) is leptokurtic, but the more observations in a sample the more closely the t-distribution resembles the normal curve. Because there is more area in the tails of a t-distribution, special comparisons are needed to use the t-distribution as a way to test the mean of a relatively small sample. Again, Chapters 8 and 9 explore this issue in some detail, but you'll find that the leptokurtic t-distribution also has applications in regression analysis (see Chapter 12).

Figure 7.3 shows a normal curve—at any rate, one with a very small amount of kurtosis, –0.03. It also shows a somewhat leptokurtic curve, with kurtosis equal to –0.80.

Figure 7.3
Observations toward the middle of the normal curve move toward the tails in a leptokurtic curve.

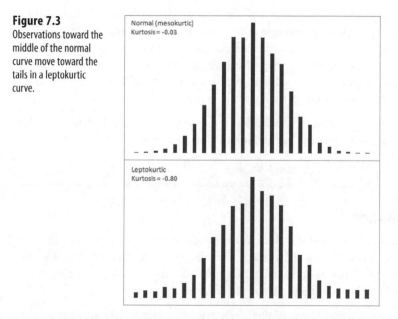

Normal (mesokurtic)
Kurtosis = -0.03

Leptokurtic
Kurtosis = -0.80

Notice that more of the area under the leptokurtic curve is in the tails of the distribution, with less occupying the middle. The t-distribution follows this pattern, and tests of such statistics as means take account of this when, for example, the population standard deviation is unknown and the sample size is small. With more of the area in the tails of the distribution, the critical values needed to reject a null hypothesis are larger than when the distribution is normal. The effect also finds its way into the construction of confidence intervals (discussed later in this chapter).

7

Quantifying Kurtosis The rationale to quantify kurtosis is the same as the rationale to quantify skewness: A number is often a more efficient descriptor than a chart. Furthermore, knowing how far a distribution departs from the normal helps the consumer of the research put other reported findings in context.

Excel offers the KURT() worksheet function to calculate the kurtosis in a set of numbers. Unfortunately there is no more consensus regarding a formula for kurtosis than there is for skewness. But the recommended formulas do tend to agree on using some variation on the z-scores raised to the fourth power.

Here's one textbook definition of kurtosis:

$$\frac{\sum_1^N z^4}{N} - 3$$

In this definition, N is the number of values in the distribution and z represents the associated z-scores: that is, each value less the mean, divided by the standard deviation.

The number 3 is subtracted to set the result equal to 0 for the normal curve. Then, positive values for the kurtosis indicate a leptokurtic distribution whereas negative values indicate a platykurtic distribution. Because the z-scores are raised to an even power, their sum (and therefore their mean) cannot be negative. Subtracting 3 is a convenient way to give platykurtic curves a negative kurtosis. Some versions of the formula do not subtract 3. Those versions would return the value 3 for a normal curve.

Excel's KURT() function is calculated in this fashion, following an approach that's intended to correct bias in the sample's estimation of the population parameter:

$$\text{Kurtosis} = \frac{N(N + 1)}{(N - 1)(N - 2)(N - 3)} \sum_1^N z^4 - \frac{3(N - 1)^2}{(N - 2)(N - 3)}$$

The Unit Normal Distribution

One particular version of the normal distribution has special importance. It's called the *unit normal* or *standard normal* distribution. Its shape is the same as any normal distribution but its mean is 0 and its standard deviation is 1. That location (the mean of 0) and spread (the standard deviation of 1) makes it a standard, and that's handy.

Because of those two characteristics, you immediately know the cumulative area below any value. In the unit normal distribution, the value 1 is one standard deviation above the mean of 0, and so 84% of the area falls to its left. The value –2 is two standard deviations below the mean of 0, and so 2.275% of the area falls to its left.

On the other hand, suppose that you were working with a distribution that has a mean of 7.63 centimeters and a standard deviation of .124 centimeters—perhaps that represents the diameter of a machine part whose size must be precise. If someone told you that one of the machine parts has a diameter of 7.816, you'd probably have to think for a moment before you realized that's one-and-one-half standard deviations above the mean. But if you're using the unit normal distribution as a yardstick, hearing of a score of 1.5 tells you exactly where that machine part is in the distribution.

So it's quicker and easier to interpret the meaning of a value if you use the unit normal distribution as your framework. Excel has worksheet functions tailored for the normal distribution, and they are easy to use. Excel also has worksheet functions tailored specifically for the unit normal distribution, and they are even easier to use: You don't need to supply the distribution's mean and standard deviation, because they're known. The next section discusses those functions, for both Excel 2010 and earlier versions.

Excel Functions for the Normal Distribution

Excel names the functions that pertain to the normal distribution so that you can tell whether you're dealing with any normal distribution, or the unit normal distribution with a mean of 0 and a standard deviation of 1.

Excel refers to the unit normal distribution as the "standard" normal, and therefore uses the letter *s* in the function's name. So the NORM.DIST() function refers to any normal distribution, whereas the NORMSDIST() compatibility function and the NORM.S.DIST() consistency function refer specifically to the unit normal distribution.

The NORM.DIST() Function

Suppose you're interested in the distribution in the population of high-density lipoprotein (HDL) levels in adults over 20 years of age. That variable is normally measured in milligrams per deciliter of blood (mg/dl). Assuming HDL levels are normally distributed (and they are), you can learn more about the distribution of HDL in the population by applying your knowledge of the normal curve. One way to do so is by using Excel's NORM.DIST() function.

NORM.DIST() Syntax

The NORM.DIST() function takes the following data as its arguments:

- **x**—This is a value in the distribution you're evaluating. If you're evaluating high-density lipoprotein (HDL) levels, you might be interested in one specific level—say, 60. That specific value is the one you would provide as the first argument to NORM. DIST().
- **Mean**—The second argument is the mean of the distribution you're evaluating. Suppose that the mean HDL among humans over 20 years of age is 54.3.
- **Standard Deviation**—The third argument is the standard deviation of the distribution you're evaluating. Suppose that the standard deviation of HDL levels is 15.

7

■ **Cumulative**—The fourth argument indicates whether you want the cumulative probability of HDL levels from 0 to x (which we're taking to be 56 in this example), or the probability of having an HDL level of specifically x (that is, 56). If you want the cumulative probability, use TRUE as the fourth argument. If you want the specific probability, use FALSE.

Requesting the Cumulative Probability

The formula

=NORM.DIST(60, 54.3, 15, TRUE)

returns .648, or 64.8%. This means that 64.8% of the area under the distribution of HDL levels is between 0 and 60 mg/dl. Figure 7.4 shows this result.

Figure 7.4
You can adjust the number of gridlines by formatting the vertical axis to show more or fewer major units.

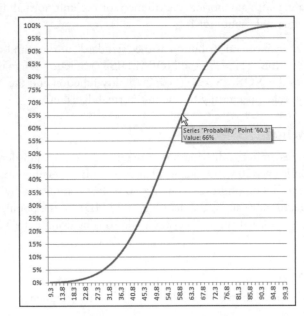

If you hover your mouse pointer over the line that shows the cumulative probability, you'll see a small pop-up window that tells you which data point you are pointing at, as well as its location on both the horizontal and vertical axes. Once created, the chart can tell you the probability associated with any of the charted data points, not just the 60 mg/dl this section has discussed. As shown in Figure 7.4, you can use either the chart's gridlines or your mouse pointer to determine that a measurement of, for example, 60.3 mg/dl or below accounts for about 66% of the population.

Requesting the Point Estimate

Things are different if you choose FALSE as the fourth, cumulative argument to NORM. DIST(). In that case, the function returns the probability associated with the specific point you specify in the first argument. Use the value FALSE for the cumulative argument if you want to know the height of the normal curve at a specific value of the distribution you're evaluating. Figure 7.5 shows one way to use NORM.DIST() with the cumulative argument set to FALSE.

Figure 7.5
The height of the curve at any point is the probability that the point appears in a random sample from the full distribution.

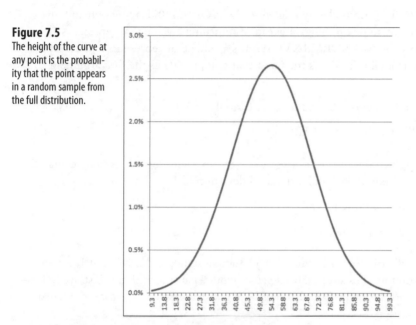

It doesn't often happen that you need a point estimate of the probability of a specific value in a normal curve, but if you do—for example, to draw a curve that helps you or someone else visualize an outcome—then setting the cumulative argument to FALSE is a good way to get it. (You might also see this value—the probability of a specific point, the height of the curve at that point—referred to as the *probability density function* or *probability mass function*. The terminology has not been standardized.)

If you're using a version of Excel prior to 2010, you can use the NORMDIST() compatibility function. It is the same as NORM.DIST() as to both arguments and returned values.

The NORM.INV() Function

As a practical matter, you'll find that you usually have need for the NORM.DIST() function after the fact. That is, you have collected data and know the mean and standard deviation of a sample or population. A question then arises: Where does a given value fall in a normal

7

distribution? That value might be a sample mean that you want to compare to a population, or it might be an individual observation that you want to assess in the context of a larger group.

In that case, you would pass the information along to NORM.DIST(), which would tell you the probability of observing up to a particular value (cumulative = TRUE) or that specific value (cumulative = FALSE). You could then compare that probability to the alpha rate that you already adopted for your experiment.

The NORM.INV() function is closely related to the NORM.DIST() function and gives you a slightly different angle on things. Instead of returning a value that represents an area—that is, a probability—NORM.INV() returns a value that represents a point on the normal curve's horizontal axis. That's the point that you provide as the first argument to NORM.DIST().

For example, the prior section showed that the formula

    =NORM.DIST(60, 54.3, 15, TRUE)

returns .648. The value 60 is at least as large as 64.8% of the observations in a normal distribution that has a mean of 54.3 and a standard deviation of 15.

The other side of the coin: the formula

    =NORM.INV(0.648, 54.3, 15)

returns 60. If your distribution has a mean of 54.3 and a standard deviation of 15, then 64.8% of the distribution lies at or below a value of 60. That illustration is just, well, illustrative. You would not normally care that 64.8% of a distribution lies below a particular value.

But suppose that in preparation for a research project you decide that you will conclude that a treatment has a reliable effect only if the mean of the experimental group is in the top 5% of the population. (This is consistent with the traditional null hypothesis approach to experimentation, which Chapters 8 and 9 discuss in considerably more detail.) In that case, you would want to know what score would define that top 5%.

If you know the mean and standard deviation, NORM.INV() does the job for you. Still taking the population mean at 54.3 and the standard deviation at 15, the formula

    =NORM.INV(0.95, 54.3, 15)

returns 78.97. Five percent of a normal distribution that has a mean of 54.3 and a standard deviation of 15 lies above a value of 78.97.

As you see, the formula uses 0.95 as the first argument to NORM.INV(). That's because NORM.INV assumes a cumulative probability—notice that unlike NORM.DIST(), the NORM.INV() function has no fourth, cumulative argument. So asking what value cuts off the top 5% of the distribution is equivalent to asking what value cuts off the bottom 95% of the distribution.

In this context, choosing to use NORM.DIST() or NORM.INV() is largely a matter of the sort of information you're after. If you want to know how likely it is that you will observe a number at least as large as X, hand X off to NORM.DIST() to get a probability. If you want to know the number that serves as the boundary of an area—an area that corresponds to a given probability—hand the area off to NORM.INV() to get that number.

In either case, you need to supply the mean and the standard deviation. In the case of NORM.DIST, you also need to tell the function whether you're interested in the cumulative probability or the point estimate.

The consistency function NORM.INV() is not available in versions of Excel prior to 2010, but you can use the compatibility function NORMINV() instead. The arguments and the results are as with NORM.INV().

Using NORM.S.DIST()

There's much to be said for expressing distances, weights, durations, and so on in their original unit of measure. That's what NORM.DIST() is for. But when you want to use a standard unit of measure for a variable that's distributed normally, you should think of NORM.S.DIST(). The *S* in the middle of the function name of course stands for *standard*.

It's quicker to use NORM.S.DIST() because you don't have to supply the mean or standard deviation. Because you're making reference to the unit normal distribution, the mean (0) and the standard deviation (1) are known by definition. All that NORM.S.DIST() needs is the z-score and whether you want a cumulative area (TRUE) or a point estimate (FALSE). The function uses this simple syntax:

    =NORM.S.DIST(z, cumulative)

Thus, the formula

    =NORM.S.DIST(1.5, TRUE)

informs you that 93.3% of the area under a normal curve is found to the left of a z-score of 1.5. (See Chapter 3, "Variability: How Values Disperse," for an introduction to the concept of z-scores.)

7

> ┌─ C A U T I O N ─────────────────────────────
>
> The compatibility function NORMSDIST() is available in versions of Excel prior to 2010. It is the only one of the normal distribution functions whose argument list is different from that of its associated consistency function. NORMSDIST() has no *cumulative* argument: It returns by default the cumulative area to the left of the z argument. Excel will warn that you have made an error if you supply a *cumulative* argument to NORMSDIST(). If you want the point estimate rather than the cumulative probability, you should use the NORMDIST() function with 0 as the second argument and 1 as the third. Those two together specify the unit normal distribution, and you can now supply FALSE as the fourth argument to NORMDIST(). Here's an example:
>
>   =NORMDIST(1,0,1,FALSE)

Using NORM.S.INV()

It's even simpler to use the inverse of NORM.S.DIST(), which is NORM.S.INV(). All the latter function needs is a probability:

    =NORM.S.INV(.95)

This formula returns 1.64, which means that 95% of the area under the normal curve lies to the left of a z-score of 1.64. If you've taken a course in elementary inferential statistics, that number probably looks familiar: as familiar as the 1.96 that cuts off 97.5% of the distribution.

These are frequently occurring numbers because they are associated with the all-too-frequently occurring "p<.05" and "p<.025" entries at the bottom of tables in journal reports—a rut that you don't want to get caught in. Chapters 8 and 9 have much more to say about those sorts of entries, in the context of the t-distribution (which is closely related to the normal distribution).

The compatibility function NORMSINV() takes the same argument and returns the same result as does NORM.S.INV().

There is another Excel worksheet function that pertains directly to the normal distribution: CONFIDENCE.NORM(). To discuss the purpose and use of that function sensibly, it's necessary first to explore a little background.

Confidence Intervals and the Normal Distribution

A *confidence interval* is a range of values that gives the user a sense of how precisely a statistic estimates a parameter. The most familiar use of a confidence interval is likely the "margin of error" reported in news stories about polls: "The margin of error is plus or minus 3 percentage points." But confidence intervals are useful in contexts that go well beyond that simple situation.

Confidence intervals can be used with distributions that aren't normal—that are highly skewed or in some other way non-normal. But it's easiest to understand what they're about in symmetric distributions, so the topic is introduced here. Don't let that get you thinking that you can use confidence intervals with normal distributions only.

The Meaning of a Confidence Interval

Suppose that you measured the HDL level in the blood of 100 adults on a special diet and calculated a mean of 50 mg/dl with a standard deviation of 20. You're aware that the mean is a statistic, not a population parameter, and that another sample of 100 adults, on the same diet, would very likely return a different mean value. Over many repeated samples, the grand mean—that is, the mean of the sample means—would turn out to be very, very close to the population parameter.

But your resources don't extend that far and you're going to have to make do with just the one statistic, the 50 mg/dl that you calculated for your sample. Although the value of 20 that you calculate for the sample standard deviation is a statistic, it is the same as the known population standard deviation of 20. You can make use of the sample standard deviation and the number of HDL values that you tabulated in order to get a sense of how much play there is in that sample estimate.

You do so by constructing a confidence interval around that mean of 50 mg/dl. Perhaps the interval extends from 45 to 55. (And here you can see the relationship to "plus or minus 3 percentage points.") Does that tell you that the true population mean is somewhere between 45 and 55?

No, it doesn't, although it might well be. Just as there are many possible samples that you might have taken, but didn't, there are many possible confidence intervals you might have constructed around the sample means, but couldn't. As you'll see, you construct your confidence interval in such a way that if you took many more means and put confidence intervals around them, 95% of the confidence intervals would capture the true population mean. As to the specific confidence interval that you did construct, the probability that the true population mean falls within the interval is either 1 or 0: either the interval captures the mean or it doesn't.

However, it is more rational to assume that the one confidence interval that you took is one of the 95% that capture the population mean than to assume it isn't. So you would tend to believe, with 95% confidence, that the interval is one of those that captures the population mean.

Although I've spoken of 95% confidence intervals in this section, you can also construct 90% or 99% confidence intervals, or any other degree of confidence that makes sense to you in a particular situation. You'll see next how your choices when you construct the interval affect the nature of the interval itself. It turns out that it smoothes the discussion if you're willing to suspend your disbelief a bit, and briefly: I'm going to ask you to imagine a situation in which you know what the standard deviation of a measure is in the population, but that you don't know its mean in the population. Those circumstances are a little odd but far from impossible.

7

Constructing a Confidence Interval

A confidence interval on a mean, as described in the prior section, requires these building blocks:

- The mean itself
- The standard deviation of the observations
- The number of observations in the sample
- The level of confidence you want to apply to the confidence interval

Starting with the level of confidence, suppose that you want to create a 95% confidence interval: You want to construct it in such a way that if you created 100 confidence intervals, 95 of them would capture the true population mean.

In that case, because you're dealing with a normal distribution, you could enter these formulas in a worksheet:

=NORM.S.INV(0.025)

=NORM.S.INV(0.975)

The NORM.S.INV() function, described in the prior section, returns the z-score that has to its left the proportion of the curve's area given as the argument. Therefore, NORM.S.INV(0.025) returns –1.96. That's the z-score that has 0.025, or 2.5%, of the curve's area to its left.

Similarly, NORM.S.INV(0.975) returns 1.96, which has 97.5% of the curve's area to its left. Another way of saying it is that 2.5% of the curve's area lies to its right. These figures are shown in Figure 7.6.

Figure 7.6
Adjusting the z-score limit adjusts the level of confidence. Compare Figures 7.6 and 7.7.

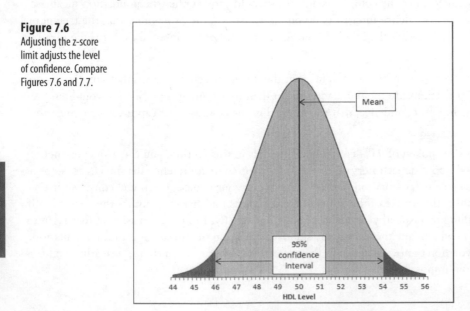

The area under the curve in Figure 7.6, and between the values 46.1 and 53.9 on the horizontal axis, accounts for 95% of the area under the curve. The curve, in theory, extends to infinity to the left and to the right, so all possible values for the population mean are included in the curve. Ninety-five percent of the possible values lie within the 95% confidence interval between 46.1 and 53.9.

The figures 46.1 and 53.9 were chosen so as to capture that 95%. If you wanted a 99% confidence interval (or some other interval more or less likely to be one of the intervals that captures the population mean), you would choose different figures. Figure 7.7 shows a 99% confidence interval around a sample mean of 50.

Figure 7.7
Widening the interval gives you more confidence that you are capturing the population parameter but inevitably results in a vaguer estimate.

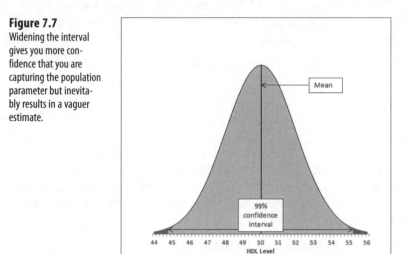

In Figure 7.7, the 99% confidence interval extends from 44.8 to 55.2, a total of 2.6 points wider than the 95% confidence interval depicted in Figure 7.6. If a hundred 99% confidence intervals were constructed around the means of 100 samples, 99 of them (not 95 as before) would capture the population mean. The additional confidence is provided by making the interval wider. And that's always the tradeoff in confidence intervals. The narrower the interval, the more precisely you draw the boundaries, but the fewer such intervals will capture the statistic in question (here, that's the mean). The broader the interval, the less precisely you set the boundaries but the larger the number of intervals that capture the statistic.

Other than setting the confidence level, the only factor that's under your control is the sample size. You generally can't dictate that the standard deviation is to be smaller, but you can take larger samples. As you'll see in Chapters 8 and 9, the standard deviation used in a confidence interval around a sample mean is not the standard deviation of the individual raw scores. It is that standard deviation divided by the square root of the sample size, and this is known as the *standard error of the mean*.

7

The data set used to create the charts in Figures 7.6 and 7.7 has a standard deviation of 20, known to be the same as the population standard deviation. The sample size is 100. Therefore, the standard error of the mean is

$$\text{Standard Error} = \frac{20}{\sqrt{100}}$$

or 2.

To complete the construction of the confidence interval, you multiply the standard error of the mean by the z-scores that cut off the confidence level you're interested in. Figure 7.6, for example, shows a 95% confidence interval. The interval must be constructed so that 95% lies under the curve and within the interval—therefore, 5% must lie outside the interval, with 2.5% divided equally between the tails.

Here's where the NORM.S.INV() function comes into play. Earlier in this section, these two formulas were used:

=NORM.S.INV(0.025)

=NORM.S.INV(0.975)

They return the z-scores –1.96 and 1.96, which form the boundaries for 2.5% and 97.5% of the unit normal distribution, respectively. If you multiply each by the standard error of 2, and add the sample mean of 50, you get 46.1 and 53.9, the limits of a 95% confidence interval on a mean of 50 and a standard error of 2.

If you want a 99% confidence interval, use the formulas

=NORM.S.INV(0.005)

=NORM.S.INV(0.995)

to return –2.58 and 2.58. These z-scores cut off one half of one percent of the unit normal distribution at each end. The remainder of the area under the curve is 99%. Multiplying each z-score by 2 and adding 50 for the mean results in 44.8 and 55.2, the limits of a 99% confidence interval on a mean of 50 and a standard error of 2.

At this point it can help to back away from the arithmetic and focus instead on the concepts. Any z-score is some number of standard deviations—so a z-score of 1.96 is a point that's found at 1.96 standard deviations above the mean, and a z-score of –1.96 is found 1.96 standard deviations below the mean.

Because the nature of the normal curve has been studied so extensively, we know that 95% of the area under a normal curve is found between 1.96 standard deviations below the mean and 1.96 standard deviations above the mean.

When you want to put a confidence interval around a sample mean, you start by deciding what percentage of other sample means, if collected and calculated, you would want to fall within that interval. So, if you decided that you wanted 95% of possible sample means to be captured by your confidence interval, you would put it 1.96 standard deviations above and below your sample mean.

But how large is the relevant standard deviation? In this situation, the relevant units are themselves mean values. You need to know the standard deviation not of the original and individual observations, but of the means that are calculated from those observations. That standard deviation has a special name, the standard error of the mean.

Because of mathematical derivations *and* long experience with the way the numbers behave, we know that a good, close estimate of the standard deviation of the mean values is the standard deviation of individual scores, divided by the square root of the sample size. That's the standard deviation you want to use to determine your confidence interval.

In the example this section has explored, the standard deviation is 20 and the sample size is 100, so the standard error of the mean is 2. When you calculate 1.96 standard errors below the mean of 50 and above the mean of 50, you wind up with values of 46.1 and 53.9. That's your 95% confidence interval. If you took another 99 samples from the population, 95 of 100 similar confidence intervals would capture the population mean. It's sensible to conclude that the confidence interval you calculated is one of the 95 that capture the population mean. It's not sensible to conclude that it's one of the remaining 5 that don't.

Excel Worksheet Functions That Calculate Confidence Intervals

The preceding section's discussion of the use of the normal distribution made the assumption that you know the standard deviation in the population. That's not an implausible assumption, but it is true that you often don't know the population standard deviation and must estimate it on the basis of the sample you take. There are two different distributions that you need access to, depending on whether you know the population standard deviation or are estimating it. If you know it, you make reference to the normal distribution. If you are estimating it from a sample, you use the t-distribution.

Excel 2010 has two worksheet functions, CONFIDENCE.NORM() and CONFIDENCE.T(), that help calculate the *width* of confidence intervals. You use CONFIDENCE.NORM() when you know the population standard deviation of the measure (such as this chapter's example using HDL levels). You use CONFIDENCE.T() when you don't know the measure's standard deviation in the population and are estimating it from the sample data. Chapters 8 and 9 have more information on this distinction, which involves the choice between using the normal distribution and the t-distribution.

Versions of Excel prior to 2010 have the CONFIDENCE() function only. Its arguments and results are identical to those of the CONFIDENCE.NORM() consistency function. Prior to 2010 there was no single worksheet function to return a confidence interval based on the t-distribution. However, as you'll see in this section, it's very easy to replicate CONFIDENCE.T() using either T.INV() or TINV(). You can replicate CONFIDENCE.NORM() using NORM.S.INV() or NORMSINV().

Using CONFIDENCE.NORM() and CONFIDENCE()

Figure 7.8 shows a small data set in cells A2:A17. Its mean is in cell B2 and the *population* standard deviation in cell C2.

Figure 7.8
You can construct a confidence interval using either a confidence function or a normal distribution function.

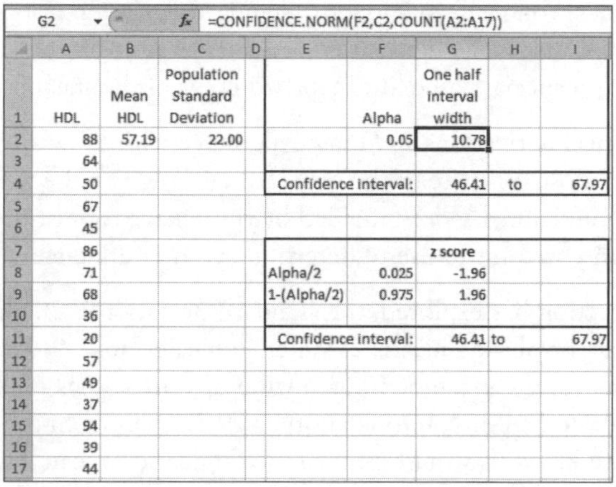

G2	▾		fx	=CONFIDENCE.NORM(F2,C2,COUNT(A2:A17))				
	A	B	C	D E	F	G	H	I
			Population			One half		
		Mean	Standard			Interval		
1	HDL	HDL	Deviation		Alpha	width		
2	88	57.19	22.00		0.05	10.78		
3	64							
4	50			Confidence interval:		46.41	to	67.97
5	67							
6	45							
7	86					z score		
8	71			Alpha/2	0.025	-1.96		
9	68			1-(Alpha/2)	0.975	1.96		
10	36							
11	20			Confidence interval:		46.41	to	67.97
12	57							
13	49							
14	37							
15	94							
16	39							
17	44							

In Figure 7.8, a value called *alpha* is in cell F2. The use of that term is consistent with its use in other contexts such as hypothesis testing. It is the area under the curve that is outside the limits of the confidence interval. In Figure 7.6, alpha is the sum of the shaded areas in the curve's tails. Each shaded area is 2.5% of the total area, so alpha is 5% or 0.05. The result is a 95% confidence interval.

Cell G2 in Figure 7.8 shows how to use the CONFIDENCE.NORM() function. Note that you could use the CONFIDENCE() compatibility function in the same way. The syntax is

=CONFIDENCE.NORM(alpha, standard deviation, size)

where *size* refers to sample size. As the function is used in cell G2, it specifies 0.05 for alpha, 22 for the population standard deviation, and 16 for the count of values in the sample:

=CONFIDENCE.NORM(F2,C2,COUNT(A2:A17))

This returns 10.78 as the result of the function, given those arguments. Cells G4 and I4 show, respectively, the upper and lower limits of the 95% confidence interval.

There are several points to note:

- CONFIDENCE.NORM() is used, not CONFIDENCE.T(). This is because you have knowledge of the population standard deviation and need not estimate it from the sample standard deviation. If you had to estimate the population value from the sample, you would use CONFIDENCE.T(), as described in the next section.

7

- Because the sum of the confidence level (for example, 95%) and alpha always equals 100%, Microsoft could have chosen to ask you for the confidence level instead of alpha. It is standard to refer to confidence intervals in terms of confidence levels such as 95%, 90%, 99%, and so on. Microsoft would have demonstrated a greater degree of consideration for its customers had it chosen to use the confidence level instead of alpha as the function's first argument.

- The Help documentation states that CONFIDENCE.NORM(), as well as the other two confidence interval functions, returns the confidence interval. It does not. The value returned is one half of the confidence interval. To establish the full confidence interval, you must subtract the result of the function from the mean and add the result to the mean.

Still in Figure 7.8, the range E7:I11 constructs a confidence interval identical to the one in E1:I4. It's useful because it shows what's going on behind the scenes in the CONFIDENCE.NORM() function. The following calculations are needed:

- Cell F8 contains the formula =F2/2. The portion under the curve that's represented by alpha—here. 0.05, or 5%—must be split in half between the two tails of the distribution. The leftmost 2.5% of the area will be placed in the left tail, to the left of the *lower* limit of the confidence interval.

- Cell F9 contains the remaining area under the curve after half of alpha has been removed. That is the leftmost 97.5% of the area, which is found to the left of the *upper* limit of the confidence interval.

- Cell G8 contains the formula =NORM.S.INV(F8). It returns the z-score that cuts off (here) the leftmost 2.5% of the area under the unit normal curve.

- Cell G9 contains the formula =NORM.S.INV(F9). It returns the z-score that cuts off (here) the leftmost 97.5% of the area under the unit normal curve.

Now we have in cell G8 and G9 the z-scores—the standard deviations in the unit normal distribution—that border the leftmost 2.5% and rightmost 2.5% of the distribution. To get those z-scores into the unit of measurement we're using—a measure of the amount of HDL in the blood—it's necessary to multiply the z-scores by the standard error of the mean, and add and subtract that from the sample mean. This formula does the addition part in cell G11:

=B2+(G8*C2/SQRT(COUNT(A2:A17)))

Working from the inside out, the formula does the following:

1. Divides the standard deviation in cell C2 by the square root of the number of observations in the sample. As noted earlier, this division returns the standard error of the mean.

2. Multiplies the standard error of the mean by the number of standard errors below the mean (–1.96) that bounds the lower 2.5% of the area under the curve. That value is in cell G8.

7

3. Adds the mean of the sample, found in cell B2.

Steps 1 through 3 return the value 46.41. Note that it is identical to the lower limit returned using CONFIDENCE.NORM() in cell G4.

Similar steps are used to get the value in cell I11. The difference is that instead of adding a negative number (rendered negative by the negative z-score –1.96), the formula adds a positive number (the z-score 1.96 multiplied by the standard error returns a positive result). Note that the value in I11 is identical to the value in I4, which depends on CONFIDENCE.NORM() instead of on NORM.S.INV().

Notice that CONFIDENCE.NORM() asks you to supply three arguments:

- **Alpha, or 1 minus the confidence level**—Excel can't predict with what level of confidence you want to use the interval, so you have to supply it.

- **Standard deviation**—Because CONFIDENCE.NORM() uses the normal distribution as a reference to obtain the z-scores associated with different areas, it is assumed that the population standard deviation is in use. (See Chapters 8 and 9 for more on this matter.) Excel doesn't have access to the full population and thus can't calculate its standard deviation. Therefore, it relies on the user to supply that figure.

- **Size, or, more meaningfully, sample size**—You aren't directing Excel's attention to the sample itself (cells A2:A17 in Figure 7.8), so Excel can't count the number of observations. You have to supply that number so that Excel can calculate the standard error of the mean.

You should use CONFIDENCE.NORM() or CONFIDENCE() if you feel comfortable with them and have no particular desire to grind it out using NORM.S.INV() and the standard error of the mean. Just remember that CONFIDENCE.NORM() and CONFIDENCE() do not return the width of the entire interval, just the width of the upper half, which is identical in a symmetric distribution to the width of the lower half.

Using CONFIDENCE.T()

Figure 7.9 makes two basic changes to the information in Figure 7.8: It uses the sample standard deviation in cell C2 and it uses the CONFIDENCE.T() function in cell G2. These two basic changes alter the size of the resulting confidence interval.

Notice first that the 95% confidence interval in Figure 7.9 runs from 46.01 to 68.36, whereas in Figure 7.8 it runs from 46.41 to 67.97. The confidence interval in Figure 7.8 is narrower. You can find the reason in Figure 7.3. There, you can see that there's more area under the tails of the leptokurtic distribution than under the tails of the normal distribution. You have to go out farther from the mean of a leptokurtic distribution to capture, say, 95% of its area between its tails. Therefore, the limits of the interval are farther from the mean and the confidence interval is wider.

Figure 7.9
Other things being equal,
a confidence interval
constructed using the
t-distribution is wider
than one constructed
using the normal
distribution.

G2			f_x	=CONFIDENCE.T(F2,C2,COUNT(A2:A17))				
	A	B	C	D	E	F	G	H	I
1	HDL	Mean HDL	Sample Standard Deviation			Alpha	One half interval width		
2	88	57.19	20.97			0.05	11.17		
3	64								
4	50				Confidence interval:		46.01	to	68.36
5	67								
6	45								
7	86						t value		
8	71				Alpha/2	0.025	-2.13		
9	68				1-(Alpha/2)	0.975	2.13		
10	36								
11	20				Confidence interval:		46.01	to	68.36
12	57								
13	49								
14	37								
15	94								
16	39								
17	44								

Because you use the t-distribution when you don't know the population standard deviation, using CONFIDENCE.T() instead of CONFIDENCE.NORM() brings about a wider confidence interval.

The shift from the normal distribution to the t-distribution also appears in the formulas in cells G8 and G9 of Figure 7.9, which are:

=T.INV(F8,COUNT(A2:A17)-1)

and

=T.INV(F9,COUNT(A2:A17)-1)

Note that these cells use T.INV() instead of NORM.S.INV(), as is done in Figure 7.8. In addition to the probabilities in cells F8 and F9, T.INV() needs to know the degrees of freedom associated with the sample standard deviation. Recall from Chapter 3 that a sample's standard deviation uses in its denominator the number of observations minus 1. When you supply the proper number of degrees of freedom, you enable Excel to use the proper t-distribution: There's a different t-distribution for every different number of degrees of freedom.

Using the Data Analysis Add-in for Confidence Intervals

Excel's Data Analysis add-in has a Descriptive Statistics tool that can be helpful when you have one or more variables to analyze. The Descriptive Statistics tool returns valuable information about a range of data, including measures of central tendency and variability, skewness and kurtosis. The tool also returns half the size of a confidence interval, just as CONFIDENCE.T() does.

7

> **NOTE** The Descriptive Statistics tool's confidence interval is very sensibly based on the t-distribution. You must supply a range of actual data for Excel to calculate the other descriptive statistics, and so Excel can easily determine the sample size and standard deviation to use in finding the standard error of the mean. Because Excel calculates the standard deviation based on the range of values you supply, the assumption is that the data constitutes a sample, and therefore a confidence interval based on t instead of z is appropriate.

To use the Descriptive Statistics tool, you must first have installed the Data Analysis add-in. Chapter 4 provides step-by-step instructions for its installation. Once this add-in is installed from the Office disc and made available to Excel, you'll find it in the Analysis group on the Ribbon's Data tab.

Once the add-in is installed and available, click Data Analysis in the Data tab's Analysis group, and choose Descriptive Statistics from the Data Analysis list box. Click OK to get the Descriptive Statistics dialog box shown in Figure 7.10.

Figure 7.10
The Descriptive Statistics tool is a handy way to get information quickly on the measures of central tendency and variability of one or more variables.

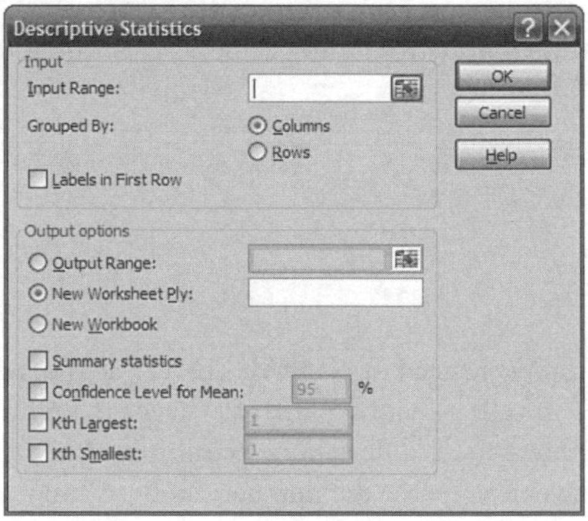

> **NOTE** To handle several variables at once, arrange them in a list or table structure, enter the entire range address in the Input Range box, and click Grouped by Columns.

To get descriptive statistics such as the mean, skewness, count, and so on, be sure to fill the Summary Statistics check box. To get the confidence interval, fill the Confidence Level for Mean check box and enter a confidence level such as **90**, **95**, or **99** in the associated edit box.

If your data has a header cell and you have included it in the Input Range edit box, fill the Labels check box; this informs Excel to use that value as a label in the output and not to try to use it as an input value.

When you click OK, you get output that resembles the report shown in Figure 7.11.

Figure 7.11
The output consists solely of static values. There are no formulas, so nothing recalculates automatically if you change the input data.

▲	A	B	C	D
1	HDL		HDL	
2	88			
3	64		Mean	57.1875
4	50		Standard Error	5.242629
5	67		Median	53.5
6	45		Mode	#N/A
7	86		Standard Deviation	20.97052
8	71		Sample Variance	439.7625
9	68		Kurtosis	-0.64987
10	36		Skewness	0.231449
11	20		Range	74
12	57		Minimum	20
13	49		Maximum	94
14	37		Sum	915
15	94		Count	16
16	39		Confidence Level(95.0%)	11.17
17	44			

Notice that the value in cell D16 is the same as the value in cell G2 of Figure 7.9. The value 11.17 is what you add and subtract from the sample mean to get the full confidence interval.

The output label for the confidence interval is mildly misleading. Using standard terminology, the *confidence level* is not the value you use to get the full confidence interval (here, 11.17); rather, it is the probability (or, equivalently, the area under the curve) that you choose as a measure of the precision of your estimate and the likelihood that the confidence interval is one that captures the population mean. In Figure 7.11, the confidence level is 95%.

Confidence Intervals and Hypothesis Testing

Both conceptually and mathematically, confidence intervals are closely related to hypothesis testing. As you'll see in the next two chapters, you often test a hypothesis about a sample mean and some theoretical number, or about the difference between the means of two different samples. In cases like those you might use the normal distribution or the closely related t-distribution to make a statement such as, "The null hypothesis is rejected; the probability that the two means come from the same distribution is less than 0.05."

That statement is in effect the same as saying, "The mean of the second sample is outside a 95% confidence interval constructed around the mean of the first sample."

The Central Limit Theorem

There is a joint feature of the mean and the normal distribution that this book has so far touched on only lightly. That feature is the Central Limit Theorem, a fearsome sounding phenomenon whose effects are actually straightforward. Informally, it goes as in the following fairy tale.

7

Suppose you are interested in investigating the geographic distribution of vehicle traffic in a large metropolitan area. You have unlimited resources (that's what makes this a fairy tale) and so you send out an entire army of data collectors. Each of your 2,500 data collectors is to observe a different intersection in the city for a sequence of two-minute periods throughout the day, and count and record the number of vehicles that pass through the intersection during that period.

Your data collectors return with a total of 517,000 two-minute vehicle counts. The counts are accurately tabulated (that's more fairy tale, but that's also the end of it) and entered into an Excel worksheet. You create an Excel pivot chart as shown in Figure 7.12 to get a preliminary sense of the scope of the observations.

Figure 7.12
To keep things manageable, the number of vehicles is grouped by tens.

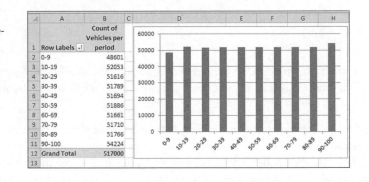

In Figure 7.12, different ranges of vehicles are shown as "row labels" in A2:A11. So, for example, there were 48,601 instances of between 0 and 9 vehicles crossing intersections within two-minute periods. Your data collectors recorded another 52,053 instances of between 10 and 19 vehicles crossing intersections within a two-minute period.

Notice that the data follows a uniform, rectangular distribution. Every grouping (for example, 0 to 9, 10 to 19, and so on) contains roughly the same number of observations.

Next, you calculate and chart the *mean* observation of each of the 2,500 intersections. The result appears in Figure 7.13.

Perhaps you expected the outcome shown in Figure 7.13, perhaps not. Most people don't. The underlying distribution is rectangular. There are as many intersections in your city that are traversed by zero to ten vehicles per two-minute period as there are intersections that attract 90 to 100 vehicles per two-minute period.

But if you take samples from that set of 517,000 observations, calculate the mean of each sample, and plot the results, you get something close to a normal distribution.

And this is termed the *Central Limit Theorem*. Take samples from a population that is distributed in any way: rectangular, skewed, binomial, bimodal, whatever (it's rectangular in

Figure 7.12). Get the mean of each sample and chart a frequency distribution of the means (refer to Figure 7.13). The chart of the means will resemble a normal distribution.

Figure 7.13

Charting means converts a rectangular distribution to a normal distribution.

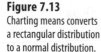

	A Mean vehicles per Intersection	B	C Row Labels	D Count of Mean vehicles per Intersection
1			Row Labels	Count of Mean vehicles per Intersection
2	47.82		40-41	1
3	43.73		41-42	1
4	51.32		42-43	14
5	49.82		43-44	29
6	47.69		44-45	47
7	52.41		45-46	103
8	48.87		46-47	155
9	52.40		47-48	208
10	45.93		48-49	296
11	52.82		49-50	326
12	47.88		50-51	334
13	45.77		51-52	337
14	54.01		52-53	258
15	48.23		53-54	174
16	49.53		54-55	108
17	54.47		55-56	60
18	54.84		56-57	29
19	47.82		57-58	13
20	45.95		58-59	5
21	47.29		59-60	2
22	50.71		Grand Total	2500

The larger the sample size, the closer the approximation to the normal distribution. The means in Figure 7.13 are based on samples of 100 each. If the samples had contained, say, 200 observations each, the chart would have come even closer to a normal distribution.

Making Things Easier

During the first half of the twentieth century, great reliance was placed on the Central Limit Theorem as a way to calculate probabilities. Suppose you want to investigate the prevalence of left-handedness among golfers. You believe that 10% of the general population is left-handed. You have taken a sample of 1,500 golfers and want to reassure yourself that there isn't some sort of systematic bias in your sample. You count the lefties and find 135. Assuming that 10% of the population is left-handed and that you have a representative sample, what is the probability of selecting 135 or fewer left-handed golfers in a sample of 1,500?

The formula that calculates that *exact* probability is

$$\sum_{i=1}^{135} \binom{1500}{i}(0.1^i)(0.9^{1500-i})$$

or, as you might write the formula using Excel functions:

=SUM(COMBIN(1500,ROW(A1:A135))*(0.1^ROW(A1:A135))* (0.9^(1500-ROW(A1:A135))))

(The formula must be array-entered in Excel, using Ctrl+Shift+Enter instead of simply Enter.)

7

That's formidable, whether you use summation notation or Excel function notation. It would take a long time to calculate its result by hand, in part because you'd have to calculate 1,500 factorial.

When mainframe and mini computers became broadly accessible in the 1970s and 1980s, it became feasible to calculate the exact probability, but unless you had a job as a programmer, you still didn't have the capability on your desktop.

When Excel came along, you could make use of BINOMDIST(), and in Excel 2010 BINOM.DIST(). Here's an example:

    =BINOM.DIST(135,1500,0.1,TRUE)

Any of those formulas returns the exact binomial probability, 10.48%. (That figure may or may not make you decide that your sample is nonrepresentative; it's a subjective decision.) But even in 1950 there wasn't much computing power available. You had to rely, so I'm told, on slide rules and compilations of mathematical and scientific tables to get the job done and come up with something close to the 10.48% figure.

Alternatively, you could call on the Central Limit Theorem. The first thing to notice is that a dichotomous variable such as handedness—right-handed versus left-handed—has a standard deviation just as any numeric variable has a standard deviation. If you let p stand for one proportion such as 0.1 and $(1 - p)$ stand for the other proportion, 0.9, then the standard deviation of that variable is as follows:

$$\sqrt{p(1 - p)}$$

That is, the square root of the product of the two proportions, such that they sum to 1.0. With a sample of some number n of people who possess or lack that characteristic, the standard deviation of that number of people is

$$\sqrt{np(1 - p)}$$

and the standard deviation of a distribution of the handedness of 1,500 golfers, assuming 10% lefties and 90% righties, would be

$$\sqrt{(1500)(.1)(.9)}$$

or 11.6.

You know what the number of golfers in your sample who are left-handed should be: 10% of 1,500, or 150. You know the standard deviation, 11.6. And the Central Limit Theorem tells you that the means of many samples follow a normal distribution, given that the samples are large enough. Surely 1,500 is a large sample.

Therefore, you should be able to compare your finding of 135 left-handed golfers with the normal distribution. The observed count of 135, less the mean of 150, divided by the standard deviation of 11.6, results in a z-score of –1.29. Any table that shows areas under the normal curve—and that's any elementary statistics textbook—will tell you that a z-score of

–1.29 corresponds to an area, a probability, of 9.84%. In the absence of a statistics textbook, you could use either

>=NORM.S.DIST(–1.29,TRUE)

or, equivalently

>=NORM.DIST(135,150,11.6,TRUE)

The result of using the normal distribution is 9.84%. The result of using the exact binomial distribution is 10.48%: slightly over half a percent difference.

Making Things Better

The 9.84% figure is called the "normal approximation to the binomial." It was and to some degree remains a popular alternative to using the binomial itself. It used to be popular because calculating the nCr combinations formula was so laborious and error prone. The approximation is still in some use because not everyone who has needed to calculate a binomial probability since the mid-1980s has had access to the appropriate software. And then there's cognitive inertia to contend with.

That slight discrepancy between 9.84% and 10.48% is the sort that statisticians have in past years referred to as "negligible," and perhaps it is. However, other constraints have been placed on the normal approximation method, such as the advice not to use it if either *np* or *n(1–p)* is less than 5. Or, depending on the source you read, less than 10. And there has been contentious discussion in the literature about the use of a "correction for continuity," which is meant to deal with the fact that things such as counts of golfers go up by 1 (you can't have 3/4 of a golfer) whereas things such as kilograms and yards are infinitely divisible. So the normal approximation to the binomial, prior to the accessibility of the huge amounts of computing power we now enjoy, was a mixed blessing.

The normal approximation to the binomial hangs its hat on the Central Limit Theorem. Largely because it has become relatively easy to calculate the exact binomial probability, you see normal approximations to the binomial less and less. The same is true of other approximations. The Central Limit Theorem remains a cornerstone of statistical theory, but (as far back as 1970) a nationally renowned statistician wrote that it "does not play the crucial role it once did."

Testing Differences Between Means: The Basics

One typical use of inferential statistics is to test the likelihood that the difference between the means of two groups is due to chance. Several situations call for this sort of analysis, but they all share the name *t-test*.

You'll find as many reasons to run t-tests as you have groups to contrast. For example, in different disciplines you might want to make these comparisons:

- **Business**—The mean profit margins of two product lines.
- **Medicine**—The effects of different cardiovascular exercise routines on the mean blood pressure of two groups of patients.
- **Economics**—The mean salaries earned by men and by women.
- **Education**—Test scores achieved by students on a test after two different curricula.
- **Agriculture**—The crop yields associated with the use of two different fertilizers.

You'll notice that each of these examples has to do with comparing *two* mean values, and that's characteristic of t-tests. When you want to test the difference in the means of exactly two groups, you can use a t-test.

It might occur to you that if you had, say, three groups to compare, it would be possible to carry out three t-tests: Group A versus B, A versus C, and B versus C. But doing so would expose you to a greater risk of an incorrect conclusion than you think you're running. So when the means of three or more groups are involved, you don't use t-tests. You use another technique instead, usually the analysis of variance (ANOVA) or, equivalently, multiple regression analysis (see Chapters 10 through 13).

The reverse is not true, though. Although you need to use ANOVA or multiple regression instead of t-tests with three or more means, you can also use ANOVA or multiple regression when you are dealing with two means only. Then, your choice of technique is more a matter of personal preference than of any technical issue.

Testing Means: The Rationale

Chapter 3, "Variability: How Values Disperse," discussed the concept of variability—how values disperse around a mean, and how one way of measuring whether there is great variability or only a little is by the use of the standard deviation. That chapter noted that after you've worked with standard deviations for a while, you develop an almost visceral feel for how big a difference a standard deviation represents.

Chapter 3 also hinted that you can make more rigorous interpretations of the difference between two means than simply noting, "They're 1.5 standard deviations apart. That's quite a difference." This chapter develops that hint into a more objective framework. In discussing differences that are measured in standard deviation units, Chapter 3 discussed z-scores:

$$z = (X - \overline{X})/\sigma$$

In words, a z-score is the difference between a specific value and a mean, divided by the standard deviation. Note the use of the Greek symbol σ (lowercase sigma), which indicates that the z-score is formed using the population standard deviation rather than using a sample standard deviation, which is symbolized using the Roman character s.

Now, that specific value symbolized as X isn't necessarily a particular value from a sample. It could be some other, hypothetical value. Suppose you're interested in the average age of the population of sea turtles in the Gulf of Mexico. You suspect that the 2010 oil well disaster in the Gulf killed off more of the older sea turtles than it did young adult turtles. In this case, you would begin by stating two hypotheses:

- One hypothesis, often called the *null hypothesis*, is normally the one you expect your research findings to reject. Here, it would be that the mean age of turtles in the Gulf is the same as the mean age of turtles worldwide.

- Another hypothesis, often called the *alternative* or *research hypothesis*, is the one that you expect to show is tenable. You might frame it in different ways. One way is, "Gulf turtles now have a lower mean age than turtles worldwide." Alternatively, "Gulf turtles have a different mean age than turtles worldwide."

The hypotheses are structured so that they cannot both be true: It can't be the case, for example, that the mean age of Gulf turtles is the same as the mean age of sea turtles worldwide, and that the mean age of Gulf turtles is different from the mean age of sea turtles worldwide. Because the hypotheses are framed so as to be mutually exclusive, it is possible to reject one hypothesis and therefore regard the other hypothesis as tenable.

> **NOTE**
>
> We use the term *population* frequently in discussing statistical analysis. Don't take the word too literally: it's used principally as a conceptual device to keep the discussion more crisp. Here, we're talking about two possible populations of sea turtles: those that live in the Gulf of Mexico and those that live in other bodies of water. In another sense, they constitute one population: sea turtles. But we're interested in the effects of an event that might have resulted in one older population of turtles that live outside the Gulf, and one younger population that lives in the Gulf. Did the event result in two populations with different mean ages, or do the turtles still belong to what is, in terms of mean age, a single population?

Suppose that your null hypothesis is that Gulf turtles have the same mean age as all sea turtles, and your alternative hypothesis is that the mean age of Gulf turtles is smaller than the mean age of all sea turtles.

You count the carapace rings on a sample of 16 turtles from the Gulf, obtained randomly and independently, and estimate the average age of your sample at 45 years. Can you reject the hypothesis that the average age of turtles in the Gulf of Mexico is actually 55 years, thought by some researchers to be the average age of all the world's sea turtles?

Using a z-Test

Before you can answer that question, you would need to know what test to apply. Do you know the standard deviation of the age of the world's sea turtles? It could be that enough research has been done on the age of sea turtles worldwide that you have at hand a credible, empirically derived and generally accepted value of the standard deviation of the age of sea turtles.

Perhaps that value is 20. In that case you could use the following equation for a z-score:

$$z = \frac{(55 - 45)}{20}$$

$$z = 0.5$$

You have adopted a null hypothesis that the average age of sea turtles in the Gulf of Mexico is 55, the same age as all sea turtles. You have taken a sample of those Gulf turtles, and calculated a mean age of 45. What is the likelihood that you would obtain a sample average of 45 if the population average is 55?

If you took many, many samples of turtles from the Gulf and calculated the mean age of each sample, you would wind up with a sampling distribution of means. That distribution would be normal and its mean would be the mean of the population you're interested in; furthermore, if your null hypothesis is correct, that mean would be 55. So, when you apply the formula

$$z = (X - \bar{X}) / \sigma$$

for a z-score, the X represents not an individual observation but a sample mean. The $\overline{X}$ represents not a sample mean but a population mean. And the σ represents not the standard deviation of individual observations but the standard deviation of the sample means.

In other words, you are treating a sample mean as an individual observation. Your population is not the population of individual observations, but a population of sample means. The standard deviation of that population of sample means is called the *standard error of the mean*, and it can be estimated with two numbers:

- The standard deviation of the individual observations in your sample. (Or, as just discussed, the known standard deviation of the population. You can use either, but your choice has implications for the type of test you run; see **Using the t-Test instead of the z-Test** later in this chapter.) In this example, that's the standard deviation of the ages of the turtles you sampled from the Gulf of Mexico.

- The sample size. Here, that's 16: Your sample consisted of 16 turtles.

Understanding the Standard Error of the Mean

Suppose that you take two observations from a population and that together they constitute one sample. The two observations are taken randomly and are independent of one another. You can repeat that process many times, taking two observations from the population and treating each pair of observations as a sample. Each sample has a mean:

$$\overline{X} = \frac{(X_1 + X_2)}{2}$$

The population variance is represented as σ^2 (recall from Chapter 3 that the variance is the square of the standard deviation). So the variance of many sample means, each based on two observations, can be written as follows:

$$\sigma^2_{\overline{x}} = \sigma^2_{(x_1 + x_2)/2}$$

In this example, we are taking the mean of two observations: dividing their sum by 2, or equivalently multiplying their sum by 0.5. We won't do it here, but it's not difficult to show that when you multiply a variable by a constant, the resulting variance is the original variance times the square of the constant. More exactly:

$$\sigma^2_{(X_1 + X_2)/2} = 0.5^2 \times \sigma^2_{(X_1 + X_2)}$$

And therefore:

$$\sigma^2_{\overline{x}} = 0.5^2 \times \sigma^2_{(X_1 + X_2)}$$

When two variables, such as X_1 and X_2 here, are independent of one another, the variance of their sum is equal to the sum of their variances:

$$\sigma^2_{(X_1 + X_2)} = \sigma^2_{X_1} + \sigma^2_{X_2}$$

Plugging that back into the prior formula we get this:

$$\sigma^2_{\bar{x}} = 0.5^2 \times (\sigma^2_{X_1} + \sigma^2_{X_2})$$

The variance of the first member in each of many samples, $\sigma^2_{X_1}$, equals the variance of the population from which the samples are drawn, σ^2_x. The variance of the second member of all those samples also equals σ^2_x. Therefore:

$$\sigma^2_{\bar{x}} = 0.5^2 \times (\sigma^2_x + \sigma^2_x)$$

$$\sigma^2_{\bar{x}} = 0.5^2 \times 2\sigma^2_x$$

$$\sigma^2_{\bar{x}} = \sigma^2_x / 2$$

More generally, substituting n to represent the sample size, we get the following:

$$\sigma^2_{\bar{x}} = \sigma^2_x / \text{n}$$

In words, the variance of the means of samples from a population is equal to the variance of the population divided by the sample size.

You don't see the term used very often, but the expression $\sigma^2_{\bar{x}}$ is referred to as the *variance error of the mean*. Its square root is shown as $\sigma_{\bar{x}}$ and referred to as the *standard error of the mean*—that's a term that you see fairly often. It's easy to get using this formula:

$$\sigma_{\bar{x}} = \frac{\sigma_x}{\sqrt{n}}$$

> **NOTE**
>
> The term *standard error* has historically been used to denote the standard deviation of something other than individual observations: For example, the standard error of the mean, as used here, refers to the standard deviation of sample means. Other examples are the standard error of estimate in regression analysis and the standard error of measurement in psychometrics.
>
> When you run across *standard error*, just bear in mind that it is a standard deviation, but that the individual data points that make up the statistic are not normally the original observations, but are observations that have already been manipulated in some fashion.

I repeat this because it's particularly important: The symbol $\sigma_{\bar{x}}$ is the standard error of the mean. It is *calculated* by dividing the sample variance (or, if known, the population variance) by the sample size and taking the square root of the result. It is *defined* as the standard deviation of the means calculated from repeated samples from a population.

Because you can calculate it from individual observations, you need take only one sample. Use that sample's variance as an estimator of the population variance. Armed with that information and the sample size, you can estimate the value of the standard deviation of the means of repeated samples without actually taking them.

Using the Standard Error of the Mean

Figure 8.1 shows how two populations might look if you were able to get at each member of the turtle population and put its age on a chart. The curve on the left shows the ages of the population of turtles in the Gulf of Mexico, where the mean age is 45 years. That mean age is indicated in the figure by the heavy dashed vertical line.

Figure 8.1
The standard deviation of the values that underlie the charts is 20.

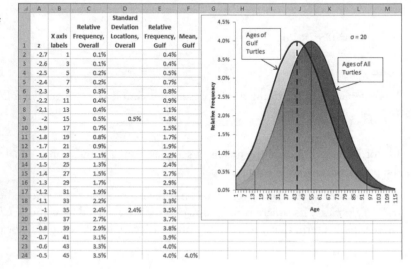

z	X axis labels	Relative Frequency, Overall	Standard Deviation Locations, Overall	Relative Frequency, Gulf	Mean, Gulf
-2.7	1	0.1%		0.4%	
-2.6	3	0.1%		0.4%	
-2.5	5	0.2%		0.5%	
-2.4	7	0.2%		0.7%	
-2.3	9	0.3%		0.8%	
-2.2	11	0.4%		0.9%	
-2.1	13	0.4%		1.1%	
-2	15	0.5%	0.5%	1.3%	
-1.9	17	0.7%		1.5%	
-1.8	19	0.8%		1.7%	
-1.7	21	0.9%		1.9%	
-1.6	23	1.1%		2.2%	
-1.5	25	1.3%		2.4%	
-1.4	27	1.5%		2.7%	
-1.3	29	1.7%		2.9%	
-1.2	31	1.9%		3.1%	
-1.1	33	2.2%		3.3%	
-1	35	2.4%	2.4%	3.5%	
-0.9	37	2.7%		3.7%	
-0.8	39	2.9%		3.8%	
-0.7	41	3.1%		3.9%	
-0.6	43	3.3%		4.0%	
-0.5	45	3.5%		4.0%	4.0%

Visualizing the Underlying Distributions

Figure 8.1 shows five other, thinner vertical lines. They belong to the curve on the right. They represent the location of, from left to right, 2 σ below the mean, 1 σ below the mean, the mean itself, 1 σ above the mean, and 2 σ above the mean.

> **NOTE** Designing the charts in Figure 8.1 takes a little practice. I discuss what's involved later in this chapter.

Notice that the mean of the left curve is at Age 45 on the horizontal axis. This matches the finding that you got from your sample. But the important point is that in terms of the right curve, which represents the ages of the population of all the world's sea turtles, Age 45 falls between 1 σ below its mean, at Age 35, and the mean itself, at Age 55. In standard deviation terms, the mean age of Gulf turtles, 45, is not at all far from the mean age of all sea turtles, 55. The two means are only half a standard deviation apart.

So it doesn't take much to go with the notion—the null hypothesis—that the Gulf turtles' ages came from the same population as the rest of the turtles' ages. You can easily chalk the ten-year difference in the means up to sampling error.

But there's a flaw in that argument: It uses the wrong standard deviation. The standard deviation of 20 used in the charts in Figure 8.1 is the standard deviation of individual ages. And you're not comparing the ages of individuals to a mean, you're comparing one mean to another mean. Therefore, the proper standard deviation to use is the standard error of the mean. Figure 8.2 shows the effect of using the standard error of the mean instead of the standard deviation.

Figure 8.2
With a sample size of 16, the standard error is four times smaller than the standard deviation.

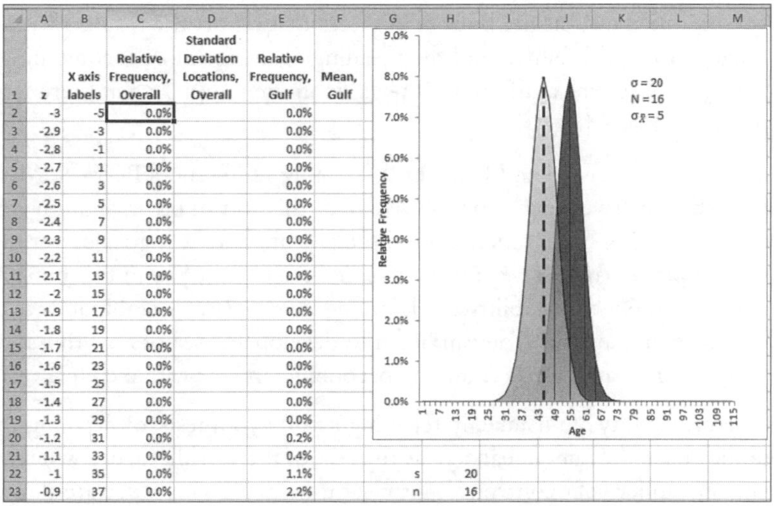

The curves shown in Figure 8.2 are much narrower than those in Figure 8.1. This is as it should be: The standard deviation used in Figure 8.2 is the standard error of the mean, which is always smaller than the standard deviation of individual observations for sample sizes greater than 1. That's clear if you keep in mind the formula for the standard error of the mean, shown in the last section and repeated here:

$$\sigma_{\bar{x}} = \frac{\sigma_x}{\sqrt{n}}$$

The curve on the right in Figure 8.2 still uses thin vertical lines to show the locations of one and two standard errors above and below the mean. Because the standard errors are smaller than the standard deviations, they cling more closely to the curve's mean than do the standard deviations in Figure 8.1.

But the means themselves are in the same locations, 45 years and 55 years, in both figures: Changing from the standard deviation of individual ages to the standard error of mean ages has no effect on the means themselves.

The net effect is that the mean age of the Gulf turtles is farther from the mean of all sea turtles when the distance is measured in standard errors of the mean. In Figure 8.2, the mean age of Gulf turtles, 45, is two standard errors below the mean of all sea turtles, whereas the means are only half a standard deviation apart in Figure 8.1. With the context provided in Figure 8.2, it's much more difficult to dismiss the difference as due to sampling error—that is, to continue to buy into the null hypothesis of no difference between the overall population mean and the mean of the population of Gulf turtles.

Error Rates and Statistical Tests

Even if you're fairly new to inferential statistics, you've probably seen footnotes such as "p<.05" or "p<.01" at the bottom of tables that report the results of empirical research. The *p* stands for "probability," and the meaning of the footnote is something such as, "The probability of observing a difference this large in the sample, when there is no difference in the population, is .05."

This book in general and Chapter 9, "Testing Differences Between Means: Further Issues," in particular have much more to say about this sort of error, and how to manipulate and control it using Excel functions and tools. Unhelpfully, it goes by various different names, such as *alpha, Type I error* and *significance level*. (I use *alpha* in this book, because *Type I error* does not imply a probability level, and *significance level* is ambiguous as to the sort of significance in question.) You can begin to develop an idea of how this sort of error works by looking again at Figure 8.2 and by becoming familiar with a couple of Excel functions.

The probability of mistakenly rejecting a null hypothesis, of deciding that Gulf turtles really do not have the same mean age as the rest of the world's turtles when they actually do, is entirely under your control. You can set it by fiat: You can declare that you are willing to make this kind of error five times in 100 (.05) or one time in 100 (.01) or any other fraction that's larger than zero and less than 1. This decision is called *setting the alpha level*.

Setting alpha is just one of the decisions you should make before you even see your experimental data. You should also make other decisions such as whether your alternative hypothesis is directional or nondirectional. Again, Chapter 9 goes into more depth about these issues.

For now, suppose that you had begun by specifying an alpha level of .05 for your statistical test. In that case, given the data you collected and that appears in Figure 8.1 and 8.2, your decision rule would tell you to reject the null hypothesis of no difference between the Gulf turtle population's age and that of all sea turtles. The likelihood of observing a sample mean of 45 when the population mean is 55, given a standard error of 5, is only .02275 or 2.275%.

That's less than half the probability of incorrectly rejecting the null hypothesis that you said you were willing to accept when you adopted a .05 value for alpha at the outset. By adopting .05 as your alpha level, you said that you were willing to reject a null hypothesis 5% of the time at most, when in fact it is true. In this case, that means you would be willing to conclude there's a difference between the mean age of all Gulf turtles and all sea turtles, when in fact there is no difference, in 5% of the samples you might take.

The result you obtained would occur not 5% of the time, but only 2.275% of the time, when no difference in mean age exists. You were willing to reject the null hypothesis if you got a finding that would occur only 5% of the time, and here you have one that occurs only 2.275% of the time, given that the null hypothesis is true. Instead of assuming that you happened to take a very unlikely sample, it makes more sense to conclude that the null hypothesis is wrong. (Compare this line of reasoning with that discussed in Chapter 7's section titled **Constructing a Confidence Interval**.)

You can determine the probability of getting the sample result (here, 2.275%) easily enough in Excel by using the NORM.DIST() function to return the results of a z-test. NORM.DIST() returns the probability of observing a given value in a normal distribution with a particular mean and standard deviation. Its syntax is shown here:

NORM.DIST(value, mean, standard deviation, cumulative)

In this example, you would use the arguments

NORM.DIST(45, 55, 5, TRUE)

where:

- *45* is the sample value that you are testing.
- *55* is the mean assumed by the null hypothesis.
- *5* is the standard error of the mean, the population standard deviation of 20 divided by the square root of the sample size of 16: $\sigma / \sqrt{N}$ or 20 / 4.
- *TRUE* specifies that you want the cumulative probability: that is, the total area under the normal curve to the left of the value of 45.

> **NOTE** If you're using a version of Excel prior to 2010, you should use NORMDIST() instead of NORM.DIST(). The arguments and results are the same for both versions of the function.

The value returned by NORM.DIST(45, 55, 5, TRUE) is .02275. Visually, it is the 2.275% of the area in the curve on the right, the curve for all turtles, in Figure 8.2, to the left of the sample mean, or Age 45, on its horizontal axis.

That area, .02275, is the probability that you could observe a sample mean of 45 or less *if the null hypothesis is actually true*. It is entirely possible that sampling error could cause your sample of Gulf turtles to have an average age of 45, when the population of Gulf turtles has a mean age of 55. But even though it's possible, it's improbable. More to the point, it is less probable than the alpha error rate of .05 you signed up for at the beginning of the experiment. You were willing to make the error of rejecting a true null hypothesis as much as 5% of the time, and you obtained a result that, if the null hypothesis is true, would occur only 2.275% of the time.

Therefore, you reject the null hypothesis and, in the somewhat baroque terminology of statistical testing, "entertain the alternative hypothesis."

Creating the Charts

You can teach yourself quite a bit about both the nature of a statistical test and about the data that plays into that test, by charting the data. If you're going to do that, consider charting both the actual observations (or their summaries, such as the mean and standard deviation) and the unseen, theoretical data that the test is based on (such as the population from which the sample came, or the distribution of the means of samples you didn't take).

This chapter contains several figures that show the distributions of hypothetical populations, of hypothetical samples, and of actual samples. The easiest and quickest way to understand how those charts are created is to open the Excel workbook for Chapter 8 that you can download from this book's website (www.informit.com/title/9780789747204). Select a worksheet (they're keyed to the figures) and open the chart on that worksheet by clicking it.

You can then select the data series in the chart, one by one, and note the worksheet range that the data series represents. (A border called a *range finder* surrounds the associated worksheet ranges when you select a data series in the chart.) You can also choose to format the data series to see what line and fill options are in use that give the chart its particular appearance.

> **NOTE**
> Don't neglect to see what chart type is in use. In this chapter and the next, I use both line and area charts. There are several considerations, but my choice often depends on whether I need to show one distribution behind another, so that the nature of their overlap is a little clearer.

However, the workbooks themselves don't necessarily clarify the rationale for the structure of a given chart. This section discusses the structure of the chart in Figure 8.1, which is moderately complex.

The Underlying Ranges

The chart in Figure 8.1 is based on six worksheet ranges, although only five appear on the chart. The data in Column A provides the basis for calculations in columns B through F. Columns B through F appear in the chart. The columns are structured as follows.

Column A: The z-Scores The first range is in column A. It contains the typical range of possible z-scores. Normally, that range would begin at –3.0 (or three standard deviations below the mean of 0.0) and end at +3.0 (three standard deviations above the mean). I eliminated z-scores below –2.7 because they would be associated with negative ages. Therefore, the range of z-scores on the worksheet runs from –2.7 through +3.0, occupying cells A2:A59.

One easy way to get that series of data into A2:A59 is to enter the first z-score you want to use in A2; here, that's –2.7. Enter this formula in cell A3:

    =A2 + 0.1

That returns –2.6. Copy and paste that formula into the range A4:A59 to end the series with a value of +3.0. You can use larger or smaller increments than 0.1 if you want. I find that increments of 0.1 strike a good balance between smooth lines on the chart and a data series with a manageable length.

Column B: The Horizontal Axis   Those z-scores in column A do not appear on the chart, but they form the basis for the ranges that do. It's usually better to show the scale of measurement on the chart's horizontal axis, not z-scores, so column B contains the age values that correspond to the z-scores. The values in column B are used for the horizontal axis on the chart. Excel converts z-scores to age values using this formula in cell B2:

    =A2*20 + 55

The formula takes the z-score in cell A2, multiplies it by 20, and adds 55. We want the spread on the horizontal axis to reflect the standard deviation of the values to be graphed. That standard deviation is 20, and we use it as the multiple for the z-scores. Then the formula adds the average of the values to be charted because the average of the z-scores is zero. The formula is copied and pasted into B3:B59.

I chose to add 55, the higher of the two averages, to make sure that the chart displayed positive ages only. A mean of 45 would lead to negative ages on the left end of the axis when the standard deviation is 20. (So does 55, but then there are fewer negative ages to suppress.)

Column C: The Population Values   Column C begins the calculation of the values that are shown on the chart's vertical axis. Column C's label, "Relative Frequency, Overall," indicates that the height of a charted curve at any particular point is defined by a value in this column. In this case, the curve on the chart that's labeled "Ages of All Turtles" depends on the values in column C.

The formula in cell C2 is

    =NORM.S.DIST(A2,FALSE)/10

and it requires some comment. In Excel 2010, the formula uses the NORM.S.DIST() function (if you are using an earlier version of Excel, be sure to see the following sidebar). That's the appropriate function because we are conducting a z-test. As you'll see in this chapter's section on t-tests, you use z to test the difference in means when you know the population standard deviation, and you use t when you don't.

The result of the function, whether you use NORM.S.DIST() or NORMDIST(), is divided by 10. This is due to the fact that I supplied about 60 (actually, 58) z-scores as the basis for the analysis. The total of the corresponding point estimates is very close to 10. By dividing by 10, you can format column C as percentages, which makes the vertical axis of the accompanying chart easier to interpret.

USING NORMDIST() INSTEAD OF NORM.S.DIST()

If you use a version of Excel prior to 2010, you could instead use the NORMDIST() function. The issue of back compatibility is a little painful in this instance.

For the present purpose of drawing a normal curve, we do not want the function to return the cumulative area under the curve. We want to know how high the curve is at any given point (and without getting into the integral calculus of the matter, the height of the curve at any given point on the horizontal axis is proportional to the probability of that particular score occurring). If the function returns the cumulative area, it returns the total area under the curve to the left of the point on the horizontal axis. That is very useful information but it doesn't help draw the curve. Instead of the cumulative area, we want the probability for one specific point on the horizontal axis—also termed the *point estimate*.

NORM.S.DIST() is accommodating in that regard. It has two arguments: The first is the z-score, the point on the horizontal axis of a normal curve that you're interested in. The second argument specifies whether you want the cumulative probability (TRUE) or the point estimate (FALSE), which is the curve's height and which represents the probability of observing that specific z-score.

That's well and good if you're using Excel 2010. If you're using Excel 2007 or earlier you don't have access to NORM.S.DIST(). Conceptually, the closest function in earlier versions is NORMSDIST(). But that function doesn't allow you to choose between a point estimate and the cumulative probability. NORMSDIST() takes one argument only, the z-score. It returns the cumulative probability willy-nilly.

So, if you're using a version prior to Excel 2010, you'll need to replace NORM.S.DIST() with NORMDIST(), which does allow you to specify point estimate versus cumulative. However, because NORMDIST() is intended for use with a broader range of normal distributions than the unit normal (which always has a mean of zero and a standard deviation of 1), you need to supply more information—specifically, the distribution's mean and standard deviation. To use NORMDIST() instead of NORM.S.DIST() in this particular instance, then, you would use this formula in cell C2:

```
=NORMDIST(A2,0,1,FALSE)/10
```

Column D: The Standard Deviations   It's important for the chart to show the locations of one and two (but seldom 3) standard deviations from the mean of the population. With those visible, it's easier to evaluate where the sample mean is found, relative to the location of the hypothesized population mean. Those locations appear as five thin vertical lines in the chart: -2σ, -1σ, μ, $+1\sigma$, and $+2\sigma$.

The best way to show those lines in an Excel chart is by means of a data series with only five values. You can see two of those values in cells D9 and D19 in Figure 8.1. I entered them in those rows so that they would line up with age 15 and age 35, which correspond to the z-scores −2.0 and −1.0.

Notice that the values in D9 and D19 are identical to the values in C9 and C19. In effect, I'm setting up two data series, where the second series has five of the same values in the first series. In the normal course of events, they overlap on the chart and you can see only the full series in column C. But you can call for *error bars* for the second data series. It's those error bars that form the thin vertical lines on the chart.

Why not call for error bars for the series in column C? Because then every data point in the column would have an error bar, not just the points that locate a standard deviation. I'll explain how to create error bars for a data series shortly.

Column E: The Distribution of Sample Means Column E contains the values that appear on the chart with the label "Ages of Gulf Turtles." They are identical to the values in Column B, and they are calculated in the same way, using NORM.S.DIST(). However, the curve needs to be shifted to the left by ten years, to reflect the fact that the alternative hypothesis has it that the mean age of Gulf turtles is 45, ten years less than turtles overall.

Therefore, the formula in cell E2 is

=NORM.S.DIST(A7,FALSE)/10

which points to A7 for its z-score, whereas the formula in cell C2 is

=NORM.S.DIST(A2,FALSE)/10

The effect is to left-shift the curve for Gulf turtles by ten years on the chart—each row on the worksheet represents two years of turtles' ages, so we point the function in E2 down five rows, or ten years.

Column F: The Mean of the Sample Finally, we need a data series on the chart that will show where the sample mean is located. It's shown by a heavy dashed vertical line on the chart. That line is established on the worksheet by a single value in cell F24. It appears on the chart by means of another error bar, which is attached to the data series for Column F.

Creating the Charts With the data established in the worksheet in columns A through F, as described previously, here is one sequence of steps you can use to create the chart as shown in Figure 8.1:

1. Begin by putting everything except the horizontal axis labels onto the chart: Select the range C1:F59.
2. Click the Ribbon's Insert tab and then click the Area button in the Charts area.
3. Click the button for the 2-D Area chart. A new chart appears, embedded in the active worksheet.
4. Click the legend in the right side of the chart and press Delete.
5. Click the major horizontal gridlines and press Delete. (You can skip steps 4 and 5 if you want, but the presence of the legend and the gridlines can distract attention from the main message of the chart.)

6. Now establish the labels for the chart's horizontal axis. When a chart is selected, an area labeled Chart Tools appears on the Ribbon. Click its Design tab and choose Select Data. The Select Data Source dialog box in Figure 8.3 appears.

Figure 8.3
This dialog box will seem unfamiliar if you are used to Excel 2003 or an earlier version.

Select Data Source

Chart data range: ='Fig 8.3'!$C$1:$F$59

Switch Row/Column

Legend Entries (Series)

Add | Edit | X Remove | ▲ | ▼

Relative Frequency, Overall
Standard Deviation Locations, Overall
Relative Frequency, Gulf
Mean, Gulf

Horizontal (Category) Axis Labels

Edit

1
2
3
4
5

Hidden and Empty Cells | OK | Cancel

7. The data series named Relative Frequency, Overall should be selected in the left list box. If it is not, select it now. Click the Edit button in the *right* list box. If you don't see that series name, make sure you selected C1:F59 in step 1.

8. The Axis Labels dialog box appears. You should see the flashing I-bar in the Axis Label Range box. Drag through the range B2:B59, type its address, or otherwise select it on the worksheet. Click OK to return to the Select Data Source dialog box, and then click OK again to return to the worksheet. Doing so establishes the values in the range B2:B59 as the labels for the chart's horizontal axis.

The chart should now appear very much as is shown in Figure 8.4.

Figure 8.4
Removing the legend and the gridlines makes it easier to see the overlap of the curves and the location of the standard deviations.

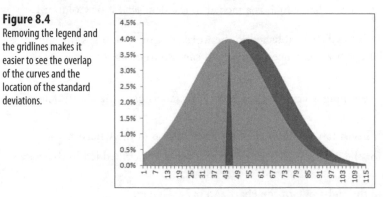

9. Steps 9 through 14 suppress the data series that represents the mean age of Gulf turtles and instead establish an error bar that displays the location of the mean age. Click the Layout tab in the Chart Tools area. Find the Current Selection area on the left end of the Ribbon and use its drop-down box to select the data series named "Mean, Gulf."

10. Choose Format Selection in the Current Selection area. A Format Data Series dialog box appears. Click Fill in its navigation bar, and then click the No Fill option button.

11. Click Border Color in the dialog box's navigation bar. Click the No Line option button and then click Close. By suppressing both the fill and the border in steps 10 and 11, you prevent the data series itself from appearing on the chart. Steps 12 through 14 replace the data series with an error bar.

12. With the Layout tab still selected, click the Error Bars drop-down arrow and choose More Error Bars Options from the drop-down menu. The Format Error Bars dialog box appears. Click the Minus and the No Cap buttons in the Vertical Error Bars window.

13. In the Error Amount pane on the Vertical Error Bars window, click the Percentage option button and set the percentage to 100%. This ensures that the error bar descends all the way to the horizontal axis.

14. Click Line Style in the Format Error Bars navigation bar. On the Line Style window, select the Dash Type you want and adjust the Width to something relatively heavy, such as 2.25. Click Close to close the Format Error Bars dialog box.

15. Steps 15 through 19 are similar to steps 9 through 14. They suppress the appearance of the data series that represents the standard deviations and replaces it with error bars. Click the Layout tab. Use the Current Selection drop-down box to select the data series named "Standard Deviation Locations, Overall."

16. Choose Format Selection. Click Fill in the Format Data Series box's navigation bar and then click the No Fill option button.

17. Click Border Color in the dialog box's navigation bar. Click the No Line option button and then click Close.

18. With the Layout tab still selected, click the Error Bars drop-down arrow and choose More Error Bars Options from the drop-down menu. Click the Minus and the No Cap buttons in the Vertical Error Bars window.

19. In the Error Amount pane on the Vertical Error Bars window, click the Percentage option button and set the percentage to 100%. Click Close to return to the worksheet. The chart should now appear as shown in Figure 8.5.

Figure 8.5
You still have to adjust the settings for the curves before the standard deviation lines make sense.

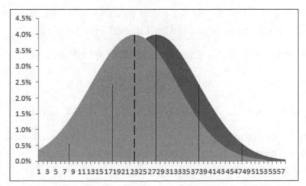

8

20. Finally, set the fill transparency and border properties so that you can see one curve behind the other. Right-click the left curve, which then becomes outlined with data markers. (You could use the Current Selection drop-down on the Layout tab instead, but the curves are much easier to locate on the chart than the mean or standard deviation series.) Choose Format Data Series from the shortcut menu.

21. Choose Fill from the navigation bar on the Format Data Series dialog box.

22. Click the Solid Fill option button in the Fill window. A Fill Color box appears. Set the Transparency to some value between 50% to 75%.

23. Click Border Color in the navigation bar. Click the Solid Line option button.

24. If you wish, you can click Border Styles in the navigation bar and set a wider border line.

25. Click Close to return to the worksheet.

26. Repeat steps 20 through 25 for the right curve. Be sure that you have selected the curve on the right: You can tell if you have done so correctly because data markers appear on the border of the selected curve.

The chart should now appear very much like the one shown in Figure 8.1.

To replicate Figure 8.2, the process is identical to the 26-step procedure just outlined. However, you begin with different definitions of the two curves in columns C and E. The formula

=NORM.DIST(B2,55,5,FALSE)

should be entered in cell C2 and copied and pasted into C3:C59. We need to specify the mean (55) and the standard error (5) because we're not using the standard unit normal distribution returned by NORM.S.DIST(). That distribution has a mean of zero and a standard deviation of 1. Therefore, we use NORM.DIST() instead, because it allows us to specify the mean and standard deviation.

Similarly, the formula

=NORM.DIST(B2,45,5,FALSE)

should be entered in cell E2 to adjust the mean from 55 to 45 for the curve that represents the Gulf sample. It should then be copied and pasted into E3:E59.

To get the means and standard deviations, enter this formula in cell D27:

=C27

Then copy and paste it into these cells: D29, D32, D35, D37, and E27.

Again, this will all be easier and quicker if you have the actual workbook from the publisher open, so that you can compare the results of the instructions given earlier with what you see in the Chapter 8 workbook.

Using the t-Test Instead of the z-Test

Chapter 3 went into some detail about the bias involved in the sample standard deviation as an estimator of the population standard deviation. There it was shown that because the sample mean is used instead of the (unknown) population mean, the sample standard deviation is smaller than the population standard deviation, and that most of that bias is removed by the use of the degrees of freedom instead of the sample size in the denominator of the variance.

Although using N − 1 instead of N acts as a bias correction, it doesn't eliminate sampling error. One of the principal functions of inferential statistics is to help you make statements about the probability of obtaining an observed statistic, under the hypothesis that a different state of nature exists.

For example, the prior two sections discussed how to determine the probability of observing a sample mean of 45 from a population whose mean is known to be 55—which is just a formal way of asking, "How likely is it that the mean age of sea turtles in the Gulf of Mexico is 45 when we know that the average age of all sea turtles is 55? Do we have two populations with different mean ages, or did we just get a bad sample of Gulf turtles?"

Those two prior sections posited a fairly unlikely set of circumstances. It is particularly unlikely that you would know the actual mean age of the world's population of sea turtles. I based the discussion on that knowledge largely because I wanted you to know the value of σ, the population standard deviation. If you know σ in these circumstances, you certainly know μ, the population mean, so I figured that I might as well give it to you.

But what if you didn't know the value of the population standard deviation? In that case, you might well estimate it using the value that you calculate for your sample: s instead of σ.

> **NOTE** It's quite plausible that you might encounter a real-world research situation in which you know a population standard deviation but might suspect that μ has changed while σ did not. This situation often comes about in manufacturing quality control. You would use the same analysis, employing NORM.DIST() and the standard error of the mean. You would substitute a hypothesized value for the mean, the second argument in NORM.DIST(), for another value that you previously knew to be the mean.

Inevitably, though, sampling error will provide you with a mis-estimate of the population standard deviation. And in that case, making reference via NORM.DIST() to the normal distribution, treating your sample statistic as a z-score, can mislead you.

Recall that a z-score is defined as follows:

$$\frac{X - \overline{X}}{\sigma}$$

Or, in the case of means, like this:

$$\frac{\overline{X} - \mu}{\sigma / \sqrt{N}}$$

In either case, you divide by σ. But if you don't know σ and use s instead, you form a ratio of this sort:

$$\frac{\overline{X} - \mu}{s/\sqrt{N}}$$

Notice that the sample standard deviation, not that of the population, is in the denominator. When you form that ratio, it is no longer a z-score but a *t-statistic*.

Furthermore, the normal distribution is the appropriate context to interpret a z-score, but it is not the appropriate point of reference for a t-statistic. A family of t-distributions provide the appropriate context and probability areas. They look very much, but not quite, like the normal distribution, and with small sample sizes this can make meaningful differences to your probability statements.

Figure 8.6 shows a t-distribution (broken line) along with a normal curve (solid line).

Figure 8.6
Notice that the t-distribution is a little shorter at the top and thicker in the tails than the normal distribution.

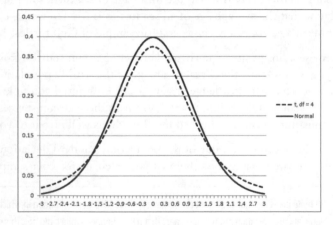

The t-distribution shown in Figure 8.6 is the distribution of t with 4 degrees of freedom. The t-distribution has a slightly different shape for every change in the number of degrees of freedom, and as the degrees of freedom gets larger the shape more nearly approaches the normal distribution.

> **NOTE**
> If you have downloaded the Excel workbooks from the publisher's website, you can open the workbook for Chapter 8. Activate the worksheet for Figure 8.6. There, change the number of degrees of freedom in cell B1 to see how the charted t-distribution changes. You'll see, for example, that the t-distribution is almost indistinguishable from the normal distribution when the degrees of freedom reaches 20 or 30.

Defining the Decision Rule

Let's make a change or two to the example of the age of sea turtles: Assume that you do not know the population standard deviation of their age, and simply want to compare the mean age in your sample with a hypothetical figure of 55 years.

You don't know the population standard deviation, and must estimate it from your sample data. You plan on a relatively small sample size of 16, so you should probably use the t-distribution as a reference rather than the normal distribution. (Compare the t-distribution with 15 degrees of freedom to the normal, as suggested in the prior note.)

Suppose that you have reason to suspect that the mean age of turtles in the Gulf of Mexico is 45, ten years younger than what you believe to be the mean age of all sea turtles. You might form an alternative hypothesis that Gulf turtles' mean age is 45, and there can be good reasons to state the alternative hypothesis with that degree of precision. More typically, a researcher would adopt a less restrictive statement. The researcher might use "Gulf turtles have a mean age less than 55" as the alternative hypothesis. After collecting and analyzing the data, they might go on to use the sample mean as the best estimate available of the Gulf turtles' mean age.

With your sample of Gulf turtles' ages, you're in a position to test your hypothesis, but before you do so you should specify alpha, the error rate that you are willing to tolerate.

Perhaps you're willing to be wrong 1 time in 20—as statisticians often phrase it, "alpha is .05." What specifically does that mean? Figure 8.7 provides a visual guide.

Figure 8.7
The area in the left tail of the right distribution represents alpha.

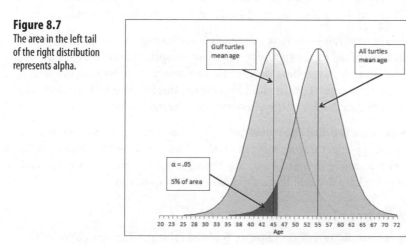

I don't mean to suggest that other figures and sections in this book aren't important, but I do think that what you see in Figure 8.7 is at least as critical for understanding inferential statistics as anything else in this or any other book.

There are two curves in Figure 8.7. The one on the right represents the distribution of the means you would calculate on many, many samples, if your null hypothesis is true: that the population mean is 55. The grand mean, the mean of all samples from the population and shown by a vertical line in that curve, shows the location of the population mean, again assuming that your null hypothesis is true.

The curve on the left represents the distribution of the means you would calculate (again, on many, many samples) if your alternative hypothesis is true: that the actual mean age is not 55 but a smaller number such as 45.

It's not possible for both curves to represent reality. If the population mean is really 55, then the curve on the left is possible only in theory. If the population mean is really 45, then the curve on the right is imaginary. (Of course, it's entirely possible that the population mean is neither 45 nor 55, but using specific values here helps to make a crisper example.)

In Figure 8.7, look closely at the left tail of the right curve, which represents the null hypothesis. Notice that there's a section in the tail that is shaded differently from the remainder of the curve. That section is bounded on the right at the value 46.2. That value separates the section in the left tail of the right curve from the rest of the curve.

Over the course of many samples from a population whose mean is 55, some samples will have mean values less than 55, some will be less than 50, some more than 60, and so on. Because we know the mean of the curve—the grand mean of those many samples—is 55 and the standard error of the mean is 5, the mathematics of the t-distribution tells us that 5% of the sample means will be less than or equal to 46.2. (For convenience, the remainder of this discussion will round 46.2 off to 46. Maybe one of the turtles lied about his age.)

That 5% is the alpha—the error rate—you have adopted. It is represented visually in Figure 8.7 by the shaded area in the left tail of the right curve. If your sample, the one that you actually take, has a mean of 46 or less, you have decided to conclude that the sample did not come from a distribution that represents the null hypothesis. Instead, you will conclude that the sample came from the distribution that represents your alternative hypothesis.

The value 46 in this example is called the *critical value*. It is the criterion associated with the error rate, so in this case if you get a sample mean of 46 or less, you reject the null hypothesis. You know that with a sample mean of 46 or less there's still a 5% chance that the null hypothesis is true, but you have decided that's a risk you're willing to run.

Finding the Critical Value for a z-Test

The prior section on z-tests did not discuss how to find the critical value that cut off 5% of the area under the curve. Instead, it simply noted that a value equal to or less than the sample mean of 45 would occur only 2.275% of the time if the null hypothesis were true.

If you knew the population standard deviation and wanted to use a z-test, you should determine the critical value for alpha—just as though you did not know the standard deviation and were therefore using a t-test. But in the case of a z-test, you would use the normal distribution, not the t distribution. In Excel you could find the critical value with the NORM.INV() function:

=NORM.INV(0.05,55,5)

The general rule for statistical distribution functions in Excel is that if the name ends in DIST, the function returns an area (interpreted as a probability). If the name ends in INV, the function returns a value along the horizontal axis of the distribution. Here, we're interested in determining the critical value: the value on the horizontal axis that cuts off 5% of the area under the normal curve.

So, we supply as the arguments to NORM.INV() these values:

- **.05**—The area we're interested in under the curve that represents the distribution.
- **55**—The mean of the distribution.
- **5**—The standard error of the mean: the standard deviation of the individual values, 20, divided by the square root of the sample size, 16.

The NORM.INV() function, given those arguments, returns 46.776. If the mean of your sample is less than that figure, you are in the 5% area of the distribution that represents the null hypothesis and, given your decision rule of adopting a .05 error rate as alpha, you can reject the null hypothesis.

Finding the Critical Value for a t-Test

If you don't know the population standard deviation and therefore are using a t-test instead of a z-test, the logic is the same but the mechanics a little different. The function you use is T.INV() rather than NORM.INV() because the t-distribution is different from the normal distribution.

Here's how you would use T.INV() in this situation:

=T.INV(0.05,15)

That formula returns a t value such that 5% of the area under the t-distribution lies to its left, just as NORM.INV() can return a z value such that 5% of the area under a normal distribution lies to its left.

However, NORM.INV() returns the critical value in the scale you define when you supply the mean and the standard deviation as two of its arguments. T.INV() is not so accommodating, and you have to see to the scale conversion yourself.

You tell T.INV() what area, or probability, you're interested in. That's the 0.05 argument in the preceding example. You also tell it the number of degrees of freedom. That's the 15 in the example. Your sample size is 16, from which you subtract 1 to get the degrees of freedom. (Recall that the shape of t-distributions varies with the degrees of freedom, so the area to the left of a given critical value does so as well.)

It's easy to convert the scale of t values to the scale you're interested in. In this example, we know that the standard error of the mean is $s/\sqrt{N}$, or 20 / 4, or 5—just as was supplied to NORM.INV(). We also know that the mean of the distribution that represents the null hypothesis is 55. So it's merely a matter of multiplying the t value by the standard error and adding the mean:

    =T.INV(0.05,15)*5+55

That formula returns the value 46.234. But the formula using NORM.INV() returned 46.776. So if you're running a t-test, you need a sample mean—a critical value—of at most 46.234 to reject the null hypothesis. If you're running a z-test, your sample mean can be as high as 46.776, as shown in the prior section.

Comparing the Critical Values

Step back a moment and review the purpose of this analysis. You know, or assume, that the world's sea turtle population has a mean age of 55. You suspect that the mean age of sea turtles in the Gulf of Mexico is 45. You have adopted an alpha level of 0.05 as protection against falsely rejecting the null hypothesis that the mean age of Gulf turtles is 55, the same as the rest of the world's sea turtles.

The preceding two sections have shown that if your sample mean is 46.776 and you're running a z-test, you can reject the null hypothesis knowing that your chance of going wrong is 5%. If you're running a t-test, your sample mean must be slightly farther away from the null's value of 55. It must be at most 46.234, about half a year younger than 46.776, if you are to reject the null with your specified alpha of 0.05.

If you glance back at Figure 8.6, you'll see that the tails of the t-distribution are slightly thicker than the tails of the normal distribution. That affords more headroom in the tails for area under the curve, and an area such as 5% is bounded by a critical value that's farther from the mean than is the case with the normal distribution. You have to go farther from the mean to get into that 5% area, and therefore reject the null hypothesis, when you use a t-test. That means that the t-test has slightly less statistical power than the z-test. The section "Understanding Statistical Power," which appears shortly, has more on that concept.

Rejecting the Null Hypothesis

Just looking at Figure 8.7, you can see that a sample with a mean value that's less than 46 is much more likely to come from the left curve, which represents your alternative hypothesis, than from the right curve, which represents your null hypothesis. A sample with a mean less than 46 is much more likely to come from the curve whose mean is 46 than from the curve whose mean is 55. Therefore, it's rational to conclude that the sample came from the left distribution in Figure 8.7. If so, the null hypothesis—in this case, that the right distribution reflects the true state of nature—should be rejected.

But there is some probability that a sample mean of 46 or less can come from the right curve. That probability in this example is 5%. Your alpha is 5%; you often see this expressed as "Your Type I error rate is 5%." (You'll see this stated in research reports as "p < .05" and as the "level of significance." It's that usage that led to the horribly ambiguous term *statistical significance*.)

Understanding Statistical Power

Figure 8.8 shows the other side of the alpha coin. Notice the area under the left curve that is shaded. That shaded area is to the left of the critical value of 46. In contrast, in Figure 8.7, the shaded, alpha area is to the left of the critical value in the *right* curve.

Figure 8.8
The sample mean appears within the area that represents the statistical power of this t-test.

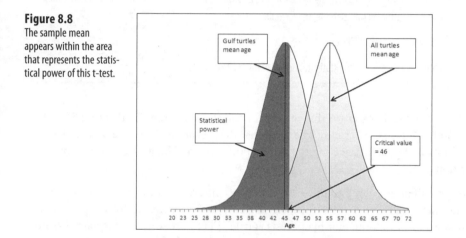

Suppose that the alternative hypothesis is true, and that Gulf turtles have a mean age of 45 years. Some of the possible samples you might take from the Gulf have a mean age greater than 46. You have already identified that number, 46, as the critical value associated with an alpha of .05, of a probability of rejecting the null hypothesis when it is true.

So a sample mean that's less than 46 causes you to reject the null hypothesis. If the null hypothesis is false, then the alternative must be true: The mean age of Gulf turtles is less than the mean age of the population of all sea turtles. Getting a sample mean that's less than 46 in this example would then represent a correct decision. That's termed *statistical power*.

You can quantify statistical power by looking to the curve that represents the alternative hypothesis; in all the figures shown so far in this chapter, that's the left curve. You want to know the area under the curve that's to the left of the critical value of 46. In this case, the power is 58%. Given the hypotheses you have set up, the value of the sample mean, and the size of the standard error of the mean, you have a 58% chance of correctly rejecting the null hypothesis.

Notice that the statistical power depends on the position of the left curve (more generally, the curve that represents the alternative hypothesis) with respect to the critical value. In this example, the farther to the left that this curve is placed, the more of it falls to the left

8

of the critical value (here, 46). The probability of obtaining a sample mean lower than 46 increases, and therefore the statistical power—which is exactly that probability—increases.

> **NOTE** This book goes into greater detail on the topic of statistical power in Chapter 9, but the quickest way to calculate, in Excel, the power of this t-test is by using the formula
>
> =T.DIST(t-statistic,df,TRUE)
>
> where the *t-statistic* is the critical value less the sample mean divided by the standard error of the mean, *df* is the degrees of freedom for the test, and *TRUE* calls for Excel to return the cumulative area under the curve. In this example, the formula
>
> =T.DIST((46-45)/5,15,TRUE)
>
> returns .5779, or 58%, the statistical power of this particular t-test.

Notice that the statistical power (in this case 58%) and the alpha rate (in this case 5%) do not total to 100%. Intuitively it's easy to expect that they'd sum to 100% because power is the probability of correctly rejecting the null hypothesis, and alpha is the probability of incorrectly doing so.

But the two probabilities belong to different curves, to different states of nature. Power is pertinent and quantifiable only when the alternative hypothesis is true. Alpha is pertinent and quantifiable only when the null hypothesis is true. Therefore, there is no special reason to expect that they would sum to 100%—they are properties of and describe different realities.

As the next section shows, though, there is a quantity that together with statistical power comprises 100% of the possibilities when the alternative hypothesis is true.

Statistical Power and Beta

You will sometimes see a reference to another sort of error rate, termed *beta*. Alpha, as just discussed, is the probability that you will reject a true null hypothesis, and is sometimes termed Type I error. Beta is also an error rate, but it is the probability that you will reject a true *alternative* hypothesis. The prior section explained that statistical power is the probability that you will reject a false null hypothesis, and therefore accept a true alternative hypothesis.

So beta is 1 – power. If the power of your statistical test is 58%, so that you will accept a true alternative hypothesis 58% of the time, then beta is 42%, and you will mistakenly reject a true alternative hypothesis 42% of the time. This latter type of error, rejecting a true alternative hypothesis, is sometimes called a *Type II* error.

Figure 8.9 illustrates the relationship between statistical power and beta.

Figure 8.9
Together, power and beta account for the entire area under the curve that represents the alternative hypothesis.

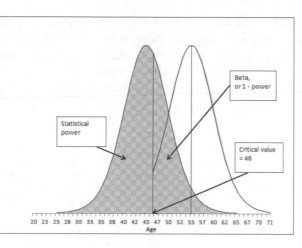

Manipulating the Error Rate

The specification of the alpha error rate is completely under your control. You can choose to set alpha at, for example, .01. In that case, only 1% of the area under the right curve would be in the shaded section, and the critical value—the value that divides alpha from the remainder of the right curve—moves accordingly. Figure 8.10 shows the result of changing alpha from .05, as in Figure 8.7, to .01.

Figure 8.10
Reducing alpha reduces the likelihood of rejecting a true null hypothesis.

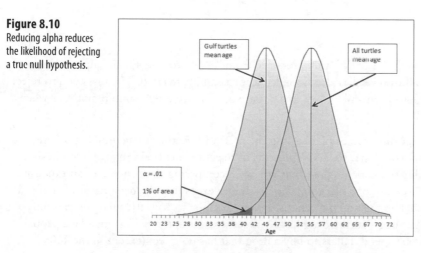

If you want to provide more protection against rejecting the null hypothesis when it's true, you can simply adopt a smaller value of alpha. In Figure 8.10, for example, alpha has been reduced to .01 from the .05 that's shown in Figure 8.7.

But notice that reducing alpha from .05 to .01 has an effect on the power of the t-test. Reducing alpha moves the critical value, in this case, to the left, from 46 in Figure 8.7 to 42 in Figure 8.10. Pushing the critical value to the left, to 42, makes it necessary for the sample mean to come in below 42 to reject the null hypothesis. That reduces the statistical power. But with alpha at .05, you can reject the null hypothesis if the sample mean is as high as 46. See the power as displayed in Figure 8.11, and compare it to Figure 8.8.

Figure 8.11
Compare to Figure 8.8, which shows the power of the t-test when alpha is set to .05.

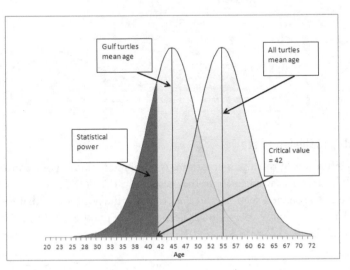

In Figure 8.11, with the critical value reduced from Age 46 to Age 42, and alpha reduced from .05 to .01, the power has also been reduced. A sample mean of 45 causes you to reject the null hypothesis when alpha is set to .05, but you don't reject the null hypothesis when alpha is set to .01.

This illustrates the importance of assessing the costs of rejecting a true null hypothesis (with a probability of alpha) vis-à-vis the costs of rejecting a true alternative hypothesis (with a probability of beta). Suppose that you were comparing the benefits of an expensive drug treatment to those of a placebo. The possibility exists that the drug has no beneficial effect—that would be the null hypothesis. If you set alpha to, say, .01, then you run only a 1% chance of deciding that the drug has an effect when it doesn't. That may save people money: They won't spend dollars to buy a drug that has no effect (except in the 1% of the time that you mistakenly reject the null hypothesis).

On the other hand, reducing alpha from .05 to .01 also reduces statistical power and makes it less likely that you will reject the null hypothesis when it is false. Then, when the drug has a beneficial effect, you stand a poorer chance of reaching the correct conclusion. You may well prevent people who could have been helped by the drug from taking it, because you will not have rejected a false null hypothesis.

Over the past 100 years it has become more a matter of tradition and convenience to use alpha levels of .01 and .05. It takes some extra work to assess the relative costs of committing either type of error, but it's worth it if your decision is based on cost-benefit analysis instead of on tradition. And because Excel makes it so easy to determine these probabilities, convenience is no excuse: You no longer need rely on tables that show critical values for only the the .01 and .05 significance levels of t-distributions with different degrees of freedom.

Chapter 9 goes more fully into using Excel's worksheet functions, particularly T.DIST(), T.DIST.RT, and T.DIST.2T, to determine those probabilities based on issues such as the directionality of your hypotheses, your choice of alpha level, and sample sizes.

8

Testing Differences Between Means: Further Issues

There are several ways to test the likelihood that the difference between two group means is due to chance, and not all of them involve a t-test. Even limiting the scope to a t-test, three general approaches are available to you in Excel:

- The T.DIST() and T.INV() functions
- The T.TEST() function
- The Data Analysis add-in

This chapter illustrates each of these approaches. You'll want to know about the T.TEST() function because it's so quick (if not broadly informative). You might decide never to use the T.DIST() and T.INV() functions directly, but you should know how to use them because they can show you step by step what's going on in the t-test. And you'll want to know how to use the Data Analysis t-test tool because it's more informative than T.TEST() and quicker to set up than T.DIST() and T.INV().

Using Excel's T.DIST() and T.INV() Functions to Test Hypotheses

The Excel 2010 worksheet functions that apply to the t-distribution are dramatically different from those in Excel 2007 and earlier. The differences have to do primarily with whether you assign alpha to the left tail of the t-distribution, the right tail, or both. Recall from Chapter 8, "Testing Differences Between Means: The Basics," that alpha, the probability of rejecting a true null hypothesis, is entirely under your control. (Beta, the probability of rejecting a true alternative hypothesis, is not fully under your control because it depends in part on the population mean if the alternative hypothesis is true—again, see Chapter 8 for more on that matter.)

As I structured the examples in Chapter 8, you suspected at the outset that the mean age of your sample of turtles from the Gulf of Mexico would be less than a hypothesized value of 55 years. You put the entire alpha into the left tail of the curve on the right (see, for example, Figure 8.7). When you adopt this approach, you reject the possibility that the alternative could exist at the other end of the null distribution.

In that example, by placing all the error probability into the left tail of the null distribution, you assumed that Gulf turtles are not on average older than the total population of turtles: Their mean is either smaller than (the alternative hypothesis) or not reliably different from (the null hypothesis) the mean of the total population. This is called a *one-tailed* or a *directional* hypothesis.

On the other hand, when you make a *two-tailed* or *nondirectional* hypothesis, your alternative hypothesis does not specify whether one group's mean will be larger or smaller than that of the other group. The null hypothesis is the same, no difference in the population means, but the alternative hypothesis is something such as "The population mean for the experimental group is different from the population mean for the control group"—"different from" rather than "less than" or "greater than."

The difference between directional and nondirectional hypotheses might seem picayune, but it makes a major difference to the statistical power of your t-tests.

Making Directional and Nondirectional Hypotheses

The main benefit to making a directional hypothesis, as the example in Chapter 8 did, is that doing so increases the power of the statistical test. But there is also a responsibility you assume when you make a directional hypothesis.

Suppose that, just as in Chapter 8, you made a directional hypothesis about the mean age of Gulf turtles: that their mean age would be lower than that of all sea turtles. Presumably you had good reason for this hypothesis, that the oil spill there in 2010 would have a harmful effect on turtles, killing older turtles disproportionately. Your null hypothesis, of course, is that there is no difference in the mean ages.

You put all 5% of the alpha into the left tail of the distribution that represents the null hypothesis, as shown in Figure 8.7, and doing so results in a critical value of 46. A sample mean above 46 means that you continue to regard the null hypothesis as tenable (while recognizing that you might be missing a genuine difference). A sample mean below 46 means that you reject the null hypothesis (while recognizing that you might be doing so erroneously).

But what if you get a sample mean of 64? That's as far above the null hypothesis mean of 55 as the critical value of 46 is below it. Given your null hypothesis that the Gulf mean and the population mean are both 55, isn't it as unlikely that you'd get a sample mean of 64 as that you'd get one of 46?

Yes, it is, but that's irrelevant. When you adopted your alternative hypothesis, you made it a directional one. Your alternative stated that the mean age of Gulf turtles is less than, not equal to, and not more than, the mean age of the rest of the world's population of turtles. And you adopted a 0.05 alpha level.

Now you obtain a sample mean of 64. If you therefore reject your null hypothesis, you are changing your alpha level after the fact. You are changing it from 0.05 to 0.10, because you are putting half your alpha into the left tail of the distribution that represents the null hypothesis, and half into the right tail. Because 5% of the distribution is in the left tail, 5% must also be in the right tail, and your total alpha is not 0.05 but 0.10.

Okay, then why not change things so that the left tail contains 2.5% of the area under the curve and the right tail does too? Then you're back to a total alpha level of 5%.

But then you've changed the critical value. You've moved it farther away from the mean, so that it cuts off not 5% of the area under the curve, but 2.5%. And the same comment applies to the right tail. The critical values are now not 46 and 64, but 44 and 66, and you can't reject the null hypothesis whether you get a sample mean of 45 or 65.

You can see the kind of logical and mathematical difficulties you can get into if you don't follow the rules. Decide whether you want to make a directional or nondirectional hypothesis. Decide on an alpha level. Make those decisions before you start seeing results, and stick with them. You'll sleep better. And you won't leave yourself open to a charge that you stacked the deck.

Using Hypotheses to Guide Excel's t-Distribution Functions

This section shows you how to choose an Excel function to best fit your null and alternative hypotheses. The previous chapter's example entailed a single group t-test, which compared a sample mean to a hypothetical value. This section discusses a slightly more complicated example, which involves not one but two groups.

Figure 9.1 shows scores on a paper-and-pencil driving test, in cells B2:C11. Participants, who were all ticketed for minor traffic infractions, were selected randomly and randomly assigned to either an experimental group that attended a class on traffic laws or a control group that did nothing special.

Figure 9.1

Note from the Name box that the range B2:B11 has been named ExpGroup.

	A	B	C	D	E	F	G
		ExpGroup	▾		f_x	62	
1		Experimental Group	Control Group		Sum of Squares Within	5431.2	=DEVSQ(ExpGroup)+DEVSQ(ControlGroup)
2		62	65		Pooled within groups variance	301.73333	=F1/(COUNT(ExpGroup)-1+COUNT(ControlGroup)-1)
3		60	60		Standard Error of difference in means	7.768	=SQRT(F2*(1/10+1/10))
4		45	77		t	2.240	=(B13-C13)/F3
5		67	37		Critical value	1.734	=T.INV(0.95,18)
6		90	26		p(t[18])	0.019	=1-T.DIST(F4,18,TRUE)
7		82	13		p(t[18])	0.019	=T.TEST(ExpGroup,ControlGroup,1,2)
8		46	58				
9		63	61				
10		60	46				
11		77	35				
12							
13	Mean	65.2	47.8				

Making a Directional Hypothesis

Suppose first that the researcher believes that the class could have increased the test scores but could not have decreased them. The researcher makes the directional hypothesis that the experimental group will have a larger mean than the control group. The null hypothesis is that there is no difference between the groups as assessed by the test.

The researcher also decides to adopt a 0.05 alpha rate for the experiment. It costs $100 per student to deliver the training, but the normal procedures such as flagging a driver's license cost only $5 per participant. Therefore, the researcher wants to hold the probability of deciding the program has an effect, when it really doesn't, to one chance in 20, which is equivalent to an alpha rate of 0.05.

After the class was finished, both groups took a multiple choice test, with the results shown in Figure 9.1.

This researcher believes in running a t-test by taking the long way around, and there's a lot to be said for that. By taking things one step at a time, it's possible to look at the results of each step and see if anything looks irrational. In turn, if there's a problem, it's easier to diagnose, find, and fix if you're doing the analysis step by step.

Here's an overview of what the researcher does at this point. Remember that the alpha level has already been chosen, the directionality of the hypothesis has been set (the experimental group is expected to do better, not just differently, on the test than the control group), and the data has been collected and entered as in Figure 9.1. These are the remaining steps:

1. For convenience, give names to the ranges of scores in B2:B11 and C12:C11 in Figure 9.1.
2. Recalling from Chapter 3, "Variability: How Values Disperse," that the variance is the average squared deviation from the mean, calculate and total up the squared deviations from each group's mean.
3. Get the pooled variance from the squared deviations calculated in step 2.
4. Calculate the standard error of the mean differences from the pooled variance.
5. Calculate the t-statistic using the observed mean difference and the result of step 4.
6. Use T.INV() to obtain the critical t-statistic.
7. Compare the t-statistic to the critical t-statistic. If the computed t-statistic is smaller than the critical t-statistic for an alpha of 0.05, regard the null hypothesis as tenable. Otherwise, reject the null hypothesis.

The next few sections explore each of these seven steps in more detail.

Step 1: Name the Score Ranges   To make it easier to refer to the data ranges, begin by naming them. There are various ways to name a range, and some ways offer different options than others. The simplest method is the one used here. Select the range B2:B11, click in the Name box (at the left end of the Formula Bar), and type the name **ExpGroup**. Press Enter. Select C2:C11, click in the Name box, and type the name **ControlGroup**. Press Enter.

Step 2: Calculate the Total of the Squared Deviations You are after what's called a *pooled* variance in order to carry out the t-test. You have two groups, the experimental and the control, and each has a different mean. According to the null hypothesis, both groups can be thought of as coming from the same population, and differences in the group means and the group standard deviations are due to nothing more than sampling error.

However, much of the sampling error that exists can be mitigated to some degree by pooling the variability in each group. That process begins by calculating the sum of the squared deviations of the experimental group scores around their mean, and the sum of the squared deviations of the control group scores around their mean.

Excel provides a worksheet function to do this: DEVSQ(). The formula

=DEVSQ(B2:B11)

calculates the mean of the values in B2:B11, subtracts each of the ten values from their mean, squares the results, and totals them. If you don't trust me, and if you don't trust DEVSQ(), you could instead use this array formula (don't forget to enter it with Ctrl+Shift+Enter):

=SUM((B2:B11-AVERAGE(B2:B11))^2)

Using the names already assigned to the score ranges, the formula

=DEVSQ(ExpGroup)+DEVSQ(ControlGroup)

returns the total of the squared deviations from the experimental group's mean, plus the total of the squared deviations from the control group's mean.

The result of this step appears in cell F1 of Figure 9.1. The formula itself, entered as text, is shown in cell G1.

Step 3: Calculate the Pooled Variance Again, the variance can be thought of as the average of the squared deviations from the mean. We can calculate a pooled variance using the total squared deviations with this formula:

=F1/(COUNT(ExpGroup)-1+COUNT(ControlGroup)-1)

That formula uses the sum of the squared deviations, in cell F1, as its numerator. The formula divides that sum by the number of scores in the Experimental group, plus the number of scores in the Control group, less one for each group.

That's why I just said that the variance "can be thought of" as the average squared deviation. It can be helpful conceptually to think of it in that way. But using Excel's COUNT() function, you divide by the group size minus 1, instead of by the actual count, so the computed variance is not quite equal to the conceptual variance. The difference becomes smaller and smaller as the group size increases, of course.

If you think back to Chapter 3, which discussed the reason to divide by the degrees of freedom instead of by the actual count, you'll recall that the formula loses one degree of freedom because calculating the mean (and sticking to that mean as the deviations are calculated) exerts a constraint on the values. In this case, we're dealing with two groups, hence two means, and we lose two (not just one) degrees of freedom in the denominator of the variance.

NOTE   Why not use the overall variance of the two groups combined? If that were appropriate, you could use the single formula

=VAR.S(B2:C11)

to get the variance of all 20 values. In fact, we want to divide, or *partition*, that total variance in two: one component that is due to the difference between the means of the groups, and one component that is due to the variability of individual scores around each group's mean. It's that latter, "within-groups" variance that we're after here. Using the deviations of all the observations from the grand mean does not result in a purely within-group variance estimate.

Step 4: Getting the Standard Error of the Difference in Means   Let's recall Chapter 3 once again: The standard error of the mean is a special kind of standard deviation. It is the standard deviation that you would calculate if you took samples from a population, calculated the mean of each sample, and then calculated the standard deviation of those means. Although that's the definition, you can estimate the standard error of the mean from just one sample: It is the standard deviation of your single sample divided by the square root of its sample size. Similarly, you can estimate the variance error of the mean by dividing the variance of your sample by the sample size.

The standard error of the mean is the proper divisor to use when you have only one mean to test against a known or hypothesized value, such as the example in Chapter 8 where the mean of a sample was tested against a known population parameter.

In the present case, though, you have two groups, not just one, and the proper divisor is not the standard error of the mean, but the standard error of the *difference* between two means. That is the value that the first steps in this process have been working toward. As a result of step 3, you have the pooled within-groups variance.

To convert the pooled variance to the variance error, you must divide the pooled within-groups variance by the sample sizes of both groups. Because, as you'll see, the groups may consist of different numbers of subjects, the more general formula is as follows, where N as usual indicates the sample size:

$$s_w^2 \left(1/N_1 + 1/N_2 \right)$$

(The formula, of course, simplifies if both groups have the same number of subjects. And as you'll also see, an equal number of subjects also makes the interpretation of the statistical test more straightforward.)

That prior equation returns the variance error of the difference between two means. To get the standard error of the difference, as shown in cell F3 of Figure 9.1, simply take its square root:

$$\sqrt{s_w^2 \left(1/N_1 + 1/N_2 \right)}$$

Step 5: Calculate the t-Statistic   This step takes less time than any other, assuming that you've done the proper groundwork. Just subtract one group mean from the other and divide the result by the standard error of the mean difference. You'll find the formula and the result for this example, 2.24, in cell F4 of Figure 9.1.

It's an easy step to take but it's one that masks some minor complexity, and that can be a little confusing at first. Except in the very unlikely event that both groups have the same mean value, the t-statistic will be positive or negative depending on whether you subtract the larger mean from the smaller or vice versa.

It can happen that you'll get a large, negative t-statistic when your hypotheses led you to expect either a positive one or no reliable difference. For example, you might test an auto tire that you expect to raise mileage, and you phrase your alternative hypothesis accordingly. But when the results come in and you subtract the control group mean mpg from the experimental group mean mpg, you wind up with a negative number, hence a negative t-statistic. It gets worse if the t-statistic is something like –5.1: a value that is highly improbable if the null hypothesis is true.

That kind of result is more likely due to confused logic or incorrect math than it is to an inherently improbable research outcome. So, if it occurs, the first thing you should do is verify that you phrased your hypotheses to conform to your understanding of the treatment effect. Then you should check your math—including the way that you presented the data to Excel's functions and tools. If you've handled those matters correctly, all you can do is swallow your surprise, continue to entertain the null hypothesis, and plan your next experiment using the knowledge you've gained in the present one.

Be careful about this sort of thing if and when you use the Data Analysis t-test tools. They subtract whatever values you designate as Variable 2 from the values you designate as Variable 1. It doesn't matter to that tool whether your alternative hypothesis is that Variable 2's mean will be larger, or Variable 1's. Variable 2 is always subtracted from Variable 1. It's helpful to be aware of this when you apply the Variable 1 and Variable 2 designations.

Step 6: Determine the Critical Value Using T.INV()   You need to know the critical value of t: the value that you'll compare to the t-statistic you calculated in step 5. To get that value, you need to know the degrees of freedom and the alpha level you have adopted.

The degrees of freedom is easy. It's the denominator of the standard error of the mean difference: that is, it's the total sample size of both groups, minus 2. This example has ten observations in each group, so the degrees of freedom is 10 + 10 – 2, or 18.

You have already specified an alpha of 0.05 and a directional alternative hypothesis that states the experimental group will have a higher mean than the control group. The situation appears graphically in Figure 9.2.

Figure 9.2
This directional hypothesis places all of alpha in the right tail of the left distribution.

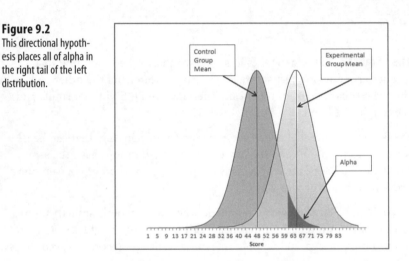

To find the value that divides the alpha area from the rest of the left distribution, enter this formula:

=T.INV(0.95,18)

That formula returns 1.73, the critical value for this situation, the smallest value that your calculated t-statistic can be if you are to reject the null hypothesis at your chosen level of alpha.

Notice that your alpha is .05 but the formula uses .95 as the first argument to the T.INV() function. The T.INV() function (as well as the TINV() compatibility function) returns the t value for which the percent under the curve lies to the left. In this case, 95% of the area of the t-distribution with 18 degrees of freedom lies to the left of the t value 1.73. Therefore, 5% of the area under the curve lies to the right of 1.73, and that 5% is your alpha rate.

To convert the t value to the scale of measurement used on the chart's horizontal axis, just multiply the t value by the standard error of the mean differences and add the control group mean. Those values are shown in Figure 9.1, in cells F3 (standard error) and C13 (control mean). The result is a value of 61, in this example's original scale of measurement.

Suppose that your treatment was not intended to improve drivers' scores on a test on traffic laws but their golf scores. Your null hypothesis, as before, would probably be that the post-treatment mean scores are the same, if the treatment were administered to the full population. But your alternative hypothesis might well be that the treatment group's mean score is *lower* than that of the control group. With the same alpha rate as before, 0.05, the change in the direction of your alternative hypothesis is shown in Figure 9.3.

Figure 9.3
The experimental group's mean still exceeds the critical value.

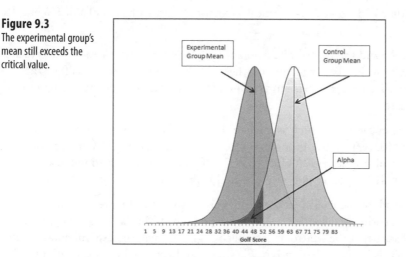

Now, the critical value of t that divides the alpha area from the rest of the area under the control group's distribution of sample means has 5% of the area to its left, not 95% as in the prior example. You can find out what the t value is by using this formula:

=T.INV(.05,18)

The alpha rate is the same in both examples, and both examples use a directional hypothesis. The degrees of freedom is the same in both cases. The sole difference is the direction of the alternative hypothesis—in Figure 9.3 you expect the experimental group's mean to be lower, not higher, than that of the control group.

One way to deal with this situation is as shown in Figure 9.3. The area that represents alpha is placed in the left tail of the control group's distribution, bordered by the critical value that separates the 5% alpha area from the remaining 95% of the area under the curve. When you want 5% of the area to appear to the left of the critical value, you would use 0.05 as the first argument to T.INV(). When you want 95% of the area to appear to the left of the critical value, use 95% as the first argument. T.INV() responds with the critical value that you specify with the probability you're interested in, along with the degrees of freedom that defines the shape of the curve.

The t-distribution has a mean of zero and it is symmetric (although, as Chapter 8 discussed, it is not the same as the normal distribution). Earlier in this section you saw that the formula

=T.INV(0.95,18)

returns 1.73. Because the t-distribution has a zero mean and is symmetric, the formula

=T.INV(0.05,18)

returns −1.73. Either 1.73 or −1.73 is a critical value for a t-test with an alpha of 5% and 18 degrees of freedom.

I included Figure 9.3 and the related discussion of the placement of the area that represents alpha primarily to provide a better picture of where and how your hypotheses affect the placement of alpha. This chapter gets more deeply into that matter when it takes up nondirectional hypotheses.

But suppose you're in a situation such as the one shown in Figure 9.3. As it's set up, you might subtract the (larger) control group mean from the (smaller) experimental group mean and compare the result to the critical value of −1.73. If you got a calculated t-statistic that is farther from 0 than −1.73, you would reject the null hypothesis.

But you could also adopt the viewpoint that things are as shown in Figure 9.2, except that the labels for the experimental and control group are swapped. Your alternative hypothesis could just as well state that the control group mean is greater than the experimental group. If you do that, alpha is located where it is in Figure 9.2 and you need not deal with negative critical values for t.

Step 7: Compare the t-Statistic to the Critical t-Statistic   You calculated the observed t-statistic as 2.24 in step 5. You obtained the critical value of 1.73 in step 6. Your observed t-statistic is larger than the critical value and so you reject the null hypothesis with 95% confidence (that 95% is, of course, 1 − alpha).

Completing the Picture with T.DIST()

So far this section has discussed the use of the T.INV() function to get a critical value, given an alpha and degrees of freedom. The other side of that coin is represented by the T.DIST(), the T.DIST.RT(), and the T.DIST.2T() functions.

When you use one of those three T.DIST functions, you specify a critical value rather than an alpha value. You still must supply the degrees of freedom. Here's the syntax for T.DIST():

=T.DIST(x, df, cumulative)

where *x* is a t value, *df* is the degrees of freedom, and *cumulative* specifies whether you want all the area under the curve to the left of the t-statistic or the probability associated with that t-statistic itself (that's the relative height of the curve at the point defined by the t statistic). So, using the figures from the prior section, the formula

=T.DIST(1.73,18,TRUE)

returns 0.95. Ninety-five percent of the area under a t-distribution with 18 degrees of freedom lies to the left of a t value of 1.73.

Because the t-distribution is symmetric, both the formulas

=1 - T.DIST(1.73,18,TRUE)

and

=T.DIST(-1.73,18,TRUE)

return 0.05, and you might want to use them if your hypotheses were as suggested in Figure 9.3—that is, alpha is in the left tail of the control group's distribution. If your situation were similar to that shown in Figure 9.2, with alpha in the right tail of the control group distribution, you might find it more convenient to use this form of T.DIST():

=T.DIST.RT(1.73,18)

It also returns 0.05. Using the .RT as part of the function's name indicates to Excel that you're interested in the area in the right tail of the t-distribution. Notice that there is no cumulative argument as there is in T.DIST(). The function assumes that you want to obtain the cumulative area to the right of the critical value. Again, because of the symmetry of the t-distribution, you can get the curve's height at 1.73 by using this (which you would also use for its height at −1.73):

=T.DIST(1.73,18,FALSE)

The final form of the T.DIST() function is T.DIST.2T(), which returns the *combined* areas in the left and right tails of the t distribution. It's useful when you are making a nondirectional hypothesis (see Figure 9.5 in the next section). The syntax is

=T.DIST.2T(x, df)

where, again, x refers to the t value and df to the degrees of freedom, and there is no cumulative argument. This usage of the function

=T.DIST.2T(1.73,18)

returns 0.10. That's because 5% of the area under the t-distribution with 18 degrees of freedom lies to the right of 1.73, and 5% lies to the left of −1.73. I do not believe you will find that you have much use for T.DIST.2T, in large measure because with nondirectional hypotheses you are as interested in a negative t value as a positive one, and T.DIST.2T, like

9

the pre-2010 function TDIST(), cannot cope with a negative value as its first argument. It is more straightforward to use T.DIST() and T.DIST.RT().

Using the T.TEST() Function

The T.TEST() function is a quick way to arrive at the probability of a t-statistic that it calculates for you. In that sense, it differs from T.DIST(), which requires you to supply your own t-statistic and degrees of freedom; then, T.DIST() returns the associated probability. And T.INV() returns the t-value that's associated with a given probability and degrees of freedom.

Regardless of the function you want to use, you must always supply the degrees of freedom, either directly in T.DIST() and T.INV() or indirectly, as you'll see, in T.TEST(). The next section discusses how degrees of freedom in two-group tests differs from degrees of freedom in Chapter 8's one-group tests.

Degrees of Freedom in Excel Functions

Regardless of the Excel function you use to get information about a t-distribution, you must always specify the number of degrees of freedom. As discussed in Chapter 8, this is because t-distributions with different degrees of freedom have different shapes. And when two distributions have different shapes, the areas that account for, say, 5% of the area under the curve have different boundaries, also termed *critical values*.

For example, in a t-distribution with 5 degrees of freedom, 5% of its area lies to the right of a t-statistic of 2.01. In a t-distribution with six degrees of freedom, 5% of its area lies to the right of a t-statistic of 1.94. (As the number of degrees of freedom increases, the t-distribution becomes more and more similar to the normal distribution.)

> **NOTE**
> You can check me on those figures by using T.INV(.95,5) and T.INV(.95,6).

So you must tell Excel how many degrees of freedom are involved in your particular t-test. When you estimate a population standard deviation from a sample, the sample size is N and the number of degrees of freedom is N – 1. The degrees of freedom in a t-test is calculated similarly.

In the case of a t-test, N means the number of cases in a group. So if you are testing the mean of one sample against a hypothesized value (as was done in Chapter 8), the degrees of freedom to use in the t-test is the number of records in the sample, minus one. If you are testing the mean of one sample against the mean of another sample (as was done in the prior section), the degrees of freedom for the test is $N_1 + N_2 - 2$: You lose one degree of freedom for each group's mean.

Equal and Unequal Group Sizes

There is no reason you cannot run a t-test on groups that contain different numbers of observations. That statement applies no matter whether you use T.DIST() and T.INV() or T.TEST(). If you work your way once again through the examples provided in this chapter's first section, you'll see that there is no calculation that requires both groups to have the same number of cases.

However, there are two issues that pertain to the use of equal group sizes in t-tests. These are discussed in detail later in this chapter, but here's a brief overview.

Dependent Groups t-Tests

Sometimes you want to use a t-test on two groups whose members can be paired in some way. For example, you might want to compare the mean score of one group of people before and after a treatment. In that case, you can pair Joe's pretest score with his posttest score, Mary's pretest score with her posttest score, and so on.

If you take to heart the discussion of experimental design in Chapter 6, "Telling the Truth with Statistics," you won't regard a simple pretest-posttest comparison as necessarily a valid experiment. But if you have arranged for a proper comparison group, you can run a t-test on the pretest scores versus the posttest scores. The t-test takes the pairing of observations into account. And because each pretest score can be paired with a posttest score, your two groups by definition have the same number of observations—you'll see next why that's important.

Other ways that you might want to pair the observations in two groups include family relationships such as father-son and brother-sister, and members of pairs matched on some other variable who are then randomly assigned to one of the two groups in the t-test.

The Data Analysis add-in has a tool that performs a dependent groups t-test. The add-in refers to it as T-Test: Paired Two Sample for Means.

Unequal Group Variances

One of the assumptions of the t-test is that the populations from which the two groups are drawn have the same variance. Although that assumption is made, both empirical research and theoretical work have shown that violating the assumption makes little or no difference when the two groups are the same size.

However, suppose that the two populations have different variances—say, 30 and 10. If the two groups have different sample sizes and the larger group is sampled from the population with the larger variance, then the probability of mistakenly rejecting a true null hypothesis is *smaller* than T.DIST() would lead you to expect. If the larger group is sampled from the population with the smaller variance, the probability of mistakenly rejecting a true null hypothesis is *larger* than you would otherwise expect.

Figure 9.4 shows what can happen.

Figure 9.4
Different group sizes and different variances combine to increase or decrease the standard error of mean differences.

	A	B	C	D	E	F	G	H	I	J	K	L	M
1	Group 1	Group 2			Group 1	Group 2		Group 3	Group 4			Group 3	Group 4
2	1	15		N	30	10		3	1		N	30	10
3	0	6		Variance	10.1	30.2		2	5		Variance	30.2	10.1
4	8	8		Sum of Sq Dev	291.5	272.1		3	7		Sum of Sq Dev	875.9	90.5
5	2	1		Pooled Variance	14.7			4	0		Pooled Variance	25.3	
6	6	0		Variance Error	0.4			14	0		Variance Error	0.6	
7	3	12		Standard Error	0.6			3	0		Standard Error	0.8	
8	7	11						1	4				
9	5	1						11	9				
10	0	2						0	5				
11	9	1						1	4				
12	0							11					
13	7							14					
14	6							6					
15	9							0					
16	9							0					
17	2							18					
18	9							2					
19	1							14					
20	0							1					
21	5							2					
22	7							1					
23	1							11					
24	1							3					
25	5							11					
26	7							6					
27	1							1					
28	7							11					
29	6							2					
30	5							14					
31	6							2					

Individual scores in columns A and B are summarized in columns D through F. Group 1 has 30 observations and a variance of 10.0; Group 2 has 10 observations and a variance of 30.1. The larger group has the smaller variance.

Individual scores in columns H and I are summarized in columns L and M. Groups 3 and 4 have the same numbers of observations as 1 and 2, but their variability has been reversed: the larger group now has the larger variance.

Even though the group sizes are the same in both instances, and the variances are the same size, the standard error of the difference in means is noticeably smaller in cell E7 than it is in cell L7. That results in an *underestimate* of the standard error in the population. Group 1 has three times the observations as Group 2, and therefore its lower variability has a greater effect on the standard error in row 7 than does Group 2's larger variability. The net effect is, in the long run, an underestimate of the standard error in the population.

When the standard error is smaller, you do not need as large a difference between means to conclude that the observed difference is reliable, and that you are in the region of the curve where you will reject the null hypothesis. (See Figure 9.12 for a demonstration of that effect.) Because you tend to be working with an underestimate of the population variability in this situation—larger group, smaller variance—you will conclude that the difference is reliable more often than you think you will when the null hypothesis is false.

Now consider the situation shown in columns H through M in Figure 9.4. The larger group now has the larger variance. Because it has more observations, it once again contributes more of its variability to the eventual standard error calculation in cell L7. The effect is to make the standard error larger than otherwise; in fact, it is 25% larger than in cell E7.

Now the standard error will be larger than in the population in the long run. You will reject the null hypothesis less frequently than you think you will when it is false.

I have made the differences in group sizes and variances fairly dramatic in this example. One group is three times as large as the other, and one variance is three times as large as the other. These are differences that you're unlikely to encounter in actual empirical research. Even if you do, the effect is not a large one. However, it could make a difference, and Excel's T.TEST() function has an accepted method of handling the situation. See the subsequent section, "Using the Type Argument" for more information.

The Data Analysis add-in has a tool that incorporates the latter method. It is named T-Test: Two-Sample Assuming Unequal Variances.

Notice that because a dependent groups t-test by definition uses two groups that have equal sample sizes, the issue of unequal variances and error rate doesn't arise. Having equal group sizes means that you don't need to worry about the equal variance assumption.

The T.TEST() Syntax

The syntax for the T.TEST() function is

=T.TEST(Array1, Array2, Tails, Type)

This syntax is quite different from that for T.DIST() and T.INV(). There is no x argument, which is the t value that you supply to T.DIST(), and there is no probability argument, which is the area that you supply to T.INV(). Nor is there a degrees of freedom argument, as there is for both T.DIST() and T.INV().

The reason that those arguments are missing in T.TEST() is that you tell Excel where to find the raw data. If you were using T.TEST() with the problem shown in Figure 9.1, for example, you might supply B2:B11 as the Array1 argument, and C2:C11 as the Array2 argument. The fact that you are supplying the raw data to the T.TEST() function has these results:

■ The T.TEST() function is capable of doing the basic calculations itself. It can count the degrees of freedom because it knows how many values there are in Array1 and Array 2.

■ It can calculate the pooled within-groups variance and the standard error of the mean differences. It can calculate the mean of each array. Therefore, it can calculate a t-statistic.

■ Because it can calculate the t-statistic and degrees of freedom itself by looking at the two arrays, T.TEST() can and does return the probability of observing that calculated t-statistic in a t-distribution with that many degrees of freedom.

Identifying T.TEST() Arrays

The T.TEST() function returns only a probability level: the probability that you would observe a difference in the means of two groups as large as you have observed, assuming that there is no difference between the groups in the populations from which the samples came (in the example shown in Figure 9.1, between people who get the training and people who don't).

With the data as shown in Figure 9.1, you could enter this formula in some blank cell (in that figure it's in cell F6):

=T.TEST(ExpGroup,ControlGroup,1,2)

> **NOTE** If you're using Excel 2007 or earlier, use the compatibility function TTEST() instead (note the absence of the period in the function name).

Array1 and Array2 are two arrays of values whose means are being compared. In the example, Array1 is a range of cells that has been given the name ExpGroup; that range is B2:B11. Array2 is a range of cells that has been given the name ControlGroup, and it's C2:C11. The means and standard deviations of the two groups, calculated separately using the AVERAGE() and STDEV.S() functions, are in the range B13:C14. They are there strictly for your information; they have nothing to do with the T.TEST() function or its use.

Using the Tails Argument

The Tails argument concerns the directionality of your hypotheses. The present example assumes that the treatment will not decrease the score on a traffic test, compared to a control group. Therefore, the researcher expects that the experimental group will score well enough on the test that the only concern is whether the experimental mean is high enough that chance can be ruled out as an explanation for the outcome. The hypothesis is directional.

This situation is similar to the hypotheses that were used in the prior section, in which the experimenter believed that the treatment would leave the experimental group higher (or lower) on the outcome measure than the control group. The hypotheses were directional.

If the experimenter's alternative hypothesis were that the experimental group's mean would be different from that of the control group (not higher than or lower than, just different), then the alternative hypothesis is nondirectional.

Setting the Tails Argument to 1 In Figure 9.2, the experimenter has adopted .05 as alpha. The right tail of the left curve contains all of alpha, which is .05 or 5% of the area under the left curve. Figure 9.2 is a visual representation of the experimenter's decision rule, which in words is this:

> *I expect that the treatment will raise the experimental group's mean score on the test above the control group's mean score. But if the two population means are really the same, I want to protect myself against deciding that the treatment was effective just because chance—that is, sampling error—worked in favor of the experimental group.*

So I'll set the bar at a point where only 5% of the possible sample experimental means are above it, given that the experimental and control means in the populations are really the same. The T.TEST() function will tell me how much of the area under the left control group curve exceeds the mean of the experimental group.

Given the data shown in Figure 9.1, the experimenter rejects the null hypothesis that the two means are the same. The alternative hypothesis is therefore tenable: that the experimental mean in the full population is greater than the control mean in the full population.

Notice the value 0.019 in cell F7 of Figure 9.1. It shows the result of the T.TEST() function. Cell G7 shows that the function's third argument, Tails, is equal to 1. That tells Excel to report the error probability in one tail only. So when Excel reports the result of T.TEST() at 0.019, it is saying that, in this example, 1.9% of the area is found above, and only above, the experimental group mean.

Interpreting the T.TEST() Result   It's important to recognize that the value returned by T.TEST() is not the same as alpha, although the two quantities are conceptually related. As the experimenter, you set alpha to a value such as .01, .025, .05, and so on.

In contrast, the T.TEST() function returns the percentage of the left curve that falls to the right of the right curve's mean. That percentage might be less than or equal to alpha, in which case you reject the null hypothesis; or it might be greater than alpha, in which case you continue to regard the null hypothesis as tenable.

In Figure 9.2, the value 0.019 is represented as the area under the left, control group curve that exceeds the experimental group mean. Only 1.9% of the time would you get an experimental group mean as large as this one when the experimental and control population means were really the same.

The experimenter set alpha at .05. The experimental group's mean was even farther from the control group's mean than is implied by an alpha of .05 (the critical value that divides the charted alpha region from the rest of the control group's distribution). So the experimenter can reject the null hypothesis at the .05 level of confidence—*not* at the .019 level of confidence. Once you have specified an alpha and an alternative hypothesis, you stick with it.

For example, suppose that the experimental group's mean score had been not 65.2 but 30.4. That's as far below the control group mean as the actual result is above the control group mean. Is that a "statistically significant" finding? In a sense, yes it is. It would occur at about the same 1.9% of the time that the actual finding did, given that the means are equal in the populations.

But the experimenter adopted the alternative hypothesis that the experimental group's mean would be higher than the treatment group's mean. That alternative implied that the error rate, the entire .05 or 5%, should be put in the right tail of the control group's curve. An experimental group mean of 30.4 does not exceed the minimum value for that alpha region, and so the alternative hypothesis must be rejected. The null hypothesis, that the group means are equal, must be retained even though a startlingly low experimental group mean came about.

> **NOTE**
>
> There is another important point regarding figures such as .019, as the probability of a finding such as a difference between means. The very use of a figure such as .019 or 1.9% implies a degree of precision in the research that almost surely isn't there. To achieve that precision, all the assumptions must be met perfectly—the underlying distributions must be perfectly congruent with the theoretical distributions, all observations must be perfectly independent of one another, groups must have started out exactly equivalent on the outcome measure, and so on. Otherwise, measuring probabilities in thousandths is false precision.
>
> Therefore, assuming that you have chosen your alpha rate rationally to begin with, it's better practice to report your findings in terms of that alpha rate rather than as a number that implies a degree of precision that's not available to you.

Setting the Tails Argument to 2   Now suppose that the experimenter had a somewhat more modest view of the treatment effect, and admitted it's possible that instead of raising the experimental group's scores, the treatment might lower them. In that case, the null hypothesis would remain the same—that the population means are the same—but the alternative hypothesis would be different. Instead of stating that the experimental group mean is higher than the control group mean, the alternative hypothesis would state that it is different from the control group mean: that is, either higher or lower than the control group mean, and the experimenter won't predict which.

Figure 9.5 illustrates this concept.

Figure 9.5
The area that represents alpha is divided between the two tails of the distribution that represents the control group sample mean.

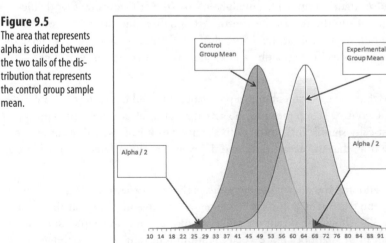

> **NOTE** Some people refer to a directional test as *one tailed* and a nondirectional test as *two tailed*. There's nothing wrong with that terminology if you're sure you're talking about a t-test. But the usage can create confusion when you start thinking about the analysis of variance, or ANOVA, which is used to test more than two means. In ANOVA you might test nondirectional hypotheses by means of a one-tailed F-test.

Figure 9.5 represents a nondirectional decision rule. Here it is in words:

> *I expect that the treatment group's mean will differ from the experimental group's mean. I don't know if the treatment will add to their knowledge and increase their test scores, or if it will confuse them and lower their test scores. But if the two group means are really the same in their respective populations, I want to protect myself against deciding that the treatment mattered just because chance—that is, sampling error—pushed the experimental group's scores up or pulled them down.*
>
> *Therefore, I'll set not just one but two bars. Under my null hypothesis, the experimental and control means in the populations are really the same. I'll place the upper bar so that only 2.5% of the curve's area is above it, and the lower bar so that only 2.5% of the curve's area is below it. That way, I still run only one chance in 20 of rejecting a true null hypothesis, and I don't have to commit myself about whether the treatment helps or hurts.*

This is called a *nondirectional test* because the experimenter is not setting an alternative hypothesis that states that the experimental mean will be higher than the mean of the control group; nor does the alternative state that the experimental mean will be lower. All the alternative hypothesis states is that the two means will be different beyond an amount that can be reasonably attributed to chance. The test is also sometimes termed a *two-tailed test* because the error rate, alpha, is split between the two tails of the curve that represents the possible control group sample means. In this example, alpha is still .05, but .025 is in the left tail and .025 is in the right tail.

In this situation, the experimenter can reject the null hypothesis if the experimental group's mean falls below the lower critical value or above the upper critical value. This differs from the decision rule used with directional hypotheses, which can force the experimenter to regard the null hypothesis as tenable even though the experimental mean might fall improbably far from the control group mean, in an unexpected direction.

There's a cost to nondirectional tests, though. Nondirectional tests allow for more possibilities than directional tests, but their statistical power is lower. Compare the upper critical value in Figure 9.2 with that in Figure 9.5. In Figure 9.2, the directional test puts all of alpha into the right tail, and so doing places the critical value at about 61. In Figure 9.5, the nondirectional test puts only half of alpha, .025, into the right tail, and so doing raises the critical value from about 61 to a little over 67.

When a critical value moves away from the mean of the sampling distribution that represents the comparison group, the power of the statistical test is reduced. Compare Figures 9.6 and 9.7.

Figure 9.6
The experimental group mean exceeds the critical value because the entire alpha is allocated to the right tail of the left curve.

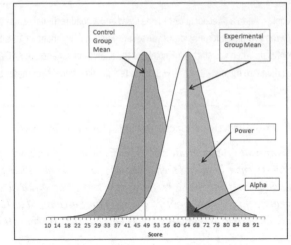

In Figure 9.6, notice that the experimental group mean is just barely above the critical value of 64: It's within the region defined by the statistical power of this t-test, so the test has enough sensitivity to reject the null hypothesis.

Figure 9.7
The upper critical value has moved right, reducing power, because alpha has been divided between two tails of the left curve.

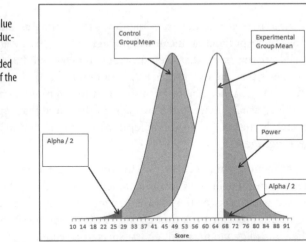

In Figure 9.7, the experimenter has made a nondirectional hypothesis. If alpha remains at .05, this means that .025 instead of .05 of the area under the left curve defines the upper critical value. That moves the critical value to the right, as compared to the situation depicted in Figure 9.6, and in turn that reduces the test's statistical power.

In general, making a directional hypothesis increases a test's statistical power when the experimenter has good reason to expect that the outcome will favor one group or the other. The tradeoff is that a directional hypothesis won't support a decision to reject the null when the experimental group's mean differs from the control group's mean, but in an unexpected direction.

Again, the syntax of the T.TEST() function is as follows:

=T.TEST(Array1, Array2, Tails, Type)

In the T.TEST() function, you state whether you want Excel to examine one tail only or both tails. If you set Tails to 1, Excel returns the area of the curve beyond the calculated t statistic in one tail. If you set Tails to 2, Excel returns the total of the areas to the right of the t statistic and to the left of the negative of the t-statistic. So if the calculated t is 3.7, T.TEST() with two tails returns the area under the curve to the left of -3.7 plus the area to the right of +3.7.

Using the Type Argument

The fourth Type argument to the T.TEST() function tells Excel what kind of t-test to run, and your choice involves some assumptions that this chapter has as yet just touched on.

Most tests that support statistical inference make assumptions about the nature of the data you supply. These assumptions are usually due to the mathematics that underlies the test. In practice:

- You can safely ignore some assumptions.
- Some assumptions get violated, but there are procedures for dealing with the violation.
- Some assumptions must be met or the test will not work as intended.

The Type argument in the T.TEST() function pertains to the second sort of assumption: When you specify a Type, you tell Excel which assumption you're worried about and thus which procedure it should use to deal with the violation.

The theory of t-tests makes three distinct assumptions about the data you have gathered.

Normal Distributions The t-test assumes that both samples are taken from populations that are distributed normally on the measure you are using. If your outcome measure were a nominal variable such as Ill versus Healthy, you would be violating the assumption of normality because there are only two possible values and the measure cannot be distributed normally.

This assumption belongs to the set that you can safely ignore in practice. Considerable research has investigated the effect of violating the normality assumption and it shows that the presence of underlying, non-normal distributions has only a trivial effect on the results of the t-test. (Statisticians sometimes say that the t-test is *robust* with respect to the violation of the assumption of normality, and the studies just mentioned are referred to as the *robustness studies*.)

Independent Observations The t-test assumes that the individual records are independent of one another. That is, the assumption is that the fact that you have observed a value in one group has no effect on the likelihood of observing another value in either group.

Suppose you were testing the status of a gene. If Fred and Judy are brother and sister, the status of Fred's gene might well mirror the status of Judy's gene (and vice versa). The observations would not be independent of one another, whether they were in the same group or in two different groups.

This is an important assumption both in theory and in practice: The t-test is not robust with respect to the violation of the assumption of independence of observations. However, you often find that quantifiable relationships exist *between* the two groups.

For example, you might want to test the effect of a new type of car tire on gas mileage. Suppose first that you acquire, say, 20 new cars of random makes and models and assign them, also at random, to use either an existing tire or the new type. But with that small a sample, random assignment is not necessarily an effective way to equate the two groups of cars.

> **NOTE** Even one outlier in either group can exert a disproportionate influence on that group's mean value when there are only 10 randomly selected cars in the group. Random selection and assignment are usually helpful in equating groups, but from time to time you happen to get 19 subcompacts and one HumVee.

Now suppose that you acquire two cars from each of ten different model lines. Then you randomly assign one car from each model-pair to get four tires of an existing type, and the other car in the pair to get four tires of your new type. The layout of this experiment is shown in Figure 9.8.

Figure 9.8
As you saw in Chapter 4, "How Variables Move Jointly: Correlation," you can pair up observations in a list by putting them in the same row.

	A	B	C	D	E	F	G	H	I	J
	Car	Tire A	Tire B			Tire A			Tire B	
1	model	mpg	mpg		Statistic	mpg			mpg	
2	1	15.4	19.0		Average	26.75	=AVERAGE(TireA)		31.18	=AVERAGE(TireB)
3	2	37.2	38.7		Variance	83.40	=VAR.S(TireA)		83.44	=VAR.S(TireB)
4	3	18.4	26.7		Standard Deviation	9.13	=STDEV.S(TireA)		9.13	=STDEV.S(TireB)
5	4	17.2	24.7		Standard Error of the Mean	2.89	=SQRT(F3/10)		2.89	=SQRT(I3/10)
6	5	34.1	22.2							
7	6	24.6	27.6		Correlation, Tire A with Tire B	0.68	=CORREL(TireA,TireB)			
8	7	40.7	45.4		Standard Error of Mean Difference	2.30	=SQRT(F3/10+I3/10-2*(F7*F5*I5))			
9	8	27.1	43.8		t statistic	1.93	=(AVERAGE(TireB)-AVERAGE(TireA))/F8			
10	9	19.4	28.1		p(t) with 9 df using T.DIST()	0.04	=1-T.DIST(F9,9,TRUE)			
11	10	33.4	35.6		p(t) with 9 df using T.TEST()	0.04	=T.TEST(TireA,TireB,1,1)			

In this design, the observations clearly violate the assumption of independence. The fact that one car from each model has been placed in one group means that the probability is 100% that another car, identical but for the tires, is placed in the other group. Because the only difference between the members of a matched pair is the tires, the two groups have been equated on other variables, such as weight and number of cylinders.

And because the experimenter can pair up the observations, the amount of dependence between the two groups can be calculated and used to adjust the t-test. As is shown in

Figure 9.8, the correlation in gas mileage between the two groups is a fairly high 0.68; therefore, the R-squared, the amount of shared variance in gas mileage, is almost 47%.

Because of the pairing of observations in different groups, the dependent groups t-test has one degree of freedom for each *pair*, minus 1. So in the example shown in Figure 9.8, the dependent groups t-test has 10 pairs minus 1, or 9 degrees of freedom.

Figure 9.8 also shows the result of the T.TEST() function on the two arrays in columns B and C. With nine degrees of freedom, taking into account the correlation between the two groups, the likelihood of getting a sample mean difference of 4.43 miles per gallon is only .04, if there is no difference in the underlying populations. If you had started out by setting your alpha rate to .05, you could reject the null hypothesis of no difference.

Calculating the Standard Error for Dependent Groups   One of the reasons to use a dependent groups t-test when you can do so is that the test becomes more powerful, just as using a larger value of alpha or making a directional hypothesis makes the t-test more powerful. To see how this comes about, consider the way that the standard error of the difference between two means is calculated.

Here is the formula for the variance of a variable named A:

$$s_A^2 = \sum \frac{(A_i - \overline{A})^2}{n - 1}$$

Then, if A is actually equal to X – Y, we have the following:

$$s_{x-y}^2 = \sum \frac{\left[(X_i - Y_i) - (\overline{X} - \overline{Y}) \right]^2}{n - 1}$$

Rearranging the elements in that expression results in this:

$$s_{x-y}^2 = \sum \frac{\left[(X_i - \overline{X}) - (Y_i - \overline{Y}) \right]^2}{n - 1}$$

Expanding that expression by carrying out the squaring operation, we get this:

$$s_{X-Y}^2 = \sum \frac{(X_i - \overline{X})^2}{n - 1} - 2 \sum \frac{(X_i - \overline{X})(Y_i - \overline{Y})}{n - 1} + \sum \frac{(Y_i - \overline{Y})^2}{n - 1}$$

The first term here is the variance of X. The third term is the variance of Y. The second term includes the covariance of X and Y (see Chapter 4 for information on the covariance and its relationship to the correlation coefficient.) So the equation can be rewritten as

$$s_{x-y}^2 = s_x^2 + s_y^2 - 2s_{xy}$$

or

$$s_{x-y}^2 = s_x^2 + s_y^2 - 2r_{xy}\,s_x s_y$$

Therefore, the variance of the difference between two variables can be expressed as the variance of the first variable plus the variance of the second variable, less twice the covariance. Chapter 4 also discusses the covariance as the correlation between the two variables times their standard deviations.

The only part of that you should bother to remember is that you subtract a quantity that depends on the strength of the correlation between the two variables. In the context of the dependent groups t-test, those variables might be the scores of the subjects in Group 1 and the scores of their siblings in Group 2—or the mpg attained by the car models in Group 1 and the mpg for the identical models in Group 2, and so on.

It's worth noting that when you are running an independent groups t-test, as was done in the first part of this chapter, there is no correlation between the scores on the two groups. Then the standard error of the mean differences is just the sum of the groups' variances. With equal sample sizes, the sum of the groups' variances is the same as the pooled variance discussed earlier in the chapter.

But when members of the two groups can be paired up, you can calculate a correlation and reduce the size of the standard error accordingly (refer to the final equation). In turn, this gives your test greater power. To review, here's the basic equation for the t-statistic:

$$t = \frac{\overline{X} - \overline{Y}}{s_{\overline{X}-\overline{Y}}}$$

Clearly, when the denominator is smaller, the ratio is larger. A larger t-statistic is more likely to exceed the critical value. Therefore, when you can pair up members of two groups, you can calculate the correlation on the outcome variable between the two groups. That results in a smaller denominator, because you subtract it (multiplied by 2 and by the product of the standard deviations) from the sum of the variances.

> **NOTE**   There's no need to remember the specifics of this discussion. For example, Excel takes care of all the calculations for you if you've read this book and know how to apply the built-in worksheet functions such as T.TEST(). The important point to take from the preceding discussion is that a dependent groups t-test can be a much more sensitive, powerful test than an independent groups test. We'll return to this point in Chapter 13, "Multiple Regression Analysis: Further Issues."

In a case such as the car tire example, you expect that the observations are not independent, but because you can pair up the dependent records (each model of car is represented once in each group), you can quantify the degree of dependency—that is, you can calculate the correlation between the two sets of scores because you know which score in one group goes with which score in the other group. Once you have quantified the dependency, you can use it to make the statistical test more sensitive.

That is the purpose of one of the values you can select for the T.TEST() function's Type argument. If you supply the value 1 as its Type argument, you inform Excel that the records in the two arrays are related in some way and that the correlation should factor into the function's result. So if each array contains one of two twins, then Record 1 in one array should be related to Record 1 in the second array; Record 2 in one array should be related to Record 2 in the other array, and so on.

Running the Car Example Two Ways   Figure 9.8 shows how you can run a dependent groups t-test two different ways. One way grinds the analysis out formula by formula: It's more tedious but it shows you what's going on and helps you lay the groundwork for understanding more advanced analysis such as ANCOVA.

The other way is quick—it requires only one T.TEST() formula—but all you get from it is a probability level. It's useful if you're pressed for time (or if you want to check your work), but it's not helpful if what you're after is understanding.

To review, columns A, B, and C in Figure 9.8 contain data on the miles per gallon (mpg) of ten pairs of cars. Each pair of cars occupies a different row on the worksheet, and a pair of cars consists of two cars from the same manufacturer/model. The experimenter is trying to establish whether or not the difference between the groups, type of car tire, makes a difference to mean gas mileage.

The ranges have been named TireA and TireB. The range named TireA occupies cells B2:B11, and the range named TireB occupies cells C2:C11. The range names make it a little easier to construct formulas that refer to those ranges, and to make the formulas a bit more self-documenting.

The following formulas are needed to grind out the analysis. The cell references are all to Figure 9.8.

Group Means   The mean mpg for each group appears in cells F2 and I2. The formulas used in those two cells appear in cells G2 and J2. In these samples, the cars using Tire B get better gas mileage than those using Tire A. It remains to decide whether to attribute the difference in gas mileage to the tires or to chance.

Group Variability   The variances appear in F3 and I3, and the formulas that return the variances are in cells G3 and J3. The standard deviations are in F4 and I4. The formulas themselves are shown in G4 and J4. The forms of the functions that treat the data in columns B and C as samples are used in the formulas.

Standard Error of the Mean   When you're testing a group mean against a hypothesized value (in contrast to the mean of another group) as was done in Chapter 8, you use the standard error of the mean as the t-test's denominator; the standard error of the mean is the standard deviation of many means, not of many individual observations.

When you're testing two group means against one another, you use the standard error of the *difference* between means; that is, the standard deviation of many mean differences. This example is about to calculate the standard error of the difference, but to do so it needs to use the variance error of the mean, which is the square of the standard error of the mean. That value, one for each group, appears in cells F5 and I5; the formulas are in G5 and J5.

Correlation   As discussed earlier in this chapter, you need to quantify the degree of dependence between the two groups in a dependent groups t-test. You do so in order to adjust the size of the denominator in the t-statistic. In this example, Figure 9.8 shows the correlation in cell F7 and the formula in cell G7.

Identifying the car models in cells A2:A11 is not strictly part of the t-test. But it underscores the necessity of keeping both members of a pair in the same row of the raw data: for example, Car Model 1 appears in cell B2 and cell C2; Model 2 appears in cell B3 and cell C3; and so on. Only when the data is laid out in this fashion can the CORREL() function accurately calculate the correlation between the two groups.

> **NOTE** The previous statement is not strictly true. The requirement is that each member of a pair occupy the same relative position in each array. So if you used something such as =CORREL(A1:A10,B11:B20), you would need to be sure that one pair is in A1 and B11, another pair in A2 and B12, and so on. The easiest way to make sure of this setup is to start both arrays in the same row—and that also happens to conform to the layout of Excel lists and tables.

Standard Error of the Difference Between Means   Cell F8 calculates the standard error of the difference between means, as it is derived earlier in this chapter in the section titled "Calculating the Standard Error for Dependent Groups." It is the square root of the sum of the variance error of the mean for each group, less twice the product of the correlation and the standard error of the mean of each group. The formula used in cell F8 appears in cell G8.

Calculating the t-Statistic   The t-statistic for two dependent groups is the ratio of the difference between the group means to the standard error of the mean differences. The value for this example is in cell F9 and the formula in cell G9.

Calculating the Probability   The T.DIST() function has already been discussed; you supply it with the arguments that identify the t-statistic (here, the value in F9), the degrees of freedom (9, the number of pairs minus 1), and whether you want the cumulative area under the t-distribution through the value specified by the t-statistic (here, TRUE).

In this case, 96% of the area under the t-distribution with 9 degrees of freedom lies to the left of a t-statistic of 1.93. But it's the area to the *right* of that t-statistic that we're interested in; see for example Figure 9.2, where that area appears in the curve for the control group, to the right of the mean of the experimental group.

The result of the formula in this example is .04, or 4%. An experimenter who adopted .05 as alpha, the risk of rejecting a true null hypothesis, and who made a directional alternative hypothesis, would reject the null hypothesis of no difference in the population mean mpg values.

Using the T.TEST() Function

All the preceding analysis, including the functions used in rows 2 through 10 of Figure 9.8, can be compressed into one formula, which also returns .04 in cell F11 of Figure 9.8. The full formula appears in cell G11. Its arguments include the named range that contains the individual mpg figures for Tire A and those for Tire B.

The third argument, Tails, is given as 1, so T.TEST() returns a directional test. It calculates the area to the right of the calculated t-statistic. If the Tails argument had been set to 2, T.TEST() would return .08. In that case, it would return the area under the curve to the left of a t-statistic of −1.93, plus the area under the curve to the right of a t-statistic of 1.93.

The fourth argument, Type, is also set to 1 in this example. That value calls for a dependent groups t-test.

If you open the workbook for Chapter 9, available for download from the book's website at www.informit.com/title/9780789747204, you can check the values in Figure 9.8 for cells F10 and F11. The values in the two cells are identical to 16 decimal places.

Using the Data Analysis Add-in t-Tests

The Data Analysis add-in has 19 tools, ranging alphabetically from ANOVA to z-tests. Three of the tools perform t-tests, and the three tools reflect the possible values for the Type argument of the T.TEST() function:

- Dependent Groups
- Equal Variances
- Unequal Variances

The prior major section of this chapter discussed dependent groups t-tests in some detail. It covered the rationale for dependent groups tests. It compared the use of several Excel functions such as T.DIST() to arrive at an answer with the use of a single summary T.TEST() function to arrive at the same answer.

This section shows you how to use the Data Analysis add-in tool to perform the same dependent groups t-test without recourse to worksheet functions. The tool occupies a middle ground between the labor-intensive use of several worksheet functions and the minimally informative T.TEST() function. The tool runs the function for you, so it's quick, and it shows averages, standard deviations, group counts, t-statistics, critical values, and probabilities, so it's much more informative than the single T.TEST() function.

The principal drawback to the add-in's tool is that all its results are reported as static values, so if you want or need to change or add a value to the raw data, you have to run the tool again. The results don't automatically refresh the way that worksheet functions do when their underlying data changes.

Group Variances in t-Tests

Earlier, this chapter noted that the basic theory of t-tests assumes that the populations from which the groups are sampled have the same variance. The procedure that follows from the assumption of equal variances is that two variances, one from each sample, are pooled to arrive at an estimate of the population variance. That pooling is done as shown in cells F1:F2 of Figure 9.1 and as repeated here in definitional form:

$$(\textstyle\sum x_1^2 + \sum x_2^2)/(N_1 + N_2 - 2)$$

That discussion went on to point out that both theoretical and empirical research have shown that when the two samples have the same number of observations, violating the equal variances assumption makes a negligible difference to the outcome of the t-test.

In turn, that finding implies that you don't worry about unequal variances when you're running a dependent groups t-test. By definition, the two groups have the same sample size, because each member of one group must be paired with exactly one member of the other group.

That leaves the cases in which group sizes are different and so are their variances. When the larger group has the larger sample variance, it contributes a *greater* share of *greater* variability to the pooled estimate of population variance than does the smaller group.

As a result, the standard error of the mean difference is inflated. That standard error is the denominator in the t-test, and therefore the t-ratio is reduced. You are working with an actual alpha rate that is less than the nominal alpha rate, and statisticians refer to your t-test as *conservative*. The probability that you will reject a true null hypothesis is lower than you think.

But if the larger group has the smaller sample variance, it contributes a *greater* share of *lower* variability than does the smaller group. This reduces the size of the standard error, inflates the value of the t-ratio, and in consequence you are working with an actual alpha that is larger than the nominal alpha. Statisticians would say that your t-test is *liberal*. The probability that you will reject a true null hypothesis is greater than you think.

The Data Analysis Add-in Equal Variances t-Test

This tool is the classic t-test, largely as it was originally devised in the early part of the twentieth century. It maintains the assumption that the population variances are equal, it's capable of dealing with groups of different sample sizes, and it assumes that the observations are independent of one another (thus, it does not calculate and use a correlation).

To run the equal variances tool (or the unequal variances tool or the paired sample, dependent groups tool), you must have the Data Analysis add-in installed, as described in Chapter 4. Once the add-in is installed, you can find it in the Analysis group on the Ribbon's Data tab.

To run the Equal Variances t-test, activate a worksheet with the data from your two groups, as in columns B and C in Figure 9.8, and then click the Data Analysis button in the Analysis group. You will see a list box with the names of the available data analysis tools. Scroll down until you see "t-Test: Two-Sample Assuming Equal Variances." Click it and then click OK. The dialog box shown in Figure 9.9 appears.

Figure 9.9
The t-test tools always subtract Variable 2 from Variable 1 when calculating the t-statistic.

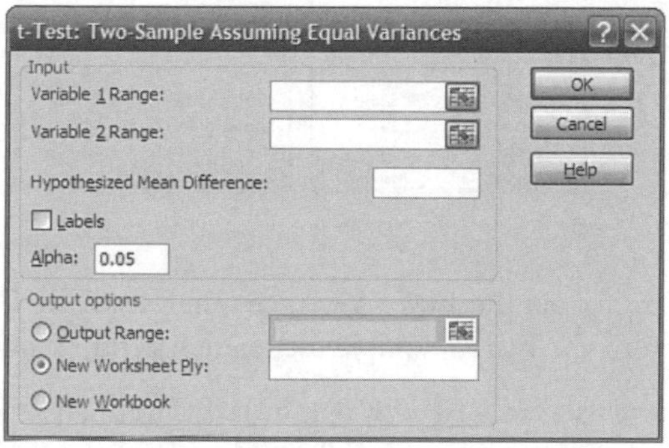

Here are a few comments regarding the dialog box in Figure 9.9 (which also apply to the dialog boxes that appear if you choose the unequal variances t-test or the paired sample t-test):

- As noted, Variable 2 is always subtracted from Variable 1. If you don't want to get caught up in the very minor logical complications of negative t-statistics, make it a rule to designate the group with the larger mean as Variable 1. So doing is *not* the same as changing a nondirectional hypothesis to a directional one after you've seen the data. You are not altering your decision rule after the fact; you are simply deciding that you prefer to work with positive rather than negative t-statistics.

- If you include column headers in your data ranges, fill the Labels check box to use those headers instead of "Variable 1" and "Variable 2" in the output.

- The caution regarding the Output Range, made in Chapter 4, holds for the t-test dialog boxes. When you choose that option button, Excel immediately activates the address box for Variable 1. Be sure to make Output Range's associated edit box active before you click in the cell where you want the output to start.

- Leaving the Hypothesized Mean Difference box blank is the same as setting it to zero. If you enter a number such as 5, you are changing the null hypothesis from "Mean

1 – Mean 2 = 0" to "Mean 1 – Mean 2 = 5." In that case, be sure that you've thought through the issues regarding directional hypotheses discussed previously in this chapter.

After making your choices in the dialog box, click OK. You will see the analysis shown in cells E1:G14 in Figure 9.10.

Figure 9.10
Note that the Paired test in columns I:K provides a more sensitive test than the Equal Variances test in columns E:G.

	Car model	Tire A mpg	Tire B mpg		t-Test: Two-Sample Assuming Equal Variances				t-Test: Paired Two Sample for Means		
1											
2	1	15.4	19.0								
3	2	37.2	38.7			Tire B mpg	Tire A mpg			Tire B mpg	Tire A mpg
4	3	18.4	26.7		Mean	31.18	26.75	Mean	31.18	26.75
5	4	17.2	24.7		Variance	83.44	83.40	Variance	83.44	83.40
6	5	34.1	22.2		Observations	10	10	Observations	10	10
7	6	24.6	27.6		Pooled Variance	83.416		Pearson Correlation	0.683	
8	7	40.7	45.4		Hypothesized Mean Difference	0		Hypothesized Mean Difference	0	
9	8	27.1	43.8		df	18		df	9	
10	9	19.4	28.1		t Stat	1.085		t Stat	1.926	
11	10	33.4	35.6		P(T<=t) one-tail	0.146		P(T<=t) one-tail	0.043	
12					t Critical one-tail	1.734		t Critical one-tail	1.833	
13					P(T<=t) two-tail	0.292		P(T<=t) two-tail	0.086	
14					t Critical two-tail	2.101		t Critical two-tail	2.262	

There are several points to note in the Equal Variances analysis in E1:G14 in Figure 9.10, particularly in comparison to the Paired Sample (dependent groups) analysis in I1:K14:

Compare the calculated t-statistic in F10 with that in J10. The analysis in E1:G14 assumes that the two groups are independent of one another. Therefore, the analysis does not compute a correlation coefficient, as is done in the "paired sample" analysis. In turn, the denominator of the t-statistic is not reduced by a figure that depends in part on the correlation between the observations in the two groups.

As a result, the t-statistic in F10 is smaller than the one in J10: small enough that it does not exceed the critical value needed to reject the null hypothesis at the .05 level of alpha either for a directional test (cell F11) or a nondirectional test (cell F13).

Also compare the degrees of freedom for the two tests. The Equal Variances test uses 18 degrees of freedom: ten from each group, less two for the means of the two groups. The Paired Sample test uses nine degrees of freedom: ten pairs of observations, less one for the mean of the differences between the pairs.

As a result, the Paired Sample t-test has a larger critical value. If the experimenter is using a directional hypothesis, the critical value is 1.734 for the Equal Variances test and 1.833 for the Paired Sample test. The pattern is similar for a nondirectional test: 2.101 versus 2.262. This difference in critical values is due to the difference in degrees of freedom: Other things being equal, a t-distribution with a smaller number of degrees of freedom requires a larger critical value.

But even though the Paired Sample test requires a larger critical value, because fewer degrees of freedom are available, it is still more powerful than the Equal Variances test because the correlation between the two groups results in a smaller denominator for the t-statistic. The weaker the correlation, however, the smaller the increase in power. You can convince yourself of this by reviewing the formula for the standard error of the difference between two means for the dependent groups t-test. See the section earlier in this chapter titled "Calculating the Standard Error for Dependent Groups."

The Data Analysis Add-in Unequal Variances t-Test

Figure 9.11 shows a comparison between the results of the Data Analysis add-in's Equal Variances test and the Unequal Variances test.

Figure 9.11
The data has been set up to return a liberal t-test.

	A	B	C	D	E	F	G	H	I	J	K
1		Tire A mpg	Tire B mpg		t-Test: Two-Sample Assuming Equal Variances				t-Test: Two-Sample Assuming Unequal Variances		
2		14.2	19.0								
3		35.5	38.7			Tire B mpg	Tire A mpg			Tire B mpg	Tire A mpg
4		16.9	26.7		Mean	31.12	26.75		Mean	31.12	26.75
5		15.8	24.7		Variance	79.39	166.00		Variance	79.39	166.00
6		32.0	22.2		Observations	20	10		Observations	20	10
7		22.5	27.6		Pooled Variance	107.23					
8		56.6	45.4		Hypothesized Mean Difference	0			Hypothesized Mean Difference	0	
9		24.9	43.8		df	28			df	13	
10		17.8	28.1		t Stat	1.090			t Stat	0.964	
11		31.3	35.6		P(T<=t) one-tail	0.142			P(T<=t) one-tail	0.176	
12			18.9		t Critical one-tail	1.701			t Critical one-tail	1.771	
13			38.6		P(T<=t) two-tail	0.285			P(T<=t) two-tail	0.353	
14			26.5		t Critical two-tail	2.048			t Critical two-tail	2.16	
15			24.6								
16			22.1								
17			27.4								
18			45.4								
19			43.8								
20			27.9								
21			35.5								

It is usual to assume equal variances in the t-test's two groups if their sample sizes are equal. But what if they are unequal? The possible outcomes are as follows:

- If the group with the larger sample size has the *larger* variance, your alpha level is smaller than you think. If the nominal alpha rate that you have chosen is 0.05, for example, the actual error rate might be 0.03. You will reject the null hypothesis less often than you should. Thus, the t-test is conservative. (The corollary is that statistical power is lower than is apparent.)

- If the group with the larger sample size has the *smaller* variance, your alpha level is greater than you think. If the nominal alpha rate that you have chosen is 0.05, for example, the actual error rate might be 0.08. You will more often erroneously conclude a difference exists in the population where it doesn't. The t-test is liberal, and the corollary is that statistical power is greater than you would expect.

Accordingly, the raw data in columns B and C in Figure 9.11 includes the following:

- The Tire B group, which has 20 records, has a variance of 79.
- The Tire A group, which has 10 records, has a variance of 166.

So the larger group has the smaller variance, which means that the t-test operates liberally—the actual alpha is larger than the nominal alpha and the test's statistical power is increased.

However, even with that added power, the Equal Variances t-test does not report a t-statistic that is greater than the critical value, for either a directional or a nondirectional hypothesis.

The main point to notice in Figure 9.11 is the difference in degrees of freedom between the Equal Variances test shown in cells E1:G14 and the Unequal Variances test in cells I1:K14. The degrees of freedom in cell F9 is 28, as you would expect. Twenty records in one group plus ten records in the other group, less two for the group means, results in 28 degrees of freedom. However, the degrees of freedom for the Unequal Variances test in cell J9 is 13, which appears to bear no relationship to the number of records in the two groups. Also note that the t-statistic itself is different: 1.090 in F10 versus 0.964 in cell J10.

The Unequal Variances test uses what's called Welch's correction, so as to adjust for the liberal (or conservative) effect of a larger group with a smaller (or larger) variance. The correction procedure involves two steps:

1. For the t-statistic's denominator, use the square root of the sum of the two variances, rather than the standard error of the mean difference.
2. Adjust the degrees of freedom in a direction that makes a liberal test more conservative, or a conservative test more liberal.

The specifics of the adjustment to the degrees of freedom are not conceptually illuminating, so they are skipped here; it's enough to state that the adjustment depends on the ratios of the groups' variances to their associated number of records.

For example, the data in Figure 9.11 involves a larger group with a smaller variance, so you expect the normal t-test to be liberal, with a higher actual alpha than the nominal alpha selected by the experimenter.

When Welch's correction is applied, the t-Test for Unequal Variances uses 13 degrees of freedom rather than 28. As the prior section noted, a t-distribution with fewer degrees of freedom has a larger critical value for cutting off an alpha area than does one with more degrees of freedom.

Accordingly, the Unequal Variances test with 13 degrees of freedom needs a critical value of 1.771 to cut off 5% of the upper tail of the distribution (cell J12). The Equal Variances test, which uses 28 degrees of freedom, cuts off 5% of the distribution at the lower critical value of 1.701 (cell F12). This is because the t-distribution is slightly leptokurtic, with thicker tails in the distributions with fewer degrees of freedom.

Visualizing Statistical Power

Both Chapter 8 and this chapter have had much to say regarding statistical power. Several factors can influence how sensitive a t-test is to experimental data: the size of the treatment effect, the sample sizes, the standard deviation of the outcome measure, the size of alpha, and the directionality of the hypotheses.

Those factors all act together to influence power. Figure 9.12 shows a worksheet that can help you visualize the effects of those factors.

Figure 9.12
The spinners enable you to increase or decrease their associated values.

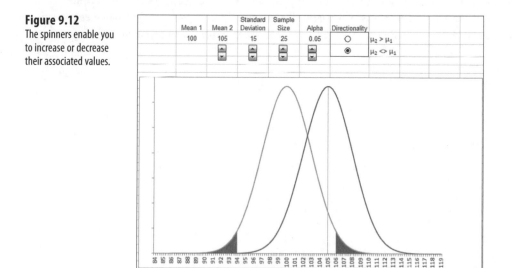

You can find the worksheet shown in Figure 9.12 in the workbook for Chapter 9 that is available on the book's website at www.informit.com/title/9780789747204.

Use it to increase or decrease the treatment effect, change sample sizes (and therefore standard errors), standard deviations (and therefore standard errors, again), and so on. When you do so, the chart redraws to show the result of the change you made.

Watch in particular what happens in the right curve that represents the experimental group. The power of the t-test, as these curves are laid out, is the area under the right curve that lies to the right of the critical value that bounds the alpha area (shown in the right tail of the left distribution).

For example, if you reduce the treatment effect by reducing Mean 2, the right curve is pulled to the left and less of it lies to the right of the critical value. Power is reduced.

Alternatively, if you decrease the size of the standard deviation, the size of the standard errors decreases. That pulls the alpha area to the left, leaving more of the area of the right curve to the right of the critical value.

When to Avoid t-Tests

The theoretical underpinnings of t-tests do not account for more than two groups. The examples in Chapters 8 and 9 have all involved an experimental group and a control group. Although this is a typical design for good experiments, it is somewhat restrictive. There are many interesting questions whose answers require the use of three or more groups: for example, a drug trial involving a group that takes a new drug, a group that takes an existing drug or a placebo, and a group that takes no medication at all.

For this sort of situation, t-tests are not appropriate. Chapter 10, "Testing Differences Between Means: The Analysis of Variance," explains why that is so, and introduces the statistical test that is designed to handle three or more groups: the analysis of variance.

Testing Differences Between Means: The Analysis of Variance

Chapter 8, "Testing Differences Between Means: The Basics," and Chapter 9, "Testing Differences Between Means: Further Issues," went into some detail about how to use z-tests and t-tests to determine the probability that two group means come from the same population. Chapter 10 tries to convince you to use a different method when you're interested in three means or more.

The need to test whether three or more means come from different populations comes up frequently. There are more than two major political organizations to pay attention to. Medical research is not limited to a comparison between a treatment and a no-treatment control group, but often compares two or more treatment arms to a control arm. There are more than two brands of car that might earn different ratings for safety, mileage, and owner satisfaction. Any one of several different strains of wheat might produce the best crop under given conditions.

Why Not t-Tests?

If you wanted to use statistical inference to test whether or not more than two sample means are likely to have different population values, it's natural to think of repeated t-tests. You could use one t-test to compare GM with Ford, another to compare GM with Toyota, and yet another to compare Ford with Toyota.

The problem is that if you do so, you're taking unfair advantage of the probabilities. The t-test was designed to compare two group means, not three, not four or more. If you run multiple t-tests on three or more means, you inflate the apparent alpha rate. That is, you might set .05 (beforehand) as the acceptable risk of rejecting a true null hypothesis, and then do so because two sample means were improbably far apart when they really come from the same population. You might think your risk of being misled by sampling error is only .05, but it's higher than that if you use several t-tests to compare more than two means.

As it happens, multiple t-tests can inflate your nominal alpha level from, say, .05 to .40. A fuller explanation will have to wait until a few relevant concepts have been discussed, but Figure 10.1 gives you the basic idea.

Figure 10.1

With every additional t-test, the cumulative probability of rejecting a true null hypothesis increases.

	A	B	C
	After comparison number	Remaining chance of not rejecting a true null	Cumulative chance of rejecting at least one true null
1	1	0.950	0.050
2	2	0.903	0.098
3	3	0.857	0.143
4	4	0.815	0.185
5	5	0.774	0.226
6	6	0.735	0.265
7	7	0.698	0.302
8	8	0.663	0.337
9	9	0.630	0.370
10	10	0.599	0.401

Suppose you have five means to compare. There are ten ways to make pairwise comparisons in a set of five means. (If J is the number of means, the general formula is J (J–1)/2.) If you set alpha at .05, then that nominal alpha rate is the actual alpha rate for one t-test.

But if you run another t-test, you have 95% of the original probability space remaining (5% is taken up by the alpha you used for the first t-test). Setting the nominal alpha to .05 for the second t-test means that the probability rejecting a true null hypothesis in either of the t-tests is .05 + (.05 × .95), or .098 (cell C3 in Figure 10.1).

Here is perhaps a more intuitive way of looking at it. Suppose you have run an experiment that collects the means of five groups on some outcome measure following treatments. You see that the largest and smallest means are improbably far apart—at any rate, far apart given the null hypothesis that the treatments had no differential effects. You choose to run a t-test on the largest and smallest means and find that so large a difference would occur less than 1% of the time if the means came from the same population.

The problem is that you have cherry-picked the two groups with the largest difference in their means, without also picking groups that may contribute substantially to the variability of the outcome measure. If you think back to Chapter 9, you'll recall that you run a t-test by dividing a mean difference by a factor that depends on the amount of variability in the groups tested. If you run an experiment that returns five means, and you compare the largest and the smallest while ignoring the others, you have stacked the deck in favor of differences in means without also allowing for possibly greater variability within groups. What you are doing is sometimes called "capitalizing on chance."

The recommended approach when your research involves more than two groups is to use the analysis of variance, or ANOVA. This approach tests all your means simultaneously, taking into account all the Within Groups variability, and lets you know whether there is a reliable difference *anywhere* in the set of means—including complex comparisons such as the mean of two groups compared to the mean of two other groups.

If the data passes that initial test, you can use follow-up procedures called *multiple comparisons* to pinpoint the source, or sources, of the significant difference that ANOVA alerted you to.

The Logic of ANOVA

The thinking behind ANOVA begins with a way of expressing each observation in each group by means of three parts:

- The grand mean of all the observations
- The mean of each group, and how far each group mean differs from the grand mean
- Each observation in each group, and how far each observation differs from the group mean

ANOVA uses these components to develop two estimates of the population variance. One is based entirely on the variability of observations within each group. One is based entirely on the variability of group means around the grand mean. If those two estimates are very different from one another, that's evidence that the groups came from different populations—populations that have different means.

Partitioning the Scores

Suppose you have three groups of people, and each group will take a different pill: a new cholesterol medication, an existing medication, or a placebo. Figure 10.2 shows how the grand mean, the mean of each group, and each person's deviation from the group mean combine to express each person's measured HDL level.

In practice, you seldom have reason to express each subject's score in this way—as a combination of the grand mean, the deviation of each group mean from the grand mean, and the subject's deviation from the group mean. But viewing the scores in this way helps lay the groundwork for the analysis.

The objective is to analyze the total variability of all the scores into two sets: variability due to individual subject scores and variability due to the differences in group means. By analyzing the variability in this way, you can come to a conclusion about the likelihood that chance caused the differences in group means. (This is the same objective that t-tests have, but ANOVA normally assesses three or more means. In fact, if there are just two groups, the F statistic you get from ANOVA is identical to the square of the ratio you get from a t-test.)

Figure 10.2
This model is the basis for many advanced statistical methods from ANOVA to logistic regression.

	A	B	C	D	E
1	Subject	Grand Mean	Group Mean	HDL value	
2	Charles	50	53	55	
3	Rob	50	53	50	
4	Pat	50	53	54	
5	Julia	50	46	48	
6	Linda	50	46	45	
7	Jodie	50	46	45	
8	Fred	50	51	50	
9	Tom	50	51	54	
10	Judy	50	51	49	
11					
12	Subject	Grand Mean	Group's Deviation from Grand Mean	Subject's Deviation from Group Mean	Calculated HDL value
13	Charles	50	3	2	55
14	Rob	50	3	-3	50
15	Pat	50	3	1	54
16	Julia	50	-4	2	48
17	Linda	50	-4	-1	45
18	Jodie	50	-4	-1	45
19	Fred	50	1	-1	50
20	Tom	50	1	3	54
21	Judy	50	1	-2	49

Figure 10.2 shows how the variation due to individual observations is separated from variation due to differences between group means. As you'll see shortly, this separation puts you in a position to evaluate the distance between means in light of the distance between the individuals that make up the means.

Figure 10.3 shows the two very different paths to estimating the variability in the data set. Row 2 contains the group means, and the differences between these means lead to the sum of squares between, in cell M2. Row 4 contains not group means but the sums of the squared deviations within each group, which lead to the sum of squares within, in cell M4.

Figure 10.3
This figure just shows the mechanics of the analysis. You don't usually manage them yourself, but turn them over to, for example, the Data Analysis add-in.

	F	G	H	I	J	K	L	M
1			Group 1	Group 2	Group 3	Sum of Squared Deviations	n	Sum of Squares
2		Groups means	53	46	51	26	3	78
3								
4		Sum of squares within groups	14	6	14	34		34
5								
6		Total variation						112
7								
8			Group 1	Group 2	Group 3	Sum of Squared Deviations	n	Sum of Squares
9		Groups means	=C2	=C5	=C8	=DEVSQ(H2:J2)	3	=K2*L2
10								
11		Sum of squares within groups	=DEVSQ(D2:D4)	=DEVSQ(D5:D7)	=DEVSQ(D8:D10)	=SUM(H4:J4)		=SUM(H4:J4)
12								
13		Total variation						=DEVSQ(D2:D10)

Figure 10.3 shows how the overall sum of squares is allocated to either individual variation or to variation between the group means.

Sum of Squares Between Groups

In Figure 10.3, the formulas themselves appear in the range H9:M13. The results of those formulas appear in the range H2:M6.

The range H2:M2 in Figure 10.3 shows how the sum of squares between group means is calculated. Each group mean appears in H2:J2 (compare with the cells C2, C5, and C8 in Figure 10.2).

Cell K2 contains the sum of the squared deviations of each group mean from the grand mean. This figure is returned using the worksheet function DEVSQ(), as shown in cell K9. The result in K2 must be multiplied by the number of individual observations in each group. Because each group has the same number of observations, this can be done by multiplying the total in K2 by 3, each group's sample size (typically represented by the letter n). The result, usually labeled *Sum of Squares Between*, appears in cell M2. Here are the specifics:

$$SS_b = 3*((53-50)^{\wedge}2 + (46-50)^{\wedge}2 + (51-50)^{\wedge}2)$$
$$SS_b = 3*(9 + 16 + 1)$$
$$SS_b = 78$$

Note that SS_b is the conventional notation for Sum of Squares Between.

Sum of Squares Within Groups

The range H4:M4 in Figure 10.3 shows how the sum of squares within groups is calculated. The function DEVSQ() is used in H4:J4 to get the sum of the squared deviations within each group from that group's mean. The range references—for example, =DEVSQ(D2:D4) in cell H4—are to cells shown in Figure 10.2.

The DEVSQ(D2:D4) function in cell H4 subtracts the mean of the values in D2:D4 from each of the values themselves, squares the differences, and sums the squared differences. Here are the specifics:

$$SS_{w1} = (55-53)^2 + (50-53)^2 + (54-53)^2$$
$$SS_{w1} = 4 + 9 + 1$$
$$SS_{w1} = 14$$

SS_w is the conventional notation for *sum of squares within*, and the numeral 1 in the subscript indicates that the formula is dealing with the first group.

After the sum of squared deviations is obtained for each of the three groups, in cells H4:J4, the sums are totaled in cell K4 and that total is carried over into cell M4. No weighting is needed as it is in M2, where the total of the squared deviations is multiplied by the sample size of three per group. The proof of this appears in a worksheet titled "MSB proof" in the workbook for Chapter 10, which you can download from the book's website at www.informit.com/title/9780789747204.

> **NOTE**
>
> Each group in this basic example has the same number of subjects. The analysis of variance handles different numbers of subjects or observations per group quite easily—automatically, in fact, if you use tools such as the Data Analysis add-in's single-factor ANOVA tool. (In this example, the type of medication taken is a *factor*. If the example also tested for differences in outcomes according to the subject's sex, that would also be termed a factor.)
>
> You often encounter two-factor, three-factor, or more complex designs, and the issue of equal group sizes then becomes more difficult to manage. Chapter 11, "Analysis of Variance: Further Issues," explores this problem in greater detail.

With this data set, the sum of squares between groups is 78, in cell M2 of Figure 10.3, and the sum of squares within groups is 34, in cell M4. Those two sums of squares total to 112, which is also the value you get using the DEVSQ() function on the full data set, as in cell M6.

Comparing Variances

What we have done here—and what every standard analysis of variance does—is break down, or *partition*, the total variation that is calculated by summing the squared deviations of every score from the grand mean. Once that's done, we can create two different, independent estimates of the total variance.

Variance Based on Sums of Squares Within Groups

Recall from Chapter 3, "Variability: How Values Disperse," that a variance is simply the sum of the squared deviations of scores from their mean, divided by the degrees of freedom. You have the sum of squares, based on variability within groups, in cell E2 of Figure 10.4. You arrive at 34 by totaling the sum of squares within each group, just as described in the prior section.

Figure 10.4
How the sums of squares within groups are accumulated.

	A	B	C	D	E	F	G	H	I
1		Group 1	Group 2	Group 3	Sum of Squared Deviations				
2	Sum of squares within groups	14	6	14	34				
3									
4					Average Variance within groups		Sum of Squares within groups	Degrees of Freedom	Mean Square within
5	Variance within group	7	3	7	5.67		34	6	5.67

Each group has 2 degrees of freedom: there are three observations per group, and you lose one degree of freedom per group because each group mean is fixed. (Chapter 3 provides the rationale for this adjustment.)

You can divide each group's sum of squares by 2 to get the variance for each group. This is done in cells B5:D5 of Figure 10.4. Each of those three variances is an estimate of the variability in the population from which the samples were drawn to create the three groups. Taking the average of the three variances in cell E5 provides an even more efficient estimate of the population variance.

A mathematically equivalent way to arrive at the total within group variance is to divide the total of the within group sums of squares by the total number of subjects less the number of groups. The total within group sum of squares is shown in cell G5 of Figure 10.4.

When the number of subjects is the same in each group, you get the total degrees of freedom for within group variation by means of N–J, where J is the number of groups and N is the total number of subjects. (The formula is easily adjusted when the groups have different numbers of subjects.) The number of subjects less the number of groups, in cell H5, is divided into the total within group sum of squares to produce the total within group variance in cell I5.

ANOVA terms this quantity "mean square within," often abbreviated as MS_w. Notice that it is identical to the average within group variance in cell E5.

Under the null hypothesis, all three groups were drawn from the same population. In that case, there is only one population mean, and any differences between the three groups' means is due to sampling error.

Therefore—still assuming that the null hypothesis is true—any differences in the within group variances are also due to sampling error: In other words, each group variance (and the average of the groups' variances) is an estimate of the variance in the population. When there is only one population mean for the scores to vary around, the three within group variances are each an estimate of the same population variance, the parameter σ^2.

Notice also—and this is important—that the estimate of the within group variation is unaffected by the distance between the group means. The within group sum of squares (and therefore the within group variance) accumulates the squared deviations of each score from its own group mean. The three group means could be 1, 2, and 3; or they could be 0, 98.6, and 100,000. It doesn't matter: The within group variation is affected only by the distances of the individual scores from the mean of their group, and therefore is unaffected by the distances between the group means.

Why is that important? Because we are about to create another estimate of the population variance that *is* based on the differences between the group means. Then we'll be able to compare an estimate based on the differences between means with an estimate that's *not* based on the differences between means. If the two estimates are very different, then there's reason to believe that the three groups are not samples from the same population, but from different populations with different means.

And that, in one paragraph, is what the logic of the analysis of variance is all about.

Variance Based on Sums of Squares Between Groups

Figure 10.5 shows how you might calculate what ANOVA calls *Mean Square Between*, or MS_b. Cells B2:D2 contain the means of the three groups, and the grand mean is in cell E2. The sum of the squared deviations of the group means (53, 46, and 51) from the grand mean (50) is in cell F2. That figure, 26, is reached with =DEVSQ(B2:D2).

Figure 10.5
The population variance as estimated from the differences between the means and the group sizes.

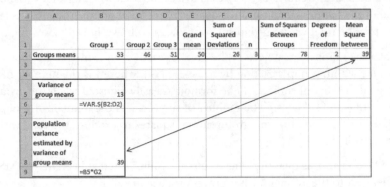

To get from the sum of the squared deviations in F2 to the Sum of Squares Between in H2, multiply F2 by G2, the number of subjects per group. The reason that this is done for the between groups variation, when it is not done for the within groups variation, is as follows.

You will find a proof of this in the workbook for Chapter 10, which can be downloaded from the book's website at www.informit.com/title/9780789747204. Activate the worksheet titled "MSB proof." The proof reaches the following equation as its next-to-last step:

$$\sum_{j=1}^{3}\sum_{i=1}^{3}\left(X_{ij}-\overline{X}_{..}\right)^2 = \sum_{j=1}^{3}\sum_{i=1}^{3}\left(X_{.j}-\overline{X}_{..}\right)^2 + \sum_{j=1}^{3}\sum_{i=1}^{3}\left(X_{.j}-\overline{X}_{.j}\right)^2$$

What happens next often puzzles students, and so it deserves more explanation than it gets in the accompanying, and somewhat terse, proof. The expression to the left of the equals sign is the sum of the squared deviations of each individual score from the grand mean. Divided by its degrees of freedom, $J * (n - 1)$, or 6 in this case, it equals the total variance in all three groups.

It also equals the total of these two terms on the right side of the equals sign:

■ The sum of the squared deviations of the group means from the grand mean:

$$\sum_{j=1}^{3}\sum_{i=1}^{3}\left(X_{.j}-\overline{X}_{..}\right)^2$$

■ The sum of the squared deviations of each score from the mean of its own group:

$$\sum_{j=1}^{3}\sum_{i=1}^{3}\left(X_{ij}-\overline{X}_{.j}\right)^2$$

Notice in the latter summation that it occurs once for each individual record, as the i index runs from 1 to 3 in each of the j = 1 to 3 groups.

However, there is no i index within the parentheses in the former summation, which operates only with the mean of each group and its deviation from the grand mean. Nevertheless, the summation sign that runs i from 1 to 3 must take effect, so the grand mean is subtracted from a group mean, the result squared, and the squared deviation is added, not just once but once for each observation in the group. And that is managed by changing

$$\sum_{j=1}^{3} \sum_{i=1}^{3} (X_j - \overline{X}_{..})^2$$

to this:

$$3 \sum_{j=1}^{3} (X_j - \overline{X}_{..})^2$$

Or more generally from

$$\sum_{j=1}^{k} \sum_{i=1}^{n} (X_j - \overline{X}_{..})^2$$

to this:

$$n \sum_{j=1}^{k} (X_j - \overline{X}_{..})^2$$

In words, the total sum of squares is made up of two parts: the squared differences of individual scores around their own group means, and the squared differences of the group means around the grand mean. The variability *within* a group takes account of each individual deviation because each individual score's deviation is squared and added.

The variability *between* groups must also take account of each individual score's deviation from the grand mean, but that is a function of the *group's* deviation from the grand mean. Therefore, the group's deviation is calculated, squared, and then multiplied by the number of scores represented by its mean.

Another way of putting this notion is to go back to the standard error of the mean, introduced in Chapter 7, "Using Excel with the Normal Distribution," in the section titled "Constructing a Confidence Interval." There, I pointed out that the standard error of the mean (that is, the standard deviation calculated using means as individual observations) can be estimated by dividing the variance of the individual scores in one sample by the sample size and then taking the square root:

$$s_{\overline{x}} = \sqrt{\frac{s^2}{n}}$$

The variance error of the mean is just the square of the standard error of the mean:

$$s_{\overline{X}}^2 = \frac{s^2}{n}$$

10

But in an ANOVA context, you have found the variance error of the mean directly, because you have two or (usually) more group means and can therefore calculate their variance. This has been done in Figure 10.5, in cell B5, giving 13 as the variance of 53, 46, and 51. Cell B6 shows the formula in cell B5: =VAR.S(B2:D2).

Rearranging the prior equation to solve for s^2, we have the following:

$$s^2 = ns_{\overline{X}}^2$$

Thus, using the figures in the present example, we have

$$s^2 = 3 \times 13$$
$$s^2 = 39$$

which is the same figure returned as MS_b in cell J2 of Figure 10.5, and, as you'll see, in cell D18 of Figure 10.7.

The F Test

To recap, in MS_w and MS_b we have two separate and independent estimates of the population variance. One, MS_w, is unrelated to the differences between the group means, and depends entirely on the differences between individual observations and the means of the groups they belong to.

The other estimate, MS_b, is unrelated to the differences between individual observations and group means. It depends entirely on the differences between group means and the grand mean, and the number of individual observations in each group.

Suppose that the null hypothesis is true: that the three groups are not sampled from different populations—populations that might differ because they received different medications that have different effects—but instead are sampled from one population, because the different medications do not have differential effects on those who take them. In that case, the observed differences in the sample means would be due to sampling error, not to any intrinsic difference in the medications that expresses itself reliably in an outcome measure.

If that's the case, we would expect a ratio of the two variance estimates to be 1.0. We would have two estimates of the same quantity—the population variance—and in the long run we would expect the ratio of the population variance to itself to equal 1.0. This, despite the fact that we go about estimating that variance in two different ways—one in the ratio's numerator and one in its denominator.

But what if the variance based on differences between group means is large relative to the variance based on deviations within groups? Then there must be something other than sampling error that's pushing the group means apart. In that case, our estimate of the population variance that we arrived at by calculating the differences between group means has been increased beyond what we would expect if the three groups were really just manifestations of the same population.

We would then have to reject the null hypothesis of no difference between the groups, and conclude that they came from at least two different populations—populations that have different means.

How large must the ratio of the two variances be before we can believe that it's due to something systematic rather than simple sampling error? The answer to that lies in the F distribution.

When you form a ratio of two variances—in the simplest ANOVA designs, it is the ratio of MS_b to MS_w—you form what's called an *F ratio*, just as you calculate a t-statistic by dividing a mean difference by the standard error of the mean. And just as with a t-statistic, you compare the calculated F ratio with an F distribution. Supplied with the value of the calculated F ratio and its degrees of freedom, the F distribution will tell you how likely your F ratio is if there is no difference in the population means.

Figure 10.7 pulls all this discussion together into one report, created by Excel's Data Analysis add-in. First, though, you have to run the ANOVA: Single Factor tool. Choose Data Analysis in the Analysis group on the Ribbon's Data tab. Select ANOVA: Single Factor from the list of tools to get the dialog box shown in Figure 10.6. (There are three ANOVA tools in the Data Analysis add-in. All the tools are available to you after you have installed the add-in as described in Chapter 4's section titled "Using the Analysis Tools.")

Figure 10.6
If your data is in Excel's list or table format, with headers as labels in the first row, use the Grouped By Columns option.

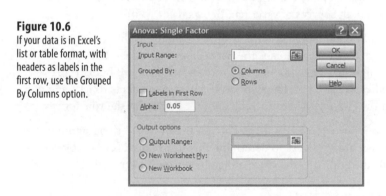

Some comments about Figure 10.7 are in order before we get to the F ratio.

The user supplied the data in cells A1:C4. The Data Analysis add-in's ANOVA: Single Factor tool was used to create the analysis in cells A7:G21.

The Source of Variation label in cell A17 indicates that the subsequent labels—in A18 and A19 here—tell you whether a particular row describes variability between or within groups. More advanced analyses call out other sources of variation. In some research reports you'll see *Source of Variation* abbreviated as *SV*. Here are the other abbreviations Excel uses:

- *SS*, in cell B17, stands for *Sum of Squares*.
- *df*, in cell C17, stands for *degrees of freedom*.
- *MS*, in cell D17, stands for *Mean Square*.

Figure 10.7
Notice that the raw data is laid out in A1:C4 so that each group occupies a different column.

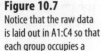

	A	B	C	D	E	F	G
1	Group 1	Group 2	Group 3				
2	55	48	50				
3	50	45	54				
4	54	45	49				
5							
6							
7	Anova: Single Factor						
8							
9	SUMMARY						
10	Groups	Count	Sum	Average	Variance		
11	Group 1	3	159	53	7		
12	Group 2	3	138	46	3		
13	Group 3	3	153	51	7		
14							
15							
16	ANOVA						
17	Source of Variation	SS	df	MS	F	P-value	F crit
18	Between Groups	78	2	39	6.882352941	0.027976	5.143253
19	Within Groups	34	6	5.666667			
20							
21	Total	112	8				

The values for sums of squares, degrees of freedom, and mean squares are as discussed in earlier sections of this chapter. For example, each mean square is the result of dividing a sum of squares by its associated degrees of freedom.

The F ratio in cell E18 is not associated specifically with the Between Groups source of variation, even though it is traditionally found in that row. It is the ratio of MS_b to MS_w and is therefore associated with both sources of variation, Between and Within.

However, the F ratio is traditionally shown on the row that belongs to the source of variation that's being tested. Here, the source is the between groups effect. In a more complicated design, you might have not just one factor (here, medication) but two or more—perhaps both medication and sex. Then you would have two effects to test, and you would find an F ratio on the row for medication and another F ratio on the row for sex.

In Figure 10.7, the F ratio reported in E18 is large enough that it is said to be significant at less than the .05 level. There are two ways to determine this from the ANOVA table, comparing the calculated F to the critical F, and calculating alpha from the critical F.

Comparing the Calculated F to the Critical F

The calculated F ratio, 6.88, is larger than the value 5.14 that's labeled "F crit" and found in cell G18. The *F crit* value is the critical value in the F distribution with the given degrees of freedom that cuts off the area that represents alpha, the probability of rejecting a true null hypothesis. If, as here, the calculated F is greater than the critical F, you know that the calculated F is improbable if the null hypothesis is true. This is just like you know that a calculated t-ratio, one that's greater than a critical t-ratio, is improbable if the null hypothesis is true.

Calculating Alpha

The problem with comparing the calculated and the critical F ratios is that the ANOVA report presented by the Data Analysis add-in doesn't remind you what alpha level you chose.

Conceptually, this issue is the same as is discussed in Chapters 8 and 9, where the relationships between decision rules, alpha, and calculated-versus-critical t-ratios were covered. The two differences here are that we're looking at more than just two means, and that we're using an F distribution rather than a normal distribution or a t-distribution.

Figure 10.8, coming up in the next section, shows a shaded area in the right tail of the curve. This is the area that represents alpha. The curve shows the relative frequency with which you will obtain different values of the F ratio assuming that the null hypothesis is true. Most of the time when the null is true you would get F ratios less than 5.143 based on repeated samples from the same population (the critical F ratio shown in Figure 10.7). Some of the time, due to sampling error, you'll get a larger F ratio even though the null hypothesis is true. That's alpha, the percent of possible samples that cause you to reject a true null hypothesis.

Just looking at the ANOVA report in Figure 10.7, you can see that the F ratios, calculated and critical, tell you to reject the null hypothesis. You have calculated an F ratio that is larger than the critical F. You are in the region where a calculated F is large enough to be improbable if the null hypothesis is true.

But how improbable is it? You know the answer to that only if you know the value of alpha. If you adopted an alpha of .05, you get a particular critical F value that cuts off the rightmost 5% of the area under the curve. If you instead adopt something such as .01 as the error rate, you'll get a larger critical F value, one that cuts off just the rightmost 1% of the area under the curve.

It's ridiculous that the Data Analysis add-in doesn't tell you what level of alpha was adopted to arrive at the critical F value. You're in good shape if you remember what alpha you chose when you were setting up the analysis in the ANOVA dialog box, but what if you don't remember? Then you need to bring out the functions that Excel provides for F ratios.

Using Excel's F Worksheet Functions

Excel provides two types of worksheet functions that pertain to the F distribution itself: the F.DIST() functions and the F.INV() functions. As with T.DIST and T.INV(), the .DIST functions return the size of the area under the curve, given an F ratio as an argument. The .INV functions return an F ratio, given the size of the area under the curve.

Using F.DIST() and F.DIST.RT()

You can use the F.DIST() function (or, in versions prior to Excel 2010, the FDIST() function) to tell you at what alpha level the *F crit* value is critical. The F.DIST() function is analogous to the T.DIST() function discussed in Chapters 8 and 9: You supply an F ratio and degrees of freedom, and the function returns the amount of the curve that's cut off by that ratio. Using the data as laid out in Figure 10.7, you could enter the following function in some empty cell on that worksheet:

    =1-F.DIST(G18,C18,C19,TRUE)

The formula requires some comments. To begin, here are the first three arguments that F.DIST() requires:

- **The F ratio itself**—In this example, that's the F crit value found in cell G18.
- **The degrees of freedom for the numerator of the F ratio**—That's found in cell C18. The numerator is MS_b.
- **The degrees of freedom for the denominator**—That's found in cell C19. The denominator is MS_w.

The fourth argument, whose value is given as TRUE in the current example, specifies whether you want the cumulative area to the left of the F ratio you supply (TRUE) or the probability associated with that specific point (FALSE). The TRUE value is used here because we want to begin by getting the entire area under the curve that's to the left of the F ratio.

The F.DIST() function, as given in the current example, returns the value .95. That's because 95% of the F distribution, with two and six degrees of freedom, lies to the left of an F ratio of 5.143. However, we're interested in the amount that lies to the right, not the left. Therefore, we subtract it from 1.

Another approach you could use is this:

    =F.DIST.RT(G18,C18,C19)

The F.DIST.RT() function returns the *right* end of the distribution instead of the left, so there's no need to subtract its result from 1. I tend not to use this approach, though, because it has no fourth argument. That forces me to remember which function uses which arguments, and I'd rather spend my energy thinking about what a function's result means than remembering its syntax.

FDIST() VERSUS F.DIST()

If an earlier version is forcing you to use FDIST() instead of F.DIST(), bear in mind that FDIST() is equivalent to F.DIST. RT(), not to F.DIST(). Annoying but inescapable, given the insistence on a sort of consistency. The consistency in this case is the insistence on returning the left portion of a distribution when the function's name ends in .DIST (that is, NORM.DIST, NORM.S.DIST, T.DIST, and so on). However, you have to work very hard to invent a situation in which you would expect the F ratio's numerator to be smaller than its denominator; in fact, if you do encounter such a situation, it's often due to mis-specifying the model for your data. The F test is a right-tailed test, unlike the z-test or the t-test, where the directionality of the difference is important.

As it is, though, keep it in mind that these two formulas are equivalent:

    =F.DIST.RT(G18,C18,C19)

    =FDIST(G18,C18,C19)

Using F.INV() and FINV()

The F.INV() function (or, in versions prior to Excel 2010, the FINV() function) returns a value for the F ratio when you supply an area under the curve, plus the number of degrees of freedom for the numerator and denominator that define the distribution.

The traditional approach has been to obtain a critical F value early on in an experiment. The researcher knows how many groups would be involved, and would have at least a good idea of how many individual observations would be available at the conclusion of the experiment. And, of course, alpha is chosen before any outcome data is available. Suppose that a researcher was testing four groups consisting of ten people each, and that the .05 alpha level was selected. Then an F value could be looked up in the appendix to a statistics textbook; or, since Excel became available, the following formula could be used to determine the critical F value:

=F.INV(.95,3,36)

Alternatively, prior to Excel 2010, you would use this one:

=FINV(.05,3,36)

These two formulas return the same value, 2.867. The older, FINV() function returns the F value that cuts off the *rightmost* 5% of the distribution; the newer F.INV() function returns the F value that cuts off the *leftmost* 95% of the distribution. Clearly, Excel has inadvertently set a trap for you. If you're used to FINV() and are converting to F.INV(), you must be careful to use the structure

=F.INV(.95,3,36)

and not the structure

=F.INV(.05,3,36)

which follows the older conventions, because if you do, you'll get the F value that cuts off the leftmost 5% of the distribution instead of the leftmost 95% of the distribution.

Back to our fictional researcher. A critical F value has been found, and the ANOVA test can now be completed using the actual data—just as is shown in Figure 10.7. The calculated F (in cell E18 of Figure 10.7) is compared to the critical F, and if the calculated F is greater than the critical F, the null hypothesis is rejected.

This sequence of events is probably helpful because, if followed, the researcher can point to it as evidence that the decision rules were adopted prior to seeing any outcome measures. Notice in Figure 10.7 that a "P-value" is reported by the Data Analysis add-in in cell F18. It is the probability, calculated from FDIST() or F.DIST(), of obtaining the calculated F if the null hypothesis is true. There is a strong temptation, then, for the researcher to say, "We can reject the null not only at the .05 level, but at the .03 level."

10

But there are at least two reasons not to succumb to that temptation. First, and most important, is that to do so implies that you have altered the decision rule after the data has come in—and that leads to capitalizing on chance.

Second, to claim a 3% level of significance instead of the *a priori* 5% level is to attribute more importance to a 2% difference than exists. There are, as pointed out in Chapter 6, "Telling the Truth with Statistics," many threats to the validity of an experiment, and statistical chance—including sampling error—is only one of them. Given that context, to make an issue of an apparent 2% difference in alpha level is straining at gnats.

The F Distribution

Just as there is a different t-distribution for every number of degrees of freedom in the sample or samples, there is a different F distribution for every combination of degrees of freedom for MS_b and MS_w. Figure 10.8 shows an example using $df_b = 3$ and $df_w = 16$.

Figure 10.8
Like the t-distribution, the F distribution has one mode. Unlike the t-distribution, it is asymmetric.

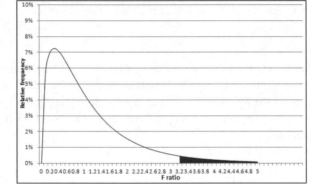

The chart in Figure 10.8 shows an F distribution for 3 and 16 degrees of freedom. The curve is drawn using Excel's F.DIST() function. For example, the height of the curve at the point where the F ratio is 1.0 is given by

=F.DIST(1,3,16,FALSE)

where the first argument, 1, is the F ratio for that point on the curve; 3 is the degrees of freedom for the numerator; 16 is the degrees of freedom for the denominator; and FALSE indicates that Excel should return the probability density function (the height of the curve at that point) rather than the cumulative density (the total probability for all F ratios from 0 through the value of the function's first argument—here, that's 1). Notice that the pattern of the arguments is similar to the pattern of the arguments for the T.DIST() function, discussed in detail in Chapter 9.

The shaded area in the right tail of the curve represents alpha, the probability of rejecting a true null hypothesis. It has been set here to .05. The curve you see assumes that the variances based on MS_b and MS_w are the same in the population, as is the case when the null hypothesis is true. Still, sampling error can cause you to get an F ratio as large as the one in this chapter's example; Figure 10.7 shows that the obtained F ratio is 6.88 (cell E18) and fully 5% of the F ratios in Figure 10.8 are greater than 3.2. (However, the distribution in Figure 10.8 is based on different degrees of freedom than the example in Figure 10.7. The change was made to provide a more informative visual example of the F distribution in Figure 10.8.)

The F distribution describes the relative frequency of occurrence of ratios of variances, and is used to determine the likelihood of observing a given ratio under the assumption that the ratio of one variance to another is 1 in the population. (George Snedecor named the F distribution in honor of Sir Ronald Fisher, a British statistician who was responsible for the development of the analysis of variance, explaining the interaction of factors—see Chapter 11—and a variety of other statistical concepts and techniques that were the cutting edge of theory in the early twentieth century.) To describe a t-distribution requires you to specify just one number of degrees of freedom, but to describe an F distribution you must specify the number of degrees of freedom for the variance in the numerator and the number of degrees of freedom for the variance in the denominator.

Unequal Group Sizes

From time to time you may find that you have a different number of subjects in some groups than in others. This situation does not necessarily pose a problem in the single-factor ANOVA, although it might do so, and you need to understand the implications if it happens to you.

Consider first the possibility that a differential dropout rate has had an effect on your results. This is particularly likely to pose a problem if you arranged for equal group sizes, or even roughly equal group sizes, and at the end of your experiment you find that you have very unequal group sizes. There are at least two reasons that this might occur:

- You used convenience or "grab" samples. That is, your groups consist of preexisting sets of people or plants or other responsive beings. There might well be something about the reasons for those groupings that caused some subjects to be missing at the end of the experiment. Because the groupings preceded the treatment you're investigating, you might inadvertently wind up assigning an outcome to a treatment when it had to do not with the treatment but with the nonrandom grouping.

- You randomly assigned subjects to groups but there is something about the nature of the treatments that causes them to drop out of one treatment at a greater rate than from other treatments. You may need to examine the nature of the treatments more closely if you did not anticipate differential dropout rates.

In either case, you should be careful of the logic of any conclusions you reach, quite apart from the statistics involved. Still, it can happen that even with random assignment, and treatments that do not cause subjects to drop out, you wind up with different group sizes. For example, if you are conducting an experiment that takes days or weeks to complete, you find people moving, forgetting to show up, getting ill, or being absent for any of a variety of reasons unrelated to the experiment. Even then, this can cause you a problem with the statistical analysis. As you will see in the next chapter, the problem is different and more difficult to manage when you simultaneously analyze two factors.

In a single-factor ANOVA, the issue pertains to the relationship between group sizes and within group variances. Several assumptions are made by the mathematics that underlie ANOVA, but just as is true with t-tests, not all the assumptions must be met for the analysis to be accurate.

One of the assumptions is that observations be independent of one another. If the fact that an observation is in Group 1 has any effect on the likelihood that another observation is in Group 1, or that it's in Group 2, the observations aren't independent. If the value of one observation depends in some way on the value of another observation, they are not independent. In that case there are consequences for the probability statements made by ANOVA, and those consequences can't be quantified. Independence of observations is an assumption that must be met.

> **NOTE** An important exception is the t-test for dependent groups and the analysis of covariance (discussed in Chapter 14, "Analysis of Covariance: The Basics"). In those cases, the dependency is deliberate and can be measured and accounted for.

Another important assumption is that the within group variances are equal. But unlike lack of independence, violating the equal variance assumption is not fatal to the validity of the analysis. Long experience and much research leads to these three general statements:

- When different within group variances exist, equal sample sizes mean that the effect on the probability statements is negligible. There are limits to this protection, though: If one within group variance is ten times the size of another, serious distortions of alpha can occur.

- If sample sizes are different and the larger samples have the smaller variances, the actual alpha is greater than the nominal alpha. You might start out by setting alpha at .05 but your chance of making a Type I error is actually, say, .09. The effect is to shift the F distribution to the right, so that the critical F value cuts off not 5% of the area under the curve but, say, 9%. Statisticians say that in this case the F test is *liberal*.

- If sample sizes are different and the larger samples have the larger variances, the opposite effect takes place. Your nominal alpha might be .05 but in actuality it is something such as .03. The F distribution has been shifted to the left and the critical F ratio cuts off only 3% of the distribution. Statisticians term this a *conservative* F test.

There is no practical way to correct this problem, other than to arrange for equal group sizes. Nor is there a practical way to calculate the actual alpha level. The best solution is to be aware of the effect (which is sometimes termed the *Behrens-Fisher problem*) and adjust your conclusions accordingly. Bear in mind that the smaller the differences between the group variances, the smaller the effect on the nominal alpha level.

Multiple Comparison Procedures

The F test is sometimes termed an *omnibus* test: That is, it tests simultaneously whether there is at least one reliable difference between any of the group means (or linear combinations of group means) that are being tested. By itself, it doesn't pinpoint which mean differences are responsible for an improbably large F ratio. Suppose you test four group means, which are 100, 90, 70, and 60, and get an F ratio that's larger than the critical F ratio for the alpha level you adopted. Probably (not necessarily, but probably) the mean of 100 is significantly different from the mean of 60—they are the highest and lowest means in an experiment that resulted in a significant F ratio. But what about 100 and 70? Is that a significant difference in this experiment? How about 90 and 60? You need to conduct multiple comparisons to make those decisions.

Unfortunately, things start to get complicated at this point. There are roughly (depending on your point of view) nine multiple comparison procedures that you can choose from. They differ on characteristics such as the following:

- Planned versus unplanned comparisons
- Distribution used (normally t, F, or q)
- Error rate (alpha) per comparison or per set of comparisons
- Simple comparisons only (that is, one group mean vs. another group mean) or complex comparisons (for example, the mean of two groups vs. the mean of two other groups)

There are other issues to consider, too, including the statistical sensitivity or power of the procedure.

For good or ill, Excel simplifies your decision because it does not always support the required statistical distribution. For example, two well regarded multiple comparison procedures are the Tukey and the Newman-Keuls. Both these procedures rely on a distribution called the *studentized range statistic*, usually referred to as *q*. Excel does not support that statistic: It does not have, for example, a Q.INV() or a Q.DIST() function.

Other methods employ modifications of, for example, the t-distribution. Dunnett's procedure modifies the t-distribution to produce a different critical value when you compare one, two, three, or more means with a control group mean. Excel does not support that sort of comparison except in the limiting case where there are only two groups. Dunn's procedure employs the t-distribution, but only for planned comparisons involving two means. When the comparisons involve more than two means, the Dunn procedure uses a modification of the t-distribution. The Dunn procedure has only slightly more statistical power than the Scheffé (see the next paragraph), which does not require planned contrasts.

Fortunately (if it was by design, I'll eat my keyboard) Excel does support two multiple-comparison procedures: planned orthogonal contrasts and the Scheffé method. The former is the most powerful of the various multiple comparison procedures (and also the most restrictive). The latter is the least powerful procedure (and gives you the most leeway in your analysis). However, you have to piece the analyses together using the available worksheet functions. The remainder of this chapter shows you how to do that.

Speaking generally, the Newman-Keuls is probably the best choice for a multiple comparison test of simple contrasts (Mean 1 vs. Mean 3, Mean 1 vs. Mean 4, Mean 2 vs. Mean 3, and so on) when you want to keep your error rate to a per-comparison basis (rather than to a per-family basis—that's much more conservative and you'll probably miss some genuine differences). The Newman-Keuls test, as mentioned previously, uses the q or *studentized range* distribution. You can find tables of those values in many intermediate statistical texts, and some websites offer you free lookups.

I suggest that you consider running your ANOVA in Excel using the Data Analysis add-in, particularly if your experimental design includes just one factor or two factors with equal group sizes. Take the output to a general statistics text and use it in conjunction with the tables you find there to complete your multiple comparisons.

> **NOTE** You could also use the freeware statistical program *R* if you must, but after a couple of years of using *R*, I find I spend more time dealing with its user interface and idiosyncratic layouts than I gain from having the occasional need for analyses that I can't do completely in Excel.

If you want to stay within what Excel has to offer, you can get just as much statistical power from planned orthogonal contrasts, which are discussed next, as from Newman-Keuls. And you can do plenty of data-snooping without planning a thing beforehand if you use Excel to run your Scheffé comparisons.

The Scheffé Procedure

The Scheffé is the most flexible of the available multiple comparison procedures. You can make as many comparisons as you want, and they need not be simply one mean compared to another. If you had five groups, for example, you could use the Scheffé procedure to compare the mean of two groups with the mean of the remaining three groups. It might make no sense to do so in the context of your experiment, but the Scheffé procedure allows it. You can also use the Scheffé with unequal group sizes, although that topic is deferred until Chapter 12, "Multiple Regression Analysis and Effect Coding: The Basics."

Furthermore, in the Scheffé procedure, alpha is shared among all the comparisons you make. If you make just one comparison and have set alpha to .05, you have a 5% chance of concluding that the difference you calculate is a reliable one, when in fact it is not. Or, if you make 20 comparisons and have set alpha to .05, then you have a 5% chance of rejecting a true null hypothesis *somewhere* in the 20 comparisons. This is very different, and much more conservative, than running a 5% chance of rejecting a true null in *each* of the comparisons.

Figure 10.9 shows how the Scheffé multiple comparison procedure might work in an experiment with two treatment groups and a control group.

Figure 10.9
The Data Analysis add-in provides the preliminary ANOVA in A9:G20.

	G24		f_x	=SQRT($C$17*(F.INV(0.95,$C$17,$C$18)))		

	A	B	C	D	E	F	G
1			HDL levels				
2		Medication A	Medication B	Placebo			
3		41	42	38			
4		47	48	38			
5		48	49	36			
6		48	50	36			
7		52	57	52			
8							
9	Anova: Single Factor						
10	SUMMARY						
11	Groups	Count	Sum	Average	Variance		
12	Medication A	5	236	47.2	15.7		
13	Medication B	5	246	49.2	28.7		
14	Placebo	5	200	40	46		
15	ANOVA						
16	Source of Variation	SS	df	MS	F	P-value	F crit
17	Between Groups	234	2	117	3.88	0.05	3.89
18	Within Groups	361.6	12	30.1			
19							
20	Total	595.73	14				
21							
22	Scheffé Method		Contrast Coefficients		Standard deviation of contrast	ψ / s_ψ	Critical Value (.05)
23		Mean 1	Mean 2	Mean 3			
24	Med A - Med B	1	-1	0	3.472	-0.576	2.788
25	Med A - Placebo	1	0	-1	3.472	2.074	2.788
26	Med B - Placebo	0	1	-1	3.472	2.650	2.788
27	(Med A + Med B)/2 - Placebo	1/2	1/2	-1	3.007	2.727	2.788

10

With the raw data laid out as shown in cells B2:D7 in Figure 10.9, you can run the ANOVA: Single Factor tool in the Data Analysis add-in to create the report shown in A9:G20. These steps will take care of it:

1. With the Data Analysis add-in installed as described in Chapter 4, "How Variables Move Jointly: Correlation," click Data Analysis in the Ribbon's Analysis group. Select ANOVA: Single Factor from the list box and click OK. The dialog box shown earlier in Figure 10.6 appears.

2. With the flashing I-bar in the Input Range edit box, drag through the range B2:D7 so that its address appears in the edit box.

3. Be sure the Columns option is chosen. (Because of the way Excel's list and table structures operate, it is very seldom that you'll want to group the data so that each group occupies a different row. But if you do, that's what the Rows option is for.)

4. If you included column labels in the input range, as suggested in step 2, fill the Labels check box.

5. Enter an alpha value in the Alpha edit box, or accept the default value. Excel uses .05 if you leave the Alpha edit box blank.

6. Click the Output Range option button. When you do so—in fact, whenever you choose a different Output option button—the add-in gives the Input Range box the

focus, and whatever you type or select next overwrites what you have already put in the Input Range edit box. Be sure to click in the Output Range edit box after choosing the Output Range option button.

7. Click a cell on the worksheet where you want the output to start. In Figure 10.9, that's cell A9.

8. Click OK. The report shown in cells A9:G20 in Figure 10.9 appears.

(To get all the data to fit in Figure 10.9, I have deleted a couple of empty rows.)

A significant result at the .05 level from the ANOVA, which you verify from cell F17 of Figure 10.9, tells you that there is a reliable difference somewhere in the data. To find it, you can proceed to one or more multiple comparisons among the means using the Scheffé method. This method is not supported directly by Excel, even with the Data Analysis add-in. In fact, no multiple comparison method is directly supported in Excel. But you can perform a Scheffé analysis by entering the formulas and functions described in this section.

The Scheffé method, along with several other approaches to multiple comparisons, begins in Excel by setting up a range of cells that define how the group means are to be combined (that is, the contrasts you look for among the means). In Figure 10.9, that range of cells is B24:D27.

The first contrast is defined by the difference between the mean for Medication A and the mean for Medication B. The mean for Medication A will be multiplied by 1; the mean for Medication B will be multiplied by –1; the mean for the Placebo will be multiplied by 0. The results are summed.

The 1's and the 0's and, if used, the fractions that are multiplied by the means are called *contrast coefficients*. The coefficients tell you whether a group mean is involved in the contrast (1), omitted from the contrast (0), or involved in a combination with other means (a coefficient such as .33 or .5). Of course, the use of these coefficients is a longwinded way of saying, for example, that the mean of Medication B is subtracted from the mean of Medication A, but there are good reasons to be verbose about it.

The first reason is that you need to calculate the standard error of the contrast. You will divide the standard error into the result of combining the means using the contrast coefficients. The general formula for the standard error of a contrast is

$$\sqrt{MS_e\left(\frac{C_1^2}{n_1} + \frac{C_2^2}{n_2} + ... + \frac{C_j^2}{n_j}\right)}$$

where MS_e is the mean square error from the ANOVA table (cell D18 in Figure 10.9) and each n is the sample size of each group.

So the standard error for the first contrast in Figure 10.9, in cell E24, is calculated with this formula:

=SQRT($D$18*(B24^2/$B$12+C24^2/$B$13+D24^2/$B$14))

> **NOTE**
>
> The mean square error just mentioned is, in the simpler ANOVA designs, the same as the within group variance you've seen so far in this chapter. There are times when you do not divide an MS_b value by an MS_w value to arrive at an F. Instead, you divide by a value that is more generally known as MS_e because the proper divisor is not a within groups variance. The proper divisor is sometimes an interaction term (see Chapter 11). The MS_e designation is just a more general way to identify the divisor than is MS_w. In the single-factor and fully crossed multiple-factor designs covered in this book, you can be sure that MS_w and MS_e mean the same thing: within group variance.

In words, this means you square each contrast coefficient and divide the result by the group's sample size. Total the results. Multiply by the MS_e, and take the square root. The conventional way to symbolize the standard error of the contrast is s_ψ, where ψ represents the contrast. (The Greek symbol ψ is represented in English as *psi*, and pronounced "sigh.")

The prior formula makes the reference to D18 absolute by means of the dollar signs: $D$18. Doing so means that you can copy and paste the formula into cells E25:E27 and keep intact the reference to D18, with its MS_e value. The same is true of the references to cells B12, B13, and B14: Each standard error in E24:E27 uses the same values for the group sizes, so $B$12, $B$13, and $B$14 are used to make the references absolute. The references to B24, C24, and D24 are left relative because you want them to adjust to the different contrast coefficients as you copy and paste the formula into E25:E27.

The contrast divided by its standard error is represented as follows:

$$\frac{\psi}{s_\psi}$$

The first ratio is calculated using this formula in cell F24:

=($D$12*B24+$D$13*C24+$D$14*D24)/E24

The formula multiplies the mean of each group (in D12, D13, and D14) by the contrast coefficient for that group in the current contrast (in B24, C24 and D24), and then divides by the standard error of the contrast (in E24). The formula is copied and pasted into F25:F27. Therefore, the cell addresses of the means in D12, D13, and D14 are made absolute: Each mean is used in each contrast. The contrast coefficients change from contrast to contrast, and their cells use the relative addresses B24, C24, and D24. This allows the coefficient addresses to adjust as the formula is pasted into different rows. The relative addressing also allows the reference to E24 to change to E25, E26 and E27 as the formula is copied and pasted into F25:F27.

The sum of the means times their coefficients is divided by the standard errors of the contrasts in F24:F27. The result of that division is compared to the critical value shown in G24:G27 (it's the same critical value for each contrast in the case of the Scheffé procedure).

> **NOTE**
>
> The prior formula includes a term that sums the products of the groups' means and their contrast coefficients. It does so explicitly by the use of multiplication symbols, addition symbols, and individual cell addresses. Excel provides two worksheet functions, SUMPRODUCT() and MMULT(), that sum the products of their arguments and would be possible to use here. However, SUMPRODUCT() requires that the two ranges be oriented in the same way (in columns or in rows) and so to use it here would mean reorienting a range on the worksheet or using the TRANSPOSE() function. MMULT() requires that you array-enter it, but with this worksheet layout it works fine. If you prefer, you can array-enter (using Ctrl+Shift+Enter) this formula
>
> =MMULT(B24:D24,$D$12:$D$14)/E24
>
> into F24, and then copy and paste it into F25:F27.

Once you have the ratios of the contrasts to the standard errors of the contrasts, you're ready to make the comparisons that tell you whether a contrast is unlikely given the alpha level you selected. You use the same critical value to test each of the ratios. Here's the general formula:

$$\sqrt{(J - 1)F_{df_b,\, df_w}}$$

In words, find the F value for the degrees of freedom between and the degrees of freedom within. Those degrees of freedom will always appear in the ANOVA table. Use the F for the alpha level you have chosen. For example, if you have set alpha at .05, you could use either the function

=F.INV(0.95,C17,C18)

in Figure 10.9 or this one:

=F.INV.RT(0.05,C17,C18)

Cells C17 and C18 contain the degrees of freedom between groups and within groups, respectively. If you use F.INV() with .95, you get the F value given that 95% of the area under the curve is to the value's left. If you use F.INV.RT() with .05, you get the same F value—you're just saying that you want to specify it such that 5% of the area is to its right. It comes to the same thing, and it's just a matter of personal preference which you use.

With that F value in hand, multiply it by the degrees of freedom between groups (cell C17 in Figure 10.9) and take the square root. Here's the Excel formula in cells G24:G27 in Figure 10.9:

=SQRT($C$17*(F.INV(0.95,$C$17,$C$18)))

This critical value can be used for any contrast you might be interested in, no matter how many means are involved in the contrast, so long as the contrast coefficients sum to zero— as they do in each contrast in Figure 10.9. (You would have difficulty coming up with a set of coefficients that do not sum to zero *and* that result in a meaningful contrast.)

In this case, none of the tested contrasts results in a ratio that's larger than the critical value. The Scheffé procedure is the most conservative of the multiple comparison procedures, in large part because it allows you to make any contrast you want, *after* you've seen the results of the descriptive analysis (so you know which groups have the largest differences in mean values) and the inferential analysis (the ANOVA's F test tells you whether there's a significant difference *somewhere*). The tradeoff is of statistical power for flexibility. The Scheffé procedure is not a powerful method: It's conservative, and it fails to regard these contrasts as significant at the .05 level. However, it gives you great leeway in deciding how to follow up on a significant F test.

> **NOTE** The second and third comparisons are so close to significance at the .05 level that I would definitely replicate the experiment, particularly given that the omnibus F test returned a probability of .05.

Planned Orthogonal Contrasts

The other approach to multiple comparisons that this chapter discusses is *planned orthogonal contrasts*, which sounds a lot more intimidating than it is.

Planned Contrasts

The *planned* part just means that you promise to decide, in advance of seeing any results, which group means, or sets of group means, you want to compare. Sometimes you don't know how to sharpen your focus until you've seen some preliminary results, and in that situation you can use one of the after-the-fact methods, such as the Scheffé procedure. But particularly in an era when very expensive medical and drug research takes place, it's not at all unusual to plan the contrasts of interest long before the treatment has been administered.

Orthogonal Contrasts

The *orthogonal* part means that the contrasts you make do not employ redundant information. You would be employing redundant information if, for example, one contrast subtracted the mean of a Group 3 from the mean of Group 1, and another contrast subtracted the mean of Group 3 from the mean of Group 2. Because the two contrasts both subtract Group 3's mean from that of another group, the information is redundant.

There's a simple way to determine whether comparisons are orthogonal if the groups have equal sample sizes. See Figure 10.10.

Figure 10.10 shows the same contrast coefficients as were used in Figure 10.9 for the Scheffé illustration. The coefficients sum to zero within a comparison. But imposing the condition that different contrasts be orthogonal means that the sum of the products of the coefficients for two contrasts also sum to zero. That's easier to see than it is to read.

Look at cell E9 in Figure 10.10. It contains 1, the sum of the numbers in B9:D9. Those three numbers are the products of contrast coefficients. Row 9 combines the contrast coefficients for contrasts 1 and 2, so cell B9 contains the product of cells B3 and B4. Similarly, cell C9 contains the product of cells C3 and C4, and D9 contains the product of D3 and D4. Summing cells B9:D9 into E9 results in 1. That means that contrasts 1 and 2 are not orthogonal to one another. Also, the mean of Group 1 is part of both those contrasts—that's redundant information, so contrasts 1 and 2 aren't orthogonal.

Figure 10.10
The products of a group's contrast coefficients must sum to zero for two contrasts to be orthogonal.

	A	B	C	D	E
1	POC	Contrast Coefficients			
2		Mean 1	Mean 2	Mean 3	Total of coefficients
3	1. Med A - Med B	1	-1	0	0
4	2. Med A - Placebo	1	0	-1	0
5	3. Med B - Placebo	0	1	-1	0
6	4. (Med A + Med B)/2 - Placebo	1/2	1/2	-1	0
7					
8	Product of coefficients for:				Total of Products
9	1 and 2	1	0	0	1
10	1 and 3	0	-1	0	-1
11	1 and 4	1/2	- 1/2	0	0
12	2 and 3	0	0	1	1
13	2 and 4	1/2	0	1	1.5
14	3 and 4	0	1/2	1	1.5

It's a similar situation in Row 10, which tests whether the contrasts in rows 3 and 5 are orthogonal. The mean of Group 2 appears in both contrasts (the fact that it is subtracted in one contrast but not in the other makes no difference), and as a result the total of the products is nonzero. Contrast 1 and Contrast 3 are not orthogonal.

Row 11 tests the contrasts in rows 3 and 6, and here we have a pair of orthogonal contrasts. The products of the contrast coefficients in row 3 and row 6 shown in B11:D11 and are totaled in E11, where you see a 0. That tells you that the contrasts defined in rows 3 and 6 are orthogonal, and you can proceed with contrasts 1 and 4: the mean of Group 1 versus the mean of Group 2, and the mean of Groups 1 and 2 taken together versus the mean of Group 3. Notice that none of the three means appears in its entirety in both contrast 1 and contrast 4.

The general rule is that if you have K means, only K – 1 contrasts that can be made from those means are orthogonal. Here, there are three means, so only two contrasts are orthogonal.

Evaluating Planned Orthogonal Contrasts

The contrasts that you calculate, the ones that are both planned and orthogonal, are calculated exactly as you calculated the contrasts for the Scheffé procedure. The numerator and denominator of the ratio, the ψ and the s_ψ, are calculated in the same way and have the same values—and therefore so do the ratios. Compare the ratios in cells F24 and F25 in Figure 10.11 with those in cells F24 and F27 in Figure 10.9.

The ratio of a contrast to its standard error is referred to as ψ / s_ψ by the Scheffé procedure, but it's referred to as a t-ratio in planned orthogonal contrasts. The differences between the two procedures discussed so far have to do solely with when you plan the contrasts and whether they are orthogonal.

Figure 10.11
Only two contrasts
are orthogonal to one
another, so only those
two appear in rows 24
and 25.

	G24	▾	f_x =T.INV.2T(0.05,$C$18)				
	A	B	C	D	E	F	G
1			HDL levels				
2		Medication A	Medication B	Placebo			
3		41	42	38			
4		47	48	38			
5		48	49	36			
6		48	50	36			
7		52	57	52			
8							
9	Anova: Single Factor						
10	SUMMARY						
11	*Groups*	*Count*	*Sum*	*Average*	*Variance*		
12	Medication A	5	236	47.2	15.7		
13	Medication B	5	246	49.2	28.7		
14	Placebo	5	200	40	46		
15	ANOVA						
16	*Source of Variation*	*SS*	*df*	*MS*	*F*	*P-value*	*F crit*
17	Between Groups	234	2	117	3.88	0.05	3.89
18	Within Groups	361.6	12	30.1			
19							
20	Total	595.73	14.00				
21							
22	POC		Contrast Coefficients		Standard deviation of contrast	t	Critical Value (.05)
23		Medication A	Medication B	Placebo			
24	Med A - Med B	1	-1	0	3.472	-0.576	2.179
25	(Med A + Med B)/2 - Placebo	1/2	1/2	-1	3.007	2.727	2.179

10

We now arrive at the point that causes the two procedures to differ statistically. You compare the t-ratios (shown in cells F24 and F25 in Figure 10.11) to the t-distribution with the same number of degrees of freedom as is associated with the MS_e in the ANOVA table; Figure 10.11 shows that to be 12 (see cell C18) for this data set. To get the critical t value with an alpha of .05 for a nondirectional comparison, you would use this formula as it's used in cell G24 of Figure 10.11:

=T.INV.2T(.05,$C$18)

> **NOTE**
> If you use any of the T.DIST functions, it's a good idea to insert the ABS function into the formula: for example, T.DIST(ABS(F24), $C$18). This is so that the t-ratio will be converted to its absolute value (a positive number) if the direction of the subtraction that the contrast coefficients call for results in a negative number. The T.DIST(), T.DIST.2T(), and T.DIST.RT() functions do not allow the first argument to be negative. This is another indication of the degree of thought that went into the design of the Excel 2010 consistency functions.

Notice that the average of Med A and Med B produces a significant result against the placebo using planned orthogonal contrasts, whereas it was not significant at the .05 level using the Scheffé procedure. This is an example of how the Scheffé procedure is more conservative and the planned orthogonal contrasts procedure is more powerful statistically. However, you can't use planned orthogonal contrasts to do what many texts call "data-snooping." That sort of after-the-fact exploration of a data set is contrary to the entire idea behind planned contrasts.

Chapter 11, coming up next, continues the discussion of how to use Excel to perform the analysis of variance, and it gets into an area that makes ANOVA an even more powerful technique: two- and three-factor analyses.

10

Analysis of Variance: Further Issues

The sort of statistical analysis that Chapters 8 through 11 examine is called *factorial analysis*. The term *factorial* in this context has nothing to do with multiplying successively smaller integers (as Excel does with its FACT() function). In the terminology used by experimental design, a factor is a variable—often measured on a nominal scale—with two or more levels to which the experimental subjects belong.

For example, the research that was depicted in the previous chapter's example and illustrated in Figure 10.11 is an experiment in which the factor—the type of treatment—has three levels: Treatment A, Treatment B, and Placebo. Each subject belongs to one of those levels, and treatment is the single factor considered in the example.

Factorial ANOVA

It's not only possible but often wise to design an experiment that uses more than just one factor. There are different ways to combine the factors. Figure 11.1 shows two of the more basic approaches: crossed and nested.

The range B5:D11 in Figure 11.1 shows the layout of a design in which two factors, Hospital and Treatment, are crossed. Every level of Hospital appears with every level of Treatment—and that's the definition of *crossed*. The intent of the design is to enable the researcher to look into every available combination of the two factors.

This type of crossing is at the heart of multifactor research. Not only are you investigating, in this example, the relative effects of different treatments on patient outcomes, you are simultaneously investigating the relative effect of different hospitals. Furthermore, you are investigating how, if at all, the two factors interact to produce outcomes that you could not identify in any other way. How else are you going to determine whether laparoscopies, as compared to more invasive surgical techniques, have different results at University Health Center than they do at Good Samaritan Hospital?

Figure 11.1
Two factors can be either crossed or nested.

	Treatment crosses Hospital	
	Hospital 1	Hospital 2
	Pt 1	Pt 7
Laparoscopy	Pt 2	Pt 8
	Pt 3	Pt 9
	Pt 4	Pt 10
Other Procedure	Pt 5	Pt 11
	Pt 6	Pt 12

	Treatment crosses Hospital MD nested within Hospital			
	Hospital 1		Hospital 2	
	MD 1	MD 2	MD 3	MD 4
	Pt 1	Pt 7	Pt 13	Pt 19
Laparoscopy	Pt 2	Pt 8	Pt 14	Pt 20
	Pt 3	Pt 9	Pt 15	Pt 21
	Pt 4	Pt 10	Pt 16	Pt 22
Other Procedure	Pt 5	Pt 11	Pt 17	Pt 23
	Pt 6	Pt 12	Pt 18	Pt 24

NOTE It's perfectly logical to term an experiment that has only one factor a "factorial" design. In another example of the many idiosyncrasies in statistical diction, though, most statisticians reserve the term *factorial* for a design with at least two factors and use any one of a variety of other terms for a design that uses one factor only.

Contrast that crossed design with the one depicted in G5:K11 of Figure 11.1. Treatment is fully crossed with Hospital as before, but an additional factor, Doctor, has been included. The levels of Doctor are *nested* within levels of Hospital: In this design, doctors do not practice at both hospitals. You can make the same inferences about Hospital and Treatment as in the fully crossed design, because those two factors remain crossed. But you cannot make the same kind of inference about different doctors at different hospitals because you have not designed a way to observe them in different institutions (and there may be no way to do so). However, there are often other advantages to explicitly recognizing the nesting.

NOTE Actually, nesting is going on in the design shown in B5:D11. Patients are nested within treatments and hospitals. This is the case for all factorial designs, where the individual subject is nested within some combination of factor levels. It's simply not traditional in statistical terminology to recognize that individual subjects are nested, except in certain designs that recognize subject as a factor.

Other Rationales for Multiple Factors

The study of interaction, or how two factors combine to produce effects that neither factor can produce on its own, is one primary rationale for using more than one factor at once. Another is efficiency: This sort of design enables the researcher to study the effects of each variable without repeating the experiment, probably with a different set of subjects.

Yet another reason is statistical power: the sensitivity of the statistical test. By including a test of two factors—or more—instead of just one factor, you often increase the accuracy of the statistical tests. Figure 11.2 shows an example of an ANOVA that tests whether there is a difference in cholesterol levels between groups that are given different treatments, or between those treatment groups and a group that takes a placebo.

Figure 11.2
There is no statistically significant difference between groups at the .05 confidence level, but compare to Figure 11.3.

	A	B	C	D	E	F	G
1		Treatment A	Treatment B	Placebo			
2		59.2	63.5	53.1			
3		57.2	59.4	57.8			
4		55.9	60.3	51			
5		53.1	56.2	50.6			
6		50.1	53.1	47.2			
7		50.2	51.3	49.9			
8							
9	Anova: Single Factor						
10							
11	SUMMARY						
12	Groups	Count	Sum	Average	Variance		
13	Treatment A	6	325.7	54.28	14.17		
14	Treatment B	6	343.8	57.30	21.34		
15	Placebo	6	309.6	51.60	12.86		
16							
17							
18	ANOVA						
19	Source of Variation	SS	df	MS	F	P-value	F crit
20	Between Groups	97.58111111	2	48.7906	3.025854	0.07871	3.68232
21	Within Groups	241.8683333	15	16.1246			
22							
23	Total	339.4494444	17				

The analysis of variance shown in Figure 11.2 was produced by Excel's Data Analysis add-in: specifically, its ANOVA: Single Factor tool (discussed in Chapter 10, "Testing Differences Between Means: The Analysis of Variance"). But Figure 11.3 shows how adding another factor makes the F test sensitive enough to decide that there is a reliable, nonrandom difference between the means for different treatments.

Figure 11.3
Adding a factor that explains some of the error variance makes the statistical test more powerful.

	A	B	C	D	E	F	G
1		Treatment A	Treatment B	Placebo			
2	Black	59.2	63.5	53.1			
3		57.2	59.4	57.8			
4	White	55.9	60.3	51			
5		53.1	56.2	50.6			
6	Asian	50.1	53.1	47.2			
7		50.2	51.3	49.9			
8							
9	ANOVA						
10	Source of Variation	SS	df	MS	F	p-value	F crit
11	Sample	195.35	2	97.67	22.47	0.00	4.26
12	Columns	97.58	2	48.79	11.22	0.00	4.26
13	Interaction	7.40	4	1.85	0.43	0.79	3.63
14	Within	39.13	9	4.35			
15							
16	Total	339.45	17				

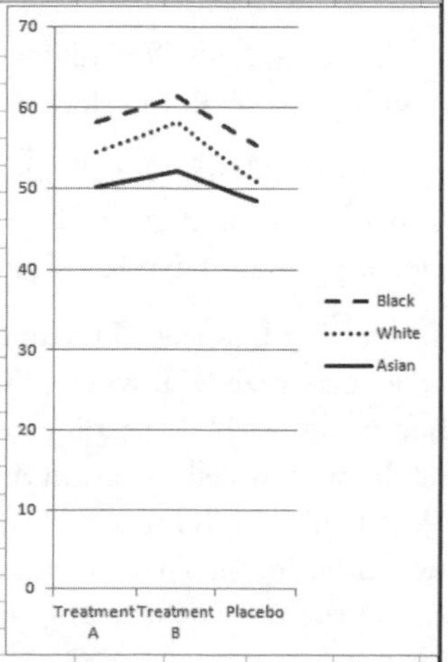

> **NOTE**
>
> I am assuming that you have already read the section in Chapter 2 titled "Understanding Formulas, Results, and Formats." That section explains why the F ratio in cell E11 might appear to be off by a couple of hundredths when you divide, by hand, the "Mean Square Sample" by the "Mean Square Within." In fact, the result is accurate to sixteen decimal places. There is no rounding error. I simply chose to show only two decimals in the numerator and denominator, instead of inflicting sixteen decimals on you in cells D11 and D14.

In Figure 11.3, the ANOVA summary table is shown in cells A9:G16. Some aspects of its structure look a little odd, and this chapter covers them in the section titled "Using the Two-Factor ANOVA Tool." The ANOVA in Figure 11.3 was produced by the Data Analysis add-in named ANOVA: Two Factor with Replication. That tool was used instead of the single-factor ANOVA tool because the example now has two factors: Treatment and Ethnicity.

The numbers for the input data are precisely the same as in Figure 11.2. The only difference is that the patient ethnicity factor has been added. But as a direct result, the Treatment effect is now significant at below the .05 level (see cell F12) and the Ethnicity factor is also significant below .05 (see cell F11).

How does that come about? If you look at the row in the ANOVA table for Between Groups in Figure 11.2, you'll see that the Mean Square Between in cell D20 is 48.79. It's the same in cell D12 in Figure 11.3. That's as it should be: Adding a factor, Ethnicity, has no effect on the mean values for Treatment, and it's the variability of the treatment means that is measured by the value of 48.79 as that factor's mean square.

However, the value of the F ratio in Figure 11.2 (3.026 in cell E20) is smaller than the F ratio in Figure 11.3 (11.22 in cell E12)—the value in Figure 11.3 is more than three times as large, even though the numerator of 48.79 is identical. The cause of the much larger F ratio in Figure 11.3 is its much smaller denominator.

In Figure 11.2, 48.79 is divided by the Mean Square Within of 16.12 to result in an F ratio of 3.026, too small to reject the null hypothesis with so few degrees of freedom.

In Figure 11.3, 48.79 is divided by the Mean Square Within of 4.35, much smaller than the value of 16.12 in Figure 11.2. The result is a much larger F ratio, 11.22, which *does* support rejecting the null hypothesis at the .05 confidence level.

Here's what happens: The amount of total variability stays the same when the Ethnicity factor is recognized. However, that Ethnicity factor accounts for 195.35 of the sums of squares that in Figure 11.2 are allocated to Mean Square Within. The remaining sums of squares for the within-cell variation drops dramatically, from 241.87 (cell B21 in Figure 11.2) to 39.13 (cell B14 in Figure 11.3). The mean square also drops, along with the sum of squares, the denominator shrinks, and the F ratio increases to the point that the observed differences among the treatment means are quite unlikely if the null hypothesis is true—and so we reject it.

And this happens to the Treatment factor because we have added the simultaneous analysis of the Ethnicity factor.

Using the Two-Factor ANOVA Tool

To use the Data Analysis add-in's ANOVA: Two Factor with Replication tool, you must lay out your data in a particular way. That way appears in Figure 11.3, and there are several important issues to keep in mind.

You must include a column on the left and a row at the top of the input data range, to hold column and row labels if you want to use them. You can leave that column and row blank if you want, but Excel expects the row and column to be there, bordering the actual numeric data. When I ran the ANOVA tool on the data in Figure 11.3, for example, the address of the data range I supplied was A1:D7, where column A was reserved for row headers and row 1 was reserved for column headers.

You must have the same number of observations in each cell. A *cell* in ANOVA terminology is the intersection of a row level and a column level. Therefore, in Figure 11.3, the range B2:B3 constitutes a cell, and so does B4:B5, and C6:C7 and so on; there are nine cells in the design.

> **NOTE** The remainder of this chapter, and of this book, attempts to distinguish between a cell in a design ("design cell") and a cell on a worksheet ("worksheet cell") where the potential for confusion exists. So a design cell might refer to a range of worksheet cells, such as B2:B3, and a worksheet cell might refer to B2.

Each design cell in your input data for the two-factor ANOVA tool must have the same number of observations. To understand how the add-in ensures that you're not trying to cheat and sneak an extra observation in one design cell or another, it's best to take a look at how the dialog box forces your hand (see Figure 11.4).

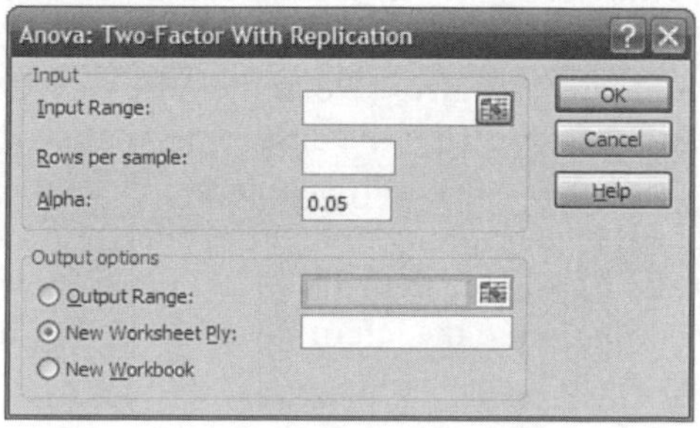

Figure 11.4
Notice that the dialog box does not ask you if you're using labels: It assumes that you are doing so.

11

The input range, as noted earlier, is A1:D7. If you fail to reserve a row and a column for column and row labels, Excel displays the cryptic complaint that "Each sample must contain the same number of rows."

That initial column for row headers excepted, the add-in assumes that each remaining column in your input range represents a different level of a factor. In Figure 11.3, for example, more data could have been added in E1:E7 to accommodate another level of the Treatment factor.

So that Excel can check that all your design's cells have the same number of observations, you're required to enter the number of "rows per sample." This is more idiosyncratic terminology: more standard would have been "observations per design cell." However, for the data in Figure 11.3, there are two observations (in this case, two patients) per design cell (or two rows per sample, if you prefer), so you would enter **2** in the Rows Per Sample text box.

You could enter **1** in the Rows Per Sample box if you wanted, and the add-in would not complain, even though with one observation per cell there can be no within-cell variance and you'll get ridiculous results. But Excel does complain if you don't provide a row and a column for headers. It's a funny world.

Missing data isn't allowed. In the Figure 11.3 example, no worksheet cell may be blank in the range B2:D7. If you leave a cell blank, Excel complains that nonnumeric data was found in the input range.

The edit box for Alpha serves the same function as it does in the ANOVA: Single Factor tool discussed in Chapter 10: It tells Excel how to determine the *F Crit* value in the output. For example, cell G12 in Figure 11.3 gives 4.26 as the value of *F Crit*, which is the value that the calculated F ratio must exceed if the differences in the group means for the Treatment factor are to be regarded as statistically significant. Excel uses the degrees of freedom and the value of alpha that you specify to find the value of *F Crit*. Suppose that you specify .05. Excel uses either the F.INV() or the F.INV.RT() function. If you prefer to think in terms of the 95% of the distribution to the left of the critical value, use F.INV():

=F.INV(0.95,2,9)

Here's the alternative if you prefer to think in terms of the 5% of the distribution to the right of the critical value:

=F.INV.RT(0.05,2,9)

In either case, Excel knows that the F distribution in question has 2 and 9 degrees of freedom. It knows about the 2 because it can count the three levels of the Treatment factor in your range of input data, and three levels less one for the grand mean results in 2 degrees of freedom. It knows about the 9 because it can count the total number of observations in your input data range (18), subtract the degrees of freedom for each of your two factors (4 in total), and subtract another 4 for the interaction (you'll see shortly how to calculate the degrees of freedom for an interaction). That leaves 10, and subtracting another 1 for the grand mean leaves 9.

In sum, you supply the alpha and the input range via the dialog box shown in Figure 11.4, and Excel can use that information to calculate the *F Crit* values to which you will compare the calculated F values.

By the way, don't read too much significance into the labels that the ANOVA: Two Factors with Replication tool puts in its ANOVA summary table. In Figure 11.3, notice that the tool uses the label "Sample" in cell A11, and the label "Columns" in cell A12.

In this particular example, *Sample* refers to the Ethnicity factor and *Columns* refers to the Treatment factor. The labels Sample and Columns are defaults and there is no way to override them, short of overwriting them after the tool has produced its output. In particular, Samples representing Ethnicity does not imply that the levels of Treatment are not samples, and Columns for levels of Treatment does not imply that levels of Ethnicity are not in rows.

Further, the two-factor ANOVA tool uses the label "Within" to indicate the source of within groups variation (cell A14 in Figure 11.3). The one-factor ANOVA tool uses the label "Within Groups." The difference in the labels does not imply any difference in the meaning of the associated statistics. Within Groups Sum of Squares, regardless of whether it's labeled "Within" or "Within Groups," is still the sum of the squared deviations of the individual observations in each design cell from that cell's mean. Later in this book, where multiple regression is discussed as an alternative approach to ANOVA, you'll see the term *Residual* used to refer to this sort of variability.

The Meaning of Interaction

The term *interaction*, in the context of the analysis of variance, means the way the factors operate jointly: They have different effects with some combinations of levels than with other combinations. Figure 11.5 shows an illustration.

I changed the input data shown in Figure 11.3 for the purpose of Figure 11.5: The scores for the two white subjects in Treatment B were raised roughly 6 points each. All the other values are the same in Figure 11.5 as they were in Figure 11.3. The result—as you can see by comparing the charts in Figure 11.3 with the chart in Figure 11.5—is that the mean value for white subjects increases to the point that it is higher than for black subjects in Treatment B.

In Figure 11.3, interaction is absent. Regardless of Treatment, blacks have the highest scores, followed by whites and then by Asians. Treatment B yields the highest scores, followed by Treatment A and then Placebo. There is no *differential* effect of Treatment according to Ethnicity.

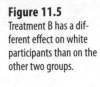

Figure 11.5
Treatment B has a different effect on white participants than on the other two groups.

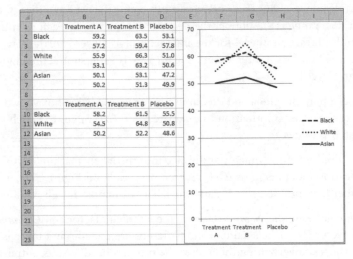

In Figure 11.5, interaction is present. Of the nine possible combinations of three treatments and three ethnicities, eight are the same as they were in Figure 11.3, but the ninth—Treatment B with whites—climbs markedly, so that whites' scores under Treatment B are higher than both blacks' and Asians'. There is a *differential* effect, an *interaction*, between ethnicity and treatment.

The researcher would not have been able to determine this if two single-factor experiments had been carried out. The data from one experiment would have shown that blacks have the highest average score, followed by whites and then by Asians. The data from the other experiment would have shown that Treatment B yields the highest scores, followed by Treatment A and then Placebo. There would have been no hint, no reason to believe, that Treatment B would have such a marked effect on whites.

The Statistical Significance of an Interaction

ANOVA terminology calls factors such as Treatment and Ethnicity in the prior example *main effects*. This helps to distinguish them from the effects of interactions.

In a design with the same number of observations in each design cell (such as the example that this chapter has discussed, which has two observations per design cell), the sums of squares, degrees of freedom, and therefore the mean squares for the main effects are identical to the results of the single-factor ANOVA. Figure 11.6 demonstrates this.

The same data set used in Figure 11.3 is analyzed three times in Figure 11.6. (In practice, you would never do this. It's being done here only to show how main effects are independent of each other and of interactions in an ANOVA with equal group sizes.) The analyses are as follows:

- The range A1:G11 runs a single-factor ANOVA with Ethnicity as the factor.
- The range A13:G23 runs a single-factor ANOVA with Treatment as the factor.
- The range I1:O16 runs a two-factor ANOVA, including the interaction term for Ethnicity and Treatment.

Figure 11.6
The main effects in the single-factor ANOVAs are the same as in the two-factor ANOVA.

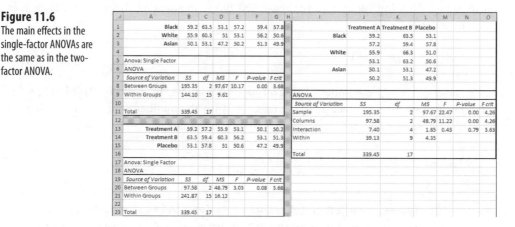

Compare the Between Groups Sum of Squares, df, and MS in worksheet cells B8:D8 with the same statistics in J11:L11. You will be comparing the variance due to Ethnicity group means in the single-factor ANOVA with the same statistics in the two-factor ANOVA. Notice that they are identical, and you'll see the same sort of thing in any ANOVA that has an equal number of observations, or *equal n's*, in each of its design cells. The analysis of the main effect in a single-factor ANOVA will be identical to the same main effect in a factorial ANOVA, up to the F ratio. The sums of squares, degrees of freedom, and mean squares will be the same in the single-factor ANOVA and the factorial ANOVA.

As a further example, compare the Between Groups Sum of Squares, df, and MS in cells B20:D20 with the same statistics in J12:L12. You will be comparing the variance due to Treatment group means in the single-factor ANOVA with the same statistics in the two-factor ANOVA. Notice that they are, again, identical.

In each case, though, the associated F ratio is different in the single-factor case from its value in the two-factor case. The reason has nothing to do with the main effect itself. It is due solely to the second factor, and to the interaction, in the two-factor analysis. The Sums of Squares for the second factor and the interaction in the two-factor analysis were part of the Within Group variation in the single-factor analysis. Moving these quantities into the interaction in the factorial ANOVA reduces the Mean Square Within, which is the denominator of the F test here. Thus, the F ratio is different. As this chapter has already pointed out, that change to the magnitude of the F ratio can convert a less sensitive test that retains the null hypothesis to a more powerful statistical test that rejects the null hypothesis.

11

Calculating the Interaction Effect

You can probably infer from this discussion that there is no difference between the single-factor and the multiple-factor ANOVA in how the sums of squares and mean squares are calculated for the main effects. Sum the squared deviations of the group means for each main effect from the grand mean. Divide by the degrees of freedom for that effect to get its mean square. Nothing about the two-factor ANOVA with equal n's changes that. Here it is again in equation form:

$$SS_{Ethnicity} = nK \sum_{j=1}^{J} (\overline{X}_{j.} - \overline{X}_{..})^2$$

In this equation, n is the number of observations (also known as "replicates") per cell, K is the number of levels of the *other* main effect, and J is the number of levels of Ethnicity. Similarly, the sum of squares for Treatment would be as follows:

$$SS_{Treatment} = nJ \sum_{k=1}^{K} (\overline{X}_{k.} - \overline{X}_{..})^2$$

> **TIP** If you ever have to do this sort of thing by hand in an Excel worksheet, remember that the DEVSQ() function is a handy way to get the sum of the squared deviations of a set of individual observations or a set of means that represent a main effect. The DEVSQ() function could replace the summation sign and everything to its right in the two prior formulas. You can see how this is done in the Excel workbooks for Chapter 10 and Chapter 11, which you can download from www.informit.com/title/9780789747204.

The interaction calculation is different—by definition, really, because there can be no factor interaction in a single-factor ANOVA. Described in words, the calculation sounds a little intimidating, so be sure to have a close look at the formula that follows. In this example, the interaction sum of squares for the Treatment and the Ethnicity main effects is the squared sum of each group mean, less the mean of each level that the group belongs to, plus the grand mean, multiplied by the number of observations per design cell.

Here's the formula:

$$SS_{TxE} = n \sum_{j=1}^{J} \sum_{k=1}^{K} (\overline{X}_{jk} - \overline{X}_{j.} - \overline{X}_{.k} + \overline{X}_{..})^2$$

Figure 11.7 repeats the data set given earlier in Figure 11.5, with increased values for whites in Treatment B so as to create a significant interaction. The data set is in A1:D7.

The range F1:L8 contains the ANOVA table for the data in A1:D7, and you can see that the interaction is now statistically significant at the .05 level. (It is not significant in Figure 11.3, but I have raised the values for whites under Treatment B for Figure 11.7; so doing makes the interaction statistically significant and also changes the sums of squares for both main effects.)

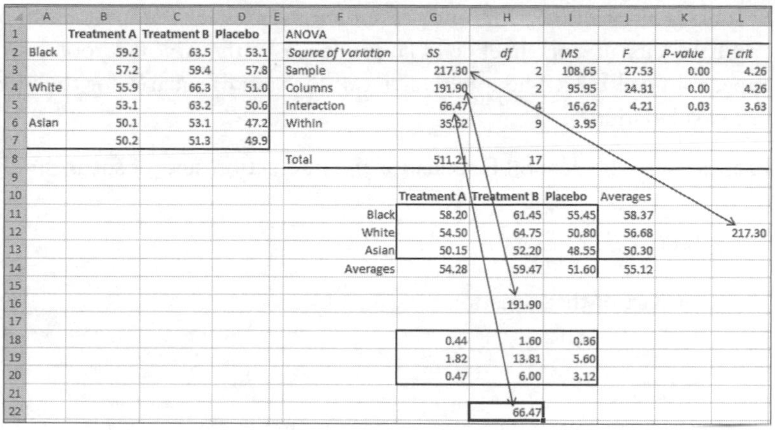

Figure 11.7
This figure shows how worksheet functions calculate the sums of squares that are the basis of the two-factor ANOVA.

	A	B	C	D	E	F	G	H	I	J	K	L
1		Treatment A	Treatment B	Placebo		ANOVA						
2	Black	59.2	63.5	53.1		*Source of Variation*	*SS*	*df*	*MS*	*F*	*P-value*	*F crit*
3		57.2	59.4	57.8		Sample	217.30	2	108.65	27.53	0.00	4.26
4	White	55.9	66.3	51.0		Columns	191.90	2	95.95	24.31	0.00	4.26
5		53.1	63.2	50.6		Interaction	66.47	4	16.62	4.21	0.03	3.63
6	Asian	50.1	53.1	47.2		Within	35.52	9	3.95			
7		50.2	51.3	49.9								
8						Total	511.2	17				
9												
10							Treatment A	Treatment B	Placebo	Averages		
11						Black	58.20	61.45	55.45	58.37		
12						White	54.50	64.75	50.80	56.68		217.30
13						Asian	50.15	52.20	48.55	50.30		
14						Averages	54.28	59.47	51.60	55.12		
15												
16								191.90				
17												
18							0.44	1.60	0.36			
19							1.82	13.81	5.60			
20							0.47	6.00	3.12			
21												
22								66.47				

In Figure 11.7, the range F10:J14 contains the group averages, the main effects averages, and their labels. For example, cell G11 contains 58.20, the average value for blacks under Treatment A. Cell J11 contains 58.37, the overall average for blacks, and cell G14 contains 54.28, the overall average for Treatment A. Cell J14 contains 55.12, the grand mean of all observations.

With that preliminary work in F10:J14, it's possible to get the sums of squares for both main effects and the interaction. After that it's easy to complete the ANOVA table, dividing the sums of squares by the degrees of freedom to get mean squares, and finally forming ratios of mean squares to get the F ratios.

First, cell L12 contains 217.30. The formula in the cell is

=2*3*DEVSQ(J11:J13)

Following the formula for the Ethnicity main effect given earlier in this section, it is the number of observations per group (2) times the number of levels of the *other* main effect (3), times the sum of the squared deviations of the Ethnicity group means from the grand mean. The result is identical to the sum of squares for Ethnicity in worksheet cell G3 of Figure 11.7, which was produced by the ANOVA: Two Factor with Replication add-in.

Similarly, cell H16 contains 191.90. The cell's formula is

=2*3*DEVSQ(G14:I14)

It is the sum of squares for the Treatment main effect, and its result is identical to the result produced by the ANOVA tool in worksheet cell G4.

The formulas in G3 and H16 both follow the general pattern given earlier by

$$SS_{Main\ Effect} = nJ \sum_{k=1}^{K} \left(\overline{X}_{k.} - \overline{X}_{..} \right)^2$$

Still using Figure 11.7, you find the sum of squares for the interaction between Treatment and Ethnicity in worksheet cell G5, produced by the ANOVA tool. Its value, 66.47, also appears in cell H22. The way to arrive at the sum of squares for the interaction requires a little explanation.

I repeat here the general formula for the interaction sum of squares:

$$SS_{TxE} = n \sum_{j=1}^{J} \sum_{k=1}^{K} \left(\overline{X}_{jk} - \overline{X}_{j.} - \overline{X}_{.k} + \overline{X}_{..} \right)^2$$

The first part of that equation

$$n \sum_{j=1}^{J} \sum_{k=1}^{K}$$

is what's represented in the formula in cell H22:

=2*SUM(G18:I20)

This formula sums across the values in the intersections of rows 18 to 20 and columns G to I, and then doubles that sum because there are two observations per design cell.

The second part of the equation

$$\left(\overline{X}_{jk} - \overline{X}_{j.} - \overline{X}_{.k} + \overline{X}_{..} \right)^2$$

represents what's in each of the cells in G18:I20. Cell G18, for example, contains this formula:

=(G11–G$14–$J11+$J$14)^2

It takes the value of cell G11 (blacks under Treatment A), subtracts the mean in G14 for everyone under Treatment A, subtracts the mean for all blacks in the experiment in J11, and adds the grand mean of all scores in J14. The result is the unique effect of being in that design cell: a black subject taking Treatment A. In terms of the general formula, cell G18 uses these values:

- $\overline{X}_{jk}$ is the cell, G11, with the mean scores of blacks under Treatment A, worksheet cells B2:B3.
- $\overline{X}_{.k}$ is the cell, G14, that contains the mean of all scores in Treatment A, worksheet cells G11:G13.
- $\overline{X}_{j.}$ is the cell, J11, that contains the mean of all blacks' scores in G11:I11.
- $\overline{X}_{..}$ is the cell that contains the grand mean of all scores, J14.

Notice that the formula in cell G18 uses relative, mixed, and absolute addressing. Once you have entered it in G18, you can drag it two columns to the right to pick up the proper formulas for blacks under Treatment B and also under Placebo, in cells H18:I18. Once the first row of three formulas has been established (in G18:I18), select those three cells and drag them down into G19:I20 using the fill handle (that's the small black square in the bottom-right corner of the selection). The formula adjusts to pick up whites and Asians under Treatment B and Placebo.

Finally, add up the values in in G18:I20. Multiply by 2, the number of observations per design cell, to get the full sum of squared deviations for the interaction in worksheet cell H22.

The degrees of freedom for the interaction is, by comparison, much easier to find. Just multiply together the degrees of freedom for each main effect involved in the interaction. In the present example, each main effect has two degrees of freedom. Therefore, the Treatment by Ethnicity interaction has four degrees of freedom. If there had been another level of Treatment, then the Treatment main effect would have had three degrees of freedom and the interaction would have had six degrees of freedom.

THE WHEEL, REINVENTED

I am aware that I have belabored these formulas beyond what's needed to complete a basic 3-by-3 analysis of variance, main effects and interaction. I'm doing it anyway for two reasons that seem pretty good to me.

One is that in keeping with most of the output provided by the Data Analysis add-in's tools, there are no formulas—just static values. A worksheet cell that contains a mean square does not contain the formula that calls for the worksheet cell with the sum of squares to be divided by the worksheet cell with the degrees of freedom. Nor does a worksheet cell that contains an F ratio contain a formula that divides a main effect mean square by a within group's mean square. All you get in the output is the result of the calculation.

That makes it hard to look more closely at what's going on, or to otherwise check on it. For example, when I'm learning a statistical procedure, I like to be able to change an observation here and an observation there, to see what effect my changes have on the outcome.

It's a useful learning technique to see what happens when you change an observation that is, at present, close to a group's mean to a value that's far from the group's mean. So doing can have a major impact on both a main effect's variance and an interaction's variance, with consequences for whether either effect takes you outside the level you've set for alpha—or makes what had been a significant effect an insignificant one.

But with the ANOVA tools in the Data Analysis add-in, you can't do that. All the results are static values. If you know what the formulas are and how they work, you can substitute them and do your own experimenting with the input data.

More important—and the second reason for emphasizing the formulas—is that I've provided *definitional* formulas in this chapter. It's fairly clear why they do what they do: For example, they accumulate squared deviations from a mean, and that's just what a variance does. Using the definitional formulas, it's easier to see the parallels between the inferential statistics and the descriptive statistics that form their underpinnings.

Unfortunately, those conceptually rich definitional formulas cause problems if you're a human being trying to apply them to real-world numbers. People rearranged the formulas a hundred years ago and in so doing made them less arduous for paper-and-pencil calculations, and less prone to serious rounding error. Even 40 years ago, when hand calculators started to feature temporary memories and square root functions, there were calculation formulas that were easier to use than the definitional formulas.

11

But although the calculation formulas were easier to use in the absence of PCs, they did not convey the concepts behind them. Here's one calculation formula, widely used back in the day:

$$\sum_{j=1}^{J} \frac{\left(\sum_{k=1}^{K} \sum_{i=1}^{n} X_{ijk} \right)^2}{n_{j.}} - \frac{\left(\sum_{k=1}^{K} \sum_{j=1}^{J} \sum_{i=1}^{n} X_{ijk} \right)^2}{n_{..}}$$

Does that look to you like a formula for the sum of squared deviations from a mean? It didn't to me in 1980 and it doesn't now. But it is. Here's what the formula for squared deviations from a mean looks like to me:

$$nJ \sum_{k=1}^{K} (\overline{X}_{k.} - \overline{X}_{..})^2$$

Take the mean of a factor level, subtract the grand mean, square the difference, sum the squared differences, and multiply to account for the number of observations and the number of levels in the other factor. Still a touch complicated but nothing like the preceding formula.

The point is that with Excel you can work with formulas that are easy to understand, without going through the kinds of labored computations that used to result in rounding errors and even more egregious, paper-and-pencil arithmetic errors. Therefore, I emphasize those definitional formulas and show you how they work out in the context of an Excel worksheet. As long as you're willing to slog through some paragraphs that might seem like over-explaining, you'll emerge with a better understanding of *why* these analyses work as they do.

And when we get around to showing how analysis of variance is just a different way of using multiple regression, you'll be better prepared to understand the relationships involved.

The Problem of Unequal Group Sizes

In ANOVA designs with two or more factors, group size matters. As it turns out, when you have the same number of observations in each design cell, there is no ambiguity in how the sums of squares are partitioned—that is, how the sums of squares are allocated to the row factor, to the column factor, to the interaction, and to the remaining within-cell sums of squares.

That's how the examples used so far in this chapter have been presented. Figure 11.8 shows another example of what's called a *balanced* design.

Figure 11.8 shows two ways of calculating the total sum of squares in the design. Recall that the total sum of squares is the total of each observation's squared deviation from the grand mean. It is the numerator of the variance, and the degrees of freedom is the denominator. Returning briefly to the logic of ANOVA, it's that total sum of squares that we want to partition, allocating some to differences in group means and, in factorial designs, to the interaction.

Figure 11.8

In a balanced design, the total sum of squares is the same whether it's calculated directly or by summing the main effects, interaction, and within-cell.

	B16	▾	*fx* =DEVSQ(C3:E8)						
	A	B	C	D	E	F	G	H	I	J
1				Patient						
2			Inpatient	Outpatient	Short Stay			Averages		
3			105	95	118		96.33	107.67	102.00	102.00
4		Medical	83	108	87		87.00	106.33	112.33	101.89
5	Treatment		101	120	101		91.67	107.00	107.17	101.94
6			88	99	105					
7		Surgical	90	108	117			SS Treatment		
8			83	112	115			0.03		
9								0.03		
10										
11	Source of variation	SS	df	MS		F		SS Patient		
12	Patient	950.78	2	475.39		4.50	633.80	153.35	163.63	
13	Treatment	0.06	1	0.06		0.00				
14	Interaction	293.44	2	146.72		1.39		SS Interaction		
15	Within groups	1266.67	12	105.56			63.79	1.12	81.81	
16	Total SS *computed directly*	2510.94					63.79	1.12	81.81	
17	Total SS *from sum of effects*	2510.94								
18								SS Within		
19							274.67	312.67	482.00	
20							26.00	88.67	82.67	

In Figure 11.8, notice cells B16 and B17. They display the same value, 2510.94, for the total sum of squares, but the two cells arrive at that value differently. Cell B16 uses Excel's DEVSQ() function on the original data set in C3:E8. As you've already seen, DEVSQ() returns the sum of the squared deviations of its arguments from their mean—the very definition of a sum of squares.

Cell B17 calculates the total sum of squares differently. It does so by adding up the sum of squares as allocated to the Patient factor, to the Treatment factor, to the interaction between the two factors, and to the remaining variability within design cells that is not associated with differences in the means of the factor levels.

Because the two ways of calculating the total sum of squares have identical results, these points are clear:

- All the variability is accounted for by the main effects, interaction, and within-group sums of squares. Otherwise, the sum of squares from totaling the main effects, interaction, and within-group sources would be *less than* the sum of squares based on DEVSQ().

- None of the variability has been counted twice. For example, it is *not* the case that some of the variability has been allocated to the Patient and also to the Patient by Treatment interaction. Otherwise, the sum of squares from totaling the main effects, interaction, and within-group sources would be *greater than* the sum of squares based on DEVSQ().

In other words, there is no ambiguity in how the sums of squares are divided up among the various possible sources of variability.

Now compare the total sums of squares calculated in Figure 11.8 with the totals in Figure 11.9.

In Figure 11.9, the design has groups whose sizes are not identical to one another: Two groups have three observations, two have four observations, and two have five. The unequal

11

design cell frequencies—often termed *unequal n's*—introduce ambiguity in how the total sum of squares is to be allocated. Notice that cell B19, which calculates the total sum of squares using DEVSQ(C3:E12), returns a smaller value (3222.00) than does cell B20, which returns 3257.28 as the total of the sums of squares for the main effects, interaction effects, and within groups.

Figure 11.9
In an unbalanced design, the total sum of squares as calculated directly differs from the total of the main effects, interaction, and within-cell.

| | B20 | | f_x | =SUM(B15:B18) | | | | | |

	A	B	C	D	E	F	G	H	I	J
1				Patient						
2			Inpatient	Outpatient	Short Stay			Averages		
3			105	95	118		96.33	110.20	101.75	103.92
4			83	108	87		87.25	106.33	111.40	102.08
5		Medical	101	120	101		91.14	108.75	107.11	103.00
6				108	101					
7				120				SS Treatment		
8		Treatment	88	99	105			10.08		
9			90	108	117			10.08		
10		Surgical	83	112	115					
11			88		105			SS Patient		
12					115		984.14	264.50	152.11	
13										
14	Source of variation	SS	df	MS	F			SS Interaction		
15	Patient	1400.75	2	700.38	7.27		54.80	1.42	157.64	
16	Treatment	20.17	1	20.17	0.21		35.43	6.75	135.49	
17	Interaction	391.53	2	195.765212	2.0323992					
18	Within cells	1444.83	15	96.3222222				SS Within		
19	Total SS computed directly	3222.00					274.67	432.80	482.75	
20	Total SS from sum of effects	3257.28					26.75	88.67	139.2	

The DEVSQ() result is inarguable: That is the total sum of squares available for allocation among the sources of variation. But a quantity of 35.28 has been counted twice and some of the surplus has been put in the sum of squares for Patient, some for Treatment, some for the interaction, and some to the remaining within-cell variability.

The underlying reason for this situation will not become clear until Chapter 12, "Multiple Regression Analysis and Effect Coding: The Basics," but it is due to the unequal n's. With one important exception, any time you have unequal n's in the cells of your design—any time that different combinations of one or more factor levels have different numbers of observations—the sums of squares in the ANOVA become ambiguous. When the sums of squares are ambiguous, so are the mean squares and therefore the F ratios, and you can no longer tell what's going on with the associated probability statements.

> **NOTE**
> An occasionally important exception to the problem I've just described is *proportional* cell frequencies. This situation comes about when each level of one factor has, say, twice as many observations as the same level on the other factor. The multiplier could be a number other than 2, of course, such as 1.5 or 2.5. The condition that must be in place is as follows: The number of observations in each design cell must equal the product of the number of observations in its row, times the number of observations in its column, divided by the total number of observations. If that condition is met, the partitioning of the sums of squares is unambiguous. You can't use Excel's Data Analysis two-factor ANOVA tool on such a data set, because it demands equal numbers of observations in each design cell. But the methods discussed in Chapter 12, including the Data Analysis Regression tool, work just fine.

Several approaches are available to you if you have a design with two or more factors, unequal n's, and disproportional frequencies. None of these approaches is consistent with the ANOVA tools in the Data Analysis add-in. These methods are discussed in Chapter 12, though, and you'll find that they are so powerful and flexible that you won't miss the ANOVA tools when you have two or more factors and unequal n's.

Repeated Measures: The Two Factor Without Replication Tool

There's a third ANOVA tool in the Data Analysis add-in. Chapters 10 and 11 have discussed the single-factor ANOVA tool and the ANOVA tool for two factors with replication. This section provides a brief discussion of the two-factor *without* replication tool.

First, a reminder: In ANOVA terminology, *replication* simply means that each design cell has more than one observation, or *replicate*. So, the name of this tool implies one observation per design cell. There is a type of ANOVA that uses one observation per design cell, traditionally termed *repeated measures analysis*. It's a special case of a design called a *randomized block*, in which subjects are assigned to blocks that receive a series of treatments. The "randomized" comes from the usual condition that treatments be randomly assigned to subjects within blocks; but this condition does not apply to a repeated measures design.

The subjects are chosen for each block based on their similarity, in order to minimize the variation among subjects within blocks: This will make the tests of differences between treatments more powerful. You often find siblings assigned to a block, or pairs of subjects who are matched on some variable that correlates with the outcome measure.

Alternatively, the design can involve only one subject per block, acting as his own control, and in that case the randomized block design is termed a *repeated measures design*. This is the design that ANOVA: Two Factor without Replication is intended to handle.

But here's what Excel's documentation as well as other books on using Excel for statistical analysis don't tell you: A randomized block design in general and a repeated measures design in particular make an additional assumption, beyond the usual ANOVA assumptions about issues such as equal cell variances. This design assumes that the covariances between different treatment levels are homogeneous: not necessarily equal, but not significantly different (the assumptions of homogeneous variances and covariances are together called *compound symmetry*). In other words, the data you obtain must not actually contradict the hypothesis that the covariances in the population are equal. If your data doesn't conform to the assumption, then your probability statements are suspect.

You can use a couple of tests to determine whether your data set meets this assumption, and Excel is capable of carrying them out. (Box's test is one, and the Geisser-Greenhouse conservative F test is another.)

However, these tests are laborious to construct, even in the context of an Excel worksheet. My recommendation is to use a software package that's specifically designed to include this sort of analysis. In particular, the multivariate F statistic in a multivariate ANOVA test does not make the assumption of homogeneity of covariance, and therefore if you arrange for

11

that test, in addition to the univariate F, you don't have to worry about Messrs. Box, Geisser, and Greenhouse.

Excel's Functions and Tools: Limitations and Solutions

This chapter has focused on two-factor designs: in particular, the study of main effects and interaction effects in balanced designs—those that have an equal number of observations in each design cell. In doing so, the chapter has made use of Excel's Data Analysis add-in and has shown how to use its ANOVA: Two Factor with Replication tool so as to carry out an analysis of variance. One limitation in particular is clear: You must have equal design cell sizes to use that tool.

In addition, the tool imposes a couple other limitations on you:

■ *It does not allow for three or more factors.* That's a standard sort of design, and you need a way to account for more than just two factors.

■ *It does not allow for nested factors.* Figure 11.1 shows the difference between crossed and nested factors, but does not make clear the implications for Excel's two-factor ANOVA tool (see Figure 11.10).

Figure 11.10
If you show the nested factor as crossed, the nature of the design becomes clearer.

	A	B	C	D	E	F	G	H	I	J	K	L	M	N
1														
2							MD 1	MD 2			MD 1	MD 2	MD 3	MD 4
3		MD 1	Pt 1	Pt 4			Pt 1	Pt 7			Pt 1	Pt 7		
4			Pt 2	Pt 5			Pt 2	Pt 8			Pt 2	Pt 8		
5	Hospital		Pt 3	Pt 6		Hospital	Pt 3	Pt 9		Hospital	Pt 3	Pt 9		
6	1	MD 2	Pt 7	Pt 10		1	Pt 4	Pt 10		1	Pt 4	Pt 10		
7			Pt 8	Pt 11			Pt 5	Pt 11			Pt 5	Pt 11		
8			Pt 9	Pt 12			Pt 6	Pt 12			Pt 6	Pt 12		
10		MD 3	Pt 13	Pt 16			Pt 13	Pt 19					Pt 13	Pt 19
11			Pt 14	Pt 17			Pt 14	Pt 20					Pt 14	Pt 20
12	Hospital		Pt 15	Pt 18		Hospital	Pt 15	Pt 21		Hospital			Pt 15	Pt 21
13	2	MD 4	Pt 19	Pt 22		2	Pt 16	Pt 22		2			Pt 16	Pt 22
14			Pt 20	Pt 23			Pt 17	Pt 23					Pt 17	Pt 23
15			Pt 21	Pt 24			Pt 18	Pt 24					Pt 18	Pt 24

As the design is laid out in Figure 11.10, in A3:D15, it's clear that MD is nested within Hospital: That is, it's *not* the case that each level of MD appears at each level of Hospital. However, although it's customary to depict the design in that way, it doesn't conform to the expectations of the ANOVA two-factor add-in. That tool wants one factor's levels to occupy different rows and the other factor's levels to occupy different columns.

If you lay the design out as the ANOVA tool wants—as shown in F2:H15 in Figure 11.10—then you're acting as though you have a fully crossed design. That design has only two levels of the MD factor, whereas in fact there are four. Certainly MDs do not limit their practices to patients in one hospital only, but the intent of the experiment is to account for MDs within hospitals, not MDs across hospitals.

The design as laid out in J2:N15 shows the nesting clearly and conforms to the ANOVA tool's requirement that one factor occupy columns and that the other occupy rows. However, that inevitably leads to empty cells, and the ANOVA tools won't accept empty cells, whether of the worksheet cell variety or the design cell variety. The ANOVA tools regard such cells as nonnumeric data and won't process them.

Here's another limitation of the Data Analysis add-in: The ANOVA tools do not provide for a very useful adjunct, one or more covariates. A *covariate* is another variable that's normally measured at the same level of measurement as the outcome or dependent variable. The use of a covariate in an analysis of variance changes it to an analysis of covariance (ANCOVA) and is intended to reduce bias in the outcome variable and to increase the statistical power of the analysis.

These difficulties—unequal group sizes in factorial designs, three or more factors, and the use of covariates—are dealt with in Chapter 12. As you'll see, the analysis of variance can be seen as a special case of something called the *General Linear Model*, which this book hinted at in the discussion surrounding Figure 10.2. Regression analysis is a more explicit way of expressing the General Linear Model, and Excel's support for regression is superb.

I have reluctantly omitted two topics in the analysis of variance from this discussion because Excel is not geared up to handle them: the statistical power of the F test and mixed models.

Power of the F Test

Chapter 9, "Testing Differences Between Means: Further Issues," goes into some detail regarding the power of t-tests: both the concept and how you can quantify it. F tests in the analysis of variance can also be discussed in terms of statistical power: how it is affected by the hypothetical differences in population means, sample sizes, the selected alpha level, and the underlying variability of numeric observations.

However, in Excel it's fairly easy to depict an alternative distribution, one that might exist if the null hypothesis is wrong, in the case of the t-test. That alternative distribution has the same shape, often normal or close to normal, as the distribution when the null hypothesis is true. That's not the case with the F distribution.

When the null hypothesis of equal group means is false, the F distribution does not just shift right or left as the t-distribution does. The F distribution stretches out to assume a different shape, and becomes what's called a *noncentral F*. To quantify the power of a given F test, you need to be able to characterize the noncentral F and compare it to the central F distribution, which applies when the null hypothesis is true. Only by comparing the two distributions can you tell how much of each lies above and below the critical F value, and that's the key to determining the statistical power of the F test.

You can determine the shape of the noncentral F distribution only through integral calculus, which is either very laborious in an Excel worksheet or requires external assistance from VBA or some other coding language. Therefore, I have chosen to omit a discussion of calculating the power of the F test from this book.

11

However, that doesn't mean you can't do it. The fundamental figures are all available, even from the Data Analysis add-in's ANOVA tools: sample sizes, factor level effects, and within-group variance. By combining those figures you can come up with what's called a *noncentrality parameter* for use in a power table that's often included as an appendix to statistics textbooks.

Mixed Models

It is possible to regard one factor in a factorial experiment as a *fixed* factor and another factor as a *random* factor. When you regard a factor as fixed, you adopt the position that you do not intend to generalize your experimental findings to other possible levels of that factor. For example, in an experiment that compares two different medical treatments, you would probably regard treatment as a fixed factor and not try to generalize to other treatments not represented in the experiment.

But in that same experiment, you might well also have a random factor such as hospital. You want to account for variability in outcomes that is due to the hospital factor, so you include it. However, you don't want to restrict your conclusions about treatments to their use at only the hospitals in your experiment, so you regard the hospitals as a random selection from among those that exist, and treat Hospital as a random factor.

If you have a random factor and a fixed factor in the same experiment, you are working with a *mixed model*.

In terms of the actual calculations, Excel's two-factor ANOVA tool with replication will work fine on a mixed model, although you do have to change the denominator of the F test for the fixed factor from the within-group mean square to the interaction mean square. But the real difficulty lies in the assumption of compound symmetry, which is also a problem for the repeated measures design. Therefore, I have chosen not to discuss mixed models beyond these few paragraphs. As I did in the section on repeated measures, I recommend that you consider different software than Excel to analyze the data in a mixed model.

Multiple Regression Analysis and Effect Coding: The Basics

12

Chapter 10, "Testing Differences Between Means: The Analysis of Variance," and Chapter 11, "Analysis of Variance: Further Issues," focus on the analysis of variance, or *ANOVA*, partly because it's a familiar approach to analyzing the reliability of the differences between three or more means, but also because Excel offers a variety of worksheet functions and Data Analysis tools that support ANOVA directly. Furthermore, if you examine the definitional formulas for components such as sum of squares between groups, it can become fairly clear how ANOVA accomplishes what it does.

And that's a good foundation. As a basis for understanding more advanced methods, it's good to know that ANOVA allocates variability according to its causes: differences between group means and differences between observations within groups. If only as a point of departure, it's helpful to be aware that the allocation of the sums of squares is neat and tidy only when you're working with equal group sizes (or proportional group sizes; see Chapter 11 for a discussion of that exception).

But as it's traditionally managed, ANOVA is very restrictive. Observations are grouped into design cells that help clarify the nature of the experimental design that's in use (review Figures 11.1 and 11.10 for examples), but that aren't especially useful for carrying out the analysis.

There's a better way. It gets you to the same place, by using stronger and more flexible methods. It's multiple regression, and it tests differences between group means using the same statistical techniques that are used in ANOVA: sums of squared deviations of factor-level means compared to sums of squared deviations of individual observations. You still use mean squares and degrees of freedom. You still use F tests.

But your method of getting to that point is very different. Multiple regression relies on correlations and their near neighbors, percentages of shared variance. It enables you to lay your data out in list format, which is a structure that Excel (along with most database management systems) handles quite smoothly. That layout enables you to deal with most of the drawbacks to using the ANOVA approach, such as unbalanced designs (that is, unequal sample sizes) and the use of covariates.

At bottom, both the ANOVA and the multiple regression approaches are based on the General Linear Model, and this chapter will have a bit more to say about that. First, let's compare an ANOVA with an analysis of the same data set using multiple regression techniques.

Multiple Regression and ANOVA

Chapter 4, "How Variables Move Jointly: Correlation," provides some examples of the use of multiple regression to predict values on a dependent variable given values on predictor variables. Those examples involved only variables measured on interval scales: for example, predicting weight from height and age. To use multiple regression with *nominal* variables such as Treatment, Diagnosis, and Ethnicity, you need a coding system that distinguishes the levels of a factor from one another, using numbers such as 1 and 0.

Figure 12.1 shows how the same data would be laid out for analysis using ANOVA and using multiple regression.

12

Figure 12.1
ANOVA expects tabular input, and multiple regression expects its input in a list format.

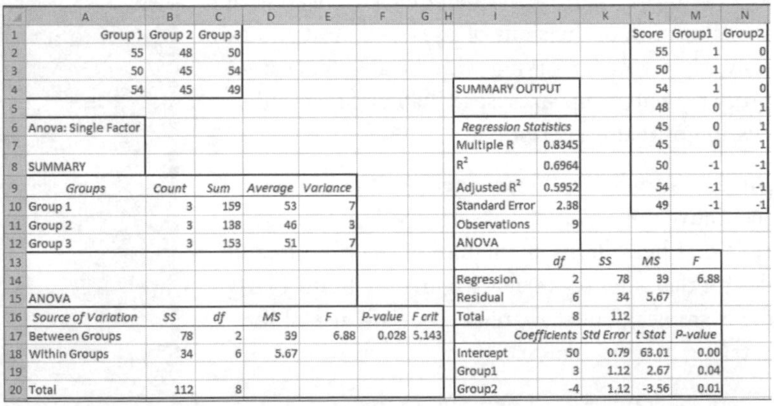

Group 1	Group 2	Group 3
55	48	50
50	45	54
54	45	49

Anova: Single Factor

SUMMARY

Groups	*Count*	*Sum*	*Average*	*Variance*
Group 1	3	159	53	7
Group 2	3	138	46	3
Group 3	3	153	51	7

ANOVA

Source of Variation	*SS*	*df*	*MS*	*F*	*P-value*	*F crit*
Between Groups	78	2	39	6.88	0.028	5.143
Within Groups	34	6	5.67			
Total	112	8				

SUMMARY OUTPUT

Regression Statistics	
Multiple R	0.8345
R^2	0.6964
Adjusted R^2	0.5952
Standard Error	2.38
Observations	9

ANOVA

	df	*SS*	*MS*	*F*
Regression	2	78	39	6.88
Residual	6	34	5.67	
Total	8	112		

	Coefficients	*Std Error*	*t Stat*	*P-value*
Intercept	50	0.79	63.01	0.00
Group1	3	1.12	2.67	0.04
Group2	-4	1.12	-3.56	0.01

Score	Group1	Group2
55	1	0
50	1	0
54	1	0
48	0	1
45	0	1
45	0	1
50	-1	-1
54	-1	-1
49	-1	-1

The data set used in Figure 12.1 is the same as the one used in Figure 10.7. Figure 12.1 shows two separate analyses. One is a standard ANOVA from the Data Analysis add-in's ANOVA: Single Factor tool, in the A6:G20 range; it is also repeated from Figure 10.7. The ANOVA tool was run on the data in A1:C4.

The other analysis is output from the Data Analysis add-in's Regression tool, in the I4:M20 range. (I should mention that to keep down the clutter in Figure 12.1, I have deleted some results that aren't pertinent to this comparison.) The Regression tool was run on the data in L1:N10.

You're about to see how and why the two analyses are really one and the same, as they always are in the equal n's case. First, though, I want to draw your attention to some numbers:

- The sums of squares, degrees of freedom, mean squares, and F ratio in the ANOVA table, in cells B17:E18, are identical to the same statistics in the regression output, in cells J14:M15. (There's no significance to the fact that the sums of squares [SS] and degrees of freedom [df] columns appear in different orders in the two tables. That's merely how the programmers chose to display the results.)

- The group means in D10:D12 are closely related to the regression coefficients in J18:J20. The regression intercept of 50 in J18 is equal to the mean of the group means, which with equal n's is the same as the grand mean of all observations. The intercept plus the coefficient for Group1, in J19, equals Group 1's mean (see cell D10). The intercept plus the coefficient for Group2, in J20, equals Group 2's mean, in cell D11. And this expression, J18 − (J19 + J20), or 50 − (−1), equals 51, the mean of Group 3 in cell D12.

- Comparing cells E17 and M14, you can see that the ANOVA divides the *mean square between groups* by the *mean square within groups* to get an F ratio. The regression analysis divides the *mean square regression* by the *mean square residual* to get the same F ratio. The only difference is in the terminology.

> **NOTE** In both a technical and a literal sense, both multiple regression and ANOVA analyze variance, so both approaches could be termed "analysis of variance." It's customary, though, to reserve the terms *analysis of variance* and *ANOVA* for the approach discussed in Chapters 10 and 11, which calculates the variance of the group means directly. The term *multiple regression* is used for the approach discussed in this chapter, which as you'll see uses a proportions of variance approach.

12

We have, then, an ANOVA that concerns itself with dividing the total variability into the variability that's due to differences in group means and the variability that's due to differences in individual observations. We have a regression analysis that concerns itself with correlations and regression coefficients between the outcome variable, here named Score, and two predictor variables in M2:N10 named Group1 and Group2.

How is it that these two apparently different kinds of analysis report the same inferential statistics? The answer to that lies in how the predictor variables are set up for the regression analysis.

Using Effect Coding

As I mentioned at the outset of this chapter, there are several compelling reasons to use the multiple regression approach in preference to the traditional ANOVA approach. The benefits come at a slight cost, one that you might not regard as a cost at all. You need to arrange your data so that it looks something like the range L1:N10 in Figure 12.1. You don't need to supply columns headers as is done in L1:N1, but it can be helpful to do so.

> **NOTE** I have given the names Group1 and Group2 to the two sets of numbers in columns M and N of Figure 12.1. As you'll see, the numbers in those columns indicate to which group a subject belongs.

The range L2:L10 contains the scores that are analyzed: the same ones as are found in A2:C4. The values in M2:N10 are the result of a coding scheme called *effect coding*. They encode information about group membership using numbers—numbers that can be used as data in a regression analysis. The ranges L2:L10, M2:M10, and N2:N10 are called *vectors*.

As it's been laid out in Figure 12.1, members of Group 1 get the code **1** in the Group1 vector in M2:M10. Members of Group 2 get the code **0** in the Group1 vector, and members of Group 3 get a **–1** in that vector.

Some codes for group membership switch in the Group2 vector, N2:N10. Members of Group 1 get a **0** and members of Group 2 get a **1**. Members of Group 3 again get a **–1**.

Once those vectors are set up (and shortly you'll see how to use Excel worksheet functions to make the job quick and easy), all you do is run the Data Analysis add-in's Regression tool, as shown in Chapter 4. You use the Score vector as the Input Y Range and the Group1 and Group2 vectors as the Input X Range. The results you get are as in Figure 12.1, in I4:J11 and I12:M20.

Effect Coding: General Principles

The effect codes used in Figure 12.1 were not just made up to bring about results identical to the ANOVA output. Several general principles regarding effect coding apply to the present example as well as to any other situation. Effect coding can handle two groups, three groups or more, more than one factor (so that there are interaction vectors as well as group vectors), unequal n's, the use of one or more covariates, and so on. Effect coding in conjunction with multiple regression handles them all.

In contrast, under the traditional ANOVA approach, two Excel tools automate the analysis for you. You use ANOVA: Single Factor if you have one factor, and you use ANOVA: Two Factors with Replication if you have two factors. The ANOVA tools, as I've noted before, cannot handle more than two factors and cannot handle unequal n's in the two factor case.

The following sections detail the general rules to follow for effect coding.

How Many Vectors

There are as many vectors for a factor as there are degrees of freedom for that factor: that is, the number of available levels for a factor, minus 1. In Figure 12.1, there is only one factor and it has three levels. Knowing the effect codes from two vectors completely accounts for group membership using nothing but 1's, 0's and –1's. Each code informs you where any subject is, relative to the three treatment groups. (We cover the presence of additional groups later in this chapter.)

Group Codes

The members of one group (or, if you prefer, the members of one level of a factor) get a code of **1** in a given vector. All but the members of one other group get a **0** on that vector. The members of that other group get a code of **–1**.

Therefore, in Figure 12.1, the code assignments are as follows:

- **The Group1 vector**—Members of Group 1 get a **1** in the vector named Group1. Members of Group 2 get a **0** because they're members of neither Group 1 nor Group 3. Members of Group 3 get a **–1**: Using effect coding, one group must get a **–1** in all vectors.

- **The Group2 vector**—Members of Group 2 get a **1** in the vector named Group2. Members of Group 1 get a **0** because they're members of neither Group 2 nor Group 3. Again, members of Group 3 get a **–1** throughout.

Figure 12.2 adds another level to the Group factor. Notice what happens to the coding.

Figure 12.2
An additional factor level requires an additional vector.

	A	B	C	D	E	F	G	H	I
1	Group 1	Group 2	Group 3	Group 4		Score	Group1	Group2	Group3
2	55	48	50	44		55	1	0	0
3	50	45	54	46		50	1	0	0
4	54	45	49	47		54	1	0	0
5						48	0	1	0
6						45	0	1	0
7						45	0	1	0
8						50	0	0	1
9						54	0	0	1
10						49	0	0	1
11						44	-1	-1	-1
12						46	-1	-1	-1
13						47	-1	-1	-1

12

In Figure 12.2, you can see that an additional level, Group 4, of the factor has been added by putting its observations in cells D2:D4. To accommodate that extra level, another coding vector has been added in column I. Notice that there are still as many coding vectors as there are degrees of freedom for this factor's effect (this is always true if the coding has been done correctly). In the vector named Group3, members of Group 1 and Group 2 get the code **0**, members of Group 3 get the code **1**, and members of Group 4 get a **–1** just as they do in vectors Group1 and Group2.

In Figure 12.2, you can see that the general principles for effect coding have been followed. In addition to setting up as many coding vectors as there are degrees of freedom:

- In each vector, a different group has been assigned the code **1**.

- With the exception of one group, all other groups have been assigned the code **0** in a given vector.

- One group has been assigned the code **-1** throughout the coding vectors.

Other Types of Coding

In this context—that is, the use of coding with multiple regression—there are two other general techniques: orthogonal coding and dummy coding. *Dummy coding* is the same as effect coding, except that there are no codes of **–1**. One group gets codes of **1** in a given vector; all other groups get **0**.

Dummy coding works, and produces the same inferential results (sums of squares, mean squares, and so on) as does effect coding, but offers no special benefit beyond what's available with effect coding. The regression equation has different coefficients with dummy coding than with effect coding. The regression coefficients with dummy coding give the difference between group means and the mean of the group that receives **0**'s throughout. Therefore, dummy coding can sometimes be useful when you plan to compare several group means with the mean of one comparison group; a multiple comparisons technique due to Dunnett is designed for that situation. (Dummy coding is also useful in logistic regression, where it can make the regression coefficients consistent with the odds ratios.)

Orthogonal coding is virtually identical to planned orthogonal contrasts, discussed at the end of Chapter 10. One benefit of orthogonal coding comes if you're doing your multiple regression with paper and pencil. Orthogonal codes lead to matrices that are easily inverted; when the codes aren't orthogonal, the matrix inversion is something you wouldn't want to watch, much less do. But with personal computers and Excel, the need to simplify matrix inversions using orthogonal coding has largely disappeared. (Excel has a worksheet function, MINVERSE(), that does it for you.)

Now that you've been alerted to the fact that dummy coding exists, this book will have no more to say about it. We'll return to the topic of orthogonal coding in Chapter 13, "Multiple Regression Analysis: Further Issues."

Multiple Regression and Proportions of Variance

Chapter 4 goes into some detail about the nature of correlation. One particularly important point is that the square of a correlation coefficient represents the proportion of shared variance between two variables. For example, if the correlation coefficient between caloric intake and weight is 0.5, then the square of 0.5, or 0.25, tells you how much variance the two variables have in common.

There are various ways to characterize this relationship. If it's reasonable to believe that one of the variables causes the other, perhaps because you know that one precedes the other in time, you might say that 25% of the variability in the subsequent variable, weight gain or loss, *is due to* differences in the precedent variable, diet.

If it's not clear that one variable causes the other, or if the direction of the causation isn't clear, for example, with variables such as crime and poverty, then you might say that crime and poverty have 25% of their *variance in common.* Shared variance, explained variance, predicted variance—all are phrases that suggest that when one variable changes in value, so does the other, with or without the presence of causation.

When you set up coded vectors, as shown in Figures 12.1 and 12.2, you create a numeric variable that has a correlation, and therefore common variance, with an outcome variable. At this point you're in a position to determine how much of the variability—the sum of squares—in the outcome variable you can attribute to the coded vector.

And that's just what you're doing when you calculate the between-groups variance in a traditional ANOVA. Back in Chapter 1, "About Variables and Values," I argued that nominal variables, variables whose values are just names, don't work well with numeric analyses such as averages, standard deviations, or correlations. But by working with the mean values associated with a nominal variable, you can get, say, the mean cholesterol level for Medication A, for Medication B, and for a placebo. Then, calculating the variance of those means tells you how much of the total sum of squares is due to differences between means.

You can also use effect coding to get to the same result via a different route. Effect coding translates a nominal variable such as Medication to numeric values (1, 0 and -1) that you can correlate with an outcome variable. Figure 12.3 applies this technique to the data presented earlier in Figure 12.1.

12

Figure 12.3
Two ways to calculate the sum of squares between groups.

L14 | fx =L12*L13

	A	B	C	D	E	F	G	H	I	J	K	L
1	Group 1	Group 2	Group 3				Score	Group1	Group2		SUMMARY OUTPUT	
2	55	48	50				55	1	0			
3	50	45	54				50	1	0		*Regression Statistics*	
4	54	45	49				54	1	0		Multiple R	0.834523
5							48	0	1		R^2	0.696429
6	Anova: Single Factor						45	0	1			
7	*Source of Variation*	*SS*	*df*	*MS*	*F*		45	0	1			*Coefficients*
8	Between Groups	78	2	39	6.88		50	-1	-1		Intercept	50
9	Within Groups	34	6	5.67			54	-1	-1		Group1	3
10							49	-1	-1		Group2	-4
11	Total	112	8									
12											R^2	0.696429
13											Total sum of squares	112
14											Sum of squares between	78

In Figure 12.3, I have removed some ancillary information from the Data Analysis add-in's ANOVA and Regression tools so as to focus on the sums of squares.

Notice that the ANOVA report in A6:E11 gives 78 as the sum of squares between groups. It uses the approach discussed in Chapters 10 and 11 to arrive at that figure.

The portion of the Regression output shown in K1:L5 shows that the multiple R^2 is 0.696 (see also cell L12). As discussed in Chapter 4, the multiple R^2 is the proportion of variance shared between (a) the outcome variable, and (b) the combination of the predictor variables that results in the strongest correlation.

Notice that if you multiply the multiple R^2 of 0.696 times the total sum of squares, 112 in cell B11, you get 78: the sum of squares between groups.

That best combination of predictor variables is shown in column G of Figure 12.4.

Figure 12.4
Getting the multiple R^2 explicitly.

	A	B	C	D	E	F	G
1	Score	Group1	Group2	3 X Group1	-4 X Group2	Intercept	Best Combination
2	55	1	0	3	0	50	53
3	50	1	0	3	0	50	53
4	54	1	0	3	0	50	53
5	48	0	1	0	-4	50	46
6	45	0	1	0	-4	50	46
7	45	0	1	0	-4	50	46
8	50	-1	-1	-3	4	50	51
9	54	-1	-1	-3	4	50	51
10	49	-1	-1	-3	4	50	51
11							
12			Multiple correlation of Score and Best Combination				0.834523
13						Multiple R^2	0.696429

To get the best combination explicitly takes just three steps (and as you'll see, it's quicker to get it implicitly using the TREND() function). You need the regression coefficients, which are shown in Figure 12.3 (cells L8:L10):

1. Multiply the coefficient for Group1 by each value for Group1. Put the result in column D.

2. Multiply the coefficient for Group2 by each value for Group2. Put the result in column E.

3. Add the intercept in column F to the values in columns D and E and put the result in column G.

> **NOTE**
> You can get the result that's shown in column G by array-entering this TREND() function in a nine-row, one-column range: TREND(A2:A10,B2:C10). That approach is used later in the chapter. In the meantime it's helpful to see the result of applying the regression equation explicitly.

As a check, the following formula is entered in cell G12:

=CORREL(A2:A10,G2:G10)

This one is entered in cell G13:

=G12^2

They return, respectively, (a) the correlation between the best combination of the predictors and the outcome variable, and (b) the square of that correlation, or R^2. Compare the values you see in cells G12 and G13 with those you see in cells L4 and L5 on Figure 12.3, which were produced by the Regression tool in the Data Analysis add-in.

Of course, if you multiply the R^2 value in cell G13 on Figure 12.4 by the total sum of squares in cell B11 on Figure 12.3, you still get the same sum of squares between groups, 78. In a single-factor analysis, the ANOVA's Sum of Squares Between Groups is identical to regression's Sum of Squares Regression.

Understanding the Segue from ANOVA to Regression

It often helps at this point to step back from the math involved in both ANOVA and regression and to review the concepts involved. The main goal of both types of analysis is to disaggregate the variability—as measured by squared deviations from the mean—in a data set into two components:

- The variability caused by differences in the means of groups that people belong to
- The remaining variability within groups, once the variability among means has been accounted for

Variance Estimates via ANOVA

ANOVA reaches its goal in part by calculating the sum of the squared deviations of the group means from the grand mean, and in part by calculating the sum of the squared deviations of the individual observations from their respective group means. Those two sums of squares are then converted to variances by dividing by their respective degrees of freedom.

Sum of Squares Within Groups   The sum of the squared deviations within each group is calculated and then summed across the groups to get the sum of squares within groups. Group means are involved in these calculations, but only to find the deviation score for each observation. The *differences* between group means are not involved.

Sum of Squares Between Groups   The between groups variance is based on the variance error of the mean—that is, the variance of the group means multiplied by the number of groups. This is converted to an estimate of the population variance by rearranging the equation for the variance error of the mean, which is

$$s_{\overline{X}}^2 = \frac{s^2}{n}$$

to this form:

$$s^2 = n s_{\overline{X}}^2$$

12

In words, the variance of all observations is equal to the variance of the group means multiplied by the number of observations in each group. (The concept of the variance error of the mean is introduced in Chapter 8, "Testing Differences Between Means: The Basics," in the section titled "Testing Means: The Rationale.")

Similarly, you get the sum of squares between groups by multiplying the sum of the squared deviations of the group means by the number of observations in each group:

$$SS_B = \sum_{j=1}^{J} n(\overline{X}_{.j} - \overline{X}_{..})^2$$

Comparing the Variance Estimates The relative size of the variance estimates—the F ratio, the estimate from between groups variability divided by the estimate from within groups variability—tells you the likelihood that the group means are really different in the population, or that their difference can be attributed to sampling error.

This is as good a spot as any to note that although a mean square is a variance, "Mean Square Between Groups" does not signify the variance of the group means. It is an estimate of the total variance of all the observations, based on the variability among the group means. In the same way, "Mean Square Within Groups" does not signify the variance of the individual observations within each group—after all, you total the sum of squares in each group. It is an estimate of the total variance of all the observations based on the variability within each group.

Therefore, you have two independent estimates of the total variance: between groups, based on differences between group means, and within groups, based on differences between individual observations and the mean of their group. If the estimate based on group means exceeds the estimate based on within cell variation by an improbable amount, it must be due to one or more differences in group means that are, under the null hypothesis, also improbably large.

Variance Estimates via Regression

Regression analysis takes a different tack. It sets up new variables that represent the subjects' membership in the different groups—these are the vectors of effect codes in Figures 12.1 through 12.4. Then a multiple regression analysis determines the proportion of the variance in the "outcome" or "predicted" variable that is associated with group membership, as represented by the effect code variables; this is the between groups variance. The remaining, unattributed variance is the within groups variance (or, as regression analysis terms it, *residual* variance). Once again you divide the between groups variance by the within groups variance to run your F test.

Or, if you work your way through it, you find that to calculate the F test, the actual values of the sums of squares and variances are unnecessary when you use regression analysis. See Figure 12.5.

Figure 12.5
You can run an F test
using proportions of variance only.

⊿	A	B	C	D	E	F	G	H	I	J	K	L	M	N	O
1	Group 1	Group 2	Group 3				Score	Group1	Group2		SUMMARY OUTPUT				
2	55	48	50				55	1	0		*Regression Statistics*				
3	50	45	54				50	1	0		Multiple R	0.8345			
4	54	45	49				54	1	0		R²	0.6964			
5							48	0	1		Adjusted R²	0.5952			
6	ANOVA						45	0	1		ANOVA				
7	*Source of Variation*	SS	df	MS	F		45	0	1			*Prop. of Variance*	df	MS	F
8	Between Groups	78	2	39	6.88		50	-1	-1		Regression	0.6964	2	0.348	6.88
9	Within Groups	34	6	5.67			54	-1	-1		Residual	0.3036	6	0.051	
10	Total	112	8				49	-1	-1		Total	1.0000	8		

> **NOTE**
> The adjusted R² is simply an estimate of what the R² might be using a different sample, one that's larger than the sample used to calculate the regression statistics. Larger samples usually do not capitalize on chance as much as smaller samples, and often result in smaller values for R².

In Figure 12.5, cells A7:E10 present an ANOVA summary of the data in A1:C4 in the traditional manner, reporting sums of squares, degrees of freedom, and the mean squares that result from dividing sums of squares by degrees of freedom. The final figure is an F ratio of 6.88 in cell E8.

But the sums of squares are unnecessary to calculate the F ratio. What matters is the *proportion* of the total variance in the outcome variable that's attributable to the coded vectors that here represent group membership. Cell L8 contains the proportion of variance, .6964, that's due to regression on the vectors, and cell L9 contains the remaining or residual proportion of variance, .3036. Divide each proportion by its accompanying degrees of freedom and you get the mean squares—or what would be the mean squares if you multiplied them by the total sum of squares, 112 (cell B10).

Finally, divide cell N8 by cell N9 to get the same F value in cell O8 that you see in cell E8. Evidently, the sum of squares is simply a constant that for the purpose of calculating an F ratio can be ignored.

You will see more about working solely with proportions of variance in Chapter 13, when the topic of multiple comparisons between means is revisited.

The Meaning of Effect Coding

Earlier chapters have referred occasionally to something called the General Linear Model, and we're at a point in the discussion of regression analysis that it makes sense to make the discussion more formal. Effect coding is closely related to the General Linear Model.

It's useful to think of an individual observation as the sum of several components:

- A grand mean
- An effect that reflects the amount by which a group mean differs from the grand mean
- An "error" effect that measures how much an individual observation differs from its group's mean

12

Algebraically this concept is represented as follows for population parameters:

$$X_{ij} = \mu + \beta_j + \varepsilon_{ij}$$

Or, using Roman instead of Greek symbols for sample statistics:

$$X_{ij} = \overline{X}_{..} + b_j + e_{ij}$$

Each observation is represented by X, specifically the ith observation in the jth group. Each observation is a combination of the following:

- The grand mean, $\overline{X}_{..}$
- The effect of being in the jth group, b_j. Under the General Linear Model, simply being in a particular group tends to pull its observations up if the group mean is higher than the grand mean, or push them down if the group mean is lower than the grand mean.
- The result of being the ith observation in the jth group, e_{ij}. This is the distance of the observation from the group mean. It's represented by the letter e because—for reasons of tradition that aren't very good—it is regarded as *error*. And it is from that usage that you get terms such as *mean square error* and *error variance*. Quantities such as those are simply the residual variation among observations once you have accounted for other sources of variation, such as group means (b_j) and interaction effects.

Various assumptions and restrictions come into play when you apply the General Linear Model, and some of them must be observed if your statistical analysis is to have any real meaning. For example, it's assumed that the e_{ij} error values are independent of one another—that is, if one observation is above the group mean, that fact has no influence on whether some other observation is above, below, or directly on the group mean. Other examples include the restrictions that the b_j effects sum to zero, as do the e_{ij} error values. This is as you would expect, because each b_j effect is a deviation from the grand mean, and each e_{ij} error value is a deviation from a group mean. The sum of such deviations is always zero.

Notice that I've referred to the b_j values as *effects*. That's standard terminology and it is behind the term *effect coding*. When you use effect coding to represent group membership, as is done in the prior section, the coefficients in a regression equation that relates the outcome variable to the coded vectors *are the b_j values*: the deviations of a group's mean from the grand mean.

Take a look back at Figure 12.1. The grand mean of the values in cells L2:L10 (identical to those in A2:C4) is 50. The average value in Group 1 is 53, so the effect—that is, b_1—of being in Group 1 is 3. In the vector that represents membership in Group 1, which is in M2:M10, members of Group 1 are assigned a **1**. And the regression coefficient for the Group1 vector in cell J19 is 3: the effect of being in Group 1. Hence, *effect coding*.

It works the same way for Group 2. The grand mean is 50 and the mean of Group 2 is 46, so the effect of being a member of Group 2 is –4. And the regression coefficient for the Group2 vector, which represents membership in Group 2 via a **1**, is –4 (see cell J20).

Notice further that the intercept is equal to the grand mean. So if you apply the General Linear Model to an observation in this data set, you're applying the regression equation. For the first observation in Group 2, for example, the General Linear Model says that it should equal

$$X_{ij} = \overline{X}_{..} + b_j + e_{ij}$$

or this, using actual values:

$$48 = 50 + (-4) + 2$$

And the regression equation says that a value in any group is found by

Intercept + (Group1 b-weight * Value on Group1) + (Group2 b-weight * Value on Group2)

or the following, using actual values for an observation in, say, Group 2:

$$50 + (3 * 0) + (-4 * 1)$$

This equals 46, which is the mean of Group 2. The regression equation does not go further than estimating the grand mean plus the effect of being in a particular group. The remaining variability (for example, having a score of 48 instead of the Group 2 mean 46) is regarded as residual or error variation.

The mean of the group that's assigned a code of **–1** throughout is found by taking the negative of the sum of the b-weights. In this case, that's –(3 + –4), or 1. And the mean of Group 3 is in fact 51, 1 more than the grand mean.

> **NOTE** Formally, using effect coding, the intercept is equal to the mean of the group means: Here, that's (53 + 46 + 51) / 3, or 50. When there is an equal number of observations per group, the mean of all observations is equal to the mean of the group means. That is not necessarily true when the groups have different numbers of observations, and then the intercept is not necessarily equal to the mean of all observations. But the intercept equals the mean of the group means even in an unequal n's design.

12

Assigning Effect Codes in Excel

Excel makes it very easy to set up your effect code vectors. The quickest way is to use Excel's VLOOKUP() function. You'll see how to do so shortly. First, have a look at Figure 12.6. The range A1:B10 contains the data from Figure 12.1, laid out as a list. This arrangement is much more useful generally than is the arrangement in A1:C4 of Figure 12.1, where it is laid out especially to cater to the ANOVA tool's requirements.

The range F1:H4 in Figure 12.6 contains another list, one that's used to associate effect codes with group membership. Notice that F2:F4 contains the names of the groups as used in A1:A10. G2:G4 contains the effect codes that will be used in the vector named Group1; that's the vector in which observations from Group 1 get a **1**. Lastly, H2:H4 contains the effect codes that will be used in the vector named Group2.

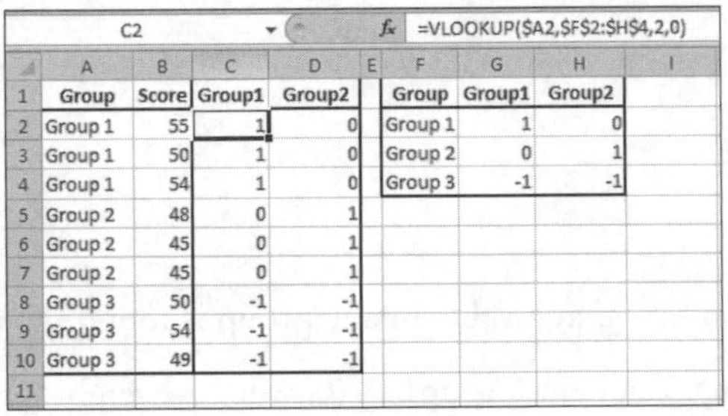

Figure 12.6
The effect code vectors in columns C and D are populated using VLOOKUP().

	A	B	C	D	E	F	G	H	I
			C2			f_x	=VLOOKUP($A2,$F$2:$H$4,2,0)		
1	Group	Score	Group1	Group2		Group	Group1	Group2	
2	Group 1	55	1	0		Group 1	1	0	
3	Group 1	50	1	0		Group 2	0	1	
4	Group 1	54	1	0		Group 3	-1	-1	
5	Group 2	48	0	1					
6	Group 2	45	0	1					
7	Group 2	45	0	1					
8	Group 3	50	-1	-1					
9	Group 3	54	-1	-1					
10	Group 3	49	-1	-1					
11									

The effect vectors themselves are found adjacent to the original A1:B10 list, in columns C and D. They are labeled in cells C1 and D1 with vector names that I find convenient and logical, but you could name them anything you wish. (Bear in mind that you can use the labels in the output of the Regression tool.)

To actually create the vectors in columns C and D, take these steps (you can try them out using the Excel file for Chapter 12, available at www.informit.com/title/9780789747204):

1. Enter this formula in cell C2:

   =VLOOKUP(A2,$F$2:$H$4,2,0)

2. Enter this formula in cell D2:

   =VLOOKUP(A2,$F$2:$H$4,3,0)

3. Make a multiple selection of C2:D2 by dragging through them.

4. Move your mouse pointer over the selection handle in the bottom-right corner of cell D2.

5. Hold down the mouse button and drag down through Row 10.

Your worksheet should now resemble the one shown in Figure 12.6, and in particular the range B1:D10.

If you're not already familiar with the VLOOKUP() function, here are some items to keep in mind. To begin, VLOOKUP() takes a value in some worksheet cell, such as A2, and looks up a corresponding value *in the first column* of a worksheet range, such as F2:H4 in Figure 12.6. VLOOKUP() returns an associated value, such as (in this example) 1, 0, or –1.

So, as used in the formula

   =VLOOKUP(A2,$F$2:$H$4,2,0)

the VLOOKUP() function looks up the value it finds in cell A2 (first argument). It looks for that value (**Group 1** in this example) in the first column of the range F2:H4 (second argument). VLOOKUP() returns the value found in column 2 (third argument) of the second argument. The lookup range need not be sorted by its first column: that's the purpose of the fourth argument, **0**, which also requires Excel to find an exact match to the lookup value, not just an approximate match.

So in words, the formula

=VLOOKUP(A2,$F$2:$H$4,2,0)

looks for the value that's in A2. It looks for it in the first column of F2:H4, the lookup range. As it happens, that value, **Group 1**, is found in the first row of the range. The third argument tells VLOOKUP() which column to look in. It looks in column 2 of F2:H4, and finds the value 1. So, VLOOKUP() returns 1.

Similarly, the formula

=VLOOKUP(A2,$F$2:$H$4,3,0)

looks for **Group 1** in the first column of F2:H4—that is, in the range F2:F4. That value is once again found in cell F2, so VLOOKUP() returns a value from that row of the lookup range.

The third argument, **3**, says to return the value found in the third column of the lookup range, and that's column H. Therefore, VLOOKUP() returns the value found in the third column of the first row of the lookup range, which is cell H2, or **0**.

Figure 12.7 shows how you could extend this approach if you had not three but four groups.

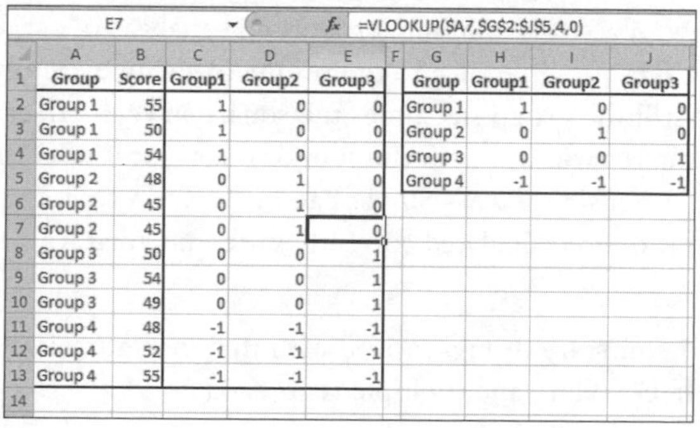

Figure 12.7
Adding a group adds a vector, and an additional column in the lookup range.

	A	B	C	D	E	F	G	H	I	J
						E7		fx =VLOOKUP($A7,$G$2:$J$5,4,0)		
1	Group	Score	Group1	Group2	Group3		Group	Group1	Group2	Group3
2	Group 1	55	1	0	0		Group 1	1	0	0
3	Group 1	50	1	0	0		Group 2	0	1	0
4	Group 1	54	1	0	0		Group 3	0	0	1
5	Group 2	48	0	1	0		Group 4	-1	-1	-1
6	Group 2	45	0	1	0					
7	Group 2	45	0	1	0					
8	Group 3	50	0	0	1					
9	Group 3	54	0	0	1					
10	Group 3	49	0	0	1					
11	Group 4	48	-1	-1	-1					
12	Group 4	52	-1	-1	-1					
13	Group 4	55	-1	-1	-1					
14										

Notice that the formula as it appears in cell E7 uses $A7 as the first argument to VLOOKUP. This reference, which anchors the argument to column A, is used so that the formula can be copied and pasted or autofilled across columns C, D, and E without losing the reference to column A. (The third argument, 4, would have to be adjusted.)

12

Notice also that the lookup range (F2:H4 in Figure 12.6 and G2:J5 in Figure 12.7) conforms to the general rules for effect coding:

- There's one fewer vector than there are levels in a factor.
- In each vector, one group has a **1**, all other groups but the last one have a **0**.
- The last group has a **–1** in all vectors.

All you have to do is make sure your lookup range conforms to those rules. Then, the VLOOKUP() function will make sure that the correct code is assigned to the member of the correct group in each vector.

Using Excel's Regression Tool with Unequal Group Sizes

Chapter 10 discussed the problem of unequal group sizes in a single-factor ANOVA. The discussion was confined to the issue of assumptions that underlie the analysis of variance. Chapter 10 pointed out that the assumption of equal variances in different groups is not a matter of concern when the sample sizes are equal. However, when the larger groups have the smaller variances, the F test is more liberal than you expect: You will reject the null hypothesis somewhat more often than you should. The size of "somewhat" depends on the magnitude of discrepancies in group sample sizes and variances.

Similarly, if the larger groups have the larger variances, the F test is more conservative than its nominal level: If you think you're working with an alpha of .05, you might actually be working with an alpha of .03. As a practical matter, there's little you can do about this problem apart from randomly discarding a *few* observations to achieve equal group sizes, and perhaps maintaining an awareness of what's happening to the alpha level you adopted.

From the point of view of actually running a traditional analysis of variance, the presence of unequal group sizes makes no difference to the results of a single-factor ANOVA. The sum of squares between is still the group size times the square of each effect, summed across groups. The sum of squares within is still the sum of the squares of each observation from its group's mean. If you're using Excel's Single Factor ANOVA tool, the sums of squares, mean squares, and F ratios are calculated correctly in the unequal n's situation. Figure 12.8 shows an example.

Compare the ANOVA summary in Figure 12.8 with that in Figure 12.9, which analyzes the same data set using effect coding and multiple regression.

There are a couple of points of interest in Figures 12.8 and 12.9. First, notice that the sum of squares between and the sum of squares within are identical in both the ANOVA and the regression analysis: Compare cells B10:B11 in Figure 12.8 with cells H11:H12 in Figure 12.9. Effect coding with regression analysis is equivalent to standard ANOVA, even with unequal n's.

Figure 12.8
There's no ambiguity about how the sums of squares are allocated in a single-factor ANOVA with unequal n's.

	A	B	C	D
1	Treatment A	Treatment B	Placebo	
2	59.2	63.5	53.1	
3	57.2	59.4	57.8	
4	55.9	60.3	51	
5		56.2	50.6	
6			47.2	
7				
8	ANOVA			
9	*Source of Variation*	*SS*	*df*	*MS*
10	Between Groups	147.84	2	73.92
11	Within Groups	93.41	9	10.38
12				
13	Total	241.25	11	

Figure 12.9
The total percentage of variance explained is equivalent to the sum of squares between in Figure 12.8.

	A	B	C	D	E	F	G	H	I
1	Group	Score	GroupA	GroupB			GroupA	GroupB	
2	Treatment A	59.2	1	0		Treatment A	1	0	
3	Treatment A	57.2	1	0		Treatment B	0	1	
4	Treatment A	55.9	1	0		Placebo	-1	-1	
5	Treatment B	63.5	0	1		SUMMARY OUTPUT			
6	Treatment B	59.4	0	1		*Regression Statistics*			
7	Treatment B	60.3	0	1		R Square	0.612814		
8	Treatment B	56.2	0	1					
9	Placebo	53.1	-1	-1		ANOVA			
10	Placebo	57.8	-1	-1				df	SS	MS
11	Placebo	51	-1	-1		Regression	2	147.84	73.92
12	Placebo	50.6	-1	-1		Residual	9	93.41	10.38
13	Placebo	47.2	-1	-1		Total	11	241.25	
14									
15		Average					*Coefficients*		
16	Treatment A	57.43				Intercept	56.41		
17	Treatment B	59.85				GroupA	1.03		
18	Placebo	51.94				GroupB	3.44		

Also notice the value of the regression equation intercept in cell G16 of Figure 12.9. It is 56.41. That is not the grand mean, the mean of all observations, as it is with equal n's, an equal number of observations in each group.

With unequal n's, the intercept of the regression equation is the average of the group averages—that is, the average of 57.43, 59.85, and 51.94. Actually, this is true of the equal n's case too. It's just that the presence of equal group sizes masks what's going on: Each mean is weighted by a constant sample size.

So, the presence of unequal n's per group poses no special difficulties for the calculations in either traditional analysis of variance or the combination of multiple regression with effect coding. As I noted at the outset of this section, you need to bear in mind the relationship between group sizes and group variances, and its potential impact on the nominal alpha rate.

It's when two or more factors are involved and the group sizes are unequal that the nature of the calculations becomes a real issue. The next section introduces the topic of the regression analysis of designs with two or more factors.

12

Effect Coding, Regression, and Factorial Designs in Excel

Effect coding is not limited to single-factor designs. In fact, effect coding is at its most valuable in factorial designs with unequal cell sizes. The rest of this chapter deals with the regression analysis of factorial designs. Chapter 13 takes up the special problems that arise out of unequal n's in factorial designs and how the regression approach helps you solve them.

Effect coding, combined with the multiple regression approach, also enables you to cope with factorial designs with more than two factors, which the Data Analysis add-in's ANOVA tools cannot handle at all. (As you'll see in Chapter 14, "Analysis of Covariance: The Basics," effect coding is also of considerable assistance in the analysis of covariance.)

To see why the regression approach is so helpful in the context of factorial designs, it's best to start with another look at correlations and their squares, the proportions of variance. Figure 12.10 shows a traditional ANOVA with a balanced design (equal group sizes).

Figure 12.10
The design is balanced: There is no ambiguity about how to allocate the sum of squares.

B17 =SUM(B13:B15)

	A	B	C	D	E	F	G
1				Patient			
2			Inpatient	Outpatient	Short Stay		
3			89	123	84		
4		Medical	84	99	109		
5	Treatment		86	117	87		
6			103	100	126		
7		Surgical	100	92	127		
8			112	93	117		
9							
10	Anova: Two-Factor With Replication						
11	ANOVA						
12	*Source of Variation*	*SS*	*df*	*MS*	*F*	*P-value*	*F crit*
13	Sample	470.222	1	470.222222	6.4561404	0.0259	4.7472
14	Columns	497.333	2	248.666667	3.4141876	0.06702	3.8853
15	Interaction	1888.44	2	944.222222	12.96415	0.001	3.8853
16							
17	Analysis for Effects	2856.000	5	571.200			
18							
19	Within	874	12	72.8333333			
20							
21	Total	3730	17				

Figure 12.11 shows the same data set as in Figure 12.10, laid out for regression analysis. In particular, the data is in Excel list form, and effect code vectors have been added. Columns D, E, and F contain the effect codes for the main Treatment and Patient effects. Columns G and H contain the interaction effects, and are created by cross-multiplying the main effects columns.

Figure 12.11 shows a correlation matrix in the range J8:P13, labeled "r matrix." It's based on the data in C1:H19. (A correlation matrix such as this one is very easy to create using the Correlation tool in the Data Analysis add-in.) Immediately below the correlation matrix is another matrix, labeled "R^2 matrix," that contains the squares of the values in the correlation matrix. The R^2 matrix shows the amount of variance shared between any two variables.

Figure 12.11
Compare the ANOVA for the regression in cells J3:O3 with the total effects analysis in cells A17:D17 in Figure 12.10.

	Treatment	Patient	Score	Tx	Pt1	Pt2	Tx Pt1	Tx Pt2		ANOVA					
1	Treatment	Patient	Score	Tx	Pt1	Pt2	Tx Pt1	Tx Pt2		ANOVA					
2	Medical	Inpatient	89	1	1	0	1	0			df	SS	MS	F	Sig F
3	Medical	Inpatient	84	1	1	0	1	0	Regression	5	2856	571.2	7.8426	0.0017	
4	Medical	Inpatient	86	1	1	0	1	0	Residual	12	874	72.833			
5	Medical	Outpatient	123	1	0	1	0	1	Total	17	3730				
6	Medical	Outpatient	99	1	0	1	0	1			r matrix					
7	Medical	Outpatient	117	1	0	1	0	1		Score	Treat1	Pt1	Pt2	T1 P1	T1 P2
8	Medical	Short Stay	84	1	-1	-1	-1	-1	Score	1					
9	Medical	Short Stay	109	1	-1	-1	-1	-1	Tx	-0.3551	1				
10	Medical	Short Stay	87	1	-1	-1	-1	-1	Pt1	-0.3592	0	1			
11	Surgical	Inpatient	103	0	1	0	0	0	Pt2	-0.1229	0	0.500	1		
12	Surgical	Inpatient	100	0	1	0	0	0	Tx Pt1	-0.1404	0	0.707	0.354	1	
13	Surgical	Inpatient	112	0	1	0	0	0	Tx Pt2	0.3944	0	0.354	0.707	0.500	1
14	Surgical	Outpatient	100	0	0	1	0	0			R^2 matrix					
15	Surgical	Outpatient	92	0	0	1	0	0		Score	Treat1	Pt1	Pt2	T1 P1	T1 P2
16	Surgical	Outpatient	93	0	0	1	0	0	Score	1					
17	Surgical	Short Stay	126	0	-1	-1	0	0	Tx	0.12606	1				
18	Surgical	Short Stay	127	0	-1	-1	0	0	Pt1	0.12904	0	1			
19	Surgical	Short Stay	117	0	-1	-1	0	0	Pt2	0.01510	0	0.25000	1		
20									Tx Pt1	0.01971	0	0.50000	0.12500	1	
21									Tx Pt2	0.15554	0	0.12500	0.50000	0.25000	1

As pointed out in the section "Variance Estimates via Regression," earlier in this chapter, you can use R^2, the proportion of variance shared by two variables, to obtain the sum of squares in an outcome variable that's attributable to a coded vector. For example, in Figure 12.11, you can see in cells K18:K19 that the two Patient vectors, Pt1 and Pt2, share 12.90% and 1.51% of their variance with the Score variable. Taken together, that's 14.41% of the Patient vector variance that's shared with the Score variable. The total sum of squares is 3730, as shown in cell L5 of Figure 12.11 (and in cell B21 of Figure 12.10). 14.41% of the 3730 is 537.67, the amount of the total sum of squares that's attributable to the Patient factor.

Except it's not. If you look at Figure 12.10, you'll find in cell B14 that 497.33 is the sum of squares for the Patient factor (labeled by the ANOVA tool, somewhat unhelpfully, as "Columns"). It's a balanced design, with an equal number (3) of observations per design cell, so the ambiguity caused by unequal n's in factorial designs doesn't arise. Why does the ANOVA table in Figure 12.10 say that the sum of squares for the Patient factor is 497.33, while the sum of the proportions of variance shown in Figure 12.11 leads to a sum of squares of 537.67?

The reason is that the two vectors that represent the Patient factor are correlated. Notice in Figure 12.11 that worksheet cell M11 shows that there's a correlation of .5 between vector Pt1 and vector Pt2, the two vectors that identify group membership for the three-level Patient factor. And in worksheet cell M19 you can see that the two vectors share 25% of their variance.

Because that's the case, we can't simply add the 12.90% (the R^2 of Pt1 with Score) and 1.51% (the R^2 of Pt2 with Score) and multiply their sum times the total sum of squares. The two Patient vectors share 25% of their variance, and so some of the 12.90% that Pt1 shares with Score *is also shared by Pt2*. We're double-counting that variance, and so we get a higher Patient sum of squares (537.67) than we should (497.33).

12

Exerting Statistical Control with Semipartial Correlations

From time to time you hear or read news reports that mention "holding income constant" or "removing education from the comparison" or some similar statistical hand-waving. That's what's involved when two coded vectors are correlated with one another, such as Pt1 and Pt2 in Figure 12.11. Here's what they're usually talking about when one variable is "held constant," and how it's usually done.

Suppose you wanted to investigate the relationship between education and attitude toward a ballot proposal in an upcoming election. You know that there's a relationship between education and income, and that there's probably a relationship between income and attitude toward the ballot proposal. You would like to examine the relationship between education and attitude, uncontaminated by the income variable. That might enable you to target your advertising about the proposal by sponsoring certain television programming whose viewers tend to be found at certain education levels.

You collect data from a random sample of registered voters and pull together this correlation matrix:

	Attitude	Education	Income
Attitude	1.0		
Education	.55	1.0	
Income	.45	.35	1.0

You would like to remove the effect of Income on the Education variable, but leave its effect on the Attitude variable. Here's the Excel formula to do that:

= (.55 − (.45 * .35)) / SQRT(1 − .35^2)

The more general version is

$$r_{1(2.3)} = \frac{r_{12} - r_{13}r_{23}}{\sqrt{1 - r_{23}^2}}$$

where the symbol $r_{1(2.3)}$ is called a *semipartial* correlation. It is the correlation of variable 1 with variable 2, with the effect of variable 3 removed from variable 2.

With the data as given in the prior correlation matrix, the semipartial correlation of Attitude with Education, with the effect of Income removed from Education only, is .42. That's .13 less than the raw, unaltered correlation of Attitude with Education.

It's entirely possible to remove the effect of the third variable from *both* the first and the second, using this general formula:

$$r_{12.3} = \frac{r_{12} - 2r_{13}r_{23}}{\sqrt{1 - r_{13}^2}\sqrt{1 - r_{23}^2}}$$

And with the given data set, the result would be .47. This correlation, in which the effect of the third variable is removed from both the other two, is called a *partial* correlation; as before, it's a semipartial correlation when you remove the effect of the third from only one of the other two.

> **NOTE**
> In yet another embarrassing instance of statisticians' inability to reach consensus on a sensible name for anything, some refer to what I have called a semipartial correlation as a *part correlation*. Everyone means the same thing, though, when they speak of partial correlations.

To solve the problem discussed in the prior section, you could use the formula given here for semipartial correlation. I'll start by showing you how you might do that with the data used in Figure 12.11. Then I'll show you how much easier—not to mention how much more elegant—it is to solve the problem using Excel's TREND() function.

Using a Squared Semipartial to get the Correct Sum of Squares

As shown in Figure 12.11, the relevant raw correlations are as follows:

	Score	Pt1	Pt2
Score	1.0		
Pt1	−0.3592	1.0	
Pt2	−0.1229	.5000	1.0

Applying the formula for the semipartial correlation, we get the following formula for the semipartial correlation between Score and Pt2, after the effect of Pt1 has been removed from Pt2:

=(−0.1229−(−0.3592*0.5))/SQRT(1−0.5^2)

This resolves to .0655. Squaring that correlation results in .0043, which is the proportion of variance that Score has in common with Pt2 after the effect of Pt1 has been partialled out of Pt2.

The squared correlation between Score and Pt1 is .129 (see Figure 12.11, cell K18). If we add .129 to .0043, we get .1333 as the combined proportion of variance shared between the two Patient vectors and the Score variable—or if you prefer, 13.3% is the percentage of variance shared by Score and the two Patient vectors—with the redundant variance shared by Pt1 and Pt2 partialled out of Pt2.

Now, multiply .1333 by 3730 (Figure 12.11, cell L5) to get the portion of the total sum of squares that's attributable to the two Patient vectors or, what's the same thing, to the Patient factor. The result is 497.33, precisely the sum of squares calculated by the traditional ANOVA in Figure 12.10's cell B14.

I went through those gyrations—dragging you along with me, I hope—to demonstrate these concepts:

- When two predictor variables are correlated, some of the shared variance with the outcome variable is redundant. You can't simply add together their R^2 values because some of the variance will be allocated twice.

- You can remove the effect of one predictor on another predictor's correlation with the outcome variable, and thus you remove the variance shared by one predictor from that shared by the other predictor.

- With that adjustment made, the proportions of shared variance are independent of one another and are therefore additive.

In prehistory, as long as 25 years ago, many extant computer programs took precisely the approach described in this section to carry out multiple regression. Suppose that you attempted the same thing using Excel with, say, eight or nine predictor variables (and you get to eight or nine very quickly when you consider the factor interactions). You'd shortly drive yourself crazy trying to establish the correct formulas for the semipartial correlations and their squares, keeping the pairing of the correlations straight in each formula.

Excel provides a wonderful alternative in the form of TREND(), and I'll show you how to use it in this context next.

Using TREND() to Replace Squared Semipartial Correlations

To review, you can use squared semipartial correlations to arrange that the variance shared between a predictor variable and the outcome variable is unique to those two variables alone: that the shared variance is not redundant with the variance shared by the outcome variable and a *different* predictor variable.

Using the variables shown in Figure 12.11 as examples, the sequence of events would be as follows:

1. Enter the predictor variable Tx into the analysis by calculating its proportion of shared variance, R^2, with Score.

2. Notice that Tx has no correlation with Pt1, the next predictor variable. Therefore, Tx and Pt1 have no shared variance and there is no need to partial Tx out of Pt1. Calculate the proportion of variance that Pt1 shares with Score.

3. Notice that Pt1 and Pt2 are correlated. Calculate the squared semipartial correlation of Pt2 with Score, partialling Pt1 out of Pt2 in order that the squared semipartial correlation consist of unique shared variance only.

Excel offers you another way to remove the effects of one variable from another: the TREND() function. This worksheet function is discussed in Chapter 4, in the section titled "Getting the Predicted Values." Here's a quick review.

One of the main uses of regression analysis is to provide a way to predict one variable's value using the known values of another variable or variables. Usually you provide known values of the predictor variables and of the outcome variable to the LINEST() function or to the Regression tool. You get back, among other results, an equation that you can use to predict a new outcome value, based on new predictor values.

For example, you might try predicting tomorrow's closing value on the Dow Jones Industrial Average using, as predictors, today's volume on the New York Stock Exchange and today's advance-decline (A-D) ratio. You could collect historical data on volume, the A-D ratio, and the Dow. You would pass that historical data to LINEST() and use the resulting regression equation on today's volume and A-D data to predict tomorrow's Dow closing.

> **NOTE**
>
> Don't bother. This is just an example. It's already been tried and there's a lot more to it—and even so it doesn't work very well.

The problem is that neither LINEST() nor the Regression tool provide you the actual predicted values. You have to apply the regression equation yourself, and that's tedious if you have many predictors, or many values to predict, or both. That's where TREND() comes in. You give TREND() the same arguments that you give LINEST() and TREND() returns not the regression equation itself, but the results of applying it.

Figure 12.12 has an example. (Remember that to get an array of results from TREND(), as here, you must array-enter it with Ctrl+Shift+Enter.)

Figure 12.12
TREND() enables you to bypass the regression equation and get its results directly.

	D2			fx	{=TREND(B2:B19,A2:A19)}			
	A	B	C	D	E	F	G	H	I	J
	Pt1	Pt2		TREND()		LINEST()			Predicted from LINEST()'s equation
1	Pt1	Pt2		TREND()		LINEST()			equation
2	1	0		0.5		0.5	0		0.5
3	1	0		0.5		0.217	0.177		0.5
4	1	0		0.5		0.25	0.75		0.5
5	0	1		0		5.333	16		0
6	0	1		0		3	9		0
7	0	1		0					0
8	-1	-1		-0.5					-0.5
9	-1	-1		-0.5					-0.5
10	-1	-1		-0.5					-0.5
11	1	0		0.5					0.5
12	1	0		0.5					0.5
13	1	0		0.5					0.5
14	0	1		0					0
15	0	1		0					0
16	0	1		0					0
17	-1	-1		-0.5					-0.5
18	-1	-1		-0.5					-0.5
19	-1	-1		-0.5					-0.5
20									

12

In Figure 12.12, you see the values of the two Patient vectors from Figure 12.11; they are in columns A and B. In column D are the results of using the TREND() function on the Pt1 and Pt2 values. TREND() first calculates the regression equation and then applies it to the variables you give it to work with. In this case, column D contains the values of Pt2 that it would predict by applying the regression equation to the Pt1 values in column A.

Because the correlation between Pt1 and Pt2 is not a perfect 1.0 or –1.0, the predicted values of Pt2 do not match the actual values.

Columns F through I in Figure 12.12 take a slightly different path to the same result. Columns F and G contain the results of the array formula

=LINEST(B2:B19,A2:A19,,TRUE)

where the relationship between the predicted variable in B2:B19 with the predictor variable in A2:A19 is analyzed. The first row of the results contains .5 and 0, which are the regression coefficient and intercept, respectively. The regression equation consists of the intercept plus the result of multiplying the coefficient times the predictor variable it's associated with. There is only one predictor variable in this instance, so the regression equation—entered in cells I2—is as follows:

=$G$2+$F$2*A2

It is copied and pasted into I2:I19, so that the predictor value multiplied by the coefficient adjusts to A3, A4, and so on.

Note that the values in columns D and I are identical. If what you're after is not the equation itself but the results of applying it, you want TREND(), as shown in column D.

For simplicity and clarity, I have used only one predictor variable for the example in Figure 12.12. But like LINEST(), TREND() is capable of handling multiple predictor variables; the syntax might be something such as

=TREND(A1:A101,B1:N101)

where your predicted variable is in column A and your predictor variables are in columns B through N.

One final item to keep in mind: If you want to see the results of the TREND() function on the worksheet (which isn't always the case), you need to begin by selecting the worksheet cells that will display the results and then array-enter the formula using Ctrl+Shift+Enter instead of simply pressing Enter.

Working with the Residuals

Figure 12.13 shows how you can use TREND() in the context of a multiple regression analysis.

Figure 12.13
The TREND() results are explicitly shown here, but it's not necessary to do so.

	A	B	C	D	E	F	G	H	I
	Score	Pt1	Pt2		Pt2 via TREND()	Residual Pt2			R^2 with Score
2	89	1	0		0.5	-0.5		Pt1	0.12904
3	84	1	0		0.5	-0.5		Pt2	0.00429
4	86	1	0		0.5	-0.5			
5	123	0	1		0	1.0		Total	0.13333
6	99	0	1		0	1.0			
7	117	0	1		0	1.0		SS Total	3730
8	84	-1	-1		-0.5	-0.5		SS due to Patient	497.3333
9	109	-1	-1		-0.5	-0.5			
10	87	-1	-1		-0.5	-0.5			
11	103	1	0		0.5	-0.5			
12	100	1	0		0.5	-0.5			
13	112	1	0		0.5	-0.5			
14	100	0	1		0	1.0			
15	92	0	1		0	1.0			
16	93	0	1		0	1.0			
17	126	-1	-1		-0.5	-0.5			
18	127	-1	-1		-0.5	-0.5			
19	117	-1	-1		-0.5	-0.5			

The data in columns A, B, and C in Figure 12.13 are taken from Figure 12.11. Column E contains the result of the TREND() function: the values of Pt2 that the regression equation between Pt1 and Pt2 returns. The array formula in E2:E19 is

=TREND(C2:C19,B2:B19)

Column F contains what are called the *residuals* of the regression. They are what remains of, in this case, Pt2 after the effect of Pt1 has been removed. The effect of Pt1 is in E2:E19, so the remainder of Pt2, its residual values, are calculated very simply in Column F with this formula in cell F2:

=C2–E2

That formula is copied and pasted into F3:F19. Now the final calculations are made in column I. (Don't be concerned. I'm doing all this just to show how and why it works, both from the standpoint of theory and from the standpoint of Excel worksheet functions. I'm about to show you how to get it all done with just a couple of formulas.)

Start in cell I2, where the R^2 between Pt1 and Score appears. It is obtained with this formula:

=RSQ(B2:B19,A2:A19)

The RSQ() worksheet function (its name is, of course, short for "r-squared") is occasionally useful, but it's limited because it can deal with only two variables. We're working with the raw R^2 in cell I2. That's because, although Tx enters the equation first in Figure 12.11, Tx and Pt1 share no variance (see cell L18 in Figure 12.11). Therefore, there can be no overlap between Tx and Pt1, as there is between Pt1 and Pt2.

Cell I3 contains the formula

=RSQ(A2:A19,F2:F19)

12

which returns the proportion of variance, R^2, in Score that's shared with the *residuals* of Pt2. We have predicted Pt2 from Pt1 in column E using TREND(). We have calculated the residuals of Pt2 after removing what it shares with Pt1. Now the R^2 of the residuals with Score tells us the shared variance between Score and Pt2, with the effect of Pt1 removed. In other words, in cell I3 we're looking at the squared semipartial correlation between Score and Pt2, with Pt1 partialled out. And we have arrived at that figure without resorting to formulas of this sort, discussed in a prior section:

$$r_{1(2.3)} = \frac{r_{12} - 2r_{13}r_{23}}{\sqrt{1 - r_{23}^2}}$$

(What we've done in Figure 12.13 might not look like much of an improvement, but read just a little further on.)

To complete the demonstration, cell I5 in Figure 12.13 contains the total of the two R^2 values in I2 and I3. That is the total proportion of the variance in Score attributable to Pt1 and Pt2 taken together.

Cell I7 contains the total sum of squares; compare it with cell L5 in Figure 12.11. Cell I8 contains the product of cells I5 and I7: the proportion of the total sum of squares attributable to the two Patient vectors, times the total sum of squares. The result, 497.33, is the sum of squares due to the Patient factor. Compare it to cell B14 in Figure 12.10: the two values are identical.

What we have succeeded in doing so far is to disaggregate the total sum of squares due to regression (cell L3 in Figure 12.11) and allocate the correct amount of that total to the Patient factor. The same can be done with the Treatment factor, and with the interaction of Treatment with Patient. It's important that you be able to do so, because you want to know whether there are significant differences in the results according to a subject's Treatment status, Patient status, or both. You can't tell that from the overall sum of squares due to the regression: You have to break it out more finely.

Yes, the ANOVA gives you that breakdown automatically, whereas Regression doesn't. But the technique of regression is so much more flexible and can handle so many more situations that the best approach is to use regression and bolster it as necessary with the more detailed analysis described here.

Next up: how to get that more detailed analysis with just a couple of formulas.

Using Excel's Absolute and Relative Addressing to Extend the Semipartials

Here's how to get those squared semipartial correlations—and thus the sums of squares attributable to each main and interaction effect—nearly automatically. Figure 12.14 shows the process.

Figure 12.14 repeats the underlying data from Figure 12.11, in the range A1:H19. The summary analysis from the Regression tool appears in the range I3:O7. The raw data in columns A:H is there because we need it to calculate the semipartials.

Figure 12.14
Effect coding and multiple regression analysis for a balanced factorial design.

	M12			fx	=(L11+M11)*L7									
	A	B	C	D	E	F	G	H	I	J	K	L	M	N	O
1	Treatment	Patient	Score	Tx	Pt1	Pt2	Tx Pt1	Tx Pt2		SUMMARY OUTPUT					
2	Medical	Inpatient	89	1	1	0	1	0							
3	Medical	Inpatient	84	1	1	0	1	0		ANOVA					
4	Medical	Inpatient	86	1	1	0	1	0			df	SS	MS	F	Sig F
5	Medical	Outpatient	123	1	0	1	0	1		Regression	5	2856	571.2	7.84	0.00173
6	Medical	Outpatient	99	1	0	1	0	1		Residual	12	874	72.8		
7	Medical	Outpatient	117	1	0	1	0	1		Total	17	3730			
8	Medical	Short Stay	84	1	-1	-1	-1	-1							
9	Medical	Short Stay	109	1	-1	-1	-1	-1				Main Effects		Interactions	
10	Medical	Short Stay	87	1	-1	-1	-1	-1			Tx	Pt1	Pt2	Tx Pt1	Tx Pt2
11	Surgical	Inpatient	103	0	1	0	0	0		Prop of Var	0.12606	0.12904	0.00429	0.02583	0.48046
12	Surgical	Inpatient	100	0	1	0	0	0		SS	470.222		497.333		1888.444
13	Surgical	Inpatient	112	0	1	0	0	0							
14	Surgical	Outpatient	100	0	0	1	0	0							
15	Surgical	Outpatient	92	0	0	1	0	0							
16	Surgical	Outpatient	93	0	0	1	0	0							
17	Surgical	Short Stay	126	0	-1	-1	0	0							
18	Surgical	Short Stay	127	0	-1	-1	0	0							
19	Surgical	Short Stay	117	0	-1	-1	0	0							

Cell K11 contains this formula:

=RSQ(C2:C19,D2:D19)

It returns the R^2 between the Score variable in column C and the Treatment vector Tx in column D. There is no partialling out to be done for this variable. It is the first variable to enter the regression, and therefore there is no previous variable whose influence on Tx must be removed. All the variance that can be attributed to Tx is attributed. Tx and Score share 12.6% of their variance.

Establishing the Main Formula

Cell L11 contains this formula, which you need enter only once for the full analysis:

=RSQ($C$2:$C$19,E2:E19–TREND(E2:E19,$D2:D19))

> **NOTE**
> You do not need to array-enter the formula, despite its use of the TREND() function. When you enter a formula that requires array entry, one of the reasons to array-enter it is that it returns results to more than one worksheet cell. For example, LINEST() returns regression coefficients in its first row and the standard errors of the coefficients in its second row. You must start by selecting the cells that will be involved, and finish by using Ctrl+Shift+Enter. In this case, though, the results of the TREND() function—although there are 18 such results—do not occupy worksheet cells but are kept corralled within the full formula. Therefore, you need not use array entry. (However, just because a formula will return results to one cell only does not mean that array entry is not necessary. There are many examples of single-cell formulas that must be array-entered if they are to return the proper result. I've been using array formulas in Excel for almost 20 years and I still sometimes have to test a new formula structure to determine whether it must be array-entered.)

The use of RSQ() in cell L11 is a little complex, and the best way to tackle a complex Excel formula is from the inside out. You could use the formula evaluator (in the Formula

12

Auditing group on the Ribbon's Formulas tab), but it wouldn't help much in this instance. Taking it from the right, consider this fragment:

TREND(E2:E19,$D2:D19)

That fragment simply returns the values shown in cells E2:E19 of Figure 12.13: the values of Pt1 that are calculated from its relationship with Tx. You don't actually see the calculated values here: They stay in the formula and out of the way.

Backing up a little, the fragment

E2:E19–TREND(E2:E19,$D2:D19)

returns the residuals: the values in E2:E19 that remain after accounting for their relationship with the values in D2:D19. These residuals are shown in Figure 12.13, cells F2:F19.

Finally, here's the full formula in cell L11:

=RSQ($C$2:$C$19,E2:E19–TREND(E2:E19,$D2:D19))

This formula calculates the R^2 between the Score variable in cells C2:C19 and the residuals of the values in E2:E19. It's the squared semipartial correlation between Score and Pt1, partialling Tx out of Pt1.

As you see, the value returned by the formula in cell L11, 0.129, is identical to the raw squared correlation between Score and Pt1 (compare with cell K18 in Figure 12.11). This is because in a balanced design using effect coding, as here, the vectors for the main effects and the interactions are mutually independent. The Tx vector is independent of, thus uncorrelated with, the Pt1 vector (and the Pt2 vector and all the interaction vectors). When two vectors are uncorrelated, there's nothing in either one to remove of its correlation with the other.

So in theory, the formula in cell L11 *could* have been

=RSQ(C2:C19,E2:E19)

because it returns the same value as the semipartial correlation does. But for practical reasons it's better to enter the formula as given, for reasons you'll see next.

Extending the Formula Automatically

If you select cell L11 as it's shown in Figure 12.14, click and hold the selection handle, and drag to the right into cell O11, the mixed and relative addresses adjust and the fixed reference remains fixed.

NOTE
The *selection handle* is the black square in the lower-right corner of the active cell.

When you do so, the formula in L11 becomes this formula in M11:

=RSQ($C$2:$C$19,F2:F19−TREND(F2:F19,$D2:E19))

The R^2 value returned by this formula is now between Score in C2:C19 and Pt2 in F2:F19—but with the effects of Tx and Pt1 partialled out of Pt2. In copying and pasting the formula from L11 to M11, the references adjusted (or failed to do so) in a few ways, as detailed next.

The Absolute Reference   The reference to $C$2:$C$19, where Score is found, did not adjust. It is an absolute reference, and pasting the reference to another cell, M11, has no effect on it.

The Relative References   The references to E2:E19 in L11 become F2:F19 in M11. The references are relative and adjust according to the location you paste them to. Because M11 is one column to the right of L11, the references change from column E to column F. In so doing, the formula turns its attention from Pt1 in column E to Pt2 in column F.

The Mixed Reference   The reference to $D2:D19 in L11 becomes $D2:E19 in M11. It is a mixed reference: the first column, the D in $D2, is fixed by means of the dollar sign. The second column, the D in D19, is relative because it's not immediately preceded by a dollar sign. So when the formula is pasted from column L to column M, $D2:D19 becomes $D2:E19. That has the effect of predicting Pt2 (column F) from both Tx (column D) and Pt1 (column E).

This is exactly what we're after. Each time we paste the formula one column to the right, we shift to a new predictor variable. Furthermore, we extend the range of the predictor variables that we want to partial out of the new predictor. In the downloaded copy of the workbook for Chapter 12, you'll find that by extending the formula out to column O, the formula in cell O11 is

=RSQ($C$2:$C$19,H2:H19−TREND(H2:H19,$D2:G19))

and is extended all the way out to capture the final interaction vector in column H.

This section of Chapter 12 developed a relatively straightforward way to calculate shared variance with the effect of other variables removed, by means of the TREND() function and residual values. We can now apply that method to designs that have unequal n's. As you'll see, unequal n's sometimes bring about unwanted correlations between factors, and sometimes are the result of existing correlations. In either case, regression analysis of the sort introduced in this chapter can help you manage the correlations and, in turn, make the partition of the variability in the outcome measure unambiguous. The next chapter takes up that topic.

12

Multiple Regression Analysis: Further Issues

Chapter 12, "Multiple Regression Analysis and Effect Coding: The Basics," discusses the concept of using multiple regression analysis to address the question of whether group means differ more than can reasonably be explained by chance. The basic idea is to code nominal variables such as type of medication administered, or sex, or ethnicity, so as to represent them as numeric variables. Coded in that way, nominal variables can be used as input to multiple regression analysis. You can calculate correlations between independent variables and the outcome variable—and, what's equally important, between the independent variables themselves. From there it's a short step to testing whether chance is a reasonable explanation for the differences you observe in the outcome variable.

This chapter explores some of the issues that arise when you go beyond the basics of using multiple regression to analyze variance. In particular, it's almost inevitable for you to encounter unbalanced factorial designs—those with unequal numbers of observations per design cell. Finally, this chapter discusses how best to use the worksheet functions, such as LINEST() and TREND(), that underlie the Data Analysis add-in's more static Regression tool.

Solving Unbalanced Factorial Designs Using Multiple Regression

An unbalanced design can come about for a variety of reasons, and it's useful to classify the reasons according to whether the imbalance is caused by the factors that you're studying or the population from which you've sampled. That distinction is useful because it helps point you toward the best way to solve the problems that the imbalance in the design presents. This chapter has more to say about that in a later section. First, let's look at the results of the imbalance.

Figure 13.1 repeats a data set that also appears in Figures 12.10 and 12.11.

Figure 13.1

This design is balanced: It has an equal number of observations in each group.

	A	B	C	D	E	F	G	H	I	J	K	L	M	N	O	P
1	Treatment	Patient	Score	Tx		Pt1	Pt2	Tx Pt1	Tx Pt2				r matrix, balanced design			
2	Medical	Inpatient	89	1	1	0		1	0			Score	Tx	Pt1	Pt2	Tx Pt1	Tx Pt2
3	Medical	Inpatient	84	1	1	0		1	0	Score	1				
4	Medical	Inpatient	86	1	1	0		1	0	Tx	-0.3551	1			
5	Medical	Outpatient	123	1	0	1		0	1	Pt1	-0.3592	0	1		
6	Medical	Outpatient	99	1	0	1		0	1	Pt2	-0.1229	0	0.5	1	
7	Medical	Outpatient	117	1	0	1		0	1	Tx Pt1	0.1607	0	0	0	1
8	Medical	Short Stay	84	1	-1	-1		-1	-1	Tx Pt2	0.6806	0	0	0	0.5	1
9	Medical	Short Stay	109	1	-1	-1		-1	-1						
10	Medical	Short Stay	87	1	-1	-1		-1	-1						
11	Surgical	Inpatient	103	-1	1	0		-1	0						
12	Surgical	Inpatient	100	-1	1	0		-1	0						
13	Surgical	Inpatient	112	-1	1	0		-1	0						
14	Surgical	Outpatient	100	-1	0	1		0	-1						
15	Surgical	Outpatient	92	-1	0	1		0	-1						
16	Surgical	Outpatient	93	-1	0	1		0	-1						
17	Surgical	Short Stay	126	-1	-1	-1		1	1						
18	Surgical	Short Stay	127	-1	-1	-1		1	1						
19	Surgical	Short Stay	117	-1	-1	-1		1	1						

In Figure 13.1, the data is presented as a balanced factorial design: that is, two or more factors with an equal number of observations per cell. For the purposes of this example, in Figure 13.2 one observation has been moved from one group to another. The observation that has a Score of 93 and is shown in Figure 13.1 in the group defined by a Surgical treatment on an Outpatient basis has in Figure 13.2 been moved to the Short Stay patient basis.

Figures 13.1 and 13.2 also show two correlation matrices. They show the correlations between the outcome measure Score and the effect vectors Tx, Pt1, and Pt2, and their interactions. Figure 13.1 shows the matrix with the correlations for the data in the balanced design in the range J2:P8. Figure 13.2 shows the correlation matrix for the unbalanced design, also in the range J2:P8.

Figure 13.2

Moving an observation from one group to another results in unequal group sizes: an unbalanced design.

	A	B	C	D	E	F	G	H	I	J	K	L	M	N	O	P
1	Treatment	Patient	Score	Tx		Pt1	Pt2	Tx Pt1	Tx Pt2				r matrix, unbalanced design			
2	Medical	Inpatient	89	1	1	0		1	0			Score	Tx	Pt1	Pt2	Tx Pt1	Tx Pt2
3	Medical	Inpatient	84	1	1	0		1	0	Score	1				
4	Medical	Inpatient	86	1	1	0		1	0	Tx	-0.3551	1			
5	Medical	Outpatient	123	1	0	1		0	1	Pt1	-0.3019	0.0655	1		
6	Medical	Outpatient	99	1	0	1		0	1	Pt2	-0.0318	0.1374	0.5579	1	
7	Medical	Outpatient	117	1	0	1		0	1	Tx Pt1	0.1107	-0.0655	-0.0730	-0.0720	1
8	Medical	Short Stay	84	1	-1	-1		-1	-1	Tx Pt2	0.5948	-0.1374	-0.0720	0.0189	0.5579	1
9	Medical	Short Stay	109	1	-1	-1		-1	-1						
10	Medical	Short Stay	87	1	-1	-1		-1	-1						
11	Surgical	Inpatient	103	-1	1	0		-1	0						
12	Surgical	Inpatient	100	-1	1	0		-1	0						
13	Surgical	Inpatient	112	-1	1	0		-1	0						
14	Surgical	Outpatient	100	-1	0	1		0	-1						
15	Surgical	Outpatient	92	-1	0	1		0	-1						
16	Surgical	Short Stay	93	-1	-1	-1		1	1						
17	Surgical	Short Stay	126	-1	-1	-1		1	1						
18	Surgical	Short Stay	127	-1	-1	-1		1	1						
19	Surgical	Short Stay	117	-1	-1	-1		1	1						

Variables Are Uncorrelated in a Balanced Design

Compare the two correlation matrices in Figures 13.1 and 13.2. Notice first that most correlations in Figure 13.1, based on the balanced design, are zero. In contrast, all the correlations in Figure 13.2, based on the unbalanced design, are nonzero.

All correlation matrices contain what's called the *main diagonal*. It is the set of cells that shows the correlation of each variable with itself, and that therefore always contains values of 1.0. In Figures 13.1 and 13.2, the main diagonal of each correlation matrix includes the cells K3, L4, M5, N6, O7, and P8. No matter whether a design is balanced or unbalanced, a correlation matrix always has 1's in its main diagonal. It must, by definition, because the main diagonal of a correlation matrix always contains the correlation of each variable with itself.

Figure 13.1 has almost exclusively 0's below the main diagonal and to the right of the column for Score. These statements are true of a correlation matrix in a balanced design where effect coding is in use:

- The correlations between the main effects are zero. See cells L5 and L6 in Figure 13.1.
- The correlations between the main effects and the interactions are zero. See cells L7:N8 in Figure 13.1.
- A main effect that requires two or more vectors has nonzero correlations between its vectors. This is also true of unbalanced designs. See cell M6 in Figures 13.1 and 13.2. (Recall from Chapter 12 that a main effect has as many vectors as it has degrees of freedom. Using effect coding, a factor that has two levels needs just one vector to define each observation's level, and a factor that has three levels needs two vectors to define each observation's level.)
- Interaction vectors that involve the same factors have nonzero correlations. This is also true of unbalanced designs. See cell O8 in Figures 13.1 and 13.2.

Those correlations of zero in Figure 13.1 are very useful. When two variables are uncorrelated, it means that they share no variance. In Figure 13.1, Treatment and Patient Status are uncorrelated—you can tell that from the fact that the Tx vector (representing Treatment, which has two levels) has a zero correlation with both the Pt1 and the Pt2 vectors (representing Patient Status, which has three levels). Therefore, whatever variance that Treatment shares with Score is unique to Treatment and Score, and is not shared with the Patient Status variable. There is no ambiguity about how the variance in Score is to be allocated across the predictor variables, Treatment and Patient Status.

This is the reason that, with a balanced design, you can add up the sum of squares for all the factors and their interactions, add the within group variance, and arrive at the total sum of squares. There's no ambiguity about how the variance of the outcome variable gets divided up, and the total of the sums of squares equals the overall sum of squared deviations of each observation from the grand mean.

13

Variables Are Correlated in an Unbalanced Design

But if the design is unbalanced, if not all design cells contain the same number of observations, then there will be correlations between the vectors that would otherwise be uncorrelated. In Figure 13.2, you can see that Tx is correlated at –0.302 and –0.032 with Pt1 and Pt2, respectively (cells K5:K6). Because Treatment now is correlated with Patient Status, it shares variance with Patient Status. (More precisely, because the Tx, Pt1, and Pt2 vectors are now correlated with one another, they have variance in common.)

In turn, the variance that Treatment shares with Score can't be solely attributed to Treatment. The three predictor vectors are correlated, and therefore share some of their variance, and therefore have some variance in common with Score.

The same is true for the other predictor variables. Merely shifting one observation from the Patient Status of Outpatient to Short Stay causes all the correlations that had previously been zero to be nonzero. Therefore, they now have variance in common. Any of that common variance might also be shared with the outcome variable, and we're dealing once again with ambiguity: How do we tell how to divide the variance in the outcome variable between Treatment and Patient Status? Between Treatment and the Treatment by Patient Status interaction? The task of allocating some proportion of variance to one predictor variable, and some to other predictor variables, depends largely on the design of the research that gathered the data.

There are ways to complete that task, and we're coming to them shortly. First, let's return to the nice, clean, unambiguous balanced design to point out a related reason that equal group sizes are helpful.

Order of Entry Is Irrelevant in the Balanced Design

Figures 13.3 and 13.4 continue the analysis of the balanced data set in Figure 13.1.

Figures 13.3 and 13.4 look somewhat complex, but there are really only a couple of crucial points to take away from them.

In both figures, the range J1:O21 contains a regression analysis and a traditional analysis of variance for the data in the range C2:H19. There are three observations in each cell, so the design is balanced.

Cells J3:O7 contain the partial results of using the Data Analysis add-in's Regression tool. As discussed in the final section of Chapter 12, the correlations between main effects vectors in a balanced design are zero. But there are correlations between vectors that represent the same factor: In this case, there is a correlation between vector Pt1 and vector Pt2 for the Patient Status factor. Squared semipartial correlations in L11:O11 of Figures 13.3 and 13.4 remove from each vector as it enters the analysis any variance that it shares with vectors that have already entered.

Therefore, the sums of squares attributed to each factor and the interaction (cells K12, M12, and O12) are unique and unambiguous. They are identical to the sums of squares reported in the traditional analysis of variance shown in J14:O21 in Figures 13.3 and 13.4.

Figure 13.3
In this analysis, Treatment enters the regression equation before Patient Status.

	A	B	C	D	E	F	G	H	I	J	K	L	M	N	O
1	Treatment	Patient	Score	Tx	Pt1	Pt2	Tx Pt1	Tx Pt2		SUMMARY OUTPUT					
2	Medical	Inpatient	89	1	1	0	1	0							
3	Medical	Inpatient	84	1	1	0	1	0		ANOVA					
4	Medical	Inpatient	86	1	1	0	1	0			df	SS	MS	F	Sig F
5	Medical	Outpatient	123	1	0	1	0	1		Regression	5	2856	571.2	7.84	0.002
6	Medical	Outpatient	99	1	0	1	0	1		Residual	12	874	72.8		
7	Medical	Outpatient	117	1	0	1	0	1		Total	17	3730			
8	Medical	Short Stay	84	1	-1	-1	-1	-1							
9	Medical	Short Stay	109	1	-1	-1	-1	-1			Main Effects			Interactions	
10	Medical	Short Stay	87	1	-1	-1	-1	-1			Tx	Pt1	Pt2	Tx Pt1	Tx Pt2
11	Surgical	Inpatient	103	-1	1	0	-1	0		Prop of Var	0.126	0.129	0.004	0.026	0.480
12	Surgical	Inpatient	100	-1	1	0	-1	0		SS	470.222		497.333		1888.444
13	Surgical	Inpatient	112	-1	1	0	-1	0							
14	Surgical	Outpatient	100	-1	0	1	0	-1		ANOVA					
15	Surgical	Outpatient	92	-1	0	1	0	-1		SV	SS	df	MS	F	P-value
16	Surgical	Outpatient	93	-1	0	1	0	-1		Treatment	470.222	1	470.222	6.456	0.026
17	Surgical	Short Stay	126	-1	-1	-1	1	1		Patient	497.333	2	248.667	3.414	0.067
18	Surgical	Short Stay	127	-1	-1	-1	1	1		Interaction	1888.444	2	944.222	12.964	0.001
19	Surgical	Short Stay	117	-1	-1	-1	1	1		Effects	2856.000	5	571.200		
20										Within	874	12	72.833		
21										Total	3730	17			

Now, compare the proportions of variance shown in cells K11:O11 of Figure 13.3 with the same cells in Figure 13.4.

Figure 13.4
Patient Status enters the regression equation first in this analysis.

	A	B	C	D	E	F	G	H	I	J	K	L	M	N	O
1	Treatment	Patient	Score	Pt1	Pt2	Tx	Tx Pt1	Tx Pt2		SUMMARY OUTPUT					
2	Medical	Inpatient	89	1	0	1	1	0							
3	Medical	Inpatient	84	1	0	1	1	0		ANOVA					
4	Medical	Inpatient	86	1	0	1	1	0			df	SS	MS	F	Sig F
5	Medical	Outpatient	123	0	1	1	0	1		Regression	5	2856	571.2	7.84	0.002
6	Medical	Outpatient	99	0	1	1	0	1		Residual	12	874	72.8		
7	Medical	Outpatient	117	0	1	1	0	1		Total	17	3730			
8	Medical	Short Stay	84	-1	-1	1	-1	-1							
9	Medical	Short Stay	109	-1	-1	1	-1	-1			Main Effects			Interactions	
10	Medical	Short Stay	87	-1	-1	1	-1	-1			Pt1	Pt2	Tx	Tx Pt1	Tx Pt2
11	Surgical	Inpatient	103	1	0	-1	-1	0		Prop of Var	0.129	0.004	0.126	0.026	0.480
12	Surgical	Inpatient	100	1	0	-1	-1	0		SS		497.333	470.222		1888.444
13	Surgical	Inpatient	112	1	0	-1	-1	0							
14	Surgical	Outpatient	100	0	1	-1	0	-1		ANOVA					
15	Surgical	Outpatient	92	0	1	-1	0	-1		SV	SS	df	MS	F	P-value
16	Surgical	Outpatient	93	0	1	-1	0	-1		Patient	497.333	2	248.667	3.414	0.067
17	Surgical	Short Stay	126	-1	-1	1	1	1		Treatment	470.222	1	470.222	6.456	0.026
18	Surgical	Short Stay	127	-1	-1	-1	1	1		Interaction	1888.444	2	944.222	12.964	0.001
19	Surgical	Short Stay	117	-1	-1	-1	1	1		Effects	2856.000	5	571.200		
20										Within	874	12	72.833		
21										Total	3730	17			

Notice that in Figures 13.3 and 13.4 the predictor variables appear in different orders in the analysis shown in cells J9:O12. In Figure 13.3, Treatment enters the regression equation first via its Tx vector. The Treatment variable shares 0.126 of its variance with the Score outcome. Because Treatment enters the equation first, all of the variance it shares with Score is attributed to Treatment. No one made a decision to give the variable that's entered first all its available variance: It's just the way that multiple regression works. You don't have to live with that, though. You might want to adjust Treatment for Patient Status even if Treatment enters the equation first. A later section in this chapter, "Managing Unequal Group Sizes in a True Experiment," deals with that possibility.

13

Next, the two Patient Status vectors, Pt1 and Pt2, enter the regression equation, in that order. They account, respectively, for 0.129 and 0.004 of the variance in Score. The variables Pt1 and Pt2 are correlated, and the variance attributed to Pt2 is reduced according to the amount of variance already attributed to Pt1. (See the section titled "Using TREND() to Replace Squared Semipartial Correlations" in Chapter 12 for a discussion of that reduction using the squared semipartial correlation.)

Compare those proportions for Patient Status, 0.129 and 0.004, in Figure 13.3 with the ones shown in Figure 13.4, cells K11:L11. In Figure 13.4, it is Patient Status, not Treatment, that enters the equation first. All the variance that Pt1 shares with Score is attributed to Pt1. It is identical to the proportion of variance shown in Figure 13.3, because Pt1 and Treatment are uncorrelated: The sample size is the same in each group. Therefore, there is no ambiguity in how the variance in Score is allocated, and it makes no difference whether Treatment or Patient Status enters the equation first. When two predictor variables are uncorrelated, the variance that each shares with the outcome variable is unique to each predictor variable.

It's also a good idea to notice that the regression analysis in cells J3:O7 and the traditional ANOVA summary in cells J14:O21 return the same aggregate results. In particular, the sum of squares, degrees of freedom, and the mean square for the regression in cells K5:M5 are the same as the parallel values in cells K19:M19. The same is true for the residual variation in K6:M6 and K20:M20 (labeled "Within" in the traditional ANOVA summary).

The only meaningful difference between the ANOVA table that accompanies a standard regression analysis and a standard ANOVA summary table is that the regression analysis usually lumps all the results for the predictors into one line labeled "Regression." A little additional work of the sort described in Chapter 12 and in this chapter is often needed.

But the findings are the same in the aggregate. Total up the sums of squares for Treatment, Patient, and their interaction in K16:K18, and you get the same total as is shown for the Regression sum of squares in L5.

The next section discusses how these results differ when you're working with an unbalanced design.

Order Entry Is Important in the Unbalanced Design

For contrast, consider Figures 13.5 and 13.6. Their analyses are the same as in Figures 13.3 and 13.4, except that Figures 13.5 and 13.6 are based on the unbalanced design shown in Figure 13.2.

The data set used in Figures 13.5 and 13.6 is no longer balanced. It is the same as the one shown in Figure 13.2, where one observation has been moved from the Patient Status of Outpatient to Short Stay. As discussed earlier in this chapter, that one move causes the correlations of Score with Patient Status and with the interaction variables to change from their values in the case of the balanced design (Figure 13.1). It also changes the correlations between all the vectors, which causes them to share variance: the correlations are no longer zero.

Figure 13.5

The Treatment variable enters the equation first and shares the same variance with Score as in Figures 13.3 and 13.4.

	A	B	C	D	E	F	G	H	I	J	K	L	M	N	O
1	Treatment	Patient	Score	Tx	Pt1	Pt2	Tx Pt1	Tx Pt2		SUMMARY OUTPUT					
2	Medical	Inpatient	89	1	1	0	1	0							
3	Medical	Inpatient	84	1	1	0	1	0		ANOVA					
4	Medical	Inpatient	86	1	1	0	1	0				df	SS	MS	F	Sig F
5	Medical	Outpatient	123	1	0	1	0	1		Regression		5	2171.917	434.3833	3.3455	0.04016
6	Medical	Outpatient	99	1	0	1	0	1		Residual		12	1558.083	129.8403		
7	Medical	Outpatient	117	1	0	1	0	1		Total		17	3730			
8	Medical	Short Stay	84	1	-1	-1	-1	-1							
9	Medical	Short Stay	109	1	-1	-1	-1	-1				**Main Effects**			**Interactions**	
10	Medical	Short Stay	87	1	-1	-1	-1	-1			Tx	Pt1	Pt2	Tx Pt1	Tx Pt2
11	Surgical	Inpatient	103	-1	1	0	-1	0		Prop of Var	0.126	0.078	0.04288	0.006	0.330
12	Surgical	Inpatient	100	-1	1	0	-1	0		SS	470.222		450.736		1250.959
13	Surgical	Inpatient	112	-1	1	0	-1	0							
14	Surgical	Outpatient	100	-1	0	1	0	-1		ANOVA					
15	Surgical	Outpatient	92	-1	0	1	0	-1		SV	SS	df	MS	F	P-value
16	Surgical	Short Stay	93	-1	-1	-1	1	1		Treatment	470.222	1	470.222	3.622	0.081
17	Surgical	Short Stay	126	-1	-1	-1	1	1		Patient	450.736	2	225.368	1.736	0.218
18	Surgical	Short Stay	127	-1	-1	-1	1	1		Interaction	1250.959	2	625.479	4.817	0.022
19	Surgical	Short Stay	117	-1	-1	-1	1	1		Effects	2171.917	5	434.383		
20										Within	1558.083	12	129.840		
21										Total	3730	17			

The one correlation that does not change between the balanced and the unbalanced designs is that of Treatment and Score. The proportion of variance in Score that's attributed to Treatment is 0.126 in Figure 13.3 (cell K11), where Tx is entered first, and in Figure 13.4 (cell M11), where Tx is entered third. Two reasons combine to ensure that the correlation between Treatment and Score remains at –0.3551, and the shared variance at 0.126, even when the balanced design is made unbalanced:

■ Moving one subject from Outpatient to Short Stay changes neither that subject's Score value nor the Treatment value. Because neither variable changes its value, the correlation remains the same.

■ In Figure 13.5, where Treatment is still entered into the regression equation first, the proportion of shared variance is still 0.126. Although there is now a correlation between Treatment and Patient Status (cells L5 and L6 in Figure 13.2), Treatment loses none of the variance it shares with Patient Status. Because it's entered first, it keeps all the shared variance that's available to it.

Figure 13.6 shows what happens when Patient Status enters the equation before Treatment in the unbalanced design.

In the balanced design, the vector Pt1 correlates at –0.3592 with Score (see Figure 13.1, cell K5). In the unbalanced design, one value in Pt1 changes with the move of one subject from Outpatient to Short Stay, so the correlation between Pt1 and Score changes (as does the correlation between Pt2 and Score). In Figures 13.1 and 13.2, you can see that the correlation between Pt1 and Score changes from –0.3592 to –0.3019 as the design becomes unbalanced.

The square of the correlation is the proportion of variance shared by the two variables, and the square of –0.3019 is 0.0911. However, in the unbalanced design analysis in Figure 13.5,

13

the proportion of variance shown as shared by Score and Pt1 is 0.078 (see cell L11). That's because Tx and Pt1 themselves share some variance, and because Treatment is already in the equation, it has laid claim to all the variance it shares with Score.

Figure 13.6
The proportions of variance for all effects are different here than in Figures 13.3 through 13.5.

	A	B	C	D	E	F	G	H	I	J	K	L	M	N	O
1	Treatment	Patient	Score	Pt1	Pt2	Tx	Tx Pt1	Tx Pt2		SUMMARY OUTPUT					
2	Medical	Inpatient	89	1	0	1	1	0							
3	Medical	Inpatient	84	1	0	1	1	0		ANOVA					
4	Medical	Inpatient	86	1	0	1	1	0			df	SS	MS	F	Sig F
5	Medical	Outpatient	123	0	1	1	0	1		Regression	5	2171.917	434.3833	3.3455	0.04016
6	Medical	Outpatient	99	0	1	1	0	1		Residual	12	1558.083	129.8403		
7	Medical	Outpatient	117	0	1	1	0	1		Total	17	3730			
8	Medical	Short Stay	84	-1	-1	1	-1	-1							
9	Medical	Short Stay	109	-1	-1	1	-1	-1			Main Effects			Interactions	
10	Medical	Short Stay	87	-1	-1	1	-1	-1			Pt1	Pt2	Tx	Tx Pt1	Tx Pt2
11	Surgical	Inpatient	103	1	0	-1	-1	0		Prop of Var	0.091	0.027	0.129	0.006	0.330
12	Surgical	Inpatient	100	1	0	-1	-1	0		SS		441.010	479.948		1250.959
13	Surgical	Inpatient	112	1	0	-1	-1	0							
14	Surgical	Outpatient	100	0	1	-1	0	-1		ANOVA					
15	Surgical	Outpatient	92	0	1	-1	0	-1		SV	SS	df	MS	F	P-value
16	Surgical	Short Stay	93	-1	-1	-1	1	1		Patient	441.010	2	220.505	1.698	0.224
17	Surgical	Short Stay	126	-1	-1	-1	1	1		Treatment	479.948	1	479.948	3.696	0.079
18	Surgical	Short Stay	127	-1	-1	-1	1	1		Interaction	1250.959	2	625.479	4.817	0.023
19	Surgical	Short Stay	117	-1	-1	-1	1	1		Effects	2171.917	5	434.383		
20										Within	1558.083	12	129.840		
21										Total	3730	16			

But in Figure 13.6, where Pt1 enters the equation first, the Pt1 vector accounts for 0.091 of the variance of the Score outcome variable (see cell K11). There are two points to notice about that value:

- It is the square of the correlation between the two variables, –0.3019.
- It is not equal to the proportion of variance allocated to Pt1 when Pt1 enters the equation *after* Tx.

With Pt1 as the vector that enters the regression equation first, it claims all the variance that it shares with the outcome variable, Score, and that's the square of the correlation between Pt1 and Score. Because Pt1 in this case—entering the equation first—cedes none of its shared variance to Treatment, Pt1 gets a different proportion of the variance of Score than it does when it enters the equation after Treatment.

About Fluctuating Proportions of Variance

Intuitively, you might think that in an unbalanced design, where correlations between the predictor variables are nonzero, moving a variable up in the order of entry would increase the amount of variance in the outcome variable that's allocated to the predictor. For example, in Figures 13.5 and 13.6, the Pt1 vector is allocated 0.078 of the variance in Score when it's entered after the Tx vector, but 0.091 of the Score variance when it's entered first.

And things often turn out that way, but not necessarily. Looking again at Figures 13.5 and 13.6, notice that the Tx vector is allocated 0.126 of the variance in Score when it's entered first, but 0.129 of the variance when it's entered third. So, although some of the variance that it shares with Score is allocated to Pt1 and Pt2 in Figure 13.6, Tx still shares a larger proportion of variance when it is entered third than when it is entered first.

There's no general rule about it. As the order of entry is changed, the amount and direction that shared variance fluctuates depends on the magnitude and the direction of the correlations between the variables involved.

From an empirical viewpoint, that's well and good. You want the numbers to determine the conclusions that you draw, even if the way they behave seems counterintuitive. Things are even better when you have equal group sizes. Then, as I've pointed out several times, the correlations between the predictor variables are zero, there is no shared variance between the predictors to worry about, and you get the nice, clean results in Figures 13.3 and 13.4, where the order of entry makes no difference in the allocation of variance to the predictors.

But it's worrisome when the design is unbalanced, group sizes are unequal, and predictor variables are correlated. It's worrisome because you don't want to insert yourself into the mix. Suppose you decide to force Patient Status into the regression equation before Treatment, increasing the proportion of variance attributed to Patient Status so that differences between, say, Inpatient and Outpatient meet your criterion for alpha. You don't want what is possibly an arbitrary decision on your part (to move Patient Status up) to affect your decision to treat the difference as real rather than the result of sampling error.

You can adopt some rules that help make your decision less arbitrary. To discuss those rules sensibly, it's necessary first to discuss the relationship between predictor correlations and group sizes from a different viewpoint.

Experimental Designs, Observational Studies, and Correlation

Chapter 4, "How Variables Move Jointly: Correlation," discusses the problems that arise when you try to infer that causation is present when all that's really going on is correlation. One of those problems is the issue of directionality: Does a person's attitude toward a given social issue cause him or her to identify with a particular political party? Or does an existing party affiliation cause the attitude to be adopted? The problem of group sizes and correlations between vectors is a case in which there is causality present, but its direction varies.

Suppose you're conducting an experiment—a true experiment, one in which you have selected participants randomly from the population you're interested in and have assigned them at random to equally sized groups. You then subject the groups to one or more treatments, perhaps with double-blinding so that neither the subjects nor those administering the treatments know which treatment is in use. This is true experimental work, the so-called gold standard of research.

But during the month-long course of the experiment, unplanned events occur. Slipping past your random selection and assignment, a brother and sister not only take part but are assigned to the same treatment, invalidating the assumption of independence of observations. An assistant inadvertently administers the wrong medication to one subject, converting him from one treatment group to another. Three people have such bad reactions to their treatment that they quit. Equipment fails. And so on.

13

The result of this attrition is that what started out as a balanced factorial design is now an unbalanced design. If you're testing only one factor, then from the viewpoint of statistical analysis it's not a cause for great concern. As noted in Chapter 10, you may have to take note of the Behrens-Fisher problem, but if the group variances are equivalent, there's no serious cause for worry about the statistical analysis.

If you have more than one factor, though, you have to deal with the problem of predictor vectors and the allocation of variance that this chapter has discussed, because ambiguity in how to apportion the variance enters the picture. One possible method is to randomly drop some subjects from the experiment until your group sizes are once again equal. That's not always a feasible solution, though. If the subject attrition has been great enough and is concentrated in one or two groups, you might find yourself having to throw away a third of your observations to achieve equal group sizes.

Furthermore, the situation I've just described results in unequal group sizes for reasons that are due to the fact of the experiment and how it is carried out. There are ways to deal with the unequal group sizes mathematically. One is discussed in Chapter 12, which demonstrates the use of squared semipartial correlations to make shared variance unique. But that sort of approach is appropriate only if it's the experiment, not the population from which you sampled, that causes the groups to have different numbers of subjects. To see why, consider the following situation, which is very different from the true experiment.

You are interested in the joint effect of sex and political affiliation on attitude toward a bill that's under discussion in the House of Representatives. You take a telephone survey, dialing phone numbers randomly, establishing first that whoever answers the call is registered to vote. You ask their sex, their party affiliation, and whether they favor the bill. When it comes time to tabulate the responses, you find that your sample is distributed by party and by sex as shown in Figure 13.7.

Figure 13.7
The differences in group sizes are due to the nature of the population, not the research.

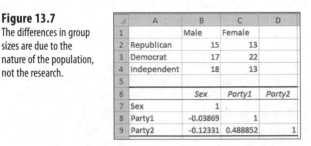

In the population, there tends to be a relationship between sex and political affiliation. Women are more likely than men to identify themselves as Democrats. Men are more likely to identify themselves as Republicans or Independents. Obviously, you're not in a position to experimentally manipulate the sex or the political party of your respondents, as you do when you assign subjects to treatments: You have to take them as they come.

Your six groups have different numbers of subjects, and any regression analysis will be subject to correlations between the predictor variables. The range A6:D9 in Figure 13.7 shows the correlations between the effect-coded vectors for sex and political party. They are correlated, and you'll have to deal with the correlations between sex and party when you allocate the variance in the outcome variable (which is not relevant to this issue and is not shown in Figure 13.7).

You could randomly discard some respondents to achieve equal group sizes. You would have to discard 20 respondents to get to 13 per group, and that's 20% of your sample—quite a bit. But more serious is the fact that in doing so you would be acting as though there were no relationship between sex and political affiliation in the population. That's manipulating substantive reality to achieve a statistical solution, and that's the wrong thing to do.

Let's review the two situations:

- A true experiment in which the loss of some subjects and, in consequence, unequal group sizes are attributable to aspects of the treatments. Correlations among predictors come about because the nature of the experiment induces unequal group sizes.

- An observational study in which the ways the population classifies itself results in unequal group sizes. Those unequal group sizes come about because the variables are correlated.

So causation is present here, but its direction depends on the situation.

In the first case, you would not be altering reality to omit a few subjects to achieve equal group sizes. But you could do equally well without discarding data by using the technique of squared semipartial correlations discussed in this chapter and in Chapter 12. By forcing each variable to contribute unique variance, you can deal with unequal group sizes in a way that's unavailable to you if you use traditional analysis of variance techniques. In this sort of situation it's usual to observe the unique variance while switching the order of entry into the regression equation. An example follows shortly.

In the second case, the observational study in which correlations in the population cause unequal group sizes, it's unwise to discard observations in pursuit of equal group sizes. However, you still want to eliminate the ambiguity that's caused by the resulting correlations among the predictors. Various approaches have been proposed and used, with varying degrees of success and of sense.

13

> **NOTE** Approaches such as forward inclusion, backward elimination, and stepwise regression are available, and may be appropriate to a situation that you are confronted with. Each of these approaches concerns itself with repeatedly changing the order in which variables are entered into, and removed from, the regression equation. Statistical decision rules, usually involving the maximization of R^2, are used to arrive at a solution. In the Excel context, the use of these methods inevitably requires VBA to manage the repetitive process. Because this book avoids the use of VBA as much as possible—it's not a book about programming—I suggest that you consult a specialized statistics application if you think one of those approaches might be appropriate.

One approach that deserves serious consideration in an observational study with unequal group sizes is what Kerlinger and Pedhazur term the *a priori ordering* approach (refer to *Multiple Regression in Behavioral Research*, 1973). You consider the nature of the predictor variables that you have under study and determine if one of them is likely to have *caused* the other, or at least preceded the other. In that case, there may be a strong argument for following that order in constructing the regression equation.

In the sex-and-politics example, it is possible that a person's sex might exert some influence, however slight, on his or her choice of political affiliation. But our political affiliation does not determine our sex. So there's a good argument in this case for forcing the sex vector to enter the regression equation before the affiliation vectors. You can do that simply by the left-to-right order in which you put the variables on the Excel worksheet. Both the Regression tool in the Data Analysis add-in and the worksheet functions concerned with regression, such as LINEST() and TREND(), enter the leftmost predictor vector first, then the one immediately to its right, and so on.

Before discussing how to do that it's important to take a closer look at the information that the LINEST() worksheet function makes available to you.

Using All the LINEST() Statistics

I have referred to the worksheet function LINEST() in this and prior chapters, but those descriptions have been sketchy. We're at the point that you need a much fuller discussion of what LINEST() can do for you.

Figure 13.8 shows the LINEST() worksheet function acting on the data set most recently shown in Figure 13.6, in the range C1:H19. The data set is repeated on the worksheet in Figure 13.8.

Figure 13.8
LINEST() always returns #N/A error values below its second row and to the right of its second column.

M10 =(J7/5)/(K7/K6)

	A	B	C	D	E	F	G	H
1	Treatment	Patient	Score	Pt1	Pt2	Tx	Tx Pt1	Tx Pt2
2	Medical	Inpatient	89	1	0	1	1	0
3	Medical	Inpatient	84	1	0	1	1	0
4	Medical	Inpatient	86	1	0	1	1	0
5	Medical	Outpatient	123	0	1	1	0	1
6	Medical	Outpatient	99	0	1	1	0	1
7	Medical	Outpatient	117	0	1	1	0	1
8	Medical	Short Stay	84	-1	-1	1	-1	-1
9	Medical	Short Stay	109	-1	-1	1	-1	-1
10	Medical	Short Stay	87	-1	-1	1	-1	-1
11	Surgical	Inpatient	103	1	0	-1	-1	0
12	Surgical	Inpatient	100	1	0	-1	-1	0
13	Surgical	Inpatient	112	1	0	-1	-1	0
14	Surgical	Outpatient	100	0	1	-1	0	-1
15	Surgical	Outpatient	92	0	1	-1	0	-1
16	Surgical	Short Stay	93	-1	-1	-1	1	1
17	Surgical	Short Stay	126	-1	-1	-1	1	1
18	Surgical	Short Stay	127	-1	-1	-1	1	1
19	Surgical	Short Stay	117	-1	-1	-1	1	1

	J	K	L	M	N	O
2	LINEST for Score by Main Effects and Interaction					
3	12.514	-5.319	-4.014	2.931	-5.903	101.569
4	4.066	3.838	2.741	4.066	3.838	2.741
5	0.582	11.395	#N/A	#N/A	#N/A	#N/A
6	3.346	12.000	#N/A	#N/A	#N/A	#N/A
7	2171.917	1558.083	#N/A	#N/A	#N/A	#N/A
10		F ratio via SS		3.346		
12		F ratio via R^2		3.346		
14		R^2 via SS		0.582		

You can obtain the regression coefficients only, if that's all you're after, by selecting a range consisting of one row and as many columns as there are columns in your input data. Then type a formula such as this one:

=LINEST(A2:A20,B2:E20)

Then array-enter the formula by the keyboard combination Ctrl+Shift+Enter instead of simply Enter. If you want all the available results, you'll need to select a range with five rows, not just one, and you'll also need to set a LINEST() argument to TRUE. That has been done in Figure 13.8, where the formula is as follows:

=LINEST(C2:C19,D2:H19,,TRUE)

The meanings of the third argument (which is not used here) and the fourth argument are discussed later in this section.

Using the Regression Coefficients

Let's take a closer look at what's in J3:O7, the analysis of the main effects Treatment and Patient Status and their interaction. Chapter 4 discusses the data in the first two rows of the LINEST() results, but to review, the first row contains the coefficients for the regression equation, and the second row contains the standard errors of the coefficients.

LINEST()'s most glaring drawback is that it returns the coefficients in the reverse order that the predictor variables exist on the worksheet. In the worksheet shown in Figure 13.8, column D contains the first Patient Status vector, Pt1; column E contains the second Patient Status vector, Pt2; and column F contains the only Treatment vector, Tx. Columns G and H contain the vectors that represent the interaction between Patient Status and Treatment by obtaining the cross-products of the three main effects vectors. So, reading left to right, the underlying data shows the two Patient Status vectors, the Treatment vector, and the two interaction vectors.

However, the LINEST() results reverse this order. The regression coefficient for PT1 is in cell N3, for Pt2 in M3, and Tx in L3. K3 contains the coefficient for the first interaction vector, and J3 for the second interaction vector. The intercept is always in the rightmost column of the LINEST() results (assuming that you began by selecting the proper number of columns to contain the results).

You make use of the regression coefficients in combination with the values on the predictors to obtain a predicted value for Score. For example, using the regression equation based on the coefficients in J3:O3, you could predict the value of Score for the subject in row 2 with this equation (O3 is the intercept and is followed by the product of each predictor value with its coefficient):

=O3+N3*D2+M3*E2+L3*F2+K3*G2+J3*H2

13

Given the length of the formula, plus the fact that the predictor values run left to right while their coefficients run right to left, you can see why TREND() is a good alternative if you're after the results of applying the regression equation.

Using the Standard Errors

The second row of the LINEST() results contains the standard errors of the regression coefficients. They are useful because they tell you how likely it is that the coefficient, in the population, is actually zero. In this case, for example, the coefficient for the second Patient Status vector, Pt2, is 2.931 while its standard error is 4.066 (cells M3:M4 in Figure 13.8). A 95% confidence interval on the coefficient spans zero (see the section titled "Constructing a Confidence Interval" in Chapter 7, "Using Excel with the Normal Distribution"). In fact, the coefficient is within one standard error of zero and there's nothing to convince you that the coefficient in the population *isn't* zero.

So what? Well, if the coefficient is really zero, there's no point in keeping it in the regression equation. Here it is again:

=O3+N3*D2+M3*E2+L3*F2+K3*G2+J3*H2

The coefficient for Pt2 is in cell M3. If it were zero, then the expression M3*E2 would also be zero and would add literally nothing to the result of the equation. You might as well omit it from the analysis. If you do so, the predictor's sum of squares and degree of freedom are pooled into the residual variance. This pooling can reduce the residual mean square, if only slightly, making the statistical tests slightly more powerful. However, some statisticians adhere to the "never pool rule," and prefer to avoid this practice. If you do decide to pool by dropping a predictor that might well have a zero coefficient in the population, you should report your results both with and without the predictor in the equation so that your audience can make up its own mind.

Dealing with the Intercept

The intercept is the point on the vertical axis where a charted regression line crosses— *intercepts*—that axis. In the normal course of events, the intercept is equal to the mean of the outcome variable; here, that's Score.

With effect coding, the intercept is actually equal to the mean of the group means. Chapter 12 points out that if you have three group means whose values are 53, 46, and 51, then the regression equation's intercept with effect coding is 50. (With equal cell sizes, the grand mean of the individual observations is also 50; see the section titled "Multiple Regression and ANOVA" in Chapter 12.)

The third argument to LINEST(), which Excel terms *const*, takes the value TRUE or FALSE; if you omit the argument, as is done in Figure 13.8, the default value TRUE is used. The TRUE value causes Excel to calculate the intercept, sometimes called the *constant*, normally. If you supply FALSE instead, Excel forces the intercept in the equation to be zero.

Recall from Chapter 2, "How Values Cluster Together," that the sum of the squared deviations is smaller when the deviations are from the mean than from any other number. If you tell Excel to force the intercept to zero, the result is that the squared deviations are not from the mean, but from zero, and their sum will therefore be larger than it would be otherwise. It can easily happen that, as a result, the sum of squares for the regression becomes larger than the sum of squares for the residual. (Furthermore, the residual sum of squares gains a degree of freedom, making the mean square residual smaller.) All this can add up to an apparently and spuriously larger R^2 and F ratio for the regression than if you allow Excel to calculate the intercept normally.

If you force the intercept to zero, other and worse results can come about, such as negative sums of squares. A negative sum of squares is theoretically impossible, because a squared quantity must be positive, and therefore the sum of squared quantities must also be positive.

In some applications of regression analysis, particularly in the physical sciences and where the predictors are continuous rather than coded categorical variables, the grand mean is *expected* to be zero. Then, it may make sense to force the intercept to zero.

But it's more likely to be senseless. If you expect the outcome variable to have a mean of zero anyway, then a rational sample will tend to return a zero (or close to zero) intercept even if you don't make Excel interfere. So there's little to gain and much to lose by forcing the intercept to zero by setting LINEST()'s third argument to FALSE.

Understanding LINEST()'s Third, Fourth, and Fifth Rows

If you want LINEST() to return statistics other than the coefficients for the regression equation, you must set LINEST()'s fourth and final argument to TRUE. FALSE is the default, and if you don't set the fourth argument to TRUE, then LINEST() returns only the coefficients.

If you set the fourth argument to TRUE, then LINEST() returns the coefficients and standard errors discussed earlier, plus six additional statistics. These additional figures are *always* found in the third through fifth rows and in the first two columns of the LINEST() results. This means that you must begin by selecting a range that's five rows high. (As you can see in Figure 13.8, the third through fifth rows contain #N/A to the right of the second column of LINEST() results.)

> **TIP**
> You should also begin by selecting as many columns for the LINEST() results as there are columns in the input range: One column for each predictor and one for the predicted variable. LINEST() does not return a coefficient for the predicted variable, but it does return one for the intercept. So, if your input data is in columns A through F, and if you want the additional statistics, you should begin by selecting a six-column range such as G1:L5 before array-entering the formula with the LINEST() function.

The statistics found in the third through fifth rows and in the first and second columns of the LINEST() results are detailed next.

Column 1, Row 3: The Multiple R^2

R^2 is an enormously useful statistic and is defined and interpreted in several ways. It's the square of the correlation between the outcome variable and the best combination of the predictors. It expresses the proportion of variance shared by that best combination and the outcome variable. The closer it comes to 1.0, the better the regression equation predicts the outcome variable, so it helps you gauge the accuracy of a prediction made using the regression equation. It is integral to the F test that assesses the reliability of the regression. Differences in R^2 values are useful for judging whether it makes sense to retain a variable in the regression equation.

It's hard to see the point of performing a complete regression analysis without looking first at the R^2 value. Doing so would be like driving from San Francisco to Seattle without first checking that your route points north.

Column 2. Row 3: The Standard Error of Estimate

The standard error of estimate gives you a different take than R^2 on the accuracy of the regression equation. It tells you how much dispersion there is in the residuals, which are the differences between the actual values and the predicted values. The standard error of estimate is the standard deviation of the residuals, and if it is relatively small then the prediction is relatively accurate: The predicted values tend to be close to the actual values.

It's actually a little more complicated than that. Although you'll see in various sources the standard error of estimate defined as the standard deviation of the residuals, it's not the familiar standard deviation that divides by N–1. The residuals have fewer degrees of freedom because they are constrained by not just one statistic, the mean, but by the number of predictor variables.

Here's one formula for the standard error of estimate:

$$\sqrt{\frac{ss_{res}}{N - k - 1}}$$

That is the square root of the sum of squares of the residuals, divided by the number of observations (N), less the number of predictors (k), less 1. As you'll see later, all these figures are reported by LINEST().

The statistics returned by LINEST() in its third through fifth rows are all closely related. For example, the formula just given for the standard error of estimate uses the value in the fifth row, second column (the residual sum of squares), and in the fourth row, second column (the degrees of freedom for the residual). Here's another formula for the standard error of estimate:

$$\sqrt{(1 - R^2)\frac{ss_Y}{N - k - 1}}$$

Notice that the latter formula uses the sum of squares of the *raw* scores, not the residuals, as does the former formula. The residuals, the differences between the predicted and the actual scores, are a measure of the inaccuracy of the prediction. That inaccuracy is accounted for in the latter formula in the form of $(1-R^2)$, the proportion of variance in the outcome variable that is *not* predicted by the regression equation.

Some sources give this formula for the standard error of estimate:

$$\sqrt{1 - R^2} s_Y$$

The latter formula is a good way to conceptualize, but not to calculate, the standard error of estimate. Conceptually, you can consider that you're multiplying a measure of the amount of unpredictability, $\sqrt{1 - R^2}$, by the standard deviation of the outcome variable (Y) to get a measure of the variability of the predicted values. But the proper divisor for the sum of squares of Y is not (N–1), as is used with the sample standard deviation, but (N–k–1), taking account of the *k* predictors. If N is very large relative to k, it makes little difference, and many people find it convenient to think of the standard error of estimate in these terms.

Column 1, Row 4: The F Ratio

The F ratio for the regression is given in the first column, fourth row of the LINEST() results. You can use it to test the likelihood of obtaining by chance an R^2 as large as LINEST() reports, when there is no relationship in the population between the predicted and the predictor variables. To make that test, use the F ratio reported by LINEST() in conjunction with the number of predictor variables (which is the degrees of freedom for the numerator) and N–k–1 (which is the degrees of freedom for the denominator). You can use them as arguments to the F.DIST() or the F.DIST.RT() function, discussed at some length in Chapter 10, to obtain the exact probability. LINEST() also returns (N–k–1), the degrees of freedom for the denominator (see later).

More relationships among the LINEST() statistics involve the F ratio. There are two ways to calculate the F ratio from the other figures returned by LINEST(). You can use the equation

$$\frac{ss_{reg}/df_1}{ss_{res}/df_2}$$

where SS_{reg} is the sum of squares for the regression and SS_{res} is the sum of squares for the residual. (Together they make up the total sum of squares.) The sums of squares are found in LINEST()'s fifth row: The SS_{reg} is in the first column and the SS_{res} is in the second column. The df_1 figure is simply the number of predictors. The df_2 figure, (N–k–1), is in the fourth row, second column of the LINEST() results, immediately to the right of the F ratio for the full regression.

So, using the range J3:O7 in Figure 13.8, you could get the F ratio with this formula:

=(J7/5)/(K7/K6)

Why should you calculate the F ratio when LINEST() already provides it for you? No reason that you should. But seeing the figures and noticing how they work together not only helps people understand the concepts involved, it also helps to make abstract formulas more concrete.

Another illuminating exercise involves calculating the F ratio without ever touching a sum of squares. Again, using the LINEST() results found in J3:O7 of Figure 13.8, here's a formula that calculates F relying on R^2 and degrees of freedom only:

=(J5/5)/((1–J5)/K6)

This formula does the following:

1. It divides R^2 by 5 (the degrees of freedom for the numerator, which is the number of predictors).
2. It divides $(1–R^2)$ by $(N–k–1)$, the degrees of freedom for the dominator.
3. It divides the result of (1) by the result of (2).

More generally, this formula applies:

$$F = \frac{R^2/k}{(1 - R^2)/(N - k - 1)}$$

If you examine the relationship between F and R^2, and how R^2 is calculated using the ratio of the SS_{reg} to the sum of SS_{reg} and SS_{res}, you will see how the F ratio for the regression is largely a function of how well the regression equation predicts, as measured by R^2. To convince yourself this is so, download the workbook for Chapter 13 from www.informit.com/title/9780789747204. Then examine the contents of cell M12 on the worksheet for Figure 13.8.

Degrees of Freedom for the F Test in Regression

LINEST() returns in its fourth row, second column the degrees of freedom for the denominator of the F test of the regression equation. As in traditional analysis of variance, the degrees of freedom for the denominator is $(N–k–1)$, although the figure is arrived at a little differently because traditional analysis of variance does not convert factors to coded vectors.

The degrees of freedom for the numerator is the number of predictor vectors. Why not the number of predictor vectors minus 1? Because using effect coding you have already eliminated one degree of freedom. If a factor has three levels, it requires only two vectors to completely describe the group membership for that factor.

Managing Unequal Group Sizes in a True Experiment

Figure 13.9 shows several analyses of the data set used in this chapter. The design is unbalanced, as it is in Figures 13.5 and 13.6, and I will show one way to deal with the proportions of variance to ensure that each variable is allocated unique variance only.

Figure 13.9
Unique variance proportions can be determined by subtraction.

	K23		f_x =J11-M18									
	C	D	E	F	G	H	I	J	K	L	M	N	O
1	Score	Pt1	Pt2	Tx	Tx Pt1	Tx Pt2		LINEST for Score by Main Effects and Interaction					
2	89	1	0	1	1	0		12.514	-5.319	-4.014	2.931	-5.903	101.569
3	84	1	0	1	1	0		4.066	3.838	2.741	4.066	3.838	2.741
4	86	1	0	1	1	0		0.582	11.395	#N/A	#N/A	#N/A	#N/A
5	123	0	1	1	0	1		3.346	12.000	#N/A	#N/A	#N/A	#N/A
6	99	0	1	1	0	1		2171.917	1558.083	#N/A	#N/A	#N/A	#N/A
7	117	0	1	1	0	1							
8	84	-1	-1	1	-1	-1			LINEST for Main Effects				
9	109	-1	-1	1	-1	-1		-5.214	4.474	-7.102	102.769		
10	87	-1	-1	1	-1	-1		3.371	5.011	4.745	3.371		
11	103	1	0	-1	-1	0		0.247	14.165	#N/A	#N/A		
12	100	1	0	-1	-1	0		1.530	14.000	#N/A	#N/A		
13	112	1	0	-1	-1	0		920.958	2809.042	#N/A	#N/A		
14	100	0	1	-1	0	-1							
15	92	0	1	-1	0	-1		LINEST for Treatment			LINEST for Patient Status		
16	93	-1	-1	-1	1	1		-5.111	102.667		3.530	-7.003	102.670
17	126	-1	-1	-1	1	1		3.364	3.364		5.199	4.959	3.523
18	127	-1	-1	-1	1	1		0.126	14.274		0.118	14.808	#N/A
19	117	-1	-1	-1	1	1		2.308	16.000		1.006	15.000	#N/A
20								470.222	3259.778		441.010	3288.990	#N/A
21													
22								Source	Prop of R^2	SS	df	MS	F
23								Treatment	0.129	479.948	1	479.948	3.696
24								Patient Status	0.121	450.736	2	225.368	1.736
25								Interaction	0.335	1250.959	2	625.479	4.817
26								Residual	0.418	1558.083	12	129.840	

Each of the instances of LINEST() in Figure 13.9 uses Score as the predicted or outcome variable. The four instances differ as to which vectors are used as predictors:

- The range J2:O6 uses all five vectors as predictors. The array formula used to return those results is =LINEST(C2:C19,D2:H19,,TRUE).

- The range J9:M13 uses only the main effects, leaving the interactions out. The array formula used is =LINEST(C2:C19,D2:F19,,TRUE).

- The range J16:K20 uses only the Treatment vector. The array formula is =LINEST(C2:C19,F2:F19,,TRUE).

- The range M16:O20 uses only the two Patient Status vectors. The array formula is =LINEST(C2:C19,D2:E19,,TRUE).

Suppose there's good reason to regard the data and the underlying design shown in Figure 13.9 as a true experiment. In that case, there's a strong argument for assigning unique proportions of variance to each predictor. The problem of the order of entry of the variables into the regression equation remains, though, as discussed earlier in the section titled "Order Entry Is Important in the Unbalanced Design."

13

That problem can be solved by adjusting the variance attributed to each variable for the variance that could be attributed to the other variables. Here's how that works out with the analyses in Figure 13.9.

We'll be arranging to assign to each factor only the variance that can be uniquely attributed to it; therefore, it doesn't matter which factor we start with, and this example starts with Treatment. (The same outcome results if you start with Patient Status, and that would be a good test of your understanding of these procedures.)

The range J9:M13 in Figure 13.9 contains the LINEST() results from regressing Score on the two main effects, Treatment and Patient Status. All the variance in Score that can be attributed to the main effects, leaving aside the interaction for the moment, is measured in cell J11: R^2 is 0.247.

The range M16:O20 shows the results of regressing Score on Patient Status alone. The R^2 for that regression is 0.118 (cell M18).

By subtracting the variance attributable to Patient Status from the variance attributable to the main effects of Treatment and Patient Status, you can isolate the variance due to Treatment alone. That is done in cell K23 of Figure 13.9. The formula in K23 is =J11–M18 and the result is 0.129.

Similarly, you can subtract the variance attributable to Treatment from the variance attributable to the main effects, to determine the amount of variance attributable to Patient Status. That's done in cell K24 with the formula =J11–J18, which returns the value 0.121.

Finally, the proportion of variance attributable to the Treatment by Patient Status interaction appears in cell K25, with the formula =J4–J11. That's the total R^2 for Score regressed onto the main effects and the interaction, less the R^2 for the main effects alone.

The approach outlined in this section has the effect of removing variance that's shared by the outcome variable and one predictor from the analysis of another predictor. But this approach has drawbacks. For example, the total of the sums of squares in L23:L26 of Figure 13.9 is 3739.73, whereas the total sum of squares for the data set is 3730 (add the SS_{reg} to the SS_{res} in the fifth row of any of the LINEST() analyses in Figure 13.9). The reason that the two calculations are not equal is the adjustment of the proportions of variance by subtraction.

This isn't a perfect situation, and there are other approaches to allocating the total sum of squares in an unbalanced design. The one described here is a conservative one. It's a thorny problem, though. There is not now and never has been complete consensus on how to allocate the sum of squares among correlated predictors.

Managing Unequal Group Sizes in Observational Research

One of those other approaches to the problem is more appropriate for an observational study in which you can reasonably assume that one predictor causes another, or at least precedes it in time. In that case you might well be justified in assigning all the variance shared between the predictors to the one that has greater precedence.

Figure 13.10 shows how you would manage this with the same data used in prior figures in this chapter, but assuming that the data represents different variables.

Figure 13.10
Under this approach the proportions of variance sum to 1.0.

	C	D	E	F	G	H	I	J	K	L	M	N	O
	K23			▼			f_x	=J18					
1	Score	Pt1	Pt2	Tx	Tx Pt1	Tx Pt2		LINEST for Score by Main Effects and Interaction					
2	89	1	0	1	1	0		12.514	-5.319	-4.014	2.931	-5.903	101.569
3	84	1	0	1	1	0		4.066	3.838	2.741	4.066	3.838	2.741
4	86	1	0	1	1	0		0.582	11.395	#N/A	#N/A	#N/A	#N/A
5	123	0	1	1	0	1		3.346	12.000	#N/A	#N/A	#N/A	#N/A
6	99	0	1	1	0	1		2171.917	1558.083	#N/A	#N/A	#N/A	#N/A
7	117	0	1	1	0	1							
8	84	-1	-1	1	-1	-1		LINEST for Main Effects					
9	109	-1	-1	1	-1	-1		-5.214	4.474	-7.102	102.769		
10	87	-1	-1	1	-1	-1		3.371	5.011	4.745	3.371		
11	103	1	0	-1	-1	0		0.247	14.165	#N/A	#N/A		
12	100	1	0	-1	-1	0		1.530	14.000	#N/A	#N/A		
13	112	1	0	-1	-1	0		920.958	2809.042	#N/A	#N/A		
14	100	0	1	-1	0	-1							
15	92	0	1	-1	0	-1		LINEST for Sex			LINEST for Political Affiliation		
16	93	-1	-1	-1	1	1		-5.111	102.667		3.530	-7.003	102.670
17	126	-1	-1	-1	1	1		3.364	3.364		5.199	4.959	3.523
18	127	-1	-1	-1	1	1		0.126	14.274		0.118	14.808	#N/A
19	117	-1	-1	-1	1	1		2.308	16.000		1.006	15.000	#N/A
20								470.222	3259.778		441.010	3288.990	#N/A
21													
22								Source	Prop of R²	SS	df	MS	F
23								Sex	0.126	470.222	1	470.222	3.622
24								Pol Affiliation	0.121	450.736	2	225.368	1.736
25								Interaction	0.335	1250.959	2	625.479	4.817
26								Residual	0.418	1558.083	12	129.840	

The only difference in how the sum of squares is allocated in Figures 13.9 and 13.10 is that in Figure 13.10 the first variable, Sex, is not adjusted for the second variable, Political Affiliation. However, Political Affiliation is adjusted so that the variance it shares with Score is independent of Sex.

Also, the variance associated with the interaction of Sex with Political Affiliation is adjusted for the main effects. (This was also done in Figure 13.9.) That adjustment is managed by subtracting the variance explained by all the main effects, cell J11 in Figure 13.9, from the variance explained by all the predictors, cell J4. There are exceptions, but it's normal to remove variance shared by main effects and interactions from the interactions and allow it to remain with the main effects.

The result of using the directly applicable variance in the Sex variable is to make the total of the sums of squares for the main and interaction effects, plus the residual, equal the total sum of squares. Cells L23:L26 in Figure 13.10 sum to the total sum of squares, 3730, unlike in Figure 13.9. Therefore, the proportion of explained variance, cells K23:K26 in Figure 13.10, sum to 1.000, whereas in Figure 13.9 the proportions of variance sum to 1.003.

Compare the proportions of variance and the sums of squares in Figure 13.10 with those reported in Figure 13.5. The labels for the variables are different, but the underlying data is the same. So are the variance proportions and the sums of squares.

13

In the range K11:O12 of Figure 13.5, the first variable is unadjusted for the second variable, just as in Figure 13.10, and the sums of squares are the same. The second variable is Patient Status in Figure 13.5 and Political Affiliation in Figure 13.10. That variable is adjusted so that it is not allocated any variance that it shares with the first variable, and again the sums of squares are the same. The same is true for the interaction of the two variables.

The difference between the two figures is the method used to arrive at the adjustments for the second and subsequent variables. In Figure 13.10, the proportions of variance for Political Affiliation and for the interaction were obtained by subtracting the variance of variables already in the equation. The sums of squares were then obtained by multiplying the proportion of variance by the total sum of squares.

Figure 13.11 repeats for convenience the ANOVA table from Figure 13.5 along with the associated proportions of variance.

Figure 13.11
The proportions of variance also sum to 1.0 using squared semipartial correlations.

| K24 | fx | =RSQ($C$2:$C$19,E2:E19-TREND(E2:E19,$D2:D19))+RSQ($C$2:$C$19,F2:F19-TREND(F2:F19,$D2:E19)) |

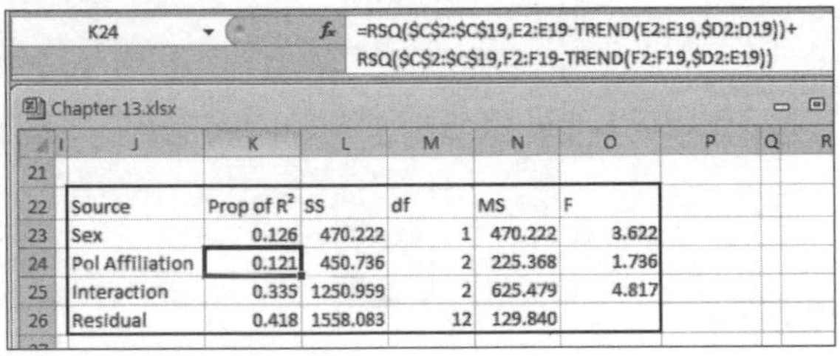

Source	Prop of R²	SS	df	MS	F
Sex	0.126	470.222	1	470.222	3.622
Pol Affiliation	0.121	450.736	2	225.368	1.736
Interaction	0.335	1250.959	2	625.479	4.817
Residual	0.418	1558.083	12	129.840	

In contrast to Figure 13.10, the proportions of variance shown in Figure 13.11 were obtained by squared semipartial correlations: correlating the outcome variable with each successive predictor variable after removing from the predictor the variance it shares with variables already in the equation.

The two methods are equivalent mathematically. If you give some thought to each approach, you will see that they are equivalent logically—each involves removing shared variance from predictors as they enter the regression equation—and that's one reason to show both methods in this chapter.

The methods used in Figures 13.5 and 13.10 are also equivalent in the ease with which you can set them up. That's not true of Figure 13.9, though, where you adjust Treatment for Patient Status. It is a subtle point, but you calculate the squared semipartial correlations by using Excel's RSQ() function, which cannot handle multiple predictors. Therefore, you must combine the multiple predictors first by using TREND() as an argument to RSQ()—see Chapter 12 for the details. However, TREND() cannot handle predictors that aren't contiguous on the worksheet, as would be the case if you wanted to adjust the vector named Pt2 for Tx and for Pt1.

In that sort of case, where Excel imposes additional constraints on you due to the requirements of its function arguments, it's simpler to run LINEST() several times, as shown in Figure 13.9, than it is to try to work around the constraints.

Nevertheless, many people prefer the conciseness of the approach that uses squared semi-partial correlations and use it where possible, resorting to the multiple LINEST() approach only when the design of the analysis forces them to adopt it.

If you have worked your way through the concepts discussed in Chapters 12 and 13—and if you've taken the time to work through how the concepts are managed using Excel worksheet functions—then you're well placed to understand the topic of Chapters 14 and 15, the analysis of covariance. As you'll see, it's little more than an extension of multiple regression using nominal scale factors to multiple regression using interval scale covariates.

Analysis of Covariance: The Basics

14

The very term *analysis of covariance* sounds mysterious and forbidding. And there are enough ins and outs to the technique (usually called *ANCOVA*) that this book spends two chapters on it—as it does with t-tests, ANOVA, and multiple regression. This chapter discusses the basics of ANCOVA, and Chapter 15, "Analysis of Covariance: Further Issues," goes into some of the special approaches that the technique requires and issues that can arise.

Despite taking two chapters to discuss here, ANCOVA is simply a combination of techniques you've already read about and probably experimented with on Excel worksheets. To carry out ANCOVA, you supply what's needed for an ANOVA or, equivalently, a multiple regression analysis with effect coding: that is, an outcome variable and one or more factors with levels you're interested in. You also supply what's termed a *covariate*: an additional numeric variable, usually measured on an interval scale, that covaries (and therefore correlates) with the outcome variable. This is just as in simple regression, in which you develop a regression equation based on the correlation between two variables.

In other words, all that ANCOVA does is combine the technique of linear regression, discussed in Chapter 4, "How Variables Move Jointly: Correlation," along with TREND() and LINEST(), with the effect coding vectors discussed in Chapter 12, "Multiple Regression Analysis and Effect Coding: The Basics," and Chapter 13, "Multiple Regression Analysis: Further Issues." At its simplest, ANCOVA is little more than adding a numeric variable to the vectors that, via effect coding, represent categories, as discussed in Chapters 12 and 13.

The Purposes of ANCOVA

Using ANCOVA instead of a t-test or ANOVA can help in two general ways: by providing greater power and by reducing bias.

Greater Power

Using ANCOVA rather than ANOVA can reduce the size of the error term in an F test. Recall from Chapter 11, "Analysis of Variance: Further Issues," in the section titled "Factorial ANOVA," that adding a second factor to a single-factor ANOVA can cause some variability to be removed from the error term and to be attributed instead to the second factor. Because the error term is used as the denominator of the F ratio, a smaller error term normally results in a larger F ratio. A larger F ratio means that it's less likely that the results were due to chance—the unpredictable vagaries of sampling error.

The same effect can occur in ANCOVA. Some variability that would otherwise be assigned to the error term (often called the *residual error* when you're using multiple regression instead of traditional ANOVA techniques) is assigned to the outcome measure's relationship with a covariate. The error sum of squares is reduced and therefore the residual mean square is also reduced. The result is a larger F ratio: a more sensitive, statistically powerful test of the differences in group means.

> **NOTE**
> Don't be misled by the term *analysis of covariance* into thinking that the technique places covariance into the same role that variance occupies in the analysis of variance. The route to hypothesis testing is the same in both ANOVA and ANCOVA: The F test is used in both, and an F test is the ratio of two variances. But in analysis of covariance, the relationship of the outcome variable to the covariate is quantified, and used to increase power and decrease bias—hence the term ANCOVA, primarily to distinguish it from ANOVA.

Bias Reduction

ANCOVA can also serve what's called a *bias reduction* function. If you have two or more groups of subjects, each of which will receive a different treatment (or medication, or course of instruction, or whatever it is that you're investigating), you want the groups to be equivalent at the outset. Then, any difference at the end of treatment can be chalked up to the treatment (or, as we've seen, to chance). The best way to arrange for that equivalence is random assignment.

But random assignment, especially with smaller sample sizes, doesn't ensure that all groups start on the same footing. Assuming that assignment of subjects to groups is random, then ANCOVA can give random assignment an assist, and help equate the groups. This result of applying ANCOVA can increase your confidence that mean differences you see subsequent to treatment are in fact due to treatment and not to some preexisting condition.

Using ANCOVA for bias reduction—to statistically equate group means—can be misleading, though: not because it's especially tricky mathematically, but because the research has to be designed and implemented properly. Chapter 15 has more to say about that issue.

First, let's look at a couple of examples.

Using ANCOVA to Increase Statistical Power

Figure 14.1 contains data from a shockingly small medical experiment. The figure analyzes the data in two different ways that return the same results. I provide both analyses—multiple regression and traditional analysis of variance—to demonstrate once again that with balanced designs the two approaches are equivalent.

Figure 14.1
These analyses indicate that the difference in group means might be due to sampling error alone.

H18 {=LINEST(B2:B21,C2:C21,,TRUE)}

	A	B	C	D	E	F	G	H	I	J	K	L	M
1	Group	Y	Coded Group		Group 1	Group 2		SUMMARY					
2	Medication	41.46	1		41.46	39.97		*Groups*	*Count*	*Sum*	*Average*	*Variance*	
3	Medication	62.32	1		62.32	42.00		Group 1	10	737.11	73.711	227.34	
4	Medication	69.00	1		69.00	49.93		Group 2	10	630.95	63.095	250.88	
5	Medication	69.89	1		69.89	59.15							
6	Medication	71.03	1		71.03	60.97		ANOVA					
7	Medication	72.27	1		72.27	61.69		*Source*	*SS*	*df*	*MS*	*F*	*P-value*
8	Medication	82.95	1		82.95	76.33		Between	563.50	1	563.50	2.36	0.14
9	Medication	87.95	1		87.95	77.14		Within	4304.02	18	239.11		
10	Medication	88.79	1		88.79	80.43							
11	Medication	91.45	1		91.45	83.34		Total	4867.52	19			
12	Control	39.97	-1										
13	Control	42.00	-1					LINEST()					
14	Control	49.93	-1					5.31	68.40				
15	Control	59.15	-1					3.46	3.46				
16	Control	60.97	-1					0.12	15.46				
17	Control	61.69	-1					2.36	18				
18	Control	76.33	-1					563.50	4304.02				
19	Control	77.14	-1										
20	Control	80.43	-1		SV	SS	df	MS	F	p of F			
21	Control	83.34	-1		Treatment	563.50	1	563.50	2.36	0.14			
22					Residual	4304.02	18	239.11					

Figure 14.1 shows a layout similar to one you've seen several times in Chapters 12 and 13:

- Group labels in column A that indicate the type of treatment administered to subjects
- Values of an outcome variable in column B
- A coded vector in column C that enables you to use multiple regression to test the differences in the means of the groups, as measured by the outcome variable

ANOVA Finds No Significant Mean Difference

In this case, the independent variable has only two values—medication and control—so only one coded vector is needed. The range H14:I18 shows the results of this array formula:

=LINEST(B2:B21,C2:C21,,TRUE)

As discussed in Chapters 12 and 13, the LINEST() function, in combination with the effect coding in column C and the general linear model, provides the data needed for an analysis of variance. That analysis has been pieced together in the range E20:J22 of Figure 14.1. The sums of squares in cells F21:F22 come from cells H18:I18 in the LINEST() results. The degrees of freedom in cell G21 comes from the fact that there is only one coded vector, and in cell G22 from cell I17. As usual, the mean squares in H21:H22 are calculated by dividing the sums of squares by the degrees of freedom.

The F ratio in I21 is formed by dividing the mean square for treatment by the residual mean square. (Notice that the figures are the same in I8:K9, despite the use of the traditional terminology "Between" and "Within.") The probability of obtaining an F ratio this large because of sampling error, when the group means are identical in the population, is in J21.

Notice that the calculated F ratio in I21 is the same as that returned by LINEST() in cell H17, and by the Data Analysis add-in in L8. The probability in cell J21 is obtained by means of the formula

    =F.DIST.RT(I21,G21,G22)

which makes use of the ratio itself and the degrees of freedom for its numerator and denominator. See the section titled "Using F.DIST() and F.DIST.RT()" in Chapter 10, "Testing Differences Between Means: The Analysis of Variance," for more information.

The p value in cell J21 states that you can expect to obtain an F ratio as large as 2.36, with 1 and 18 degrees of freedom, as often as 14% of the time when the population values of the treatment group's mean and the control group's mean are the same.

Still in Figure 14.1, the range H7:M11 shows a traditional analysis of variance produced by Excel's Data Analysis add-in, specifically by its ANOVA: Single Factor tool, which requires that the input data be laid out with each group occupying a different column (or if you prefer, a different row). This has been done in the range E1:F11. Notice that the sums of squares, degrees of freedom, mean squares, F ratio, and probability of the F ratio are identical to those reported by or calculated from the LINEST() analysis.

The ANOVA: Single Factor tool provides some information that LINEST() doesn't, at least not directly. The descriptive statistics reported by the add-in are in I3:L4, and the group means are of particular interest, because unlike ANOVA, ANCOVA routinely and automatically adjusts them. (Only when the groups have the same means on the *covariate* does ANCOVA fail to adjust the means on the outcome variable.)

> **NOTE**
>
> The LINEST() worksheet function also returns the group means, indirectly, if you're using effect coding. A coded vector's regression coefficient plus the intercept equals the mean of the group that's assigned 1's in that vector. So in Figure 14.1, the coefficient plus the intercept in H14:I14 equals 73.71, the mean of the Medication group. This aspect of effect coding is discussed in the section titled "Multiple Regression and ANOVA" in Chapter 12.

The main point to come away with from Figure 14.1 is that standard ANOVA techniques tell you it's quite possible that the difference between the group means, 73.7 and 63.1, is due to sampling error.

Adding a Covariate to the Analysis

Figure 14.2 adds another source of information, a *covariate*.

Figure 14.2
ANCOVA traditionally refers to the outcome variable as Y and the covariate as X.

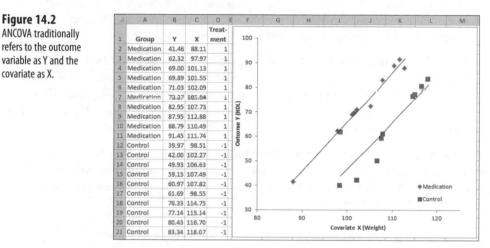

In Figure 14.2, a covariate has been added to the underlying data, in column C. I have labeled the covariate as X, because most writing that you may come across concerning ANCOVA uses the letter X to refer to the covariate. Later in this chapter, you'll see that it's important to test what's called the *treatment by covariate interaction*, which might be abbreviated as something such as *Group 1 by X* or *Group 2 by X*. There, it's useful to have a letter such as X stand in for the actual name of the covariate in the interaction's label.

We want to use ANCOVA to test group mean differences in the outcome variable (conventionally designated as Y) after any effect of the covariate on the outcome variable has been accounted for.

The chart in Figure 14.2 shows the relationship between the outcome variable (suppose it's HDL cholesterol levels in adolescents) and the covariate (suppose it's the weight in pounds of those same children). Each group is charted separately, and you can see that the relationship is about the same in each group: The trendlines are very nearly parallel. You'll soon see why that's important, and how to test for it statistically. For now, simply be aware that the question of parallel trendlines is the same as that of treatment by covariate interaction mentioned earlier in this section.

You can check explicitly whether the groups have different means on the covariate, and you should do so, but by simply glancing at the chart's horizontal axis you can see that there's

14

just a moderate difference between the two groups as measured on the covariate X (weight). As it happens, the average weight of the Medication group is 103.9 and that of the Control group is 108.6. This is just the sort of difference that tends to come about when a relatively small number of subjects is assigned to groups at random.

It's not the dramatic difference that you can get from preexisting groupings, such as people enrolled in weight loss programs versus those who are not. It is not the vanishingly small difference that comes from randomly assigning thousands of subjects to one of several groups. It's the moderately small difference that's due to the imperfect efficiency of the random assignment of a relatively small number of subjects.

And that makes a situation such as the one depicted in Figures 14.1 and 14.2 an ideal candidate for ANCOVA. You can use it to make minor adjustments to the means of the outcome measure (HDL level) by equating the groups on the covariate (weight). So doing gives random assignment to groups an assist (ideally, random assignment equates the groups, but what's ideal isn't necessarily real).

You can also use ANCOVA to improve the sensitivity, or power, of the F test. Recall from Figure 14.1 that using ANOVA—and thus using no covariate—no reliable difference between the two groups was found. Figure 14.3 shows what happens when you use the covariate to beef up the analysis.

Figure 14.3
This analysis notes the increment in R^2 due to adding a predictor, as discussed in Chapter 13.

I15 f_x =K8*K11

	A	B	C	D	E	F	G	H	I	J	K	L	M	N
1	Group	Y	X	Treat-ment				Y on X, Total				Y on X and Treatment		
2	Medication	41.46	88.11	1				1.52	-93.30			9.90	1.95	-138.52
3	Medication	62.32	97.97	1				0.34	36.51			1.35	0.18	19.46
4	Medication	69.00	101.13	1			R^2	0.52	11.36		R^2	0.88	5.74	#N/A
5	Medication	69.89	101.55	1				19.71	18			65.32	17	#N/A
6	Medication	71.03	102.09	1				2544.1503	2323.37			4307.07	560.45	#N/A
7	Medication	72.27	105.04	1										
8	Medication	82.95	107.73	1					Increase in R2		0.36			
9	Medication	87.95	112.88	1										
10	Medication	88.79	110.49	1										
11	Medication	91.45	111.74	1				Total Sum of Squares:			4867.52			
12	Control	39.97	98.51	-1										
13	Control	42.00	102.27	-1				SV	SS	df	MS	F	p	
14	Control	49.93	106.63	-1				Covariate	2544.15	1	2544.15	77.17	1E-07	
15	Control	59.15	107.49	-1				Treatment	1762.92	1	1762.92	53.47	1E-06	
16	Control	60.97	107.82	-1				Residual	560.45	17	32.97			
17	Control	61.69	98.55	-1										
18	Control	76.33	114.75	-1										
19	Control	77.14	115.14	-1										
20	Control	80.43	116.70	-1										
21	Control	83.34	118.07	-1										

14

Figure 14.3 displays two instances of LINEST(). The instance in the range H2:I6 uses this array formula:

=LINEST(B2:B21,C2:C21,,TRUE)

This instance analyzes the relationship between Y (HDL level) and X (weight). For convenience, the R^2 value is called out in the figure. Cell H4 shows that 0.52 or 52% of the variance in Y is shared with X; another way of stating this is that variability in weight explains 52% of the variability in HDL.

The other instance of LINEST() is in L2:N6, and it analyzes the relationship between Y and the best combination of the covariate and the coded vector. (The phrase "best combination" as used here means that the underlying math calculates the combination of the covariate and the coded vector that has the highest possible correlation with Y. Chapter 4 goes into this matter more fully.)

The R^2 value in cell L4 is 0.88. By including the coded vector in the regression equation as a predictor, along with the covariate X, we can account for 0.88 or 88% of the variance in Y. That's an additional 36% of the variance in Y, over and above the 52% already accounted for by the covariate alone.

This book has already made extensive use of the technique of comparing variance explained before and variance explained after one or more predictors are added to the equation. Chapter 13 in particular uses the technique because it's so useful in the context of unbalanced designs. Statisticians have a keen ear for the *bon mot* and an appreciation of the desirability of consensus on a concise, descriptive terminology. Therefore, they have coined terms such as *models comparison approach*, *incremental variance explained*, and *regression approach* when they mean the method used here.

Regardless of the technique's name, it puts you in a position to reassess the reliability of, in this example, the difference in the mean HDL levels of the two groups. Using ANOVA alone, an earlier section in this chapter showed that the difference could be attributed to sampling error as much as 14% of the time.

But the ANCOVA in Figure 14.3, in the range H13:M16, changes that finding substantially. The cells in question are H15:M15. The total sum of squares of the outcome variable appears in cell K11, using this formula:

```
=DEVSQ(B2:B21)
```

We know from comparing the R^2 values from the two instances of LINEST() that the treatment vector accounts for 36% of the variability in Y after X has entered the equation; that value appears in cell K8. Therefore, the formula

```
=K8*K11
```

entered in cell I15 gives us the sum of squares due to Treatment. Converted to a mean square and then to the numerator of the F ratio in cell L15, this result is highly unlikely to occur as a result of sampling error, and an experimenter would conclude that the treatment has a reliable effect on HDL levels after removing the effect of differences in the covariate weight from the outcome measure.

14

Be sure to notice that the F ratio's denominator in Figure 14.3 is 32.97 (cell K16), but in Figure 14.1 it's 239.11 (cell H22). Most of the variability that's assigned to residual variation in Figure 14.1 is assigned to the covariate in Figure 14.3, thus increasing the F ratio and making the test much more sensitive.

Figure 14.4 provides further insight into how it can happen that an ANOVA fails to return a reliable difference in group means while an ANCOVA does so.

Figure 14.4
The adjustment of the means combined with the smaller residual error makes the F test much more powerful.

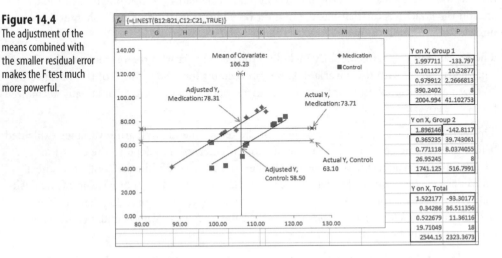

The Group Means Are Adjusted

In Figure 14.4, notice the vertical line labeled "Mean of Covariate" in the chart. It is located at 106.23 on the horizontal X axis; that value, 106.23, is the grand mean of all subjects on the covariate, Weight. The vertical line representing the mean of the covariate is crossed by two diagonal regression lines. Each regression line (in Excel terminology, *trendline*) represents the relationship in each group, Medication or Control, between the covariate Weight and the outcome variable HDL.

The point on the vertical axis at which each regression line crosses the mean of the covariate is where that group's HDL mean would be if the two groups had started out with the same mean Weight. This is how ANCOVA goes about adjusting group means on an outcome variable as if they started out with equal means on the covariate.

In general, you use ANCOVA to take the relationship between the covariate and the outcome measure as a starting point. You can draw a line that represents the relationship, just as the regression lines are drawn for each group in Figure 14.4. There is a point where each regression line crosses the vertical line that represents the covariate's mean. That point is where the group's mean on the outcome variable would be if the group's mean on the covariate were equal to the grand mean on the covariate.

So, in Figure 14.4, you can see that the actual Y mean of the Control group is 63.1. It is shown in the chart as the lower of the two horizontal lines. But the regression line indicates that if the Control group's covariate mean were slightly lower (106.23 instead of its actual 108.59) then the Control group's mean on Y, the HDL outcome measure, would be 58.5 instead of its observed 63.1.

Similarly, the regression line for the Medication group crosses the grand mean of the covariate at 78.31. If the Medication group's mean on the covariate were 106.23 instead of its actual 103.87, then we would expect its HDL mean to be 78.31.

Therefore, the combined effect of each group's regression line and its actual mean value on the weight covariate is to push the group HDL means farther apart, from 73.71 − 63.10 = 10.61, to 78.31 − 58.50 = 19.81.

With the group means farther apart, the sum of squares attributable to the difference between the means becomes larger, and therefore the numerator of the F test also becomes larger—the result is a more statistically powerful test.

In effect, the process of adjusting the group means says, "Some of the treatment effect has been masked by the fact that the two groups did not start out on an equal footing. There's a relationship between weight and HDL, and the Medication group started out with a handicap because its lower mean weight masked the treatment effect. The regression of HDL on weight enables us to view the difference between the two groups as though they had started out on an equal footing prior to the treatment."

Calculating the Adjusted Means

It's usually helpful to chart your data in Excel, regardless of the type of analysis you're doing, but it's particularly important to do so when you're working with the regression of one variable on another (and with the closely related issue of correlations, as discussed in Chapter 4). In the case of ANCOVA, where you're working with the relationship between an outcome variable and a covariate in more than one group, charting the data as shown in Figure 14.4 helps you visualize what's going on with the analysis—for example, the adjustment of the group means as discussed in the prior section.

But it's also good to be able to calculate the adjusted means directly. Fortunately, the formula is fairly simple. For a given group, all you need are the following values (they are not all displayed in Figure 14.4 but you can verify them by downloading Chapter 14's workbook from www.informit.com/title/9780789747204):

- The group's observed mean value on the outcome variable. For the data in Figure 14.4, that's 63.1 in the Control group.

- The regression coefficient for the covariate. In Figure 14.4, that's 1.947. (It's easy to get the regression coefficient, but it's not immediately apparent how to do so. More on that shortly.)

- The group's mean value on the covariate. In this example, that's 108.59 in the Control group.

14

■ The grand mean value on the covariate. In Figure 14.4, that's 106.23.

With those four numbers in hand, here's the formula for the Control group's adjusted mean. (You can get the adjusted mean for any group by substituting its actual mean value on the outcome variable and on the covariate.)

$$\hat{Y}_j = \overline{Y}_j - b(\overline{X}_j - \overline{X})$$

The symbols in the formula are as follows:

■ $\hat{Y}_j$ is the adjusted mean of the outcome variable for the *j*th group.

■ $\overline{Y}_j$ is the actual, observed mean of the outcome variable for the *j*th group.

■ *b* is the common regression coefficient for the covariate.

■ $\overline{X}_j$ is the mean of the covariate for the *j*th group.

■ $\overline{X}$ is the grand mean of the covariate.

Using the actual values for the Control group in Figure 14.4, we have the following:

$$58.5 = 63.1 - 1.947 * (108.59 - 106.23)$$

Where did the figure 1.947 for the common regression coefficient come from? It's the average of the two separate regression coefficients calculated for each group. This is sometimes called the *pooled* or the *common* regression coefficient. In Figure 14.4, it's the average of the values in cells O2 and O9.

If you're interested in getting the individual adjusted scores in addition to the adjusted group means, you can use the following simple modification of the formula given earlier:

$$\hat{Y}_{ij} = Y_{ij} - b(X_{ij} - \overline{X})$$

In this case, the symbols are as follows:

■ $\hat{Y}_{ij}$ is the adjusted value of the outcome variable for the *i*th subject in the *j*th group.

■ Y_{ij} is the actual, observed value of the outcome variable for the *i*th subject in the *j*th group.

■ *b* is the common regression coefficient for the covariate.

■ X_{ij} is the value of the covariate for the *i*th subject in the *j*th group.

■ $\overline{X}$ is the grand mean of the covariate.

A Common Regression Slope

In the course of preparing to write this book, I looked through 11 statistics texts on my shelves, each of which I have used as a student, as a teacher, or both. Several of those texts discuss the fact that a statistician uses a common regression coefficient to adjust group means, but nowhere could I find a discussion of *why* that's done—nothing to supply as a reference, so I'll cover it here.

Refer to Figure 14.4 and notice the two sets of LINEST() results. Cell O2 contains the regression coefficient for the covariate based on the data for the Medication group, 1.998. Cell O9 contains the regression coefficient for the covariate calculated from the data for the Control group, 1.896. Although close, the two are not identical.

A fundamental assumption in ANCOVA is that the regression slopes—the coefficients—in each group are the same in the population, and that any difference in the observed slopes is due to sampling error. In fact, in the example we've used so far in this chapter, the two coefficients of 1.998 and 1.896 are only 0.102 apart. Later in this chapter I'll show you how to test whether the difference between the coefficients is real and reliable, or just sampling error.

You might intuitively think that the way to get the common regression line would be to ignore the information about group membership and simply regress the outcome variable on the covariate for all subjects. Figure 14.5 shows why that's not a workable solution.

Figure 14.5
When the group means differ on either the outcome or the covariate, the regression becomes less accurate.

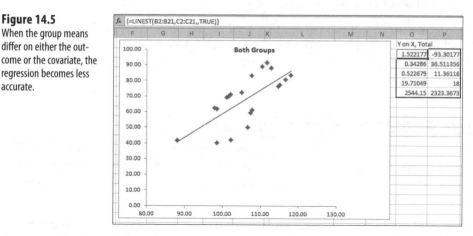

The same data for the outcome variable and the covariate appears in Figure 14.5 as in Figure 14.4. But even a visual inspection tells you that the relationship between the two variables is not as strong when all the data is combined: The markers that represent the individual observations are farther from the regression line in Figure 14.5 than is the case in Figure 14.4. The reason is that the two groups, Medication and Control, have little overlap on the outcome variable (plotted on the vertical axis). In Figure 14.5, the same regression equation that is based on ten Medication group units with a higher mean on the outcome variable must also be based on the ten observations with a lower mean on the outcome variable.

14

In the sort of situation presented by this data, it is not that a common regression line has a markedly different coefficient than the regression lines calculated for each group. The coefficients are quite close. Figure 14.4 shows that the coefficient for the Medication group alone is 1.998 (cell O2); for the Control group, it's 1.896 (cell O9). As you will see in cell H10 of Figure 14.6, the coefficient is 1.948 when the group membership is included in the equation. What matters is that if you use a single regression line as calculated and shown in Figure 14.5, the deviations of the individual observations are greater than if you use two regression lines, both with the same slope *but different intercepts*, as shown in Figure 14.4.

Therefore, you can lose accuracy if you use a single regression based on all the data. The solution is to use a common regression slope. Take the average of the regression coefficients calculated for the covariate in each group: cells O2 and O9 in Figure 14.4. At first glance this may seem like a quick-and-dirty guesstimate, but it's actually the best estimate available for the common regression line.

Suppose that you converted each observation to a z-score: that is, subtract each group's mean from each individual score and divide the result by the group's standard deviation. This has the effect of rescaling the scores on both the covariate and the outcome variable to have a mean of 0 and a standard deviation of 1.

Having rescaled the data, if you calculate the total regression as in Figure 14.5, the coefficient for the covariate will be identical to the average of the coefficients in the single group analyses. (This holds only if the groups have the same number of observations, so that the design is balanced.)

Testing for a Common Regression Line

Why is it so important to have a common regression line? It's largely a question of interpreting the results. It's convenient to be able to use the same coefficient for each group; that way, you need change only the group means on the outcome measure and the covariate to calculate each group's adjusted mean.

There are ways to deal with the situation in which the data suggests that the regression coefficient between the covariate and the outcome variable is different in different groups. This book does not discuss those techniques, but if you are confronted with that situation, you can find guidance in *The Johnson-Neyman Technique, Its Theory and Application*, by Palmer Johnson and Leo Fay (Biometrika, December 1950), and in *The Analysis of Variance and Alternatives*, by B. E. Huitema (Wiley, 1980). Obviously these references predate the existence of Excel, but the discussion of using LINEST() and other worksheet functions in this chapter and the next positions you to make use of the techniques if necessary.

The question of determining whether you can assume a common regression coefficient remains (you may see this topic discussed as *homogeneity of regression coefficients* in other material on ANCOVA). Figure 14.6 illustrates the approach, which you'll recognize from earlier situations in which we have evaluated the significance of incremental variance that's attributable to variables added to the regression equation.

14

Figure 14.6

If the additional variance can be attributed to sampling error, it's reasonable to assume a common regression coefficient.

	B	C	D	E	F	G	H	I	J	K	L	M
			Treat-	X by								
1	Y	X	ment	Treatment								
2	41.46	88.11	1	88.11		Y on X, Treatment and X by Treatment interaction						
3	62.32	97.97	1	97.974		0.0508	4.507	1.947	-138.304			
4	69.00	101.13	1	101.132		0.1880	20.031	0.188	20.031			
5	69.89	101.55	1	101.551		0.8854	5.905	#N/A	#N/A			
6	71.03	102.09	1	102.087		41.1983	16	#N/A	#N/A			
7	72.27	105.04	1	105.039		4309.6158	557.902	#N/A	#N/A			
8	82.95	107.73	1	107.725								
9	87.95	112.88	1	112.884		Y on X and Treatment						
10	88.79	110.49	1	110.486		9.9043	1.948	-138.52				
11	91.45	111.74	1	111.741		1.3544	0.183	19.461				
12	39.97	98.51	-1	-98.514		0.8849	5.742	#N/A				
13	42.00	102.27	-1	-102.267		65.3232	17	#N/A				
14	49.93	106.63	-1	-106.626		4307.0722	560.445	#N/A				
15	59.15	107.49	-1	-107.485								
16	60.97	107.82	-1	-107.824		Source of Variation	Prop. of variance	SS	df	MS	F	p
17	61.69	98.55	-1	-98.554		R^2 increment	0.0005	2.54	1	2.54	0.07	0.79
18	76.33	114.75	-1	-114.75		Residual	0.1146	557.9	16	34.87		
19	77.14	115.14	-1	-115.136								
20	80.43	116.70	-1	-116.695								
21	83.34	118.07	-1	-118.071								

The formula bar shows: H17 f_x =G5-G12

Figure 14.6 contains a new vector in column E. It represents the interaction of the Treatment vector—medication or control—with the covariate. It's easily created: You simply multiply a value in the Treatment vector by the associated value in the covariate's vector. If there is additional information that column E's interaction vector can provide, it will show up as an increment to the proportion of variance already explained by the information about treatment group membership and the covariate, Weight.

If there is a significant amount of additional variance in the outcome measure HDL that is explained by the interaction vector, you should consider using the Johnson-Neyman techniques, and those discussed in Huitema's book, both mentioned earlier.

However, the analysis in Figure 14.6 shows that in this case there's little reason to believe that including the factor-covariate interaction explains a meaningful amount of additional variance in the outcome measure. In that case, it's rational to conclude that the slope of the regression between the covariate and the outcome variable is the same in both groups.

The comparison of models in the range G16:M18 tests that increment of variance, as follows: LINEST() is used in G3:J7 to analyze the regression of the HDL outcome measure on all the available predictors: the weight covariate, the treatment, and the weight by treatment interaction. LINEST() returns the R^2 value in its third row, first column, so the total proportion of variance in the outcome measure that's explained by those three predictors is 0.8854.

LINEST() is used once again in G10:I14 to test the regression of HDL on the covariate and the treatment factor only, omitting the weight by treatment interaction. In this analysis, R^2 in cell G12 turns out to be 0.8849. The difference between the two values for R^2 is 0.0005, shown in cell H17 of Figure 14.6. That's half of a thousandth of the variance, so you wouldn't regard it as meaningful. However, the formal test appears in G16:M18.

14

Cell H17 is obtained by subtraction, the R^2 in G12 from that in G5. The proportion of the variance that remains in the residual, "error" term is also obtained by subtraction: 1.0 less the total proportion of variance explained in the full model, the R^2 in cell G5.

It's not necessary to involve a sum of squares column in the analysis, but to keep the analysis on familiar ground, the sums of squares are shown in I17:I18. Both values are the product of the proportion of variance explained in column H and the total sum of squares. Notice these alternatives:

- You can obtain the total sum of squares with the formula =DEVSQ(B2:B21), substituting for B2:B21 whatever worksheet range contains your outcome measure. You can also get the total sum of squares from the sum of squares (regression) plus the sum of squares (residual); these values are found both in G7:H7 and in G14:H14.

- You can obtain the incremental sum of squares by taking the difference in the sum of squares (regression) for the two models. In Figure 14.6, for example, you could subtract cell G14 from cell G7 to get the incremental sum of squares.

The degrees of freedom for the R^2 increment is the difference in the number of predictor vectors in each analysis. In this case, the full model has three vectors: the covariate, the treatment, and the covariate by treatment interaction. The restricted model has two vectors: the covariate and the treatment. So, 3 – 2 = 1, and the R^2 increment has 1 df.

The degrees of freedom for the denominator is the number of observations, less the number of vectors for the full model, less 1 for the grand mean. In this case, that's 20 – 3 – 1 = 16.

As usual, the mean squares are formed by the ratio of the sum of squares to the degrees of freedom. Finally, the F ratio is the mean square for the R^2 increment divided by the mean square for the residual. In this case, the p value of .79 indicates that 79% of the area in an F distribution with 1 and 16 df falls to the right of the obtained F ratio: clear evidence that the covariate by factor interaction is simply sampling error.

Note that you could dispense with the sums of squares entirely by dividing each proportion of variance by the associated degrees of freedom and then forming the F ratio using the results:

$$0.07 = (0.0005 \,/\, 1) \,/\, (0.1146 \,/\, 16)$$

This is generally true, not just for the test of a factor by covariate interaction. The route to an F test via sums of squares is due largely to the reliance on adding machines in the early part of the twentieth century. As tedious, cumbersome, and error prone as those methods were, they were more tractable than repeatedly calculating entire regression analyses to determine the differences in proportions of explained variance that result. As late as the 1970s, books on regression analysis showed how different regression equations could be obtained from the overall analysis by piecing together intercepts and coefficients. This approach saved time and had some pedagogical value, but 40 years later it's much more

14

straightforward to use the LINEST() function repeatedly, with different sets of predictors, and to test the resulting difference in R^2 values.

Removing Bias: A Different Outcome

The adjustment of the group means in the prior example was combined with the increased sensitivity of the F test, due to the allocation of variance to the covariate instead of to residual variation. The result was that the difference between the group means, initially judged non-significant, became one that was likely reliable, and not merely due to sampling error.

Things can work out differently. It can happen that differences between group means that an ANOVA judges significant turn out to be unreliable when you run an ANCOVA instead—even with the increased sensitivity due to the use of a covariate. Figure 14.7 has an example.

Figure 14.7
An additional factor level requires an additional coded vector.

H15 fx {=LINEST(B2:B19,C2:D19,,TRUE)}

	A	B	C	D	E	F	G	H	I	J	K	L	M	N	O
1	Group	Y	Treatment Vector 1	Treatment Vector 2		Med 1	Med 2	Control		SUMMARY					
2	Med 1	51.6	1	0		51.6	54.8	54.4		*Groups*	*Count*	*Sum*	*Average*	*Variance*	
3	Med 1	25.6	1	0		25.6	52	65.2		Med 1	6	278	46.4	218.56	
4	Med 1	40.8	1	0		40.8	43.2	72		Med 2	6	339	56.53	85.74	
5	Med 1	45.6	1	0		45.6	64	59.2		Control	6	393	65.53	136.99	
6	Med 1	44	1	0		44	69.6	56.8							
7	Med 1	70.8	1	0		70.8	55.6	85.6		ANOVA					
8	Med 2	54.8	0	1						*Source*	*SS*	*df*	*MS*	*F*	*P-value*
9	Med 2	52	0	1						Between	1099.5	2	549.77	3.74	0.048
10	Med 2	43.2	0	1						Within	2206.4	15	147.10		
11	Med 2	64	0	1											
12	Med 2	69.6	0	1						Total	3306	17			
13	Med 2	55.6	0	1											
14	Control	54.4	-1	-1					LINEST()						
15	Control	65.2	-1	-1				0.38	-9.76	56.16					
16	Control	72	-1	-1				4.04	4.04	2.86					
17	Control	59.2	-1	-1				0.33	12.13	#N/A					
18	Control	56.8	-1	-1				3.74	15	#N/A					
19	Control	85.6	-1	-1				1099.54	2206.43	#N/A					
20															
21						SV	SS	df	MS	F	p of F				
22						Treatment	1099.54	2	549.77	3.74	0.048				
23						Residual	2206.43	15	147.10						

Compare Figure 14.7 with Figure 14.1. Two differences are fairly clear: Figure 14.1 depicts an analysis with one factor that has two levels. Figure 14.7's analysis uses a factor that has three levels: a control group as before, but two experimental medications instead of just one. That additional factor level simply means that there's an additional vector, and therefore an additional regression line to test.

The other meaningful difference between Figure 14.1 and 14.7 is that the initial ANOVA in Figure 14.1 indicates no reliable difference between the Medication and Control group means on the outcome variable named Y, which measures each subject's HDL. The subsequent ANCOVA that begins with Figure 14.2 shows that the means are adjusted to be farther apart, and the residual mean square is reduced enough that the result is a reliable difference between the two means.

But in Figure 14.7, the ANOVA indicates a reliable difference somewhere in the group means if the experimenter set alpha to .05. (Recall that neither ANOVA nor ANCOVA by itself pinpoints the source of a reliable difference. All that a significant F ratio tells you is that there is a reliable difference somewhere in the group means. But when there are only two groups, as in Figure 14.1, the possibilities are limited.) In Figure 14.7, both the traditional ANOVA summary in J8:O12, and the regression approach in H15:J19 and F21:K23, indicate that at least one significant difference in group means exists. The F ratio's p-value of .048 is smaller than the alpha of .05.

So what's the point of using ANCOVA in this situation? The answer begins with the analysis in Figure 14.8, which adds a covariate in column C to the layout in Figure 14.7.

Figure 14.8
The factor by covariate interaction again fails to contribute meaningful shared variance.

	A	B	C	D	E	F	G	H	I	J	K	L
				Treatment	Treatment	X by						
1	Group	Y	X	Vector 1	Vector 2	T1	X by T2					
2	Med 1	51.6	94.8	1	0	94.8	0					
3	Med 1	25.6	52.8	1	0	52.8	0					
4	Med 1	40.8	134.4	1	0	134.4	0					
5	Med 1	45.6	163.2	1	0	163.2	0					
6	Med 1	44	86.4	1	0	86.4	0					
7	Med 1	70.8	189.6	1	0	189.6	0					
8	Med 2	54.8	115.2	0	1	0	115.2					
9	Med 2	52	151.2	0	1	0	151.2					
10	Med 2	43.2	138	0	1	0	138					
11	Med 2	64	176.4	0	1	0	176.4					
12	Med 2	69.6	166.8	0	1	0	166.8					
13	Med 2	55.6	123.6	0	1	0	123.6					
14	Control	54.4	111.6	-1	-1	-112	-111.6					
15	Control	65.2	87.6	-1	-1	-87.6	-87.6					
16	Control	72	175.2	-1	-1	-175	-175.2					
17	Control	59.2	133.2	-1	-1	-133	-133.2					
18	Control	56.8	201.6	-1	-1	-202	-201.6					
19	Control	85.6	218.4	-1	-1	-218	-218.4					
20												
21	0.036634	0.03		-0.540595	-6.258676		Source	Prop of Var	df	Prop / df	F	Prob of F
22	0.130888	0.09		3.2046459	3.3764652		R² increment	0.023	2	0.011	0.375	0.69
23	0.634642	10		0.6117822	9.5746475		Residual	0.365	12	0.030		
24	4.168901	12		7.3540769	14							
25	2098.104	1208		2022.5302	1283.4343							

Figure 14.8 contains an analysis that is a necessary preliminary to subsequent figures. It uses the models comparison approach to test whether there is a reliable difference in the regression slopes of HDL on Weight within each group. The range A21:B25 contains the first two columns of a LINEST() analysis of HDL (Y) regressed onto all the prediction vectors in C2:G19. The total proportion of HDL that's predicted by those vectors appears in cell A23: 63.46% of the variance in HDL is associated with the covariate, the two treatment vectors, and the factor by covariate interaction in columns F and G.

Another instance of LINEST is in D21:E25, where HDL is regressed onto the covariate and the two treatment vectors, leaving the factor by covariate interaction out of the analysis. In this case, cell D23 shows that 61.18% of the variance in HDL is associated with the covariate and the treatment factor.

14

The increment in explained variance (or R^2) from putting the covariate by factor interaction in the equation is therefore 63.46% – 61.18%, or 2.3%, as shown in cell H22. The remaining values in the models comparison are as follows:

- The unexplained proportion of variance—the residual—in cell H23 is 1.0 minus the proportion of explained variance in the full model, shown in cell A23.

- The degrees of freedom for the R^2 increment is the number of prediction vectors in the full model (5) minus the number of prediction vectors in the restricted model (3), resulting in 2 df for the comparison's numerator.

- The degrees of freedom for the denominator is the number of observations (18) less the number of vectors for the full model (5) less one for the grand mean (1), resulting in 12 df for the comparison's denominator.

- The column headed "Prop / df" (H21:H23) is not a mean square, because we're not bothering to multiply and divide by the constant total sum of squares in this analysis. We simply divide the increment in R^2 by its df and the residual proportion by its df. If you multiplied each of those by the total sum of squares, you would arrive at two mean squares, but their F ratio would be identical to the one shown in cell K22.

- The F ratio in cell K22 is less than one and therefore insignificant, but to complete the analysis I show in cell L22 the probability of that F ratio if the factor by covariate interaction were due to true population differences instead of simple sampling error.

I belabor this analysis of parallel regression slopes (or, if you prefer, common regression coefficients) here for several reasons. One is that it's an important check, and Excel makes it very easy to carry out. All you have to do is run LINEST() a couple of times, subtract one R^2 from another, and run an F test on the difference.

The second reason is that in this chapter's first example, I postponed running the test for homogeneity of regression coefficients until after I had discussed the logic of and rationale for ANCOVA and illustrated its mechanics using Excel. In practice you should run the homogeneity test before other tasks such as calculating adjusted means. If you have within-group regression coefficients that are significantly different, there's little point in adjusting the means using a common coefficient. Therefore, I wanted to put the test for a common slope here, to demonstrate where it should occur in the order of analysis.

Because in this example we're dealing with regression coefficients that do not differ significantly across groups, we can move on to examining the regression lines. See Figure 14.9.

Notice the table in the range A21:D23 of Figure 14.9. It provides the mean weight—the covariate X—for each of the three groups at the outset of the study. Clearly, random assignment of subjects to different groups has failed to equate the groups as to their mean weight at the outset. *When group means differ on the covariate, and when the covariate is correlated with the outcome measure, then the group means on the outcome measure will be adjusted as though the groups were equivalent on the covariate.*

14

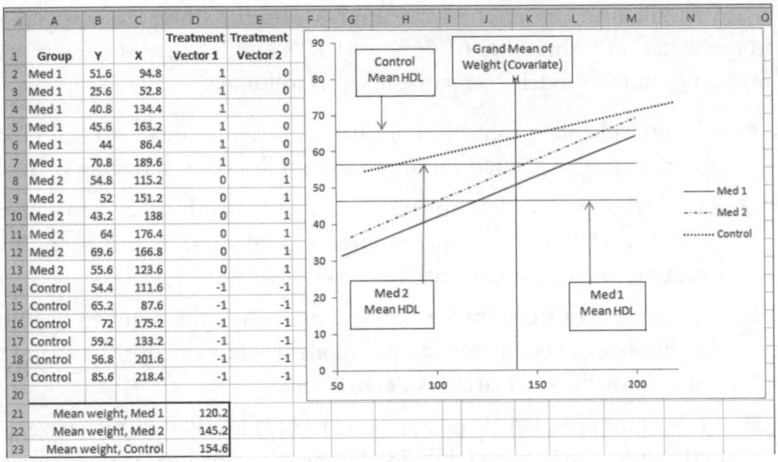

	Group	Y	X	Treatment Vector 1	Treatment Vector 2
2	Med 1	51.6	94.8	1	0
3	Med 1	25.6	52.8	1	0
4	Med 1	40.8	134.4	1	0
5	Med 1	45.6	163.2	1	0
6	Med 1	44	86.4	1	0
7	Med 1	70.8	189.6	1	0
8	Med 2	54.8	115.2	0	1
9	Med 2	52	151.2	0	1
10	Med 2	43.2	138	0	1
11	Med 2	64	176.4	0	1
12	Med 2	69.6	166.8	0	1
13	Med 2	55.6	123.6	0	1
14	Control	54.4	111.6	-1	-1
15	Control	65.2	87.6	-1	-1
16	Control	72	175.2	-1	-1
17	Control	59.2	133.2	-1	-1
18	Control	56.8	201.6	-1	-1
19	Control	85.6	218.4	-1	-1
20					
21	Mean weight, Med 1			120.2	
22	Mean weight, Med 2			145.2	
23	Mean weight, Control			154.6	

Figure 14.9
The regression slopes adjust the observed means to show the expected HDL if each group started with the same average weight.

You can see this effect in Figure 14.9, just as you can in Figure 14.4. In Figure 14.4, the Medication group weighed less than the Control group, but its HDL was higher than that of the Control group. The adjustment's effect was to push the means farther apart.

But in Figure 14.9, the Med 1 group has the lowest mean of 120.2 on the covariate and also has the lowest unadjusted mean on the HDL outcome measure, about 46. (See the lowest horizontal line in the chart.) Furthermore, the Control group has the highest mean of 154.6 on the covariate and also has the highest unadjusted mean on the HDL measure, about 66. (See the highest horizontal line in the chart.)

Under those conditions, and with the covariate and the outcome measure correlated positively within each group, the effect is to close up the differences between the group means. Notice that the regression lines are closer together where they cross the vertical line that represents the grand mean of the covariate: where the groups would be on HDL if they started out equivalent on the weight measure.

So the adjusted group means are closer together than are the raw means. Figure 14.7 shows that the group raw means are significantly different at the .05 alpha level. Are the adjusted means also significantly different? See Figure 14.10.

Compare Figure 14.10 with Figure 14.3. Structurally the two analyses are similar, differing only in that Figure 14.3 has just one treatment vector, whereas Figure 14.10 has two. But they have different input data and different results. Both regress the outcome measure Y onto the covariate X, and in a separate analysis they regress Y onto the covariate plus the treatment. The result in Figure 14.3 is to find that the group means on the outcome measure are significantly different somewhere, in part because the raw means are pushed apart by the regression adjustments.

In contrast, the result in Figure 14.10 shows that differences in the raw means that were judged significantly different by ANOVA are, adjusted for the regression, possibly due to sampling error. The ANCOVA summary in H11:M16 assigns some shared variance to the covariate (47%, or 1560.74 in terms of sums of squares), but not enough to reduce the residual enough that the F ratio for the treatment factor is significant at a level that most would accept as meaningful.

Figure 14.10
With the group means adjusted closer together, there is no longer a significant difference.

I15 f_x =K8*K11

	A	B	C	D	E	F	G	H	I	J	K	L	M	N	O
1	Group	Y	X	Treatment Vector 1	Treatment Vector 2			Y on X, Total				Y on X and Treatment			
2	Med 1	51.6	94.8	1	0			0.22	25.89			-0.54	-6.26	0.18	31.43
3	Med 2	25.6	52.8	1	0			0.06	8.37			3.20	3.38	0.06	8.11
4	Med 3	40.8	134	1	0		R^2	0.47	10.44		R^2	0.61	9.57	#N/A	#N/A
5	Med 1	45.6	163	1	0			14.31	16			7.35	14	#N/A	#N/A
6	Med 1	44	86.4	1	0			1560.742	1745.22			2022.53	1283.43	#N/A	#N/A
7	Med 1	70.8	190	1	0										
8	Med 2	54.8	115	0	1				Increase in R2		0.14				
9	Med 2	52	151	0	1										
10	Med 2	43.2	138	0	1										
11	Med 2	64	176	0	1			Total Sum of Squares:			3305.96				
12	Med 2	69.6	167	0	1										
13	Med 2	55.6	124	0	1			SV	SS	df	MS	F	p		
14	Control	54.4	112	-1	-1			Covariate	1560.74	1	1560.74	17.02	0.001		
15	Control	65.2	87.6	-1	-1			Treatment	461.79	2	230.89	2.52	0.116		
16	Control	72	175	-1	-1			Residual	1283.43	14	91.67				
17	Control	59.2	133	-1	-1										
18	Control	56.8	202	-1	-1										
19	Control	85.6	218	-1	-1										

In Figure 14.10, I could have left the sum of squares and the mean square columns out of the analysis in H11:M16 and followed the strict proportion of variance approach used in Figure 14.8, cells G21:L23. I include them in Figure 14.10 just to demonstrate that either can be used—depending mainly on whether you want to follow a traditional layout and include them, or a more sparse layout and omit them.

Chapter 15 looks at some special considerations concerning the analysis of covariance, including multiple comparisons following a significant finding in ANCOVA, and multiple covariates.

Analysis of Covariance: Further Issues

The final chapter in this book builds on Chapter 14, "Analysis of Covariance: The Basics." This chapter looks at some special considerations concerning the analysis of covariance, including a closer look at adjusting means using a covariate, multiple comparisons following a significant finding in ANCOVA, multiple covariates and factorial designs.

Adjusting Means with LINEST() and Effect Coding

There's a special benefit to using LINEST() in conjunction with effect coding to run your ANCOVA. Doing so makes it much easier to obtain the adjusted means than using any traditional computation methods. Of course you want the adjusted means for their intrinsic interest—"What would my results have looked like if all the groups had begun with the same mean value on the covariate?" But you also want them because the F ratio from the ANCOVA might indicate one or more reliable differences among the adjusted group means. If so, you'll want to carry out a multiple comparisons procedure to determine which adjusted means are reliably different. (See Chapter 10, "Testing Differences Between Means: The Analysis of Variance," for a discussion of multiple comparisons following an ANOVA.)

Figure 15.1 shows the data and preliminary analysis for a study of auto tires. It is known that a tire's age, even if it has just been sitting in a warehouse, contributes to its deterioration. One way to measure that deterioration is by checking for evidence of cracking on the tire's exterior.

You decide to test whether the different types of stores that sell tires contribute to the deterioration of the tires, apart from that expected on the basis of the tires' ages. You examine twelve different tires for the degree of deterioration as evidenced by the amount of surface cracking you can see. You examine four tires from each of three types of store: retailers that specialize in tires, auto dealers whose repair facilities sell tires, and repair garages. You come away with the findings shown in Figure 15.1.

Figure 15.1

A visual scan of the data indicates that an ANCOVA would be a reasonable next step.

	A	B	C	D	E	F	G	H	I	J	K	L
1		Retail Outlet			Auto Dealer			Garage			Total	
2		Degree of Cracking	Tire Age		Degree of Cracking	Tire Age		Degree of Cracking	Tire Age		Degree of Cracking	Tire Age
3		41	23		53	56		63	91			
4		59	30		66	65		71	98			
5		63	52		75	70		84	102			
6		81	60		88	83		94	119			
7												
8	Mean	61	41.25		70.5	68.5		78	102.5		69.83	70.75

By looking at the relationship between the mean degree of cracking and the mean tire age at each type of store, you can tell that as the age increases, so does the degree of cracking. You decide to test the mean differences in cracking among store types, using tire age as a covariate. The first step, as discussed in Chapter 14, is to check whether the regression coefficients between cracking and age are homogeneous in the three different groups. That test appears in Figure 15.2.

There are several aspects to note regarding the data in Figure 15.2.

Figure 15.2

A data layout similar to this is needed for analysis by LINEST().

	A	B	C	D	E	F	G	H	I	J	K	L
C16			f_x	=B16*(J6+K6)								
1	Store Type	Degree of Cracking	Tire Age	Store Vector 1	Store Vector 2	Factor by Covariate 1	Factor by Covariate 2			LINEST(), All Vectors		
2	Retail Outlet	41	23	1	0	23	0				0.22	-0.23
3	Retail Outlet	59	30	1	0	30	0				0.23	0.19
4	Retail Outlet	63	52	1	0	52	0		R^2		0.92	5.94
5	Retail Outlet	81	60	1	0	60	0				13.57	6
6	Auto Dealer	53	56	0	1	0	56				2395.78	211.89
7	Auto Dealer	66	65	0	1	0	65					
8	Auto Dealer	75	70	0	1	0	70			LINEST(), No Interaction Vector		
9	Auto Dealer	88	83	0	1	0	83				2.93	20.86
10	Garage	63	91	-1	-1	-91	-91				2.40	4.77
11	Garage	71	98	-1	-1	-98	-98		R^2		0.90	5.83
12	Garage	84	102	-1	-1	-102	-102				22.93	8.00
13	Garage	94	119	-1	-1	-119	-119				2335.99	271.68
14												
15	Source	Prop of Var	SS	df	MS	F	p of F					
16	Factor by covariate	0.02	59.79	2	29.90	0.85	0.47					
17	Residual	0.08	211.89	6	35.31							

The individual observations have been realigned in Figure 15.2 so that they occupy two columns, B and C: one for tire surface cracking and one for age. Figure 15.1 shows the data in two columns that span three different ranges, one range for each type of store (columns B, C, E, F, H, and I).

I organized the data shown in Figure 15.1 to appear as it might in a report, where the emphasis is visual interpretation rather than statistical analysis. I rearranged it in Figure 15.2 to a list layout, which is appropriate for every method of analysis and charting available in Excel. You could use a list layout to get the analysis in Figure 15.1 with a pivot table, and also the LINEST() analyses in Figure 15.2.

Four vectors have been added in Figure 15.2 from column D through column G. Columns D and E contain the familiar effect codes to indicate the type of store associated with each tire. The vectors in columns F and G are created by multiplying the covariate's value by the value of each of the factor's vectors. So, for example, cell F2 contains the product of cells C2 and D2, and cell G2 contains the product of cells C2 and E2.

The vectors in columns F and G represent the interaction between the factor, Store Type, and the covariate, Tire Age. Any variability in the outcome measure that the interaction vectors explain is due either to a real difference in the regression slopes between cracking and age in the different types of store, or to sampling error. The ANCOVA usually starts with a test of whether the regression lines differ at different levels of the factor.

To make that test, we use LINEST() twice. Each instance returns the amount of variability in the outcome measure, or R^2, that's explained by the following:

- The full model (covariate, factor, and factor-covariate interaction)
- The restricted model (covariate and factor only)

The difference in the two measures of explained variance is attributable to the factor-covariate interaction. In Figure 15.2, the instance of LINEST() for the full model is in the range J2:K6. The cell with the R^2 is labeled accordingly, and shows that 0.92, or 92%, of the variance in the outcome measure is explained by all five predictor vectors.

By comparison, the instance of LINEST() in the range J9:K13 represents the restricted model and omits the interaction vectors in columns F and G from the analysis. The R^2 in cell J11 is 0.90, so the covariate and the factor vectors alone account for 90% of the variance in the outcome measure. Therefore, the interaction of the covariate with the factor accounts for a scant 2% of the variance in the outcome.

Despite the fact that so little variance is attributable to the interaction, it's best to complete the analysis. That's done in the range A16:G17 of Figure 15.2. There you can find a traditional ANOVA summary that tests the 2% of variance explained by the factor-covariate interaction against the residual variance. (You can get the residual proportion of variance by subtracting the R^2 in cell J4 from 1.0. Equivalently, you can get the residual sum of squares from cell K6.)

Notice from the p-value in cell G16 that this F ratio with 2 and 6 degrees of freedom can be expected by chance about half the time. Therefore, we retain the assumption that the regression slope of the outcome variable on the covariate is the same in each store type, in the population, and that any differences among the three regression coefficients is merely sampling error.

NOTE

You might wonder why the results of the two instances of LINEST() in Figure 15.2 each occupy only two columns: LINEST() calculates results for as many columns as there are predictor vectors, plus one for the intercept. So, for example, the results in J2:K6 could occupy J2:O6. That's six columns: five for the five vectors in columns C:G and one for the intercept. I wanted to save space in the figure, and so I began by selecting J2:K6 and then array-entered the formula with the LINEST() function. The focus here is primarily on R^2 and secondarily on the sums of squares, and those values occupy only the first two columns of LINEST() results. The remaining columns would have displayed only the individual regression coefficients and their standard errors, and at the moment they are not of interest (but they become so in Figure 15.5).

TIP

You might want to keep this in your hip pocket: You need not show all the possible results of LINEST(), and you can suppress one or more rows or columns simply by failing to select them before array-entering the formula. However, once you have displayed a row or column of LINEST() results, you cannot subsequently delete it except by deleting the entire range of LINEST() results. If you attempt to do so, you'll get the Excel error message "You cannot change part of an array."

The next step is to perform the ANCOVA on the Tire Age covariate and the Store Type factor. Figure 15.3 shows that analysis.

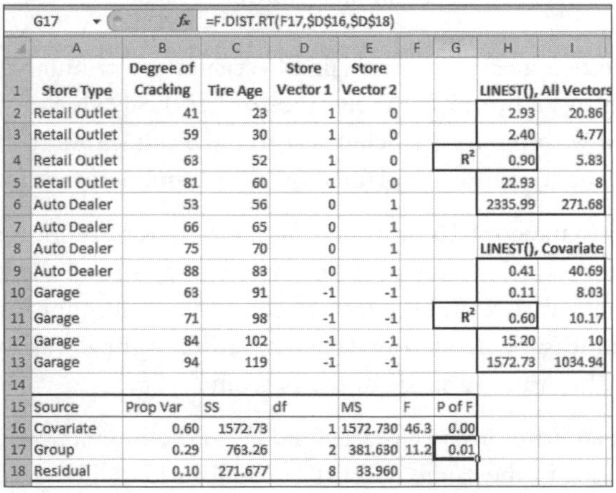

G17 =F.DIST.RT(F17,$D$16,$D$18)

	A	B	C	D	E	F	G	H	I
1	Store Type	Degree of Cracking	Tire Age	Store Vector 1	Store Vector 2			LINEST(), All Vectors	
2	Retail Outlet	41	23	1	0			2.93	20.86
3	Retail Outlet	59	30	1	0			2.40	4.77
4	Retail Outlet	63	52	1	0		R^2	0.90	5.83
5	Retail Outlet	81	60	1	0			22.93	8
6	Auto Dealer	53	56	0	1			2335.99	271.68
7	Auto Dealer	66	65	0	1				
8	Auto Dealer	75	70	0	1			LINEST(), Covariate	
9	Auto Dealer	88	83	0	1			0.41	40.69
10	Garage	63	91	-1	-1			0.11	8.03
11	Garage	71	98	-1	-1		R^2	0.60	10.17
12	Garage	84	102	-1	-1			15.20	10
13	Garage	94	119	-1	-1			1572.73	1034.94
14									
15	Source	Prop Var	SS	df	MS	F	P of F		
16	Covariate	0.60	1572.73	1	1572.730	46.3	0.00		
17	Group	0.29	763.26	2	381.630	11.2	0.01		
18	Residual	0.10	271.677	8	33.960				

Figure 15.3
The relationships between the covariate and the outcome, and between the factor and the outcome, are both reliable.

Two instances of LINEST() are needed in Figure 15.3 to test the relationship between the covariate and the outcome measure, and between the factor plus the covariate, and the outcome measure.

The range H2:I6 shows the first two columns of a LINEST() analysis of the regression of the outcome measure on the covariate and on the two factor vectors. Cell H4 shows that 0.90 of the variance in the outcome variable is explained by the covariate and the factor. (This analysis is of course identical to the one shown in J9:K13 of Figure 15.2.)

The second instance of LINEST() in Figure 15.3, in H9:I13, shows the regression of the outcome variable on the covariate only. The covariate explains 0.60 of the variability in the outcome measure, as shown in cell H11. Note that this figure, 0.60 or 60%, is repeated in cell B16 as part of the full ANCOVA analysis.

The difference between the R^2 for the covariate and the factor, and the R^2 for the covariate alone, is 0.29, or 29% of the variance in the outcome measure. This difference is attributable to the factor, Store Type.

The sums of squares in the range C16:C18 contribute little to the analysis—including them works out to little more than multiplying and dividing by the same constant when the F ratio is computed. But it's traditional to include them.

The degrees of freedom are counted as discussed several times in Chapter 14. The covariate accounts for 1 df and the factor accounts for as many df as there are levels, minus 1. (It is not accidental that the number of vectors for each source of variation is equal to the number of df for that source.) The residual degrees of freedom is the total number of observations, less the number of covariates and factor vectors, less 1. Here, that's 12 – 3 – 1, or 8.

As usual, dividing the sum of squares by the degrees of freedom results in the mean squares. The ratio of the mean square for the covariate to the mean square residual gives the F ratio for the covariate; the F ratio for the factor is, similarly, the result of dividing the mean square for the factor by the mean square for the residual.

(You could dispense with the sums of squares, divide the proportion of variance explained by the associated df, and form the same F ratios using the results of those divisions. This method is discussed in Testing for a Common Regression Line, in Chapter 14.)

An F ratio for the Store factor of 11.2 (see cell F17 in Figure 15.3) with 2 and 8 df occurs by chance, due to sampling error, 1% of the time (cell G17). Therefore, there is a reliable difference somewhere in the adjusted means. With only two means, it would be obvious where to look for a significant difference. With three or more means, it's more complicated. For example, one mean might be significantly different from the other two, which are not significantly different. Or all three means might differ significantly. With four or more groups, the possibilities become more complex yet, and include questions such as whether the average of two group means is significantly different from the average of two other group means. These kinds of considerations, and their solutions, are discussed in Chapter 10, in the section titled "Multiple Comparison Procedures."

But what you're interested in, following an ANCOVA that returns a significantly large F ratio for a factor, is comparing the *adjusted* means. Because multiple comparisons involve the use of residual (also known as *within-cell*) variance, some modification is needed to account for the variation associated with the covariate.

In Chapter 14, one way to obtain adjusted group means in Excel was discussed. That was done in order to provide conceptual background for the procedure. But there is an easier way, provided you're using LINEST() and effect coding to represent group membership (as this book has done for the preceding three chapters). We'll cover that method next.

Effect Coding and Adjusted Group Means

Figure 15.4 shows again how to arrive at adjusted group means using traditional methods following a significant F ratio in an ANCOVA.

Figure 15.4

These figures represent the recommended calculations to adjust group means using the covariate in a traditional ANCOVA.

	F18	▼		f_x	=B18-C18*(D18-E18)							
	A	B	C	D	E	F	G	H	I	J	K	L
1		Retail Outlet			Auto Dealer			Garage				
2		Degree of Cracking	Tire Age		Degree of Cracking	Tire Age		Degree of Cracking	Tire Age			
3		41	23		53	56		63	91			
4		59	30		66	65		71	98			
5		63	52		75	70		84	102			
6		81	60		88	83		94	119		Total	
7												
8	Mean	61	41.25		70.5	68.5		78	102.5		69.83	70.75
9												
10	Σx^2		7733			19150			42450		69333	
11	$(\Sigma x)^2/N$		6806.25			18769			42025		67600.25	
12											Σx^2_w	1732.75
13												
14	Σxy	10849			19812			32445			63106	
15	$\Sigma x \Sigma y/N$	10065			19317			31980			61362	
16											Σxy_w	1744
17		Group Means, Y	Common Beta	Group Means, X	Grand Mean, X	Adjusted Group Means, Y						
18		61	1.0065	41.25	70.75	90.69					b_w	1.0065
19		70.5	1.0065	68.5	70.75	72.76						
20		78	1.0065	102.5	70.75	46.04						

A lot of work must be done if you're using traditional approaches to running an analysis of covariance. In Figure 15.4, the following tasks are illustrated:

■ The unadjusted group means for the outcome measure (tire cracking) and the covariate (tire age), along with the grand mean for both variables, are calculated and shown in row 8.

■ For each group, the sum of the squares of the covariate is found (row 10). These sums are accumulated in cell K10.

■ For each group, the sum of the covariate is found, squared, and divided by the number of observations in that group. Those values, in cells C11, F11, and I11, are accumulated in cell K11.

■ The difference between the values in K10 and K11 is calculated and stored in K12. This quantity is often referred to as the *covariate total sum of squares*.

■ The cross-products of the covariate and the outcome measure and calculated and summed for each group in B14, E14, and H14. They are accumulated into K14.

- Within each group the total of the covariate is multiplied by the total of the outcome measure, and the result is divided by the number of subjects per group. The results are accumulated in K15.

- The difference between the values in K14 and K15 is calculated and stored in K16. The quantity is often referred to as the *total cross-product*.

- The total cross-product in K16 is divided by the covariate total sum of squares in K12. The result, shown in K18, is the common regression coefficient of the outcome measure on the covariate, and symbolized as b_w.

- Lastly, the formula given toward the end of Chapter 14 is applied to get the adjusted group means. In Figure 15.4, the figures are summarized in B18:F20. The common regression coefficient in cells C18:C20 is multiplied by the difference between the group means on the covariate in D18:D20 less the grand mean on the covariate in E18:E20. The result is subtracted from the unadjusted group means in B18:B20 to get the adjusted group means in F18:F20.

That's a fair amount of work. See Figure 15.5 for a quicker way.

Figure 15.5
Using effect coding with equal sample sizes results in the regression coefficients that equal the adjustments.

	C16	▾	f_x	=B16+H2						
	A	B	C	D	E	F	G	H	I	J
	Store Type	Degree of Cracking	Tire Age	Store Vector 1	Store Vector 2			LINEST(), All Vectors		
1										
2	Retail Outlet	41	23	1	0		2.931275	20.8582	1.006493	-1.37602
3	Retail Outlet	59	30	1	0		2.399824	4.766098	0.139995	10.04651
4	Retail Outlet	63	52	1	0		0.895816	5.827488	#N/A	#N/A
5	Retail Outlet	81	60	1	0		22.92909	8	#N/A	#N/A
6	Auto Dealer	53	56	0	1		2335.99	271.677	#N/A	#N/A
7	Auto Dealer	66	65	0	1					
8	Auto Dealer	75	70	0	1					
9	Auto Dealer	88	83	0	1					
10	Garage	63	91	-1	-1					
11	Garage	71	98	-1	-1					
12	Garage	84	102	-1	-1					
13	Garage	94	119	-1	-1					
14										
15		Grand Mean, Y	Adjusted Group Means, Y							
16	Retail Outlet	69.833333	90.69							
17	Auto Dealer	69.833333	72.76							
18	Garage	69.833333	46.04							

Compare the values of the adjusted means in Figure 15.5, cells C16:C18, with those in Figure 15.4, cells F18:F20. They are identical. In Figure 15.5, though, they are calculated by adding the regression coefficient from the LINEST() analysis to the grand mean of the outcome variable. So, in Figure 15.5, these calculations are used: The grand mean of the outcome measure is put in B16:B18 using the formula =AVERAGE($B$2:$B$13). With ANOVA (not ANCOVA), the intercept returned by LINEST() with effect coding is the grand mean of the outcome measure. That is not generally the case with ANCOVA, however, because the presence of the covariate changes the nature of the regression equation. Therefore, we calculate the grand mean explicitly and put it in B16:B18.

The regression coefficient returned by LINEST() with effect coding represents the *effect* of being in a particular group—that is, the deviation from the grand mean that is associated with being in the group assigned 1's in a given vector. That's actually a fairly straightforward concept, but it's very difficult to describe crisply in English. The situation is made more complex, and unnecessarily so, by the order in which LINEST() returns its results. To help clarify things, let's consider two examples—but first a little background.

In Chapter 4, "How Variables Move Jointly: Correlation," in a sidebar rant titled "LINEST() Runs Backward," I pointed out that LINEST() returns results in an order that's the reverse of the order of its inputs. In Figure 15.5, then, the left-to-right order in which the vectors appear in the worksheet is covariate first in column C, then factor vector 1 in column D, then factor vector 2 in column E.

However, in the LINEST() results shown in the range G2:J6, the left-to-right order is as follows: first factor vector 2 (coefficient in G2), then factor vector 1 (coefficient in H2), then the covariate (coefficient in I2). The equation's intercept is always the rightmost entry in the first row of the LINEST() results and is in cell J2.

In Figure 15.5, an observation that belongs to the Retail Outlet store type gets the value 1 in the vector labeled Store Vector 1. That vector's regression coefficient is found in cell H2, so the adjusted mean for Retail Outlets is found with this formula in cell C16: =B16+H2.

Similarly, the regression coefficient for Store Vector 2—the rightmost vector in Figure 15.5—is found in cell G2—the leftmost coefficient in the LINEST() results. So the adjusted mean for the Auto Dealer store type (the type that's assigned 1's in the Store Vector 2 column) is found in cell C17 with the formula =B17+G2.

What of the third group in Figure 15.5, Garage? Observations in that group are not assigned a value of 1 in either of the store type vectors. In accordance with the conventions of effect coding, when you have three or more groups, one of them is assigned 1 in none of the factor vectors but a –1 in each of them. That's the case here with the Garage level of the Store factor.

The treatment of that group is a little different. To find the adjusted mean of that group, you subtract the sum of the other regression coefficients from the grand mean. Therefore, the formula used in Figure 15.5, cell C18, is =B16-(G2+H2).

Given the difficulty presented by LINEST() in associating a particular regression coefficient with the proper prediction vector, this process is a little complicated. But consider all the machinations needed by traditional techniques, shown in Figure 15.4, to get the adjusted means. In comparison, the approach shown in Figure 15.5 merely requires you to get the grand mean of the outcome variable, run LINEST(), and add the grand mean to the appropriate regression coefficient. Again, in comparison, that's pretty easy.

Multiple Comparisons Following ANCOVA

If you obtain an F ratio for the factor in an ANCOVA that indicates a reliable difference among the adjusted group means, you will often want to perform subsequent tests to determine which means, or combinations of means, differ reliably. These tests are called *multiple comparisons* and have been discussed in the section titled "Multiple Comparison Procedures" in Chapter 10. You might find it useful to review that material before undertaking the present section. The multiple comparison procedures are discussed further here, for two reasons:

- The idea is to test the differences between the group means as adjusted for regression on the covariate. You saw in the prior section how to make those adjustments, and it simply remains to plug the adjustments into the multiple comparison procedure properly.

- The multiple comparison procedure relies in part on the mean square error, typically termed the *residual error* when you're using multiple regression to perform the ANOVA or ANCOVA. Because some of what was the residual error in ANOVA is allocated to the covariate in ANCOVA, it's necessary to adjust the multiple comparison formulas so that they use the proper value for the residual error.

Using the Scheffé Method

Chapter 10, this book's introductory chapter on the analysis of variance, shows how to use multiple comparison procedures to determine which of the possible contrasts among the group means bring about a significant overall F ratio. For example, with three groups, it's quite possible to obtain an improbably large F ratio due solely to the difference between the means of Group 1 and Group 2; the mean of Group 3 might be halfway between the other two means and significantly different from neither.

The F ratio that you calculate with the analysis of variance doesn't tell you where the reliable difference lies: only that there is at least one reliable difference. Multiple comparison procedures help you pinpoint where the reliable differences are to be found. Of course, when you have only two groups, it's superfluous to conduct a multiple comparison procedure. With just two groups there's only one difference.

Figure 10.9 demonstrates the use of the Scheffé method of multiple comparisons. The Scheffé is one of several methods that are termed *post hoc* multiple comparisons. That is, you can carry out the Scheffé after finding that the F ratio indicates the presence of at least one reliable difference in the group means, without having specified beforehand which comparisons you're interested in. There is another class of *a priori* multiple comparisons, which are more powerful statistically than a post hoc comparison, but you must have planned which comparisons to make before seeing your outcome data. (One type of a priori comparison is demonstrated in Figure 10.11.)

Figure 15.6 shows how the Scheffé method can be used following an ANCOVA. As noted in the prior section, you must make some adjustments because you're running the multiple comparison procedure on the adjusted means, not the raw means, and also because you're using a different error term, one that has almost certainly shrunk because of the presence of the covariate.

Figure 15.6
LINEST() analyses replace the ANOVA tables used in Figure 10.9.

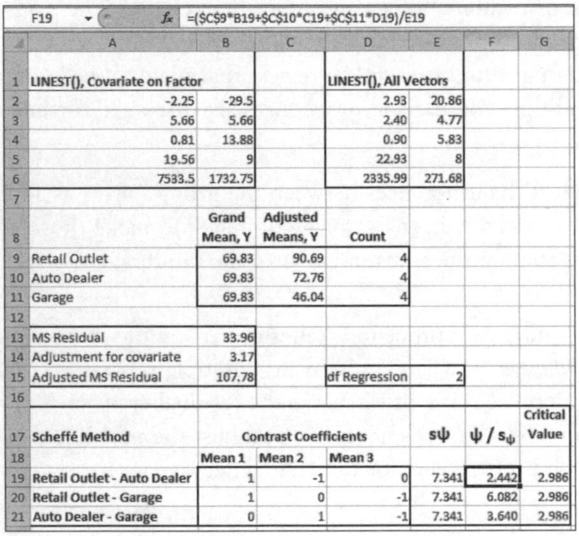

F19		▾	⊙	f_x	=($C$9*B19+$C$10*C19+$C$11*D19)/E19			
	A	B	C	D	E	F	G
1	LINEST(), Covariate on Factor			LINEST(), All Vectors			
2		-2.25	-29.5		2.93	20.86		
3		5.66	5.66		2.40	4.77		
4		0.81	13.88		0.90	5.83		
5		19.56	9		22.93	8		
6		7533.5	1732.75		2335.99	271.68		
7							
8		Grand Mean, Y	Adjusted Means, Y	Count			
9	Retail Outlet	69.83	90.69	4			
10	Auto Dealer	69.83	72.76	4			
11	Garage	69.83	46.04	4			
12							
13	MS Residual	33.96					
14	Adjustment for covariate	3.17					
15	Adjusted MS Residual	107.78		df Regression	2		
16							
17	Scheffé Method		Contrast Coefficients		sψ	ψ / sψ	Critical Value
18		Mean 1	Mean 2	Mean 3			
19	Retail Outlet - Auto Dealer	1	-1	0	7.341	2.442	2.986
20	Retail Outlet - Garage	1	0	-1	7.341	6.082	2.986
21	Auto Dealer - Garage	0	1	-1	7.341	3.640	2.986

Figure 10.9 shows the relevant descriptive statistics and the traditional analysis of variance table that precedes the use of a multiple comparison procedure. You can, if you wish, use Excel's Data Analysis add-in—specifically, the ANOVA Single Factor and the ANOVA Two Factor with Replication tools—to obtain the preliminary analyses. Of course, if the F ratio is not large enough to indicate a reliable mean difference somewhere, you would stop right there: There's no point in testing for a reliable mean difference when the ANOVA or the ANCOVA tells you there isn't one to be found.

Figure 15.6 does not show the results of using the Data Analysis add-in because it isn't capable of dealing with covariates. As you've seen, the LINEST() worksheet function is fully capable of handling a covariate along with factors, and it's used twice in Figure 15.6:

- To analyze the outcome variable Degree of Cracking by the covariate Tire Age and the factor Store Type (the range D1:E6)
- To analyze the covariate by the factor Store Type (the range A1:B6)

You'll see shortly how the instance of LINEST() in A1:B6, which analyzes the covariate by the factor, comes into play in the multiple comparison.

As you've seen in Figure 15.5, with equal group sizes and effect coding, the adjusted group means equal the grand mean of the outcome variable plus the regression coefficient for the vector. Figure 15.6 repeats this analysis in the range B9:C11, because the adjusted means are needed for the multiple comparison. The group sizes are also needed and are shown in D9:D11.

Adjusting the Mean Square Residual

In Figure 15.6, the range B13:B15 shows an adjustment to the residual mean square. If you refer back to Figure 10.9 (and also Figure 10.10), you'll note that the residual mean square is used in the denominator for the multiple comparison. For the purpose of the omnibus F test, no special adjustment is needed. You simply allocate some of the variability in the outcome measure to the covariate and work with the reduced mean square residual as the source of the F ratio's denominator.

But when you're conducting a multiple comparison procedure, you need to adjust the mean square residual from the ANCOVA. When you are using the mean square residual to test not all the means, as in the ANCOVA, but in a follow-up multiple comparison, it's necessary to adjust the mean square residual to reflect the differences between the groups *on the covariate*.

To do so, begin by getting the residual mean square from the regression of the outcome variable on the covariate and the factor. This is done using the instance of LINEST() in the range D2:E6. In cell B13, the ratio of the residual sum of squares to the residual degrees of freedom is calculated, using this formula:

=E6/E5

Then the quantity in cell B14 is calculated, using this formula:

=1+(A6/(E15*B6))

In words: Divide the regression sum of squares for the covariate on the factor (cell A6) by the product of the degrees of freedom for the regression (cell E15) and the residual sum of squares for the covariate on the factor (cell B6).

Then, multiply the residual mean square from the analysis of the outcome variable by the adjustment factor. In cell B15, that's handled by this formula:

=B13*B14

> **NOTE**
>
> Notice, by the way, that if there are no differences among the group means on the covariate, the adjustment is the equivalent of multiplying the mean square residual by 1.0. When the groups have the same mean on the covariate, the regression sum of squares for the covariate on the factor is 0.0, and the value calculated in cell B14 must therefore equal 1.0. In that case, the adjusted mean square residual is identical to the mean square residual from the ANCOVA. There is then nothing to add back in to the mean square residual that's due to differences among the groups on the covariate.

Other Necessary Values

The number of degrees of freedom for the regression—also termed the *degrees of freedom between*—is put in cell E15 in Figure 15.6. It is equal to the number of groups, minus 1. As mentioned previously, it is used to help compute the adjustment for the mean square residual, and it is also used to help determine the critical value for the multiple comparison, in cells G19:G21.

The coefficients that determine the nature of the contrasts appear in cells B19:D21. These are usually 1's, –1's, and 0's, and they determine which means are involved in a given contrast, and to what degree. So, the 1, the –1 and the 0 in B19:D19 indicate that the mean of Group 2 is to be subtracted from the mean of Group 1, and Group 3 is not involved. If the coefficients for Groups 1 and 2 were both 1/2 and the coefficient for Group 3 were –1, the purpose of the contrast would be to compare the average of Groups 1 and 2 with the mean of Group 3.

The standard deviations of the contrasts appear in cells E19:E21. They are calculated exactly as is done following an ANOVA and as shown in Figure 10.9, with the single exception that they use the adjusted residual mean square instead of an unadjusted residual mean square for the excellent reason that in an ANOVA, there's no covariate to adjust for. That is, as I mentioned in the prior Note, when there is no covariate there is no adjustment, and when the groups have the same mean values on the covariate there's no adjustment.

The standard deviations of the contrasts simply reduce the adjusted residual mean square according to the number of observations in each group and the contrast coefficient. The mean square is a variance, so the square root of the result represents the standard error of the contrast. For example, the formula for the standard error in cell E19 is

=SQRT(B15*(B19^2/D9+C19^2/D10+D19^2/D11))

which, more generally, is as follows:

$$\sqrt{MS_{resid} \sum \frac{C_j^2}{n_j}}$$

Take the sum of the squared contrast coefficients divided by each group size. Multiply that times the (adjusted) residual mean square and take the square root. This gives you the standard deviation (or, if you prefer, the standard error) of the contrast.

In this case, the sample sizes are all equal and the sum of the squared coefficients equals 2 in each contrast, so the standard errors shown in E19:E21 are all equal. (But in Figure 10.9, the contrast coefficients for the fourth contrast were not all 1's, –1's, and 0's, so its standard error differs from the other three.)

Still in Figure 15.6, the range F19:F21 contains the ratios of the contrasts to their standard errors. The contrast is simply the sum of the coefficients times the associated means, so the formula used in cell F19 is

=($C$9*B19+$C$10*C19+$C$11*D19)/E19

TIP The absolute addressing is used so that the formula can be dragged into F20:F21 without modifying the addresses that identify the adjusted group means in C9:C11.

Completing the Comparison

The critical values to compare with the ratios in F19:F21 are in G19:G21. As in Figure 10.9, each critical value is the square root of the critical F value times the degrees of freedom for the regression. The critical value in the Scheffé method does not vary with the contrast, and the formula used in cell G19 is as follows:

=SQRT(E15*(F.INV.RT(0.05,E15,E5)))

The value in E15 is the degrees of freedom between, and the value in cell E5 is the degrees of freedom for the residual. The F.INV.RT function returns the value of the F distribution with (in this example) 2 and 8 degrees of freedom, such that 0.05 of the area under the curve is to its right. Therefore, cell F19 contains the critical value that the calculated t-ratio must surpass if you want to regard it as significant at the 95% level of confidence.

NOTE In Figure 10.9, I used F.INV() with 0.95 as an argument. Here, I use F.INV.RT() with 0.05 as an argument. I do so merely to demonstrate that the two functions are equivalent. The former returns a value that has 95% of the area under the curve to its left; the latter returns a value that has 5% of the area to its right. The two forms are equivalent, and the choice is entirely a matter of whether you prefer to think of the 95% of the time that the population values of the numerator and the denominator are equal, or the 5% of the time that they're not.

The two ratios in F20 and in F21 both exceed the critical value; the ratio in F19 does not. So the Scheffé multiple comparison procedure indicates that two contrasts (Retail Outlet vs. Garage and Auto Dealer vs. Garage) result in the overall ANCOVA F ratio that suggests at least one reliable group mean difference in tire cracking, as corrected for the covariate of tire age. There is no reliable difference for Retail Outlet vs. Auto Dealer.

The comments made in Chapter 10 regarding the Scheffé procedure hold for comparisons made following ANCOVA just as they do following ANOVA. The Scheffé is the most flexible of the multiple comparison procedures; you can specify as many contrasts as make sense to you, and you can do so after you've seen the outcome of the experiment or other research effort. The price you pay for that flexibility is reduced statistical power: Some comparisons that other methods would regard as reliable differences will be missed by the Scheffé technique. It is possible, though, that the gain in statistical power that you get from using ANCOVA instead of ANOVA more than makes up for the loss due to using the Scheffé procedure.

Using Planned Contrasts

As noted in the section on multiple comparisons in Chapter 10, you can get more statistical power if you plan the comparisons before you see the data. So doing allows you to use a more sensitive test than the Scheffé (but again, the tradeoff is one of power for flexibility).

In Figure 15.6, you can see that the Scheffé method does not regard the difference in adjusted means on the outcome measure for Retail Outlet vs. Auto Dealer as a reliable one. The calculated contrast divided by its standard error, in cell F19, is smaller than the critical value shown in cell G19. So you conclude that some other mean difference is responsible for the significant F value for the full ANCOVA, and the comparisons in F20:G21 bear this out.

The analysis in Figure 15.7 presents a different picture.

Figure 15.7

A planned contrast generally has greater statistical power than a post hoc contrast.

C18	f_x =SQRT(B13*((1/E9+1/E10)+(D9-D10)^2/B14))			
	A	B	C	D	E
1	LINEST(), Covariate on Factor			LINEST(), All Vectors	
2	-2.25	-29.5		2.93	20.86
3	5.66	5.66		2.40	4.77
4	0.81	13.88		0.90	5.83
5	19.56	9		22.93	8
6	7533.5	1732.75		2335.99	271.68
7					
8		Grand Mean, Y	Adjusted Means, Y	Raw Means, X	Count
9	Retail Outlet	69.83	90.69	41.25	4
10	Auto Dealer	69.83	72.76	68.5	4
11	Garage	69.83	46.04	102.5	4
12					
13	MS Residual	33.96			
14	SS Residual, covariate	1732.75			
15					
16					
17		Mean difference	Denominator	t ratio	Critical t
18	Retail Outlet - Auto Dealer	17.93	5.62	3.19	1.86

The planned contrast shown in Figure 15.7 requires just slightly less information than is shown for the Scheffé test in Figure 15.6. One added bit of data required is the actual group means on the covariate (X, or in this case Tire Age).

Figure 15.7 extracts the required information from the LINEST() analyses in A2:B6 and D2:E6, and from the descriptive statistics in B9:E11. The residual mean square in cell B13 is the ratio of the residual sum of squares (cell E6) for the outcome measure on the covariate and the factor, to the residual degrees of freedom (cell E5).

Cell B14 contains the residual sum of squares of the covariate on the factor, and is taken directly from cell B6.

The comparison is actually carried out in Row 18. Cell B18 contains the difference between the adjusted means on the outcome measure of the retail outlets and the auto dealers. It serves as the numerator of the t-ratio. More formally, it is the sum of the contrast coefficients (1 and –1) times the associated group means (90.69 and 72.76). So, (1 × 90.69) + (–1 × 72.76) equals 17.93.

The denominator of the t-ratio in cell C18 is calculated as follows:

=SQRT(B13*((1/E9+1/E10)+(D9-D10)^2/B14))

More generally, that formula is

$$\sqrt{MS_{resid}\left[\frac{2}{n} + \frac{(\overline{X}_1 - \overline{X}_2)^2}{SS_{resid(x)}}\right]}$$

The t-ratio itself is in cell D18 and is the result of dividing the difference between the adjusted means in cell B18 by the denominator calculated in cell C18. Notice that its value, 3.19, is greater than the critical value of 1.86 in cell E18. The critical value is easily obtained with this formula:

=T.INV(0.95,E5)

Cell E5 contains 8, the residual degrees of freedom that results from regressing the outcome measure on the covariate and the factor. So the instance of T.INV() in cell E5 requests the value of the t-distribution with 8 degrees of freedom such that 95% of the area under its curve lies to the left of the value returned by the function.

Because the calculated t-ratio in cell D18 is larger than the critical t-value in cell E18, you conclude that the mean value of tire cracking, adjusted for the covariate of tire age, is greater in the population of retail outlets than in the population of auto dealers. Because of the argument used for the T.INV() function, you reach this conclusion at the 95% level of confidence.

So by planning in advance to make this comparison, you can use an approach that is more powerful and may declare a comparison reliable when a post hoc approach such as the Scheffé would fail to do so. Some constraints are involved in using the more powerful procedure, of course. The most notable of the constraints is that you won't cherry-pick certain comparisons after you see the data, and then proceed to use an approach that assumes the comparison was planned in advance.

The Analysis of Multiple Covariance

The title of this section sounds kind of highfalutin, but the topic builds pretty easily on the foundation discussed in Chapter 14. The notion of *multiple covariance* is simply the use of two or more covariates in an ANCOVA instead of the single covariate that has been demonstrated in Chapter 14 and thus far in the present chapter.

The Decision to Use Multiple Covariates

There are a couple of mechanical considerations that you'll want to keep in mind, and they are covered later in this section. First, it's important to consider again the purposes of adding one or more covariates to an ANOVA so as to run an ANCOVA.

The principal reason to use a covariate is to reallocate variability in the outcome variable. This variability, in an ANOVA, would be treated as error variance and would contribute to the size of the denominator of the F ratio. When the denominator increases without an accompanying increase in the numerator, the size of the ratio decreases; in turn, this reduces the likelihood that you'll have an F ratio that indicates a reliable difference in group means.

Adding a covariate to the analysis allocates some of that error variance to the covariate instead. This normally has the effect of reducing the denominator of the F ratio and therefore increasing the F ratio itself.

Adding the covariate doesn't help things much if its correlation with the outcome variable is weak—that is, if it shares a small proportion of its variance with the outcome variable so that the R^2 between the covariate and the outcome variable is small. If the R^2 is small, then there's little variance in the outcome variable that can be reallocated from the error variance to the covariate. In a case like that, there's little to be gained.

Suppose that you have an outcome variable that correlates well with a covariate, but you are considering adding another covariate to the analysis. So doing might reduce the error variance even further, and therefore give the F test even more statistical power. What characteristics should you look for in the second covariate?

As with the first covariate, there should be some decent rationale for including a second covariate. It should make good sense, in terms of the theory of the situation, to include it. In a study of cholesterol levels, it makes good sense to use body weight as a covariate. To add the street number of the patient's home address as a second covariate would be deranged, even though it might accidentally correlate well with cholesterol levels.

Then, a second covariate should correlate well with the outcome variable. If the second covariate doesn't share much variance with the outcome variable, it won't function well as a means of drawing variance out of the F ratio's error term.

Furthermore, it's best if the second covariate does *not* correlate well with the first covariate. The reason is that if the two covariates themselves are strongly related, then the first covariate will claim the variance shared with the outcome measure and there will be little left that can be allocated to the second covariate.

That's a primary reason that you don't find multiple covariates used in published experimental research as often as you find analyses that use a single covariate only. It may be straightforward to find a good first covariate. It is more difficult to find a second covariate that not only correlates well with the outcome measure, but poorly with the first covariate.

Furthermore, there are other minor problems with adding a marginal covariate. You'll lose an additional degree of freedom for the residual. Adding a covariate to a relatively small sample makes the regression equation less stable. Other things being equal, the larger the residual degrees of freedom to the number of variables in the equation, the better. To add a covariate does precisely the opposite: It adds a variable and subtracts a degree of freedom from the residual variation. So you should have a good, sound reason for adding a covariate.

Two Covariates: An Example

Figure 15.8 extends the data shown in Figure 14.10. It does so by adding a covariate to the one that was already in use.

Figure 15.8
A new covariate, X2, has been added in column D.

L8 f_x =M4-I4

	A	B	C	D	E	F	G	H	I	J	K	L	M	N	O	P	Q
1	Group	Y	X_1	X_2	Treatment Vector 1	Treatment Vector 2			Y on X_1 and X_2				Y on X_1, X_2 and Treatment				
2	Med 1	51.6	94.8	99.4	1	0			0.29	0.13			1.26	-7.17	0.30	0.08	20.39
3	Med 1	25.6	52.8	32.4	1	0			0.11	0.06			2.51	2.60	0.09	0.05	7.04
4	Med 1	40.8	134	53.3	1	0		R^2	0.65	8.81		R^2	0.79	7.32	#N/A	#N/A	#N/A
5	Med 1	45.6	163	73.8	1	0			13.78	15			12.17	13	#N/A	#N/A	#N/A
6	Med 1	44	86.4	68.3	1	0			2141.03441	1164.93			2609.25	696.71	#N/A	#N/A	#N/A
7	Med 1	70.8	190	131	1	0											
8	Med 2	54.8	115	76.7	0	1				Increase in R2		0.14					
9	Med 2	52	151	57.5	0	1											
10	Med 2	43.2	138	76.8	0	1											
11	Med 2	64	176	81.1	0	1					Total Sum of Squares:	3305.96					
12	Med 2	69.6	167	92.9	0	1											
13	Med 2	55.6	124	65.5	0	1			SV	SS	df	MS	F	p			
14	Control	54.4	112	58	-1	-1			Covariates	2141.03	2	1070.52	19.97	0.000			
15	Control	65.2	87.6	75.4	-1	-1			Treatment	468.22	2	234.11	4.37	0.035			
16	Control	72	175	121.8	-1	-1			Residual	696.71	13	53.59					
17	Control	59.2	133	95.5	-1	-1											
18	Control	56.8	202	78	-1	-1											
19	Control	85.6	218	92.3	-1	-1											

If you compare Figure 15.8 with Figure 14.10, you'll notice that the covariate X_2 was inserted immediately to the right of the existing covariate, X_1 (in Figure 14.10, it's just labeled "X"). You could add X_2 to the right of the second treatment vector, but then you'd run into a difficulty. One of your tasks is to run LINEST() to regress the outcome variable Y onto the two covariates. If the covariates aren't adjacent to one another—for example, if X1 is in column C and X2 is in column F—then you won't be able to refer to them as the *known-xs* argument in the LINEST() function.

Laid out as shown in Figure 15.8, with the covariates adjacent to one another in columns C and D, you can use the following array formula to get the LINEST() results that appear in the range I2:J6:

```
=LINEST(B2:B19,C2:D19,,TRUE)
```

This instance of LINEST() serves the same purpose as the one in H2:I6 of Figure 14.10: It quantifies the proportion of variance, R^2, in the outcome measure that can be accounted for by the covariate or covariates. In Figure 14.10, with one covariate, that proportion is 0.47. In Figure 15.8, with two covariates, the proportion is 0.65. Adding the second covariate

15

accounts for an additional 0.65 – 0.47 = 0.18, or 18% of the variance in the outcome measure—a useful increment.

The use of two vectors in the *known-xs* argument to LINEST() given previously is the second mechanical adjustment you must make to accommodate a second covariate. The first, of course, is the insertion of the second covariate's values adjacent to those of the first covariate.

The range M2:Q6 in Figure 15.8 contains the full LINEST() results, for the outcome measure Y regressed onto the covariates and the effect-coded treatment vectors. By comparing the two values for R^2 we can tell whether the use of the treatment factor vectors add a reliable increment to the variance explained by the covariates. Adding the treatment vectors increases the R^2 from 0.65 to 0.79, or 14% as shown in cell L8.

Finally—just as in Figure 14.10, but now with two covariates—we can test the significance of the differences in the treatment group means after the effects of the covariates have been removed from the regression. That analysis is found, in Figure 15.8, in I14:N16.

To make it easier to compare Figure 15.8 with Figure 14.10, I have included the sums of squares in the analysis in Figure 15.8. The total sum of squares is shown in cell L11, and is calculated using the DEVSQ() function on the outcome measure:

    =DEVSQ(B2:B19)

The sum of squares for the covariates is found by multiplying the R^2 for the covariates, 0.65, times the total sum of squares. (However, LINEST() does provide it directly in cell I6.) Similarly, the sum of squares for the treatments *after* accounting for the covariates is found by multiplying the incremental R^2 in cell L8 by the total sum of squares. The residual sum of squares is found most easily by taking it directly from the overall LINEST() analysis, in cell N6.

All the preceding is just as it was in Figure 14.10, but the degrees of freedom are slightly different. There's another covariate, so the degrees of freedom for the covariates changes from 1 in Figure 14.10 to 2 in Figure 15.8. Similarly, we lose a degree of freedom from the residual. That loss of a degree of freedom from the residual increases the residual mean square very slightly, but that is more than made up for by the reduction in the residual sum of squares. The net effect is to make the F test more powerful.

Compare the F ratio for Treatment in Figure 14.10 (2.52, in cell L15) with the one in Figure 15.8 (4.37, in cell M15). It is now large enough that, with the associated degrees of freedom, you can conclude that the group means, adjusted for the two covariates, are likely to differ in the populations at over the 95% confidence level (100% – 3.5% = 96.5%).

**degrees of freedom,
73-75, 236**

  in two-test groups, 236

**dependent group t-tests,
performing with Data
Analysis add-in tools,
249-256**

**descriptive statistics,
22-23**

**Descriptive Statistics tool
(Data Analysis add-in),
189-191**

design cells, 291-292

**DEVSQ() function,
229, 263**

**directional hypotheses,
165-167, 226-228**

  verifying with t-test,
228-234

**distributions,
t-distribution, 214**

**documentation (Excel),
problems with, 149-151**

dummy coding, 312

E

**effect coding, 310,
317-319**

  adjusted group means,
386-388

  codes, assigning in Excel,
319-322

factorial designs, 324-325

general principles, 310

  group codes, 311-312

  means, adjusting, 381-386

**Equal Variances t-Test
tool (Data Analysis
add-in), 252-254**

error rates

  alpha, manipulating,
221-223

  beta, 220

**establishing internal
validity, 152-153**

estimates of variance

  via ANOVA, 315-316

  via regression, 316-317

estimators, 74

Excel

  Data Analysis add-in tools.
See Data Analysis add-in
tools

  documentation, problems
with, 149-151

  effect codes, assigning,
319-322

  formula evaluation tool,
56-59

  formulas. *See* formulas

  functions. *See* functions

  matrix functions, 110-112

  pivot tables

    Index display, 147-148

    one-way, 113-116, 120

    two-way, 117-119,
129-139

Single Factor ANOVA
tool, 322-323

Solver, 42-43

  installing, 43

  worksheets, setting up,
44-46

**experimental designs,
multiple regression,
345-348**

**experiments, managing
unequal group sizes,
355-356**

F

**F distribution, 269,
274-275**

F ratio, 269

F tests, 268-270, 305

  calculated F, comparing to
critical F, 270

  multiple comparison
procedures, 277-278

    planned orthogonal
contrasts, 283-286

    Scheffe procedure,
278-283

  noncentral F, 305

  noncentrality parameters,
306

factorial ANOVA, 287-288

  F tests, 305

    noncentral F, 305

    noncentrality
parameters, 306